# The New World Order

This series discusses issues of cultural identity, and the proper role of national and ethnic affiliations in the world's structures of legal and political power.

# The New World Order

Sovereignty, Human Rights, and the
Self-Determination of Peoples

Edited by
Mortimer Sellers

**BERG**
Oxford/Washington, D.C.

First published in 1996 by
**Berg**
Editorial offices:
150 Cowley Road, Oxford, OX4 1JJ, UK
22883 Quicksilver Drive, Dulles, VA 20166, USA

Berg is the imprint of Oxford International Publishers Ltd.

**Library of Congress Cataloging-in-Publication Data**

A catalogue record for this book is available from the Library of Congress

**British Library Cataloguing-in-Publication Data**

A catalogue record for this book is available from the British Library

ISBN 1 85973 059 0 (Cloth)
1 85973 064 7 (Paper)

Typeset by JS Typesetting, Wellingborough, Northants.
Printed in the United Kingdom by WBC Bookbinders, Bridgend, Mid-Glamorgan.

To Cora Mary Stead Sellers

aspice venturo laetentur ut omnia saeclo
o mihi tum longae maneat pars ultima vitae
spiritus et quantum sat erit tua dicere facta

# Contents

## Contents

# Preface

The Baltimore Studies in Nationalism and Internationalism are sponsored by the Center for International and Comparative Law. The Center was established in 1994 as a research center of the University of Maryland System, affiliated with the University of Baltimore School of Law. The series discusses issues of cultural identity and the proper role of national and ethnic affiliations in the world's structures of legal and political power.

This volume grows out of a Workshop on International Organization Studies, held at Brown University in July, 1994, and jointly sponsored by the Academic Council of the United Nations System and the American Society of International Law. Lively and protracted discussions in Providence were followed by further thought and correspondence that ultimately resulted in the essays published here. David Forsythe, Hurst Hannum, Nico Schrijver, Melissa Phillips and Thomas Weiss presided over and guided the conference sessions. Without their leadership and encouragement this volume would not have been possible.

Thanks are also due to Donna Pennepacker, Administrative Aide to the Center for International and Comparative Law, and to Clement Adibe, Maxwell Chibundu, William DeMars, Lynda Frost, Catherine Iorns, Barbara Jones, Marc Moquette, Anthony Ofodile, Zoran Pajic, Raul Pangalangan, Katherine Rahman, Paula Rhodes, Gillian Robinson, William Schabas, Albrecht Schnabel, William Stanley, Zelim Tskhovrebov, Anjoo Upadhyaya and Mari Yamashita. Kathryn Earle took the lead in suggesting publication. As with all the Center's events and accomplishments, this book would not exist without the inspiration and encouragement of John Sebert, Eric Schneider and Frances Stead Sellers.

# Notes on Contributors

*Gian Luca Burci* is a Legal Officer in the United Nations Office of Legal Affairs.

*Nergis Canefe* is a doctoral candidate at York University in Ontario, Canada.

*Philippe Ch. A. Guillot* is a Lecturer in Public Law at the University of Rouen.

*Sohail H. Hashmi* is Assistant Professor of International Relations at Mount Holyoke College.

*Stephanie Lawson* is a Fellow of International Relations at the Australian National University.

*Robert McCorquodale* is a Senior Lecturer in Law at the Australian National University. He wrote his contribution to this volume while a Fellow and Lecturer in Law at St. John's College, Cambridge.

*René Provost* is Assistant Professor of Law at McGill University in Montreal, Quebec.

*Vladimir Rudnitsky* is a Legal Officer in the Codification Division of the Office of Legal Affairs at the United Nations.

*Mortimer Sellers* is Director of the Center for International and Comparative Law and Associate Professor of Law at the University of Baltimore School of Law.

*Gerry J. Simpson* is a Senior Lecturer in Law at the Australian National University. He wrote his contribution to this volume while a Lecturer in Law at the University of Melbourne.

*Nira Wickramasinghe* is a Senior Lecturer at the Department of History and Political Science, University of Colombo and a consultant at the International Centre for Ethnic Studies in Colombo, Sri Lanka.

# – 1 –

# Introduction

## Mortimer Sellers

Sovereignty, human rights and the self-determination of peoples were all taken into consideration and in some sense protected under the international order that grew out of World War II, as embodied in the Charter of the United Nations. They represented three central purposes of the United Nations Organization, laid out in the Charter's first Article – to "suppress" aggression, to "respect" self-determination and to "promote" human rights. The order in which they appear and the descending strength of the verbs reveal the relative importance of each concept in the postwar order. Sovereignty is the oldest and most established of the three concepts, having been broadly defined by Emmerich de Vattel as long ago as 1758. Self-determination acquired primary significance only after World War I and the interventions of President Woodrow Wilson. Human rights hardly played a role in international law before the Nuremberg trials.

Vattel's broad conception of state sovereignty made sense in an international order dominated by dangerous and self-interested tyrants. National autonomy protected human rights and self-determination by defending the freedom of the world's few liberal states to develop their own domestic bills of rights and democratic institutions. But the fall of the Berlin Wall and the disintegration of the Soviet Empire now open the possibility that strong state sovereignty no longer serves the purposes it first emerged to protect. Has the world entered a new era in which human rights and national self-determination should modify or supersede state sovereignty in the interests of national liberty and justice?

The idea that a New World Order must inevitably replace the old state system has gained wide currency, even among those who fear its implications. Human rights and national self-determination affect not only conceptions of state sovereignty but also each other. Human rights may challenge democratic mandates. Democracy may threaten human rights. Or democracy may threaten itself as new "peoples" claim autonomy from old nations and empires.

This volume considers the fundamental moral questions of the international legal order through the eyes of ten young scholars from nine different nations and legal traditions. Their purpose has been to define the proper relationship between national and international institutions after the Cold War, with particular reference to the protection of human rights in different local situations. More general essays begin the collection, followed by several detailed discussions of specific applications and histories. All ten authors examine the moral basis of international institutions from new perspectives, in the light of dramatically changed contemporary circumstances.

Robert McCorquodale (Chapter 2) sets out the modern conflict between state sovereignty and the self-determination of peoples, beginning with Versailles, and proposes a reconciliation grounded in human rights doctrine. McCorquodale suggests that the recent international recognition of human rights protections also entails protecting rights to "internal" self-determination as a necessary foundation for other fundamental freedoms. This usually does not mean the right to secession, but rather the opportunity to participate fully in the state's political, economic, and social processes. A state must protect all the inhabitants of its territory or face restricted sovereignty. But the existing international order properly privileges territorial integrity in the absence of serious human rights violations. McCorquodale concludes that basing self-determination on human rights protections removes some of the most contentious aspects of the (self-)identification of "peoples" and that human rights doctrine provides the best legal framework for the peaceful resolution of disputes involving the right to self-determination.

Gerry Simpson (Chapter 3) challenges the dominant "colonial" conception of self-determination in international law. He reviews rival "national," "democratic," "devolutionary" and "secessionist" senses of self-determination and concludes that each contains a disabling contradiction caused by its failure to accommodate the others. Simpson goes on to propose a new "participatory" understanding of self-determination based on the legal recognition of various forms of sovereignty. The end of empire has revealed that *all* states are imperial. Simpson's participatory self-determination rests on the idea of protecting the collective human and democratic rights of minorities and unrepresented peoples rather than encouraging claims to territorial separation or assertions of national and racial exceptionalism. By widening the possible meanings of sovereignty, Simpson hopes to facilitate the process of negotiation and accommodation that alone can reconcile competing claims to national and cultural self-expression.

Vladimir Rudnitsky (Chapter 4) shares Simpson's view that anticolonial conceptions of self-determination have limited relevance to modern political realities. But Rudnitsky regards the United Nations as the salient source of coordinated new approaches to the human rights, development and security issues raised by claims to national liberation. In his view, as global interdependence undermines the traditional autonomy of sovereign states, only the United Nations has the position and moral authority needed to develop consistent and coherent standards of self-determination. Rudnitsky suggests that this process is already under way, as reflected in the General Assembly's Declaration on the Rights of Persons belonging to National or Ethnic, Religious and Linguistic Minorities (adopted on 18 December 1992). But the declaration did not specify which social groups should be considered holders of internationally protected rights, including the right to self-determination. Rudnitsky proposes that the proper balance between self-determination and state sovereignty requires an institutional framework rather than rigid legal prescriptions. Self-determination need not necessarily imply statehood or sovereignty at all. Properly designed democratic institutions obviate the need for political separation. Rudnitsky concludes that the creation of new sovereign states should be a last resort, when all other social remedies have been applied by the United Nations.

Nergis Canefe (Chapter 5) questions the "nation-state" model of unified political community. She doubts the value of nationalism and its natural corollary, the principle of sovereignty. Instead Canefe proposes to transcend the old European identification of nationality with citizenship by distinguishing the "territorial state" from the nation. She argues that traditional state nationalism views ethnic and other minorities as (at best) anomalies to be integrated into the homogeneous nation and that the "one-state, one-nation" model promotes an endless cycle of secession and repression that transforms all minority rights into fundamental threats to the state. Canefe proposes a purely territorial allocation of civil and political rights, coupled with international protections for the identity claims of individual citizens. While granting that liberal democracy has moderated the internal excesses of some European nation-states, she holds that constitutional pluralism will not emerge elsewhere until unitary European concepts of political identity give way to more inclusive conceptions of the state.

Sohail Hashmi (Chapter 6) provides one such conception with his analysis of self-determination and secession in Islamic thought. Islamic ethics embraces the normative goal of universal community among the faithful, transcending ethnic, tribal, racial, and other national or territorial distinctions. This makes claims to national self-determination and secession problematic, at least within existing Muslim states. Islam holds that the ethical norms of justice, fraternity and peace should supersede narrow tribal identities, limiting the right to secede if secession means carving out a separate territory and not admitting other national or ethnic groups within it. Hashmi suggests that the proper Islamic remedy for oppressive regimes is revolution, not separation or departure.

Stephanie Lawson (Chapter 7) considers the same problems from the perspective of the South Pacific. In places such as Fiji and Papua New Guinea, political entities formed by European colonization brought together people of very different ethnic and cultural backgrounds. United Nations-sponsored decolonization often maximized the territorial "viability" of new states at the expense of ethnic or tribal unity. This has prevented any easy equivalence between ethnic "nations" and the state, so South Pacific ethno-nationalism has sought to unite territories with peoples by treating some citizens as outsiders. Lawson endorses a more pluralistic and inclusionary conception of "the people," which would extend political equality to all citizens regardless of religious, linguistic, or cultural identity. This should not mean denial of indigenous rights, but rather their association with other basic human rights, so that no one will suffer oppression for reasons of ethnicity, color, religion, language, gender or any other single aspect of human identity. Lawson concludes that internal sovereignty and self-determination require the inclusion not simply of "a" people, but of "the" people, in all their complexity.

René Provost (Chapter 8) compares wars of national liberation with other armed conflicts and considers the problems of "indeterminacy" and "characterization" that arise in the application of humanitarian law to conflicts that may be either "internal" or "international," depending on one's perspective. Provost explores the nature and effect of characterization by various agents. The degree of indeterminacy of a norm conditions the need for procedural mechanisms to make it more certain. Characterization may be performed by the state itself, by other states, by political organs of international organizations or by specialized bodies such as the International Committee of the Red Cross. Provost concludes that when recourse to specialized bodies offering guarantees of neutrality and legality is impossible, each of these characterizations remains valid within its proper sphere of authority. He proposes consensus-building as a solution to disagreements about characterization. Prior to consensus, agents would have to bear the risk of their own mischaracterizations. This admittedly unsatisfactory conclusion reflects the current state of international law. Provost suggests that international norms have outrun the mechanisms created to enforce them. Until the international community develops permanent bodies capable of guiding the development and application of international law, inconsistencies will be unavoidable.

Gian Luca Burci (Chapter 9) describes some international mechanisms that may serve to avert disagreements about character-ization and ameliorate situations of internal conflict. The United Nations already finds itself embroiled in peacemaking as well as peacekeeping operations in the aftermath of the Cold War. Burci analyzes these activities in the light of emerging law and practice by the United Nations in the fields of security and humanitarian assistance. States that fail to fulfill basic duties to their citizens may find their sovereign rights temporarily attenuated or held in abeyance, subject to multilateral decision-making processes. Burci concludes, however, that the secretary-general and forces under his command should concentrate on what they are naturally inclined and best suited to do: negotiate, assist, persuade and try to draw conflicting parties into a political process that can be advanced, but should not be coerced, by an external peacekeeping and humanitarian presence.

Philippe Guillot (Chapter 10) compares current practice of the United Nations to the international order of sovereign states developed since the Peace of Westphalia in 1648. Now a new directorate under the five permanent members of the Security Council seeks to advance liberal democratic solutions to internal conflicts, promoting Western standards of governance worldwide. Guillot suggests that "assistance-to-transition" operations can be found throughout the history of United Nations peacekeeping but that prodemocracy constitutional engineering developed more recently. The price of United Nations assistance and protection has become the limitation of constitutional sovereignty. Guillot concludes that the surest way to build peace is through the choice and agreement of the people concerned, ratified by a plebiscite. Nations will eventually reject imposed legal and political institutions. United Nations "solutions" not guided by local circumstances and cultural context inevitably fail and could bring the Organization down with them.

Nira Wickramasinghe (Chapter 11) also considers the risks of imposed solutions to local and regional problems, with special reference to the aid regime in Sri Lanka. The international mobility of capital, ideas, technologies, and persons has reduced the real importance of statehood and dramatically eroded the significance of nominal state sovereignty. Donor countries increasingly link development aid to human rights and other political and moral considerations. Wickramasinghe recognizes the importance of human rights, but questions the recent emergence of "good governance" as a decisive factor in aid policy and development assistance. Nations subscribing to the International Covenant on Civil and Political Rights or to the International Covenant on Economic, Social and Cultural Rights agree, in effect, to cede part of their sovereignty to world institutions. But "good governance" as defined by the World Bank would relocate authority towards subnational collectives. Wickramasinghe proposes a new role for the United Nations as a watchdog over insensitive world economic institutions, making development programs more mindful of the social, cultural, and political consequences of their intervention.

All ten of the essays collected in this volume see significant links between sovereignty, human rights, and national self-determination. Most would condition some aspects of state autonomy on respect for individual liberties and the sovereignty of the people. Vattel's basic insight that every nation must create its own system and laws survives, modified by new conceptions of what constitutes a nation. Very briefly, self-determination means that the people decide their own fate. The "people," for political purposes, should mean the inhabitants of a given territory. Yet self-determination cannot exist without the protection of certain basic human rights, including the right to develop one's group identity within the larger political community. These seem to be the basic conditions of sovereignty after the end of the Cold War.

The role of international institutions in safeguarding this New World Order is much less certain. On the one hand, the United Nations and other organizations seem to promise an impartial application of evolving doctrine against local tyrants. On the other, they threaten outside interference, without sensitivity to specific conditions and cultural context. Perhaps the common ground among contributors to this volume is a shared propensity to encourage broad international cooperation and movement, by consent, toward a shared agenda. But there remains considerable reluctance to let institutions move ahead of the consensus. The United Nations may play a leading role in developing standards, provided it respects the self-determination of its constituent states.

How, then, do younger scholars and post-Cold War attitudes differ from what went before? Perhaps in their new willingness to take human rights and self-determination seriously, even at the expense of de facto power. National and international law exist to unite the interests of states and individuals with the interests of the whole.[1] Whenever anyone is shut out of this discourse, truth is lost, justice suffers, and no one enjoys the peace and security that flow from the mutual respect of our shared humanity.

## Note

1. Cf. Cicero, *De officiis* III.vi.26.

# – 2 –

# Human Rights and Self-Determination

## Robert McCorquodale

If every ethnic, religious or linguistic group claimed Statehood, there would be no limit to fragmentation, and peace, security and economic well-being for all would become ever more difficult to achieve. One requirement for solutions to these problems lies in commitment to human rights. – Boutros-Ghali, *Agenda for Peace*

## Introduction

The above statement by the secretary-general of the United Nations expresses concern about the consequences of unlimited exercise of the right of self-determination for the future stability of the international system. At the same time, the statement points the way to resolving the many conflicts between groups, on the one hand, claiming a right of self-determination and, on the other, states insisting on absolute sovereignty over territory.[1] The solution lies in a commitment to human rights.

Human rights are central to the clarification and application of the right of self-determination. The development of the right of self-determination has been part of the international community's vigorous attempts to eradicate oppression of individuals and groups by states. The right developed in the context of increased international legal protection of human rights and universal acceptance by states that "the promotion and protection of all human rights is a legitimate concern of the international community".[2] Indeed, self-determination has been clarified as a human right in treaties and other international documents relating to human rights.

The extent of protection given by the right of self-determination has become broader and deeper than it was after World War I[3] and during decolonization.[4] It now applies to all peoples in all territories, not just colonial territories, and to all peoples within a state. Today

– 9 –

the right of self-determination extends to all peoples suffering from oppression by subjugation, domination, and exploitation by others.

But in order to resolve potentially conflicting claims and obligations concerning the right of self-determination, a coherent legal framework for it needs to be developed. The rules expounded in this framework must be capable of being applied to a variety of circumstances without creating an increased threat to international security. They must respect the rights and interests of all members of the international community. The only appropriate legal framework that meets these difficult requirements is one based on the general legal rules of international human rights law. Thus a human rights approach to the right of self-determination needs to be taken.

A human rights approach, as described in this chapter, makes clear that the right of self-determination is not an absolute right. Instead the right has limitations, both to protect the rights of others and to protect the general interests of society, especially with regard to international security. But it also makes clear that these limitations are applicable only in certain circumstances, such as where internal self-determination has already occurred and where there are compelling reasons for them in the society concerned. Similarly, the human rights approach can resolve the difficult issue of defining "peoples" entitled to the protection of the right, by its clarification of which victims can bring a claim for a violation of a right. This approach also acknowledges diversity in the exercise of the right – with a presumption against secession, as it is usually a breach of the rights of others – and allows the right to be addressed in the context of the developing standards and practices of the international community.

While the human rights approach does not make it possible to say in abstract which peoples have the right of self-determination or what the extent of any exercise of this right should be, it does provide a framework to enable every situation to be considered and all the relevant rights and interests to be taken into account, analyzed, and balanced. This balance means that the geopolitical context of the right being claimed, the particular historical circumstances surrounding the claim, and the present constitutional order of the state and of international society are acknowledged and addressed. Once this legal balancing process has been completed, the relevant political and moral forces will be able to act on the clear and coherent legal position.

In addition, the human rights approach is able to deal with the shift in the international order away from being state-based and towards a more flexible system of international law.[5] Indeed, many claims for self-determination have arisen because an unjust, state-based international legal order has failed to respond to the legitimate aspirations of peoples. The human rights approach restricts attempts to reassert the exclusivity of the state in international law at the expense of the people of a territory. This is consistent with the statement by the Secretary-General of the United Nations that "the time of absolute and exclusive sovereignty, however, has passed" and that there must be "respect for the needs of the more vulnerable groups of society. . . [and] empowerment of the unorganized, the poor, the marginalized."[6] The human rights approach offers a solution, based on a commitment to human rights, to the concerns expressed by the Secretary-General in the opening quotation of this chapter and provides a legal framework for the peaceful resolution of disputes involving the right of self-determination.

## Self-Determination as a Human Right

The link between self-determination and general human rights law should not be surprising considering the inclusion of the right in the first article of the two international human rights covenants of 1966: the International Covenant on Economic, Social and Cultural Rights (ICESCR) and the International Covenant on Civil and Political Rights (ICCPR).[7] These treaties entered into force in 1976 and have now been ratified by about two-thirds of the members of the United Nations. Subsequently, self-determination has been stated as a human right in other international and regional treaties and instruments, such as the Declaration on Principles of International Law Concerning Friendly Relations and Cooperation among States (1970),[8] the Final Act of the Conference on Security and Cooperation in Europe (CSCE) (1975),[9] and the African Charter on Human and Peoples' Rights (1981). While some jurists have argued that the right of self-determination could even form part of *jus cogens*,[10] it is certain that self-determination is now a human right in international law.

The Human Rights Committee, which was set up under the ICCPR, has acknowledged the link between the right of self-determination and general human rights law:

> The right of self-determination is of particular importance because its realization is an essential condition for the effective guarantee and observance of individual human rights and for the promotion and strengthening of those rights. It is for that reason that States set forth the right of self-determination in a provision of positive law in both Covenants [the ICCPR and the ICESCR] and placed this provision as article 1 apart from and before all of the other rights in the two Covenants.[11]

The right is considered an "essential condition" in the protection of individual rights because if peoples are being subjected to oppression they are not in a position to be able to have any of their individual rights fully protected. The right, therefore, is aimed at protecting the rights of a group as a group – as distinct from individuals within a group – and enabling groups to prosper and transmit their culture as well as to participate fully, as a group, in the political, economic, and social process. Indeed, the Secretary-General of the United Nations has stated:

> Democracy within nations requires respect for human rights and fundamental freedoms, as set forth in the Charter. . ... This is not only a political matter. The social stability needed for productive growth is nurtured by conditions in which people can readily express their will. For this, strong domestic institutions of participation are essential. Promoting such institutions means promoting the empowerment of the unorganized, the poor, the marginalized.[12]

It is this empowerment that is at the core of the purpose of the right of self-determination. The right seeks to protect each people or group as a group from oppression and so to empower them. In doing so, it forms part of the empowering process of human rights.

In addition, the development of international human rights law has meant that human rights are now accepted by the international community as not being a matter solely within a state's domestic jurisdiction.[13] In the Vienna Declaration and Programme of Action, which grew out of the United Nations World Conference on Human Rights in 1993,[14] Article 4 provides that "the promotion and protection of all human rights is a legitimate concern of the international community," and in the Concluding Document of the Moscow Conference on the Human Dimension of the CSCE,[15] the states involved "categorically and irrevocably [declared] that the commitments undertaken in the field of the human dimension of the CSCE are matters of direct and legitimate concern of all participating States and do not belong exclusively to the internal affairs of the State concerned." Therefore, how a state treats its inhabitants generally and, specifically, the extent to which it allows peoples within its territory to participate fully in its political, economic, and social process – that being its internal protection of the right of self-determination – are now a matter of international concern. So both the rationale for the protection of the right of self-determination and its integration with the protection of human rights generally allow the right to be considered under the legal rules protecting human rights.

Unfortunately for the purpose of clarification of the right of self-determination in international human rights law, the only international legal tribunal that has the jurisdiction to consider the right directly – that is, the Human Rights Committee – has chosen not to deal with complaints of breaches of Article 1 of the International Covenant on Civil and Political Rights. The reason for this is that the Human Rights Committee has interpreted Article 1 of the Optional Protocol to the ICCPR, which allows "individuals" to bring complaints to the committee against states party to the Covenant, to mean only a single person alone can bring a complaint and not groups or peoples.[16] This stance could be criticized as ignoring the reality that individuals can suffer because of a breach of the right of self-determination of a people of whom they are a member.[17] The Human Rights Committee can and does though address the right under its reporting procedure[18] as does the African Commission on Human and Peoples' Rights.[19] Yet none of the major international human rights tribunals have had to consider directly a claim alleging the abuse of the right of self-determination. Nevertheless, the framework of international human rights law offers clear, general legal rules that can be used to consider the human right of self-determination.

## The Framework of International Human Rights Law

### *General Legal Rules*

International human rights law is primarily contained in global and regional treaties, and some of this law now forms part of customary international law and so is binding on all states.[20] Indeed, there are very few states that are not party to at least one human rights treaty or instrument dealing with human rights.[21] This law has been clarified by the principal international human rights tribunals – the Human Rights Committee;[22] the European Court of (and Commission on) Human Rights, established under the European Convention for the Protection of Human Rights and Fundamental Freedoms in 1950;[23] and the Inter-American Court of (and Commission on) Human Rights, established under the American Convention on Human Rights in 1969.[24] Enough consistent and coherent legal rules are being declared by all three forums to discern a general legal framework of international human rights law.

The legal rules developed within the international human rights law framework are clear and understandable; as required of any legal rule, they give "adequate notice to those subject to an obligation of the ambit of that obligation, and to those who administer the rules, of their content."[25] These rules are concerned with the social process of balancing human rights with the requirements of society and are made so as to be responsive to developments in international society and law. The following general legal rules can be discerned within the international human rights framework: (1) Human rights are interpreted in the context of current standards; (2) Any limitations on the exercise of human rights are limitations to protect other rights or limitations to protect the general interests of society; (3) The limitations on human rights are considered narrowly, with consideration given to the circumstances of the relevant society; and (4) A victim of a violation of human rights must bring the claim.

These general rules are a simplification of the complex of specific, detailed rules set out in decisions, comments, opinions, and other statements by the principal international human rights tribunals.[26] They are also consistent with the terms of the Universal Declaration of Human Rights of 1948, the document from which all the major human rights treaties stem. Article 29 of that Declaration states:

> In the exercise of his rights and freedoms, everyone shall be subject only to such limitations as are determined by law solely for the purpose of securing due recognition and respect for the rights and freedoms of others and of meeting the just requirements of morality, public order and the general welfare in the democratic society.

While each general rule is important, those dealing with limitations on human rights require closer examination.

### Limitations on Human Rights

Some human rights are absolute, such as the right of freedom from torture and other cruel, inhuman, or degrading treatment or punishment[27] and the right of protection against acts of genocide,[28] both of which place the personal or physical integrity of an individual or a group beyond other considerations.[29] Most human rights do have some limitations, however – for example, the right of freedom of expression is subject to restrictions where necessary to protect the rights or reputations of others or to ensure national security, public order, public health, or public morals.[30]

These limitations are a recognition that individuals do not exist in a vacuum but are part of a broader society of families, groups, organizations and communities.[31] It is in the general interest of any society to create a social and legal system that is relatively stable, so enabling those within the society to conduct their affairs with some degree of assurance. The state is the body given the obligation under international law to represent the interests of all inhabitants of the society within its boundaries. In international human rights law this responsibility is manifested in limitations on human rights for the sake of upholding such general interests of society as maintaining public order and security. The international community, as the society of states and other actors on the world plane, has similar general interests it seeks to uphold, such as the maintenance of international peace and security.

International human rights law aims at balancing competing or conflicting rights and interests. There is a presumption in favor of a right, with any limitations construed narrowly because of the non-reciprocal nature of human rights treaties and the inequality in power between states and peoples.[32] Nevertheless, in reaching conclusions about the general interests of a society, an allowance is made for a "margin of appreciation"[33] to each state. This means a degree of flexibility is given to a government in determining the particular pressing needs of its state in the light of the state's constitutional and social organization, as there "cannot [be a] disregard [for] those legal and factual features which characterize the life of the society in the state."[34] The onus is on the state, however, to prove there is a "pressing social need . . . proportionate to the legitimate aim pursued" before a right will be limited.[35] If there is prima facie evidence of a violation of a right, then it will be considered to have been proved "in the absence of satisfactory evidence and explanations to the contrary submitted by the State."[36] In the same way, the tribunals have been generous in allowing a range of persons and, except under the Optional Protocol to the International Covenant on Civil and Political Rights, groups to bring claims against states.[37]

At the same time, the understanding of the content and exercise of human rights does evolve. The European Convention for the Protection of Human Rights and Fundamental Freedoms "is a living instrument which . . . must be interpreted in the light of present-day conditions."[38] Therefore, any consideration of a human right must be in the context of current international standards. Taken together, the legal rules result in the position that there are limitations on most human rights in order to protect other rights and the general interests of society; these limitations are interpreted narrowly, but consideration is given to the context of the specific society affected and of current international standards.

## The Human Rights Approach to the Right of Self-Determination

*Nature and Applicability of the Human Rights Approach*

The human rights approach to the right of self-determination seeks to apply the framework of international human rights law to that right and, using the general legal rules within the framework, to create a coherent approach to dealing with situations where conflicts about self-determination arise. In the light of the preceding discussion about self-determination as a human right and about the competing interests and developing applications of the right of self-determination, the framework of international human rights law seems to be an appropriate structure in which to consider the right.

While this framework has been based on specific treaties and largely developed through concentration on civil and political rights, its general legal rules are often applied by other international human rights forums, such as the CSCE;[39] by national legal systems when interpreting human rights;[40] and by tribunals considering economic, social, and cultural rights (which include rights protecting groups such as employees and families).[41] Therefore, this framework can be applied to the right of self-determination. Indeed, irrespective of the justifiable criticism of their decisions, it was within a general human rights framework that members of the Arbitration Committee on Yugoslavia (the Badinter Committee) set up by the states of European Community considered the issue of whether Serbian minorities in Croatia and Bosnia and Herzegovina were entitled to self-determination.[42] In other words, by its nature and interaction with other rights and aided by the flexibility of international human rights law, the right of self-determination is capable of being considered within this framework.

It has already been pointed out that the international community now applies the right of self-determination to any situation, internal or external, in which peoples are suffering from oppression by subjugation, domination or exploitation. The right of self-determination is not, however, an absolute right without any limitations. Its purpose is not directly to protect the personal or physical integrity of individuals or groups as is the purpose of absolute rights. Unlike absolute rights, the right of self-determination can, when exercised, involve major structural and institutional changes in a state and affect, often significantly, groups and individuals in and even beyond that state.[43] Therefore, the nature of the right does require some limitations to be imposed on the exercise of it. These limitations on the right of self-determination – which are designed to protect the rights of everyone (not just those seeking self-determination), as well as the general interests of the international community – can be appropriately dealt with by a human rights approach. This is because the international human rights law frame-work takes into account the limitations on rights and offers a means to consider the exercise of a right in the context of the interests of all those potentially affected by it. The framework also accommodates the need for a state to act in the interest of all the inhabitants on its territory, this being its margin of appreciation, and thus allows the state to limit the exercise of the right in order to protect itself, although such action by the state cannot be oppressive.

### *Limitations on the Right of Self-Determination to Protect the Rights of Others*

Despite the lack of express limitations on the right of self-determination in common Article 1 of the two international human rights covenants, common Article 5(1) of these covenants provides that "nothing in the present Covenant may be interpreted as implying for any State, group or person any right to engage in any activity or perform any act aimed at the destruction of any of the rights and freedoms recognized herein."

This provision, which is also in the European Convention for the Protection of Human Rights and Fundamental Freedoms and in an American Convention on Human Rights,[44] implies a limitation on the right of self-determination to the extent that any exercise of the right cannot result in the destruction (or impairment) of any of the other rights protected by the treaty. For example, the exercise of the right of self-determination may result in the violation of individual rights, such as the rights of freedom of expression and freedom of religion, and so it needs to be limited to allow each right to be protected. In the same manner, the European Court of Human Rights has said that a state cannot pursue an education policy for the entire community that is in effect "an indoctrination against parents' wishes."[45]

The particular concern of the international community with regard to this limitation has been to protect the rights of other groups affected by the exercise of the right of self-determination. In situations of external self-determination, practice now seems to stress the need for a new state to protect the rights of all the inhabitants of the territory, usually by means of constitutional guarantees. This is seen both when the new state has come into existence by independence, as with Namibia,[46] and by secession, as with the former Yugoslavia and the former republics of the U.S.S.R. It is also seen in the debate on the right of self-determination of both the Israelis and the Palestinians.[47] Indeed, the Badinter Committee considered that the rights of Serbians living in Bosnia and Herzegovina must be taken into account (as well the provisions in the Yugoslav constitution that protected minorities) before any possible right of self-determination of the Bosnians could be exercised.[48]

Above all, if there were enforceable national and international guarantees of human rights so that the rights of every person and group in each state were judicially protected, then there would probably be fewer claims of violation of the right of self-determination. For the consequence of enforcement would be that each government did represent "the whole people belonging to the territory without distinction as to race, creed or colour"[49] or any other form of discrimination,[50] and the right of self-determination would not be infringed. Both current state practice and the nature of the right of self-determination itself place limits on its exercise in order to protect the rights of others as far as possible. This is because the rights of both individuals and groups need to be protected against the possibility of oppressive acts carried out in the name of self-determination.

### Limitations on the Right of Self-Determination to Protect the General Interests of Society

Common Article 1(3) of the International Covenants on Civil and Political Rights and the International Covenant on Economic, Social, and Cultural Rights implies a limitation on the right of self-determination as it stipulates that states have an obligation to respect the right "in conformity with the provisions of the Charter of the United Nations." The relevant obligations of states under the provisions of the Charter were clarified by the Declaration on Principles of International Law. The declaration set out seven principles of international law. Besides equal rights and self-determination of peoples, these principles are: prohibition of the use of force; prohibition of intervention in the domestic jurisdiction of a state; duty to settle disputes by peaceful means; duty to cooperate with other states; sovereign equality of states; and fulfillment by states of obligations in good faith. The declaration expressly says that "in their interpretation and application the above principles are interrelated and each principle should be construed in the context of the other principles."[51]

In other words, a requirement exists to take into account all the other principles when construing the principle of the right of self-determination. For the most part, these other principles reassert the general purposes of the United Nations and principally its objective of maintaining international peace and security.[52] Thus, the general interest of the international community in preserving international peace and security creates a limitation on the right of self-determination. This general interest limiting the right is often expressed in two parts: territorial integrity of states and the maintenance of colonial boundaries (*uti possidetis juris*).

*Territorial Integrity.* A part of the general limitation on the right of self-determination is the specific limitation of territorial integrity. The Declaration on Principles of International Law specifies that the right of self-determination shall not "be construed as authorizing or encouraging any action which would dismember or impair, totally or in part, the territorial integrity or political unity of sovereign and independent States."[53] This limitation is an extension of the desire in most societies to create a social and legal system that is relatively stable. In the international community, dominated as it is by states, the stability desired primarily concerns territorial boundaries.[54] This limitation was implied by the United States as part of its decision not to recognize the independence of Lithuania in 1990–1[55] and was evident in the initial response of the European Community to the breakup of Yugoslavia.[56]

But territorial integrity cannot be asserted as a limitation in all situations. The Declaration on Principles of International Law provides that the only states that can rely on this limitation are those "conducting themselves in compliance with the principle of equal rights and self-determination of peoples . . . and thus possessed of a government representing the whole people belonging to the territory without distinction as to race, creed or colour." So a government of a state that does not represent the whole population on its territory without discrimination – such as Iraq with respect to the Kurds or South Africa with respect to the blacks – cannot succeed in limiting the right of self-determination by arguing that it would infringe the state's territorial integrity.[57] After the recognition by the international community of the disintegration of the U.S.S.R. and Yugoslavia as unitary states, it may now be that any government that is oppressive to peoples on its territory can no longer rely on the general interest of the community in protecting territorial integrity as a limitation on the right of self-determination. To allow such a limitation could legitimate oppression of peoples. Besides, state practice shows that limitations on the right of self-determination in the interest of territorial integrity are often ignored, as seen in the recognition of the independence of Bangladesh (from akistan), Singapore (from Malaysia) and Belize (despite the claims of Guatemala).[58]

It appears then that only a government of a state that allows all its peoples to decide freely their political status and economic, social, and cultural development can assert an interest in protecting its territorial integrity to limit the exercise of a right of self-determination. So territorial integrity, as a limitation on the exercise of the right of self-determination, can only apply to those states (a minority) in which the government represents the whole population in accordance with the exercise of internal self-determination.

*Uti Possidetis Juris.* Where the right of self-determination is exercised to gain independence from a colonial power or to secede from a sovereign state, the principle of *uti possidetis* may apply as a limitation on that right. The aim of this principle is to achieve territorial stability by preserving the colonial boundaries of a state. It is a limitation based on the maintenance of international peace and security, as was made clear by a chamber of the International Court of Justice: "The maintenance of the territorial status quo in Africa is often seen as the wisest course, to preserve what has been achieved by peoples who have struggled for their independence, and to avoid a disruption which would deprive the continent of the gains achieved by much sacrifice . . . [and] induced African States . . . to take account of [*uti possidetis*] in the interpretation of the principle of self-determination of peoples."[59]

This principle arose in the South American context but has begun to be applied to territorial disputes wherever they occur, including Europe.[60] In a world where boundary disputes are a constant source of instability and tension, the principle of *uti possidetis* seems to have been adopted by some international tribunals as a broad limitation on the exercise of the right of self-determination. Yet state practice is inconclusive. For example, upon winning independence from the colonial powers, British Togo was incorporated into Ghana by referendum and British and Italian Somaliland became the one state of Somalia; Belize was recognized as being independent from Guatemala; and yet the international community recognized the incorporation of Goa into India,[61] despite the colonial boundaries that had existed. This situation led the dissenting judge in the *Frontier Dispute case* to remark that "the frontiers of an independent State emerging from colonization may differ from the frontiers of the colony which it replaces . . . [as a result of] the exercise of the right of self-determination."[62] In addition, the inequities of the colonial boundaries cannot be ignored, as these boundaries were the result of administrative dispositions by colonial powers, often in complete disregard for natural geographic or ethnic boundaries.[63] These inequities often give rise to conflicts and can appear to give legitimacy to unlawful acts, simply because those unlawful acts occurred a number of years previously, as with the boundaries set for the Baltic states by the U.S.S.R.[64] Indeed, the chamber of the International Court of Justice that considered the *Land, Island and Maritime Dispute case* noted that "*uti possidetis juris* is essentially a retrospective principle, investing as international boundaries administrative limits intended originally for quite other purposes."[65]

Despite the uncertainties in the universal application of the principle of *uti possidetis*, it is a principle that does need to be considered as a limitation on the right of self-determination. It is only relevant, though in those very few situations when the exercise of the right is for secession and when that secession has an effect on a colonial boundary.

*International Peace and Security Generally.* While there are prohibitions on the use of force and intervention to protect the general interest of international society in peace and security, there has been an acceptance of the need to ease those prohibitions in order to protect those whose right of self-determination is being infringed. It is clear that those deprived of the right of self-determination can seek forcible international support to uphold that right, and it is also clear that no state is entitled to use force against them.[66] It may even be that groups seeking to exercise their right of self-determination could use armed force if that was the only means to resist forcible action against them.[67] The increase in actions taken by the international community that might be classified as humanitarian intervention, such as that in Somalia and the creation of "safe havens" for the Kurds in Iraq,[68] indicates the reduced importance given by the international community to the territorial integrity of a state when human rights, including the right of self-determination, are grossly and systematically violated.

Thus a special status has emerged with regard to the right of self-determination, one in which the usual limitations on the exercise of that right in deference to the general interests of the international community might not be applied. This status is consistent with what was the first clear international declaration upholding the right of self-determination – the Declaration on the Granting of Independence to Colonial Countries and Peoples. Issued in 1960, the declaration states that "the subjection of peoples to alien subjugation, domination and exploitation constitutes a denial of fundamental human rights, is contrary to the Charter of the United Nations and is *an impediment to the promotion of world peace and co-operation.*"[69]

Therefore, such undertakings as the military action in the Baltic states by the government of the former U.S.S.R. and the military action against Slovenia and Croatia by the government of the former Yugoslavia were violations of the right of self-determination of the peoples involved and were not justifiable limitations of that right.

There are limitations on the right of self-determination, and they have to do with what is in the general interest of society as a whole, whether within a state or within the larger community of states – that is, with maintaining peace and security. Two specific limitations proceed from this general interest, one involves protecting the territorial integrity of a state; the other, protecting colonial boundaries in keeping with the principle of *uti possidetis*. But each of these limitations is applicable to only a few of the ways in which the right of self-determination might be exercised; and, even in those instances, the limitations might not be appropriate given the particular circumstances of the claim.

### "Peoples" Protected by the Right of Self-Determination

No permanent or universal objective definition of "peoples" has yet been accepted in relation to the right of self-determination, either in theory or by state practice. This is not surprising as "nations and peoples, like genetic populations, are recent, contingent, and have been formed and reformed constantly throughout history."[70] Nevertheless, the Article 1 of the International Covenant on Civil and Political Rights and state practice reject the notion that peoples can only be defined as all the inhabitants of a state – hence the application of the right of self-determination to noncolonial territories.[71] Despite this lack of an agreed-upon definition, in the vast majority of cases it is clear who peoples are. Common identity, traditions and historical ties to a territory can be established without much trouble in most instances – for example, with the Tibetans, the Kurds, and the Yanomani. Indeed, many peoples can be identified by reference to a state's public documents or public administration, such as the Slovaks, who were given special protections under the Czechoslovak constitution or the Scots, who in law and education have court and school systems separate from those of England. The actions of a state against a particular group can also serve to identify it as a people. In instances of doubt, self-identification by a group as a people would be a primary consideration, as accepted in the Convention concerning Indigenous and Tribal People in Independent Countries (1989),[72] although this would probably not keep disputes from arising.

The human rights approach can help in defining who are peoples and reduce the grounds for dispute. While international human rights law does not as yet provide a definition of a people, it does clarify who is a victim of a breach of human rights. Disputes involving the right of self-determination rest on claims of violations of that right. By deciding a complainant is the victim of a breach of that right, who are the people entitled to the protection of that right is clarified.

The term "victim" is defined in Article 25 of the European Human Rights Convention and Article 44 of the American Human Rights Convention as including any individual, nongovernmental organization, or group of persons. Articles 55 and 56 of the African Charter on Human and Peoples' Rights do not place any restriction on the type of claimant who can register a complaint. The Optional Protocol to the ICCPR limits the term "victim" to meaning individuals, as was seen above.[73] In examining complaints, international tribunals have decided that, even if the complainant is not the direct object of a violation of rights by a state, these articles allow claims to be brought as long as the complainant is "at the risk of being directly affected by"[74] the state's action. Even a representative body, such as a church, can bring a claim "in its own capacity as a representative of its members,"[75] and claims have been accepted from many groups, such as trade unions, corporations, and prisoners (where each has suffered the same abuse of rights).[76] In consequence, a broad class of persons, both individuals and groups, can bring claims for a breach of human rights. This is consistent with the need to protect as many persons as possible from violations of human rights by a state, considering both the inequality of power between a state and its inhabitants and the nonreciprocal nature of human rights treaties.[77]

This clarification of who is a victim of a human rights violation within the framework of international human rights law can be applied to the right of self-determination. The complainant alleging a breach of that right will usually be an individual directly affected or at risk of being directly affected because of being a member of a people against whom the state is taking action; or else the complainant will be a representative body bringing a claim on behalf of a people as a whole. The representative of the people will generally be evident, though some form of international recognition may be helpful.[78] Under the human rights approach either kind of complainant could bring a claim for a violation of the right of self-determination. A decision that these complainants are victims of violations of this right would clarify who are peoples entitled to the protection of the right. But the focus is then not on the complainants alone but also on the violation of human rights. Thus the issue of who is a people becomes primarily a procedural matter in the protection of the right of self-determination and so reduces the importance of a definition of peoples as a factor in determining the application and exercise of the right.

### Exercise of the Right of Self-Determination

Too often the assumption has been that the only possible exercise of the right of self-determination is by independence – either directly from a colonial power or by secession from an independent state. This assumption is invalid. It is also dangerous, as it may create a volatile environment within states. There is rarely a clear or absolute division of peoples within a state, and such thinking can lead to conflicts by raising expectations. It can also foster claims by those elites more interested in accruing power than in ensuring respect for rights.

From the early stages of the development of the right of self-determination, many possible forms of exercise of the right have been available, with independence/secession being only one option and then only in extreme cases of oppression. In 1920, the Commission of Inquiry that considered whether the Aaland Islands were part of Finland or Sweden concluded that "the separation of a minority from the State of which it forms a part and its incorporation in another State can only be considered as an altogether exceptional solution, a last resort when the State lacks either the will or the power to enact and apply just and effective guarantees."[79]

The international community looked on colonial territories as in need of an exceptional solution. But even then independence was only one option, with free association and integration also possible,[80] and State practice restricting it in some situations such as colonial enclaves.[81] Despite the efforts of some jurists,[82] it is clear that there is no absolute right of secession. Indeed, there must be a strong presumption against secession in noncolonial situations.

Instead, the exercise of the right of self-determination can take a variety of forms, from autonomy over most policies and laws in a region or part of a state, such as with the canton system in Switzerland and, perhaps, Greenland's relationship with Denmark; to exclusive control by a people over only certain aspects of policy, such as educational, social, and cultural matters.[83] The way in which the right of self-determination is exercised will usually depend on the constitutional order of the state concerned and may challenge the present centralized structure of most states. This variety of possible ways of exercising of the right occurs because "the concept of self-determination is capable of embracing much more nuanced interpretations and applications [than just that of independent Statehood], particularly in an increasingly interdependent world in which the formal attributes of Statehood mean less and less."[84]

The human rights approach draws on this variety of interpretations and applications to put the claimed right in context. It aims at the protection of all rights and not just the right of self-determination in isolation. These rights and the general interests of society can then be balanced and a solution found that insofar as possible protects all rights in the particular circumstances. Thus, instead of secession being the only option, peoples would be able to exercise their right of self-determination by such methods as the creation of a federation; guarantees of political power to defend or promote certain group interests; the giving of special assurances (as with minority rights); providing for a specific recognized status for a group; or by "consociational democracy."[85] Yet circumstances where secession may be the appropriate form of exercise of the right might still arise. In particular, "where the majority [in a State] refuses to even recognize a substantial minority or ethnically distinct nation, and prevents it from sharing in the life of the State, external self-determination or secession may seem like the last hope for those who feel like they are treated as aliens in their own country."[86]

The human rights approach acknowledges the various ways in which the right of self-determination may be exercised and accepts that independence/secession is rarely an appropriate or necessary means of exercise, given the need to protect the rights of others and the general interests of society. As a consequence, the approach affords flexibility in finding solutions for protecting that right and resolving conflicts without dictating one solution.[87] It could even comprehend flexibility in sovereignty – for example, by giving separate British and Irish nationalities to inhabitants of Northern Ireland as a means of protecting the right of self-determination in that situation.

## Conclusion

Self-determination is defined as a human right in international law. Its purpose is to protect the rights of groups, as groups, from oppression, and its development and changing application over the years have been within the context of the development of international human rights law. The possible ways in which the right of self-determination can be legitimately exercised are now considered in terms of human rights, including their impact on the human rights of others. Therefore, the human rights approach proposed here, which applies the framework of international human rights law to the right of self-determination, is entirely consistent with the development of international law.

The legal framework of international human rights law enables competing claims and obligations concerning human rights to be resolved in a peaceful manner and respects the rights and interests of all members of the international community. It is also sufficiently flexible to allow a range of possible solutions to any related conflict. By applying this framework to the right of self-determination, solutions can be found to some conflicts and a more coherent approach to the right itself can be developed. Moreover, a commitment to applying international human rights law to the right of self-determination reinforces the acknowledgement by states that their sovereignty is not absolute at least as far as the treatment of persons and groups on their territory is concerned. It would also require acceptance by those claiming a right of self-determination that the rights of others, both individually and as a group, must be respected. Therefore, the possibility exists that the principles and procedures developed to consider human rights in the international community can be used to find a solution to conflicts connected with the right of self-determination without the consequences feared by the Secretary-General in the opening quotation arising.

## Notes

This chapter is largely based on a paper delivered by the author at the ACUNS/ASIL Summer Workshop on International Organization Studies in Providence, Rhode Island, in July 1994 and published in *I.C.L.Q.* 43 (1994): 857–885.

1. The statement is reproduced in A. Roberts and B. Kingsbury, *United Nations, Divided World*, 2nd ed. (Oxford: Oxford University Press, 1993), 470–498.
2. Article 4, Vienna Declaration and Programme of Action arising from the United Nations World Conference on Human Rights in 1993. See *International Legal Materials* 32 (1993): 1661. See also W. M. Reisman, "Sovereignty and Human Rights in Contemporary International Law" *American Journal of International Law* 82 (1990): 866.
3. In 1918 U.S. President Woodrow Wilson warned that "peoples may now be dominated and governed only by their own consent.

'Self-determination' is not a mere phrase. It is an imperative principle of action, which statesmen will henceforth ignore at their peril." See "War Aims of Germany and Austria (1918)," in R. Baker and W. Dodd (eds), *The Public Papers of Woodrow Wilson: War and Peace* 177 (1927): 182. See also the summary of Wilson's position in H. Hannum, "Rethinking Self–Determination" *Virginia Journal of International Law* 34 (1993): 2–8.

4. The bases for the statements given here on the development of the right of self-determination are provided in R. McCorquodale, "Self-Determination: A Human Rights Approach", I.C.L.Q. 43 (1994): 857–865. For an excellent analysis of the development of the right, see G. Simpson, "The Diffusion of Sovereignty: Self-Determinations in The Postcolonial Age", Chapter 3 in this volume.

5. F. Tesón, "The Kantian Theory of International Law" *Columbia Law Review* 92 (1992): 53–54, points out that the Statist conception of international law "is incapable of serving as the normative framework for present or future political realities. . . new times call for a fresh conceptual and ethical language."

6. Roberts and Kingsbury, *United Nations, Divided World*, at paragraphs 17 and 81 of statement by Boutros-Ghali.

7. Common article 1(1) provides that "all peoples have the right of self-determination. By virtue of that right they freely determine their political status and freely pursue their economic, social and cultural development."

8. The Declaration on Principles of International Law concerning Friendly Relations and Cooperation among States in accordance with the Charter of the United Nations, General Assembly Resolution 2625 (XXV), adopted 24 October 1970.

9. Other documents in the Conference on Security and Co-operation in Europe (C.S.C.E.) process have also endorsed the right of self-determination, e.g. the Document of the Copenhagen Meeting of the Conference on the Human Dimension of the C.S.C.E., 1990 and The Charter of Paris for a New Europe 1990.

10. Supporters of the view that the right of self-determination may be part of *jus cogens* include: I. Brownlie, *Principles of Public International Law,* 4th ed. (Oxford: Oxford University Press, 1991), 513; A. Cassese, *International Law in a Divided World* (Oxford: Oxford University Press, 1986), 136; J. Crawford, "The Rights of Peoples: Some Conclusions" in J. Crawford (ed.), *The Rights of Peoples*, (Oxford: Oxford University Press, 1988), 159–166; H. Gros Espiell, *The Right to Self-Determination, Implementation of*

*United Nations Resolutions* (New York: United Nations, 1978) para. 85 (where he refers to state's attitudes); and the United Kingdom's and Argentina's statements in the context of the Falklands/Malvinas dispute in *B.Y.I.L.* 53 (1982): 366–379.

11. Human Rights Committee General Comments 12 (21) para. 1 (General Assembly Official Records Doc A/39/40, pp.142–143); *emphasis* added.

12. Roberts and Kingsbury, *United Nations, Divided World*, at paragraph 81 of statement by Boutros-Ghali.

13. Hence overcoming Article 2(7) of the United Nations Charter. See A. Bloed, "Human Rights and Non-Intervention" in A. Bloed and P. van Dijk (eds), *Essays on Human Rights in the Helsinki Process* (Dordrecht: Nijhoff, 1985), 57; and Reisman, "Sovereignty and Human Rights," 866.

14. Adopted by consensus 25 June 1993 (see 32 *International Legal Materials* (1993): 1661.

15. *International Legal Materials* 30 (1991): 1670.

16. *Ominayak and the Lubicon Lake Band v. Canada* Human Rights Committee Report Doc A/45/40 Vol.II Annex IX, 1–27 (para. 32.1).

17. See also criticism by D. McGoldrick, "Canadian Indians, Cultural Rights and the Human Rights Committee," I.C.L.Q. 40 (1991): 658.

18. See D. McGoldrick, *The Human Rights Committee* (Oxford: Oxford University Press, 1991), 249–254 and also R. McCorquodale, "The United Kingdom's Compliance with Article 1 of the I.C.C.P.R." in D. Harris and S. Joseph (eds), *The International Covenant on Civil and Political Rights and the United Kingdom*, (Oxford: Oxford University Press, 1995).

19. "Guidelines for National Periodic Reports", Afr/Com' H.P.R.5(IV), Part III, reported in 5 R.A.D.I.C./Afr.J.I.C.L. (1993) 885, pp.901–905.

20. E.g. the United States Court of Appeals, Second Circuit, in *Filartiga* v. *Pena-Irala* 630 F 2nd 876 (1980): 883–885, held that the right of freedom from torture was part of customary international law.

21. See L. Henkin, "Human Rights" 8 *Encyclopaedia of Public International Law* (Max Planck, Amsterdam, 1985) 268 at 271.

22. About 25 States have ratified the A.C.H.R. (although not the United States). Individual petition is automatic on ratification (art 44) and about 15 States have recognized the jurisdiction of the Court (art 62).

23. About 35 States are parties to the E.C.H.R. The Court's juris-

diction is compulsory on ratification. Every party has also made declarations (under art 25) allowing a right of individual petition.

24. About 25 States have ratified the A.C.H.R (although not the United States). Individual petition is automatic on ratification (art 44) and about 15 States have recognized the jurisdiction of the Court (art 62).

25. L. Prott, "Cultural Rights as Peoples' Rights in International Law" in J. Crawford (ed.), *The Rights of Peoples, op cit supra* n.10, p.93.

26. There are also significant procedural rules, such as the exhaustion of local remedies and only one international human rights tribunal is to deal with the same complaint at the same time.

27. Article 7 I.C.C.P.R., article 3 E.C.H.R. and article 5(2) A.C.H.R.

28. The Convention on the Prevention and Punishment of the Crime of Genocide 1948.

29. Some rights cannot be derogated from e.g. the right to life, freedom from slavery and freedom from retrospective criminal laws; see article 4 I.C.C.P.R., article 15 E.C.H.R. and article 27 A.C.H.R. However, even where a State purports to derogate from its obligations, or to place a reservation, under a human rights treaty it is still subject to the scrutiny of the international human rights tribunals – *Belilos v. Switzerland* E.Ct.H.R. Ser A No.132 (1988), *Brannigan and McBride v. U.K.* E.Ct.H.R. Ser A No.258B (1993) and *Effect of Reservations on Entry into Force of the American Convention (Articles 74 and 75)* 67 I.L.R. 559 (1982).

30. Article 19(3) I.C.C.P.R.; article 19(2) E.C.H.R.; article 13(2) A.C.H.R. – also article 27(2) A.C.H.P.R.

31. See P. Allott, *Eunomia*, (Oxford: Oxford University Press, 1990), Chap. 3.

32. See the decision of the Inter-American Court of Human Rights in *Effect of Reservations on Entry into Force of the American Convention (Articles 74 and 75)* 67 I.L.R. 559 (1982) para. 29, quoted at n.70 below.

33. See P. van Dijk and G. van Hoof, *Theory and Practice of the European Convention on Human Rights* (Kluwer, 2nd ed., 1990) pp.585–606.

34. *Belgian Linguistics Case* E.Ct.H.R. Series A, Vol.6 (1968) para. 34–35.

35. *Handyside v. U.K.* E.Ct.H.R. Series A Vol.24 (1976) para. 48–50. See also *The Sunday Times v. U.K.* E.Ct.H.R. Series A, Vol.30 (1979).

36. *Bleir v. Uruguay* 1 Selected Decisions H.R.C. (1982) 109, at p.112.

37. See below with regard to the definition of "peoples".

38. *Tyrer v. U.K.* E.Ct.H.R. Series A, Vol.26 (1978) para.15–16.
39. See the documents arising from the C.S.C.E. Process, such as The Charter of Paris for a New Europe 1990 (30 I.L.M. 190 (1991)) and D.McGoldrick, "The Development of the Conference on Security and Co-Operation in Europe – From Process to Institution" in B. Jackson and D. McGoldrick (eds), *Legal Visions of the New Europe* (London: Graham and Trotman, 1993) p.135.
40. For example, the Zimbabwe Supreme Court in *Catholic Commission for Justice and Peace in Zimbabwe v. Attorney-General* 1993 (4) SA 239 and *S v. Ncube* 1988 (2) SA 702; the Namibian Supreme Court in *Ex parte Attorney-General, Namibia: In Re Corporal Punishment by Organs of State* 1991 (3) SA 76; and by the United Kingdom Court of Appeal in *Derbyshire County Council v. Times Newspapers* [1992] 3 W.L.R. 28.
41. See D. Harris, "The System of Supervision of the European Social Charter" in L. Betten (ed.), *The Future of European Social Policy* (1991), particularly at p.31. See also M. Häusermann, "The Realization and Implementation of Economic, Social and Cultural Rights" in D. Beddard and S. Hill (eds), *Economic, Social and Cultural Rights* (Southampton University Press, 1992) p.47 and P. Alston, "The Committee on Economic, Social and Cultural Rights" in P. Alston (ed.), *The United Nations and Human Rights: A Critical Appraisal* (Oxford: Oxford University Press, 1992) p.473. The right to education, a social and cultural right, is protected in Protocol 1 Art 2 of the E.C.H.R.
42. Opinion No.2, 3 E.J.I.L. (1992) 182–185.
43. E.g., the right of self-determination of the Kurds has impacts on Iraq, Turkey, Iran and Syria.
44. Article 17 E.C.H.R. and article 29(a) A.C.H.R.
45. *Kjeldsen, Busk Madsen and Pedersen v. Denmark* E.Ct.H.R. Ser A, Vol.23 (1976) at para. 53. See further, G. Triggs, "The Rights of 'Peoples' and Individual Rights: Conflict or Harmony?" in J. Crawford (ed.), *The Rights of Peoples, op cit supra* n.14, p.141 at p.144.
46. When Namibia became independent in 1990, the new constitution contained entrenched rights due in part to international pressure – see D. van Wyk, "The Making of the Namibian Constitution: Lessons for Africa" 24 Comp and Int L.J. of Southern Africa (1991) 341, at pp.345–346.
47. See, for example, Y. Dinstein, "Self-Determination and the Middle East Conflict" in Y. Alexander and R. Friedlander (eds), *Self-Determination: National, Regional and Global Dimensions*, (Westview Press, Boulder, 1980) and A.Cassese, "The Israel-PLO

Agreement and Self-Determination," 4 E.J.I.L. (1993) 564.

48. Opinion No.2, 3 E.J.I.L. (1992) 183–184. It also refused Bosnia's application for recognition as an independent state and found that a referendum was needed which was open to all citizens to decide the matter – Opinion No.4, 3 E.J.I.L. (1993) 74–76.

49. Declaration on Principles of International Law, *op cit supra* n.8.

50. The decision of the Estonian government to restrict the voting franchise in Estonia has been criticized as being a violation of the rights of those Russians living in Estonia for many decades – see *The Independent*, London, 3 September, 1992.

51. Declaration 2, *op cit supra* n.8.

52. Article 1(1) United Nations Charter.

53. *Op cit supra* n.8.

54. A number of treaties reflect this concern, e.g. Article 11 Vienna Convention on Succession of States in Respect of Treaties 1978.

55. *Keesing's Record of World Events*, April/May 1990, para. 37462.

56. The U.K. Foreign Secretary said in January, 1992 that "the first prize, the best prize would have been a Yugoslavia held together on the basis of consent."

57. See R. McCorquodale, "South Africa and the Right of Self-Determination" 10 S.A.J.H.R. (1994) 4.

58. See J. Maguire, "The Decolonization of Belize: Self-Determination v. Territorial Integrity," 22 Virg J.I.L. (1982) 849.

59. *Case concerning the Frontier Dispute (Burkina Faso and Mali)* I.C.J. Rep 1986 554, at p.567. The principle of *uti possidetis* was expressly adopted by the Organization of African Unity in 1964 (A.G.H./Res 16(1)) and has been upheld in *Land, Island and Maritime Dispute Case (El Salvador v. Honduras)* (Merits) I.C.J. Rep 1992 35 and by the dissenting Judge Bedjaoui of the International Arbitration Tribunal decision in *Guinea-Bissau v. Senegal* 83 I.L.R. (1989) 1. See further G. Naldi, "Case concerning the Frontier Dispute (Burkina Faso and Mali): *Uti Possidetis* in an African Perspective," 36 I.C.L.Q. (1987) 893.

60. In Opinion 3 of the Badinter Committee 3 E.J.I.L. (1992) 184–185, at p.185, the Committee considered that, unless there was contrary agreement, "former boundaries became frontiers protected by international law" due to *uti possidetis*. This decision is rightly criticized as applying a principle of international law to internal administrative boundaries – see H.Hannum, *op.cit. supra* n.3.

61. The incorporation of Goa in India in 1962 (and Ifni into Morocco in 1969) was probably an example of the rare position concerning "colonial enclaves", for which the right of self-

determination may not be applicable. However, as J.Crawford, *The Creation of States in International Law* (Oxford: Oxford University Press, 1979) n.38, at p.384, has made clear: "international practice supports [this] application in the most limited circumstances: that is, to minute territories which approximate, in the geographical sense, to 'enclaves' of the claimant state, which are ethnically and economically parasitic upon or derivative of that state, and which cannot be said in any legitimate sense to constitute separate territorial units."

62. *Op cit supra* n.59, Separate Opinion, at p.653.
63. Such as the Caprivi Strip in Namibia – a finger of land stretching to Zambia and Zimbabwe – the inclusion of which "was due to poor geographical knowledge, since the intention had been to secure access to the Zambezi for the German colony, in the [mistaken] belief that an important communications route was involved" – M.Shaw, *Title to Territory in Africa* (Oxford: Clarendon, 1986) at p.51.
64. See R. Mullerson, "The Continuity and Succession of States by Reference to the Former U.S.S.R. and Yugoslavia", 42 I.C.L.Q. (1993) 473, at p.487.
65. *Op cit supra* n.59, at p.388.
66. The Declaration on Principles of International Law, *op cit supra* n.8, provides that "every State has the duty to refrain from any forcible action which deprives peoples. . .of their right of self-determination and freedom and independence."
67. Article 7 of The Definition of Aggression (General Assembly Resolution 3314 (XXIX) 14 December 1974) and article 1 paragraph 4 of Protocol I to the Geneva Conventions of 12 August 1949 and relating to the Protection of Victims of International Armed Conflicts refer to the resistance of forcible action by peoples exercising their right of self-determination. H.Gros Espiell, *The Right to Self-Determination: Implementation of United Nations Resolutions*, *op cit supra* n.10, at p.14 concludes from this that because "a State which forcibly subjugates a people to colonial or alien [or racist] domination is committing an unlawful act expressly so defined by international law, . . .[therefore] the subject people, in the exercise of its inherent right of self-defence, may fight to defend and attain its right to self-determination."
68. Security Council Resolution 688 (5 April 1991) created "safe havens" for the Kurds north of the 36th parallel in Iraq. See R. McCorquodale, "Self-Determination beyond the Colonial Context and its Potential Impact on Africa", 4 R.A.D.I.C./ African J.I.C.L. (1992) 592, at pp.600–601; O.Schachter, "United

Nations Law in the Gulf Conflict", 85 A.J.I.L. 452 (1991) at pp.468–469; and R. McCorquodale, "The World has a Legal Duty to Protect the Kurds" *The Independent*, London, 20 April 1991, p.14

69. General Assembly Resolution 1514 (xv) art 1. emphasis added.

70. E. Kamenka, "Human Rights, Peoples' Rights" in J. Crawford (ed.), *The Rights of Peoples, op cit supra* n.10, p.127, at p.133. See also P. Allott, "The Nation as Mind Politic", 24 N.Y.U.J.I.L.P. (1992) 1361 and N. Berman, "Sovereignty in Abeyance: Self-Determination in International Law", 7 Wisconsin I.L.J. (1988) 51.

71. See criticism of the "peoples" approach to self-determination in R. McCorquodale, "Self-Determination: A Human Rights Approach", 43 I.C.L.Q. (1994) 857, at pp.866–868.

72. Art 1(2) provides that self-identification is a "fundamental criterion" of the definition of "peoples", 28 I.L.M. 1382 (1989).

73. See text at note 16.

74. *Marckx v. Belgium* E.Ct.H.R. Series A, Vol.31 (1979) at p.12.

75. *Pastor X and the Church of Scientology v. Sweden* Y.B.K. XXII (1979) 244 (European Commission of Human Rights).

76. See further, P. van Dijk and G. van Hoof, *Theory and Practice of the European Convention on Human Rights, op cit supra* n.33, pp.37–52.

77. In *Effect of Reservations on Entry into Force of the American Convention (Articles 74 and 75)* 67 I.L.R. 559 (1982) para. 29, the Inter-American Court of Human Rights held that "modern human rights treaties in general, and the [A.C.H.R.] in particular, are not multilateral treaties of the traditional type concluded to accomplish the reciprocal exchange of rights for the mutual benefit of the contracting States. Their object and purpose is the protection of the basic rights of individual human beings, irrespective of their nationality, both against the State of their nationality and all other contracting States. In concluding these human rights treaties, the States can be deemed to submit themselves to a legal order within which they, for the common good, assume various obligations, not in relation to other States, but towards all individuals within their jurisdiction." See also *Ireland v. U.K.* E.Ct.H.R. Series A, Vol.25 (1978) at para. 160.

78. Some representatives have been identified by the international community, for example, by the granting of Observer status in the United Nations and in regional bodies. The representatives of peoples can never be States "as the Charter and the two International Covenants expressly declare, [it is] a right of peoples. Not

States. Not countries. Not governments. Peoples" – Statement by the United Kingdom representative to the United Nations Commission on Human Rights, 9 February 1988, U.K.M.I.L., 59 B.Y.I.L. (1988) p.441.

79. League of Nations Doc. B7.21/68/106 (1921) at p.28.
80. See G.A. Resolution 1541 (XV) 1960, 15 December 1960.
81. Such as Goa into India and Ifni into Morocco see fn.61.
82. See, for example, L. Buchheit, *Secession: The Legitimacy of Self-Determination* (New Haven: Yale Univ Press, 1978); L.-C. Chen, "Self-Determination and World Public Order", 66 Notre Dame L.R. (1991) 1287; and L. Brilmayer, "Secession and Self-Determination: A Territorial Interpretation", 16 Yale J.I.L. (1991) 177.
83. For a more detailed examination of the various forms and their applications see H. Hannum, *Autonomy. Sovereignty and Self-Determination: The Accommodation of Conflicting Rights*, (University of Pennsilvania Press, 1990). Economic self-determination has been used in the context of sovereignty over natural resources, e.g. in art 1(2) I.C.C.P.R. and I.C.E.S.C.R.
84. S.J. Anaya, "The Capacity of International Law to Advance Ethnic or Nationality Rights Claims", 75 Iowa L.R. 837 (1990) 840, p.842.
85. This has four elements: a "grand coalition" of political leaders representative of the different groups in society; the presence of a mutual veto for the protection of minority interests; proportionality in political representation and appointments; and a high degree of autonomy for each group in running its internal affairs – A. Lijphart, *Democracy in Plural Societies* (1977).
86. H. Hannum, *op. cit. supra* n.3, at p.64.
87. The exercise of a right tends to be upheld only to the extent that it is necessary to protect those claiming the right. The European Court of Human Rights has made this clear in its application of the right to education – see the *Belgian Linguistics Case* E.Ct.H.R. Series A, Vol.6 (1968) at para. 3; *Kjeldsen, Busk Madsen and Pedersen v. Denmark* E.Ct.H.R. Ser A, Vol.23 (1976) at para. 53; and the European Commission on Human Rights has held that the right of freedom of thought and religion of conscientious objectors is not violated if reasonable alternative arrangements are available that meet the conscientious objections – see P. van Dijk and G. van Hoof, *Theory and Practice of the European Convention on Human Rights, op. cit. supra* n.33, p.400–410.

# – 3 –

# The Diffusion of Sovereignty: Self-Determinations in the Post-Colonial Age

## Gerry J. Simpson

"But do you know what a nation means?" says John Wyse.
"Yes," says Bloom.
"What is it," says John Wyse.
"A nation," says Bloom. "A nation is the same people living in the same place."
"By God, then," says Ned, laughing, "if that's so I'm a nation for I'm living in the same place for the past five years."

*James Joyce, Ulysses*

## International Law and Self-Determination

In international law, the right of self-determination is invoked more often than any other collective human right.[1] At a political level, it is proclaimed by, and on behalf of, non-state entities as diverse as the Kurds, the Quebecois, the Basques, the Scots, the Palestinians, the East Timorese, and the Tamils.[2] These groups are accorded varying degrees of political recognition in the world community. International law, too, bestows a measure of legitimacy on some of them but in a somewhat haphazard manner.[3] Too frequently, success in defending or asserting collective political and cultural rights, depends, at the international level, on the visibility of the cause or the exercise of violence in support of the claim. Often the international community only becomes involved in disputes over self-determination when there is already a threat to peace and security. This is at least partly attributable to the absence of a sophisticated and flexible principle of self-determination that could be applied before a crisis develops.

Any potential role self-determination may have had in promoting resolution of these conflicts has been diminished by two interpretive trends. The first has been toward conservative, statist, and untenable definitions of the principle. This process reached its apogee during the period when self-determination came to be identified exclusively with decolonization. As this period drew to a close and with only the vestigial peculiarities of classical colonialism remaining,[4] self-determination, as conceived by the United Nations, had been adopted as a principle without a purpose, a right apparently bereft of any potential beneficiaries.[5]

A more recent, second trend has involved the misappropriation of the label. The elasticity of self-determination has, throughout history, both ensured its longevity and diminished its legitimacy. The principle has had to be capable of surviving inconsistent application absorbing anomalies; and, ultimately, satisfying powerful strategic and political interests and realities without compromising its revolutionary appeal. In this latter role, it has frequently flattered to deceive. In effect, self-determination has most assiduously served the same state system it pretends to assail. In the process, the principle has evolved into a highly manipulable and indiscriminately employed slogan.[6] It vests those who use it with a tainted respectability[7] but is at the same time deprived of clarity and the possibility of legal content or persuasive force.[8] There is a contradiction at the heart of self-determination that does not exist in other potentially ambiguous norms of international law. While the interpretation of nonintervention, sovereignty, or domestic jurisdiction may differ, the core principle remains the same – the sanctity of the state. In the case of self-determination there is an internal opposition contained in the idea of on the one hand, state rights to self-determination and, on the other, the rights of minorities within a state to dismember or challenge it in the name of another competing norm of self-determination.

Clearly, then, self-determination at present lacks both definition and applicability.[9] If the principle is to be salvaged from "its descent into incoherence,"[10] there must be a renewal of the link between autonomy, democracy, human rights, and the right of self-determination. The way to bring about this renewal is to adopt a more liberal and expansive interpretation of the right, one that encompasses rights to autonomy, constitutional recognition, devolution, and cultural self-expression. In this way, self-determination would be galvanized and rescued from the theoretical confusion and political misuse that has dogged it in recent decades.[11]

In order to understand how the normative force of self-determination has been degraded and, more important, how this process might be reversed, it is necessary to reconceptualize the history of self-determination and, insofar as possible, dispel the myths detaching self-determination from democracy, autonomy and other forms of self-expression. By doing so, it will be possible to illustrate how neither the democratic vein nor the idea of self-determination as a human right of participation or devolution (arising out of an expanded view of sovereignty) should be viewed as being in any way novel or historical. Instead, the period in which self-determination became synonymous with decolonization was somewhat aberrant.

## The United Nations Charter System in the Era of Decolonization

The period of decolonization commenced with inclusion of the principle in the Charter of the United Nations (1945)[12] as one of the organization's major purposes. It reached its peak with the 1970 Declaration on Principles of International Law concerning Friendly Relations and Cooperation among States (1970).[13] Thus, during the past twenty-five years a heavily circumscribed right to self-determination has entered customary international law for the first time.

As will be shown, these formal developments coincided with a failure (or more likely, unwillingness) to grasp the full humanitarian potential of the principle of self-determination.[14] Consequently, the transformation from political strategy to legal right was accompanied by an unnecessary restriction of the concept's revolutionary and democratic possibilities.[15] Now, in the final decade of the twentieth century, self-determination may be exhausted as a legal right in its present form under customary international law. What we have witnessed is the shift from self-determination as an exercisable right to self-determination as a privilege.

The developments lamented above have two principal causes. First, there were the predictable and successful attempts by states in general to exclude a right of secession from the principle of self-determination. Secession was thought to have enormous disruptive potential in the newly independent postcolonial states. This meant that the evolution[16] of self-determination was attended by an abhorrence of one of its natural outcomes: secession. The threat posed by secession to the values of peace and security, as well as to the integrity of individual states, required that it be distinguished from more general rights of self-determination.

The other cause lay in the contemporaneous drive to associate self-determination with decolonization. While self-determination was always recognized as a convenient route by which the independence of the colonies might be achieved, it soon came to be identified exclusively with the process of decolonization. This identification served several purposes. First, it had the merit of aiming at morally commendable ends. Second, it reflected the severely debilitated economic position of the imperial powers. Third, it drew attention away from a right of secession by making decolonization the only legitimate goal of self-determination. Preservation of the state was in this way made compatible with ending empire.

Nonetheless, while self-determination continued to evade definition at a theoretical level, it certainly found a niche in the process of decolonization; this had the double-edged effect, though, of both securing its primacy as long as decolonization was at its most prevalent yet threatening it with obsolescence as the process reached completion.[17]

It was the quest for emancipation by the colonized Afro-Asian nations that distinguished postwar from prewar self-determination.[18] This resulted eventually in the displacement of the national model by the colonial model. Manifesting itself at first as an ill-defined yearning for freedom or independence, the desire for liberation eventually prevailed as the inspiration for the new United Nations law of self-determination.[19] The Western powers were initially averse to self-determination on the grounds that it might be used to facilitate the dismemberment of their empires.[20] Only American distaste for European colonialism prevented the European colonial states from rejecting self-determination altogether, and for a while American democratic idealism[21] came into conflict with European colonial entrenchment.[22] The British view of self-determination was unapologetically paternalistic; and though the United States was eager to display its anticolonial credentials, American support for the principle was equivocal. Meanwhile, because of a newly perceived Soviet threat, the Americans remained diffident about alienating their allies, and it was the influence of the British and the other major colonial powers that resulted in the adoption of an imprecise principle of self-determination in the Charter of the United Nations.[23]

It is a measure of how relatively insignificant the principle of self-determination was thought to be by the drafters of the Charter that mention of it appears only twice in the whole document.[24] There was certainly no right to self-determination flowing directly from the Charter.[25] Prior to 1945 international law knew of no specific right to self-determination.[26] There was no mention of it in the Covenant of the League of Nations, and until 1945 the legitimacy of colonialism was rarely questioned (except, of course, by the peoples subjected to colonial administrative control).

In the Charter the principle of self-determination was of clearly subordinate status in relation both to the prohibition on the use of force and the right of territorial integrity (Article 2(4)) as well as to the general commitment to ensuring peace and security (e.g., Chapter VII), all of which were regarded as the foundational norms of the post-war international system. In fact, the Charter is the most tentative of United Nations instruments on the matter of self-determination. Chapters XI and XII make it clear that self-determination for non-self-governing and trust territories is to proceed at a pace dictated by the colonial administrators – e.g., Article 73(b) of Chapter XI enjoins these powers "to develop self-government . . . according to the particular circumstances of each territory and its peoples and their varying stages of advancement."

In fact, the whole trusteeship scheme[27] is an exercise in legitimized colonial paternalism.[28] Article 76, for example, lays down the basic objectives of the scheme and includes among them a duty, "to promote the . . . advancement of the inhabitants of the trust territories, and their progressive development towards self-government or independence *as may be appropriate to the particular circumstances of each territory and its peoples*" (emphasis mine).[29]

In the period immediately following the adoption of the Charter the colonial powers felt little obligation to support the achievement of independence for their colonies. The British had in mind eventual independence for their overseas dominions but pledged, "to guide colonial peoples along the road to self-government *within the framework of the British Empire*."[30] The French adopted an even more controversial policy that envisaged trusteeship as the first step leading to union with France. Their position was stated clearly at the Brazzaville conference of colonial administrators in 1944: "The aims of the work of civilization accomplished by France in its colonies exclude all idea of autonomy, all possibility of evolution outside the French bloc of the Empire; the eventual establishment, even in the distant future, of self-government is to be dismissed."[31]

Portugal, the Netherlands, Belgium, and Spain pursued variations of one or both of these colonial philosophies, and even the United States, which had long been the sternest critic of Western imperialism, had reservations about self-determination for territories in its sphere of influence.[32] The Afro–Asian countries had yet to exercise much influence at the United Nations, and many of them, in dialogue with the imperial states, were often content to accept incremental steps toward independence through negotiation rather than immediate achievement of that goal. The U.S.S.R., the original sponsor of self-determination at San Francisco, continued to formally uphold the idea in its constitution[33] while denying it to a succession of nations that became either part of the U.S.S.R. itself (Lithuania, Latvia, and Estonia) or were absorbed into what became known as the Soviet bloc (e.g., Poland, Czechoslovakia, and Hungary).[34] Even the United Nations itself, in sanctioning the demarcation of Germany, Korea, and Vietnam along Cold War lines had, predictably, abrogated the principle of national self-determination in favor of the interests of peace and security. Most pertinent was the absence of any mention of self-determination or minority rights in the Universal Declaration of Human Rights proclaimed in 1948.[35]

The two decades following the drafting of the Universal Declaration was a period marked by the end of empire. The majority of colonial powers became increasingly committed to divesting their colonial territories while their more recalcitrant metropolitan counterparts were forced to subdue often violent independence movements.[36] At the same time, the Afro-Asian bloc began to find its voice at the United Nations.

## Developments After the Charter

In a resolution issued a mere two years after the Universal Declaration, the General Assembly recognized the right of self-determination as a fundamental human right.[37] In a further resolution the General Assembly decided that an international covenant on human rights should include a right of all peoples and nations to self-determination.[38] Common Articles 1(1) of the International Covenant on Civil and Political Rights and the International Covenant on Social, Economic and Cultural Rights[39] did include a right of self-determination for "peoples."[40] It is, however, unclear which "peoples" are to have this right conferred upon them or, indeed, whether "peoples" is a category distinguishable from states on the one hand and individuals on the other. During the debates in the General Assembly and the Commission on Human Rights leading up to the final drafting of the covenants, there was a certain amount of disagreement over the meaning of both "peoples" and "self-determination." The West European states opposed the inclusion of a right of self-determination on a number of grounds. Initially, they argued that since self-determination was a principle rather than a right it would be premature to include it as a right in the international covenants.[41] Representatives of these states argued, further, that the

Charter did not provide immediate self-government for trust territories through exercise of the right to self-determination[42] and that anyway the principle of self-determination was too complex to be translated into legal terms.[43] History, however, was with the new and increasingly vociferous Afro-Asian bloc, which argued that, self-determination was the most fundamental of all human rights and, as such, was a prerequisite for the enjoyment of all other rights.[44]

The language of the Covenants, like that of the various declarations concerning self-determination, can easily accommodate an expansive definition of the right of self-determination. Again, however, a narrow, more constrained interpretation prevailed. The minimum that can be safely asserted is that the right applied to states and the peoples of non-self-governing and trust territories within the meaning of the Charter. The question of secession and the right of self-determination for noncolonial peoples was raised at the discussions[45] but was eventually dismissed as a separate problem[46] or a misuse of the right of self-determination.

The Covenants were not adopted (or ready for signature and ratification) by the General Assembly until 1966, by which time the content of the right to self-determination had radically changed. Prior to 1960, the scope of the principle was more limited. Self-determination had acquired the status of a normative standard but not yet that of a fully formed right to colonial self-determination.[47] The emphasis in state practice was on progressive development toward self-determination rather than immediate realization of such a right. Two General Assembly resolutions recognizing a right to self-determination and the various drafts of the covenants are hardly conclusive of the existence in customary international law of such a right.

In 1960 the General Assembly passed two resolutions within twenty-four hours of one another that articulated a change in the essential character of the principle of self-determination.[48] In the Declaration on the Granting of Independence to Colonial Countries and Peoples, a Magna Carta[49] of decolonization, the pattern of meticulous preparation for independence set forth by the Charter was scrambled in favor of "a speedy and unconditional end to colonialism." Principle 3, the most radical departure from the Charter, states, "inadequacy of political, economic, social or educational preparedness should never serve as a pretext for delaying independence."[50] Colonialism was thus identified as the great evil in the modern world and was said to "constitute a threat to the peace," taking it outside the proscription in international law against external interference in state affairs.

A number of points can be usefully extracted from this declaration.

First, there is little in it to suggest a move towards the recognition of a right of internal self-determination, i.e., the right of representative government and freedom from discrimination. Only those territories "which have not yet attained independence" are regarded as relevant subjects for the right of self-determination even if this right must be exercised according to the "freely expressed will and desire" of the people. Second, preservation of territorial integrity (Article 6) remains an overriding norm of international law, and the artificial boundaries imposed on the colonies by the Congress of Berlin are tacitly accepted. This gave legal approval to the quite literal change of subject matter (of self-determination) from what had prior to World War II been "cultural and linguistic communities without political organization" to what had become the present "politically defined but culturally diverse colonies and ex-colonies of the developing world."[51]

General Assembly Resolution 1541,[52] passed the following day, is a cautious restatement of the chapters of the Charter of the United Nations on dependent and trust territories. In the light of its predecessor (Resolution 1514), it can be viewed as somewhat incongruous given contemporary sentiments. Resolution 1541 upholds the provisions of the Charter that Resolution 1514 appears to renounce and says nothing of the need for an immediate end to colonialism. Additionally, it provides a number of alternatives[53] to complete independence, alternatives that are conspicuously absent from the previous day's resolution. The idea of self-determination is embellished to the extent that, while it remains fully identified with decolonization, it is not necessarily deemed synonymous with independence. Alternatives to independence are offered, but these do not include a right of secession. The colonially imposed political unit remains inviolable.

The Declaration on Friendly Relations, adopted in 1970, develops the right of self-determination still further but provides few clues to how a precise definition of terms might be accomplished.[54] It is content to remain loyal to what Arangio-Ruiz calls "the big print of self-determination,"[55] failing to grapple with hidden agendas. Nevertheless, as the most recent major resolution concerning self-determination, it represents the highest development yet of United Nations law.[56] At least one writer makes the point: "It is no overstatement to say that the elaboration of the principle of self-determination in the 1970 declaration provides the cornerstone of the U.N. approach to the concept."[57] The Declaration on Friendly Relations is innovative in one very significant sense. It at least prefigures current developments in reforging the bond between democratic representation and self-determination. By 1970, self-determination had ascended to a prominent, if not predominant, position among the principles of international law.[58]

## Decolonization and Self–Determination

By the time independence had been achieved in virtually all the ex-colonial territories, it was possible to state authoritatively that a right of self-determination in colonial cases had been established. J.F. Engers noted that, "ex origine it [self-determination] is not a universal doctrine but rather a specific concept relating to the international law of decolonization."[59] Self-determination had indeed become associated with decolonization but only with a very precisely defined form of decolonization. In the era of self-determination as decolonization, some writers suggested that under the Charter of the United Nations and the series of instruments following it "peoples" had come to mean, "communities that live under (but do not share in) alien sovereignty."[60] A closer reading of the major resolutions indicates a more precise definition. The Declaration on the Granting of Independence (General Assembly Resolution 1541) relates self-determination to "the subjection of peoples to alien subjugation" and specifically mentions colonialism three times. The Declaration on the Admissibility of Intervention in Domestic Affairs and Protection of Their Independence and Sovereignty (1965) requires, "all states [to] respect the right of self-determination and independence of peoples and nations, to be freely exercised without any foreign pressure, and with absolute respect for, human rights and fundamental freedoms." Consequently all states shall contribute to the complete elimination of racial discrimination and colonialism in all its forms and manifestations.[61]

The Declaration on Friendly Relations makes a similar linkage,[62] but it is the resolution outlining the Definition of Aggression[63] that is most illustrative of the prevailing current. It applies the right of self-determination to "peoples under colonial and racist regimes or other forms of alien domination."[64] Finally, in the *Western Sahara case* the International Court of Justice repeatedly equated self-determination with decolonization.[65] Clearly then, U. Umozurike is right to say that "there is almost complete unanimity that self-determination applies to colonial peoples."[66] More than that, however, throughout the 1950s and 1960s "colonial self-determination" referred to a highly specific mode of self-determination for which the prefix colonial provides insufficient guidance.

The Afro-Asian states, and subsequently the United Nations[67] itself, subscribed to a theory of saltwater colonialism.[68] Self-determination could only apply to territories that were separated from their metropolitan parent by oceans or high seas. In this way, overland acquisitions such as those made by China and the U.S.S.R. were excluded from consideration. Excluded too were those ethnic groups within a colonial territory that regarded "the majority rule"[69] as alien or oppressive. In the absence of any requirement that there be strict adherence to internal self-determination, it was enough that the elite, no matter how oppressive or unrepresentative, was at least not tainted with the colonial stigma.

Although self-determination was attaining some measure of conceptual consistency, it could not, based as it was at the time on a saltwater definition of colonialism, be applied effectively to South African apartheid or Rhodesia after the Unilateral Declaration of Independence from Britain (U.D.I.), since neither white elite was connected to a metropolitan power. Hence, a racial element was introduced. Self-determination was to apply where a racial elite was denying representation to other racial groups. This took care of the Southern African questions but raised further ones about forms of tribal rule in the rest of Africa. In order to circumvent this difficulty an additional criterion was incorporated. Mazrui[70] termed the result "pigmentational self-determination," meaning that self-determination could only apply where there was white European or pseudo-European domination. Thus, ruling religious or racially discriminating elites in places such as Eritrea, East Pakistan (now Bangladesh), and Biafra were deemed acceptable even though the peoples indigenous to the territory regarded the controlling regime as colonial.[71]

Furthermore, there was tacit approval in the United Nations for the Moroccan absorption of Ifni, the Indonesian assimilation of West Irian, and the Indian invasion of Goa.[72] In these cases the principle of self-determination was ignored because there was no "foreign" domination where, as B. Neuberger puts it "foreign=European."[73] The Syrians argued that the dominant elite, provided it was not foreign to the whole continent, should be regarded as indigenous and therefore legitimate. Generally speaking, this was the argument most favored at the United Nations, and there was little or no support for the various peoples claiming self-determination from non-European colonial governments (e.g., Tibet, Biafra, Bangladesh).[74]

To summarize, self-determination, during the period in which the Afro-Asian voice in the United Nations and world affairs had most resonance, was defined as the right held by the majority in a colonially defined territory to external independence from colonial domination by metropolitan powers alien to the continent[75] or pseudo-European[76] colonial rule. It did not apply to ethnic groups within these territories nor to majorities that were being oppressed by indigenous "alien" elites. Neither secession nor democratic representation was regarded as part of this novel right of self-determination.[77] In this period "anticolonial results [were] deemed more important than genuine self-determination methods."[78]

Not surprisingly, some of these assumptions are now being questioned. Events in the two decades since the proclamation of the Declaration on Friendly Relations have tended to draw attention to the impoverished state of the law of self-determination as decolonization. The principle of self-determination proved unable to meet the challenges posed by successive claims to independence made on behalf of the Kurds, the Eritreans, the Basques, and other secessionist groups. Nor was it equipped to deal with the denial of internal democratic self-determination to the disenfranchised majorities of states already exercising the right to external self-determination or with the claims of disparate oppressed minorities or indigenous peoples within those states. Self-determination had been transformed from a potentially revolutionary and flexible democratic ideal into an anticolonial imperative.

## Four Challenges to Colonial Self-Determination

In the period from 1975 to 1990, decolonization declined as the dominant form of self-determination. With this decline have come increasing opportunities to fashion alternatives. The nature of the model that will replace colonial self-determination is uncertain. Ultimately, as has been argued here, the theory of colonial self-determination neither exhausted the possible expressions of group freedom nor resolved the contradictions within any single view of self-determination.[79] Colonial self-determination left a vast number of national aspirations unsatisfied. It eschewed innovative forms of self-expression (devolution); it excluded secession but failed to distinguish secession from other forms of decolonization in a morally coherent manner;[80] and, finally, it prolonged the disenfranchisement of majorities in new, often authoritarian, independent states.

A number of alternative and competing models of self-determination have now reemerged to challenge the dominant colonial practice. Each is itself a renewal of a historical movement. They are, as indicated earlier, national self-determination, democratic self-determination, devolutionary self-determination, and secession.[81]

These different forms have not in any material sense returned. Examples of national expression of self-determination (the Basque separatist movement, Acheh province in Indonesia, and Tibetan nationalism), of democratic aspiration (South Africa, Portugal, Spain), of devolutionary practices (Quebec, Scotland), and of secession (Biafra, Bangladesh) continued throughout the period of decolonization. The opportunities for such expression have, however, been dramatically enhanced by the existence of a number of changes in the international environment. First, the colonial period has more or less ended at last.[82] One of the last major official colonies, Palau, has become (nominally, at least) independent,[83] and other cases of colonialism still remaining are being recast as autonomy disputes or secessionist conflicts.[84] There is recognition that making self-determination coterminous with decolonization in the absence of colonialism would render self-determination meaningless. Second, there has been the disintegration of communism in Eastern Europe and the much-documented rise of nationalism to replace it. This has, for some, seemed to confirm, that the theater of self-determination is now Central and Eastern Europe and its dominant mode, national.

The end of the Cold War has brought with it a further significant development. The various forms of indigenous, national, and democratic self-determination are no longer perceived through the lens of bipolar strategic interest (though national interests continue to play a decisive role). This has resulted in greater experimentalism ranging from the Declaration on Principles in the Middle-East[85] to the Eritrean secession to the suggestion that self-determination is now properly transforming itself into an emerging right to democratic governance.[86]

The free play of these different forms of self-determination is likely to bring greater rewards than any one of them could on its own. Indeed, self-determination as a human need or urge cannot be satisfied by any one of these modalities exclusively. Each contains an opposing idea of self-determination that carries with it the inevitable demise of the original. This process can be seen, as described earlier, where decolonization, narrowly defined as self-determination from European, metropolitan control and exploitation, required the division of territories along colonial lines and resulted in the imposition of colonially trained elites, the continuing inequality of women in these territories, a repression of national identities and the denial of suffrage to the newly independent peoples of these states. This mixture continues to prove explosive for many African states.

What, then, of alternatives? The problems and possibilities of national and democratic theories of self-determination and of devolutionary and secessionist practices are explored below. It is argued that, though each offers a possible mode of partial and provisional satisfaction of claims to self-determination, each is also open to the critique of partiality and incompleteness.

## National Self-Determination

There are two fashionable formulations of national self-determination worth outlining. The first characterizes nationalism as the form of self-determination that is the most powerful in its emotional appeal and the least convincing in its intellectual persuasiveness.[87] In many of its manifestations nationalism is said to require active suppression of rational thought about the nature of the community as a "nation" and obsession with differentiation. From this perspective, the nation is imagined by nationalists as homogeneous, exceptional, pure, venerable, and self-evident even when it is culturally diverse, racially mixed, of recent historical provenance, and artificial. This view of nationalism grew out of its association with Nazi racial doctrine and is combined with a sense that nationalism is a rather primitive, egotistical, and embarrassing phenomenon in these interdependent, cosmopolitan times.[88] Worse, it is one whose principal manifestations seem to be brutality, tribalism, ethnic cleansing, and secession. One should, however, be wary of these descriptions. Nationalism is too often defined as the practice of group identity by our adversaries.

Another group of theorists, then, rejects the view of nationalism as mere ancestral fantasy, a collection of irrational prejudices, or an error of history.[89] An optimistic strain in this writing sees national self-determination by groups, no matter how arbitrarily constructed and historically imagined, as a form of self-expression vital to the realization of individual human ends.[90] The national identities of, for example, Quebec, Scotland, Acheh Merdeka, the Sioux, the Batwa, and the Mapuche are said to play a vital role in preserving the cultural richness of these societies. Nationalism is the politicization of this cultural identity. Indeed, in the absence of this political dimension, it is quite likely that culture atrophies. National self-determination cannot be wholly confined to cultural or aesthetic or folk settings. This has proved neither possible nor desirable in the past. Equally, nationalism in its political forms can provide a counterweight in civil society to the state nationalisms of the modern political unit. The interests of diversity, difference and community are served only when national identities abound.

It is not the purpose of this discussion to indicate a preference for one or the other of these characterizations of national self-determination but simply to note that neither resolves the contradiction posed by competing forms of self-determination. The harsher, more belligerent version fails to capture the disparate aspirations for self-expression within a group. The construction of national identity here is generally frantic, often absurd, and sometimes violent. There is little room for the diverse, participatory forms of self-determination. Nor can national self-determination in this form be accommodated within a state system in which the overwhelming preference is for self-determination through state territorial integrity. Finally, this form of national self-determination tends toward a single view of sovereignty that excludes the devolutionary forms mentioned below and is extremely hostile to secessionist movements within the "nation."[91] Unfortunately for the practice of nationalism, all nations carry within their territories other nations. The nation-state no longer exists (if it ever did). Attempts to arrange political communities along national lines are exercises in practical futility.[92] National self-determination in its crudest, most unrefined forms is the denial of a multiplicity of competing exercises of self-determination. In both procedural and substantive senses it is exclusionary and unsophisticated. Apart from the denial of territorial self-determination to other nations within an often carelessly defined national territory, there is the crucially significant rejection of other processes of self-determination from the participatory kind to devolution of power to minorities. There is the denial to people, and not only groups, of the right to realize their political ends in ways not consistent with the national self-expression. Eventually, of course, the nation-state is prey to the disruptive influence of the other methods of self-determination.

At the same time, the logic of even milder forms of national self-determination is that they must deny difference in order to assert it. But difference can only be suppressed for so long, and then the cycle of competing self-determinations begins anew.[93] In addition, the softer, more accommodating forms of national expression may suffer from harsh reaction by states. Therefore, it is impossible to view national self-expression as capable of resolving all possible self-determination disputes. There must come a point at which the secessionist option becomes a reality because national expression through cultural forms is inadequate, unprotected, or attenuated. Conversely, the exercise of national self-determination can be precipitous given the exigencies of the state system. This is when devolutionary or democratic forms might be preferable. Before turning to secession, the possibilities of these democratic and devolutionary forms of self-determination will be examined.

## Democratic Self-Determination

The democratic critique of self-determination takes as its point of departure the assumption that self-determination has tended to manifest itself in undemocratic and exclusionary forms. From at least 1950, national self-determination, the dominant variant up to that point, was relegated to a position of historical obscurity and replaced by colonial self-determination, a theory whose sole concern was with the termination of white colonial domination. Colony replaced nationality as the identifying characteristic of the subject peoples of self-determination.[94] If this reconstruction of the principle had the merit of giving it practical effect, it also initiated a period in which the democratic dimension of self-determination was severely diminished. External self-determination, meaning the right of peoples to choose the sovereignty under which they wish to live, had become the only meaning subscribed to by the majority of members in the United Nations. Internal self-determination, which emphasized the right of peoples to choose the type of government by which they wished to be represented, was regarded as an unnecessary encumbrance to the newly independent Afro-Asian states. The result was often the replacement of one ruling elite by another.[95] The United Nations never inquired as to what democratic standards were being met in the newly independent states.

Nevertheless, events in Eastern Europe, coupled with the proposed referendums in the Western Sahara and Angola, the delegitimation of an unelected Haitian government, and the principles of democracy adopted by the Conference on Security and Cooperation in Europe (CSCE) have combined to lead some writers to suggest that democracy and self-determination may again be wedded in order to secure real political participation.[96] For example, Thomas Franck, in a discussion of the relationship between self-determination and democracy, claims that there has been "a transformation of the democratic entitlement from moral prescription to international legal obligation" and that self-determination can be realized through this emerging right to democratic governance.[97] This is sympathetic to the Kantian view, which envisages a federation of sovereign states in which each state holds regular, public, universal, periodic, and free elections. In this way, each person is secured his or her right to personal political self-determination.[98]

This argument seems to assume that group self-determination is an extension of personal political self-determination. There are doubts, however, whether group rights to self-determination can be satisfied on the majoritarian model (even in the presence of minority rights) or whether individual human realization can occur in settings where these group rights are effaced. Indeed democratic self-determination, while possessing many advantages over some earlier models, cannot fully elide the contradictions from which other versions of self-determination suffer. Democracy, alone, is unlikely to be a panacea for satisfying the political interests of indigenous peoples and far less for preserving their cultural integrity.[99] Equally, democratic self-determination confronts the same obstacle as other forms of self-determination – namely, the prior choice of a relevant territory or voting population. This is an acute problem for indigenous peoples in countries where democratic decisions have led to progressive disenfranchisement of the indigenous population in the cause of national development or equal rights or rights to property (all understood as central values of the democratic model). Even when the territory is relatively undisputed, the question of citizenship can arise in complex and, potentially, insoluble ways. Estonia and Latvia, for example, have argued that the presence of Russian immigrants in these republics is a denial of self-determination, and a Latvian delegate at the Unrepresented Peoples and Nations Assembly in the Hague in 1991 went further, arguing that to allow these Russians to vote in democratic elections "would imply the end of Latvia."[100]

In addition to what might be termed the indigenous critique, feminists working in international law have been understandably ambivalent about the possibilities of self-determination in any of its classical forms. It has often been stated that an exercise of self-determination can sometimes result in the replacement of one colonial and oppressive elite with another unrepresentative and neocolonial minority. Indeed, this has been the pattern in many newly independent states. For many women, the problem is exacerbated by the fact of their virtual exclusion from policy-making in the new state. Women continue to be exploited and denied representation in liberated territories as much as they were within colonial entities. The outcomes of self-determination are too often marked by the replacement of a colonial administration by a set of locally-entrenched patriarchies.

Furthermore, states, even those in which there is the exercise of democratic self-determination, tend to be conglomerations of institutions in which males are in the vast majority. Since the creation of a state is often the preferred outcome of a self-determination struggle, it follows that the exercise of self-determination in one sphere can be part of a process of continuing gender domination in another.[101] These processes of self-determination have the effect of further weakening women politically and economically and of ensuring that their claims remain marginal to the business of self-determination.

Ultimately, democratic self-determination cannot fully resolve the challenges from indigenous, national, and devolutionary forms of self-determination and the feminist critique of self-determination as at present practiced. The mere invocation of democratic rights and minority protections is unlikely to satisfy the demands by these groups, for tangible forms of self-determination.[102]

## Devolutionary Self-Determination

Devolutionary self-determination is the name given to official arrangements that distribute power to local groups, regions, or centers. Most often these arrangements are constitutional in nature and are, in effect, concessions of sovereignty from the state to the group. Devolution, then, is a process of decentralization or noncentralization embracing the classical forms of dividing power from federalism to local government to regional autonomy. As with other forms of self-determination, devolution can be traced through a series of historical repetitions, usually accompanied by conceptual reimaginings and renamings.

Devolution has been a technique applied by institutions as diverse as the powerful territorial religious orders of the seventeenth century, the European empires of the nineteenth and twentieth centuries and the states of the New World (Canada, the United States, Australia).[103] Federalism has existed as long as there have been troublesome or independent-minded territorial groupings and relatively centralized states. The modern federal state is usually a creation of the various nations or entities within it but can also be conceived as a process of self-determination designed to avoid cataclysmic rupture in the state. Ironically, devolutionary forms of self-determination may rescue some states from eventual collapse by providing for political expression and cultural identity short of outright secession.

Both federalism and subsidiarity can be seen as devolutionary forms of self-determination. Each involves a grant of power to a local authority or group within a state as a way of enhancing the efficiency or moral basis of governance (subsidiarity) or protecting expression of political autonomy (federalism).[104] There is no question that states and supranational bodies are taking devolution very seriously indeed. Forms of devolution, sometimes in addition to already sophisticated federal guarantees, have been proposed in the United Kingdom in its dealings with Northern Ireland, Wales, and Scotland; by Canada in its dispute with Quebec, and, most notably, by the European Community in its recent approach to subsidiarity.[105] Subsidiarity is a particularly interesting form of self-determination because it does not rely on specifically national forms of self-determination or on majoritarian decision-making but rather on a localism that provides for an autonomous politics at a regional level where this is appropriate. The European Community may come to be an exemplar for reconciling self-determination with confederation if it succeeds in distributing sufficient power to both its regions and the sovereign entities that make up the community.[106] In the end, subsidiarity may be the only model capable of securing stability in the former multiethnic republics of the U.S.S.R. Unfortunately, where there is intransigence on one side and manipulation on the other, the result is unavoidably conflict. The failure to reach compromise and agreement over devolved power can be seen most notably in Chechnya today.[107]

International law, too, seems slightly more receptive to devolutionary forms of self-determination. The Draft Declaration on Indigenous Peoples, for example, establishes safeguards for original inhabitants of territories who are threatened with cultural degradation, not by merely offering up a highly abstract and aspirational right to self-determination but by establishing a series of concrete rights that allow indigenous groups to exercise the broader right of self-determination. Chief among these are land and economic rights without which a right to self-government or limited sovereignty becomes meaningless.[108] These forms of territorial devolution provide meaningful alternatives to the cycle of revolt and repression.

In other spheres, international organizations have been unwilling to engage with some of the thornier problems of devolutionary self-determination, and there have been few substantial developments pointing toward these more sophisticated understandings of self-determination short of statehood. Nevertheless, to take one institution as an example, even the Security Council has recognized the advantage in proposing or supporting devolutionary forms of self-determination. The council has recognized in successive resolutions that just such an approach is necessary in divided states such as Cyprus. Here, the traditional resolution calling for self-determination for the people of Cyprus has given way to more flexible, innovative models of power-sharing. For example, in one resolution the Council asserted that: "A Cyprus settlement must be based on a State of Cyprus with a single sovereignty and international personality . . . and comprising two politically equal communities . . . in a bi-communal and bi-zonal federation. . . ."[109] In the dispute between Abkhazia and Georgia, the

Council asserted in a resolution that a comprehensive political settlement of the conflict, including the political status of Abkhazia, was the only means by which peace could be secured.[110]

Arguably, though, it was the failure of the United Nations and the European Community to adopt the devolutionary approach that doomed the enterprise in Bosnia and Herzegovina. There is little doubt that the collective inability of the Western powers to see beyond the statist/secessionist models was partly responsible for the collapse of Bosnia and the war in Krajina.[111] The adoption of a series of extreme positions, from support for the sanctity of Yugoslavia to the recognition of the secession of its federal republics, was fatal given the aspirations of Serbian self-determination groups in Croatia and Bosnia and Croats in Bosnia. Ironically, some of the later peace proposals attempted to use devolutionary techniques to secure an end to the conflict.[112] These might well have been successful had they been proposed earlier and might conceivably have served as useful models in other areas. By the time devolutionary self-determination was conceived as a solution to the present crisis, however, it had been seriously compromised by the ethnic cleansing on which its viability eventually depended.

To summarize, devolution through the vertical distribution of government, may be a way of preempting precipitous resort to violence in situations where there are a number of national entities coexisting precariously within one state. Devolution is the dispersal of power to non-state groupings whether on the basis of regionalism, federalism, or subsidiarity.[113] As such, it may prevent a more catastrophic fracturing of government through revolution, secessionist interethnic conflict or political disintegration. The international community must choose between encouraging the constitutional provision of minority guarantees and limited self-government on the one hand and triage and belated intervention on the other.[114]

That being said, it remains to be pointed out that no matter how successful some devolutionary forms could prove to be, there is always the distinct possibility that governments will refuse to adopt them and international organizations lack the will or the capacity to impose them even at the beginning of a conflict. There is also the possibility that federalism is incompatible with certain forms of national expression.[115] In such cases it is necessary to turn to the remedy of last resort, secession.

## Secession

Naturally, any attempt to broaden the right to self-determination is likely to be resisted in an essentially statist system.[116] The right of states to maintain their territorial integrity is enshrined in the Charter of the United Nations[117] and in customary international law. Ex facie, the right of self-determination conflicts with the principle of territorial integrity.[118] But, it is not imperative that either be rejected outright for an international system based on respect for human rights and remaining relatively stable to be assured. The maintenance of territorial integrity is a preferred value given the disruptive consequences of breaches of that integrity. It cannot be an end in itself, however. It is important not to lose sight of the original rationale for territorial integrity, for, as Umozurike emphasizes, "the ultimate purpose of territorial integrity is to safeguard the interests of the peoples of a territory. The concept of territorial integrity is . . . meaningful [only] so long as it continues to fulfil that purpose to all the sections of the people."[119]

Unfortunately, in the postcolonial phase of self-determination the collective human rights of "peoples" have often been abandoned in favor of the norm of territorial integrity. This severing of the link with human rights has resulted in a theoretical crisis. The connection between human rights in general and the right to self-determination as the ultimate exercise of collective human rights must be re-established. While containing a typical admonition against breaching the territorial integrity of a state, the Declaration on Friendly Relations proclaimed in 1970 represents a tentative step toward such a reassertion. The Declaration makes territorial integrity a rebuttable presumption that can only be invoked by states that act in accordance with the principle of self-determination. A number of writers propose a right to self-determination as a remedy when the actions of the state extinguish that presumption,[120] thus furnishing the Declaration with content and resolving the tension between territorial integrity and self-determination through a reaffirmation of human rights.[121] An assertion of the right of secession would be a remedy of the last resort for peoples or groups,[122] an exercise of the ultimate collective human right as a means to secure basic individual human rights where devolutionary, democratic, and colonial models of self-determination have failed.

In this matter, there has been a perceptible shift in state practice over the last twenty years. The major postcolonial wars of self-determination, involving secession, fought by the Biafrans, Bangladeshis, and Eritreans were each regarded by the world community as matters within the domestic jurisdiction of Nigeria, Pakistan, and Ethiopia respectively. External interference was either negligible or unilateral.[123] States themselves faced with nonstate claims from minorities within their borders often used brutal counter-revolutionary methods to suppress these threats to their territorial integrity.

While these methods are still employed, and with the same counterproductive effect, more states exhausted by the endless conflict are seeking alternative means of resolving these disputes. There is little doubt, too, that the international community has become more sympathetic to secession or, at least, embryonic secessions. The events that have taken place in Iraqi Kurdistan, the former U.S.S.R., Eritrea, and in the Northern Balkans have consequences for customary international law that are difficult to gauge. This much is certain: there has been a detectable shift in emphasis away from an absolute, unconditional right to political sovereignty and territorial integrity and toward more flexible, less statist positions. The proposition that individual human rights are a matter for international concern has long been an indisputable one. There is a certain logic in making a similar claim for the collective rights of "peoples" and their claims to assert those rights effectively.

Recent developments lend some credence to the claim that a new postcolonial right to limited secession may be on the point of crystallizing. To take one, perhaps controversial, example, the U.N. sanctioned intervention on behalf of the Kurds in May 1991 was a clear breach of Iraq's territorial integrity and political sovereignty.[124] The intervention under Security Council Resolution 688 had a humanitarian objective and was justified on the grounds that the Kurds in northern Iraq were suffering massive human rights deprivations, partially inflicted by the parent state, Iraq, and that this was causing a flood of refugees into Turkey. What has become increasingly obvious is that the threat to the Kurds (and therefore to peace and security) will remain as long as they are denied a right to self-determination. Consequently, it becomes impossible and fruitless to tease out a distinction between intervention to protect individual, traditional human rights and intervention in support of the right to self-determination (possibly leading to outright secession). This is especially true when the former cannot be protected in the absence of the latter. The United Nations has in effect recognized a limited right of intervention in cases where a distinct people is suffering gross violations of human rights.[125] There was even talk of backing an autonomy agreement with international guarantees. It seems that secession is no longer regarded with quite the degree of antipathy shown toward it in the 1960s when U Thant made his famous statement condemning the practice. Recognized and, in some cases, encouraged by the international community, secessions coming one after another in the former Yugoslavia,[126] the former U.S.S.R., and in Ethiopia tend to support this view.

What we are witnessing, then, is the internationalization of the new right to self-determination. The agitations of ethnic peoples are no longer thought to be a matter of exclusive concern to the sovereign entity. The reserve domain of sovereign states no longer automatically includes a right to deal with the internal claims of peoples to self-determination free of external interference. This is particularly true in cases where ethnic conflicts are deemed to constitute a threat to the peace or where the human rights situation is particularly grave. Secession is by no means an ideal form of self-determination. It is often violent, its national dimensions can be unattractive, and it can pose a threat to peace and security. Even so, secession may be a valid response to certain situations that themselves are threats to national and international security.

## Conclusion

Defining a right to self-determination with potential application beyond the colonial context will not be simple, but self-determination must be imbued with meaning if it is to possess renewed legal relevance. The post-Charter distortion of the principle arose partly because of the attempt to outline a right of self-determination while denying rights to autonomy or devolution or democratic representation or, in extreme cases, secession. In other words, self-determination had become detached from the very modalities through which it was most likely to enjoy success. International law, if it demonstrates doctrinal flexibility and intellectual openness, can accommodate these diverse understandings and facilitate the process of negotiation that should be the mark of all competing claims to cultural and national self-expression.

## Notes

1. Compared to the right to development or the right to natural resources, the right to self-determination possesses a vastly greater public and institutional profile.

2. These are only some of the better known groups. A complete list of groups and peoples claiming self-determination would also include the Karen peoples in Burma, the Ambonese and Acheh Mederka in Indonesia, the Chittagong Hill Tribes in Bangladesh, Southern Sudan, the South Ossetians in Georgia, the Tamils in Sri Lanka, the Naga people in India, the Catholic Irish in the United Kingdom, and the Western Saharans under control by the Moroccans. The Unrepresented Nations and Peoples Organization based in the Hague has steadily expanding list of member groups that currently stands at twenty-six. All these groups are claiming some degree of self-determination and together represent some 50 million persons. See M. Olsthoorn & G. Simpson, "Self-Determination in Relation to Individual Human Rights, Democracy and the Protection of the Environment," Conference Report, U.N.P.O. Doc. GA/1993/CR/1.

3. By way of example, there is the quasi–official status of the P.L.O. and the A.N.C. at the United Nations and other multilateral agencies. Witness, also, the semiofficial recognition given to nonstate representatives such as the Dalai Lama and Jose Ramos Horta of Tibet and East Timor respectively.

4. By these are meant, for instance, the cases of St. Helena, Pitcairn, American Samoa, Anguilla, East Timor, Gibraltar, the Falkland Islands, and Hong Kong.

5. The work of the Decolonization Committee is now at last coming to an end. See Security Council Resolution 956 of 10 November 1994, terminating the trust over Palau) "satisfied that the people of Palau have freely exercised their right to self-determination in approving the new status agreement in a plebiscite."

6. See the recent claims to self-determination made by elements of the white minority in South Africa who wish to establish a white homeland (or Volksstaat) and similar claims made by the Bosnian Serbs. See J. Sharp, "Introduction: Constructing Social Reality" in E. Boonzaier and J. Sharp (eds), *South African Keywords: The Uses and Abuses of Political Concepts* (1988) as quoted in R. McCorquodale, "Self-Determination: A Human Rights Approach," n.55.

7. Even organizations as unsavory as R.E.N.A.M.O. in Mozambique, the Contras in Nicaragua, and the Khmer Rouge in Cambodia can

couch their claims in the language of self-determination. This perhaps explains the need to renew the link between self-determination and human rights law generally without collapsing one onto the other entirely. In the first case we have an insurgency army that had been sponsored by the South African government and was renowned for its brutality. See e.g. W. Gehrke, "The Mozambique Crisis: A Case for United Nations Intervention" *Cornell International Law Journal* 24 (1991): 135, 141.

8. Self-determination has been reduced to the level of rhetorical device or political slogan; predictably, increasing frequency of usage has led to diminishing meaning. Van Dyke stated the problem elegantly, twenty years ago, when he remarked, "self-determination has become an emotion-laden term in the field of human rights, a shibboleth that all must pronounce to identify themselves with the virtuous." See Van Dyke, *Human Rights, The United States and World Community*, (1970), 77. As Franck notes, however, diminished meaning brings in its train diminished impact: "Obviously rules with a readily ascertainable meaning have a better chance than those that do not regulate conduct of those to whom their rule is addressed or exert a compliance pull on their policy-making process." Self-determination suffers equally in regard to the conferring of legitimacy by process. The institutions that could have accomplished this have either developed obtuse and contradictory norms (the General Assembly see below), statist principles (the Security Council, until recently), or little beyond the colonial definitions (the International Court of Justice). See Thomas Franck, "Legitimacy in the International System," *American Journal of International Law* 82 (1988): 713, 725. See also W. Ofuatey-Kodjoe, *The Principle of Self-Determination* (1977), at viii: "it is certainly safe to assert that the removal of confusion and uncertainty from a definition tends to heighten considerably the expectation of a clear and unambiguous application of the principle."

9. This is not to deny its talismanic appeal to national liberation movements and unrepresented people.

10. See Thomas Franck, "Legitimacy in the International System," 746.

11. For a fuller description of this intellectual confusion see D. Cass, "Rethinking Self-determination: A Critical Analysis of International Legal Theory," *Syracuse Journal of International Law and Comparative* 18 (1992): 21.

12. Charter of the United Nations Articles 1(2) and 55.

13. General Assembly Resolution 2625 24 October 1970, 25

U.N.G.A.O.R. Supp. (no.28) 122, U.N. Doc.A/8028 (1970). Hereafter cited as "Declaration on Friendly Relations."

14. "Colonial liberation created some fifty new states...their formation reflecting the right of self-determination without any advance in the technique of applying the principle." See I. Bibo, *The Paralysis of International Institutions and the Remedies* (1976), 31.

15. This is not to deny that all such transformations must to an extent be restrictive. That is, after all, the nature of law. The argument here is that it need not have been restricted in quite this manner.

16. See A. Rigo Sureda, *The Evolution of the Right of Self-determination: A Study of United Nations Practice* (1973).

17. See Emerson, "Self-Determination," 459–475. A.J.I.L. 65: 1971: 459.

18. Pre-World War II self-determination was a parochial European concept not only reflecting the values of the Western nationalist tradition but also remaining European in its application. See J. Barros, *The Aaland Islands Question: Its Settlement by the League of Nations* (1968).

19. See Pomerance, *Self-Determination in Law and Practice* (1982).

20. Ironically, these same fears underpin the rejection of a right of secession by many of the states created as a result of this initial process.

21. The U.S. Government continued to emphasize "the right of all peoples to choose the form of government under which they will live." See B. Wells, *United Nations Decisions on Self-Determination* (Ann Arbor: Michigan University Microfilms, 1963), 54.

22. On the colonial question, Douglas Williams, the British colonial attaché in Washington at the time, stated his position succinctly: "most of our territories, if the principle of self-determination were applied, would simply disintegrate as administrative units and fall apart on the basis of tribal divisions." Ibid., 57.

23. Ibid., 57–64. See also Ofuatey-Kodjoe, *The Principle of Self-Determination*, 104, 105. The U.S.S.R. too, played an important role in promoting self-determination at discussions on the drafting of the charter. But Soviet support for self-determination and decolonization needs to be seen in the light of Marxist-Leninist ideology and was essentially opportunistic – the U.S.S.R. had sound strategic motives for wishing to undermine the empires of the West European states. For the U.S.S.R., national self-determination was simply an adjunct to revolutionary communism. National self-determination was envisaged as a transitional phase between the disintegration of empire and the formation of the Socialist state. National liberation and

decolonization were means for the Soviet leadership, but ends for the fledgling Afro-Asian nations. See D. Levin, "The Principle of Self-Determination in International Law," (1962) *Soviet Yearbook of International Law* (Moscow, 1962) 45, 48. Eventually, at the height of the Cold War, the Americans too began to cynically exploit self-determination movements in Nicaragua, Angola and Afghanistan with little regard for human cost.

24. Article 1(2) states one of the purposes of the United Nations to be developing "friendly relations among nations based on respect for the principle of equal rights and self-determination of peoples" and Article 55 repeats this desideratum in identical language. See Pomerance, *Self-Determination in Law and Practice.*

25. Indeed, there is some doubt whether the principle even extends to groups other than states. See H. Kelsen, *The Law of the United Nations* (1964), 20, 23. See also the submissions by the British and French representatives at the Commission on Human Rights, 8th Session (1952), to the effect that the principle referred only to relations between sovereign states. (E/CN.4/SR.253, p.6 (GB); E/CN.4/SR.255, p.8 (F). Writers frequently and rather blithely refer to a "right" of self-determination in the Charter of the United Nations. Cf. M. Lachs, "The Law in and of the United Nations: Some Reflections on the Principle of Self-determination" *Indian Journal of International Law* 1 (1961): 429, 442. Neither the wording or customary international law at the time support such a contention.

26. See Hackworth, *Digest of International Law*, 1 (1940): 74, 79; T. Lawrence, *The Principles of International Law* (1923), 54, 65; H. Smith, *Great Britain and the Laws of Nations*, Vol.I states. 34, 47, 67–76; T. Baty, *The Canons of International Law* (1930), 119, 126 (self-determination equated with independence of the state itself).

27. Charter of the United Nations, Articles 73–91, Chapters XI and XII.

28. Whether through economic self-interest or genuine concern for the chaotic consequences of premature independence.

29. There is reference made in Article 76(b) to the "freely expressed wishes of the peoples concerned" but this is followed by the phrase ". . . and as may be provided by the terms of the trustee-ship agreement." Some writers have discerned here the genesis of a right to self-determination. See, e.g., D. Ronen, *The Quest for Self-Determination* (1979) p.5.

30. See Ofuatey-Kodjoe, *The Principle of Self-Determination*, 131.

31. See J. Hatch, *A History of PostWar Africa* (1965), 37. Quoted in Ofuatey-Kodjoe, *The Principle of Self-Determination*, 132.

32. The former secretary of state, Cordell Hull claims that the purpose of the United States was, "to support the attainment of freedom for all peoples who, by their acts, show themselves worthy of it and ready for it" (quoted in Ofuatey-Kodjoe, ibid. 101. Ironically, the United States now obstructs the right of self-determination, even in pseudocolonial situations, if such an exercise is likely to interfere with its perceived strategic interests. See, R. Clark, "Free Association – A Critical View," Conference on the Future Political Status of the U.S. Virgin Islands, 26 to 27 February, 1988; W. Van Dorn, "The Compact of Free Association: An End to the Trust Territory of the Pacific Islands", *Boston University International Law Journal* 5 (1987): 213.

33. See The Soviet Constitution of 1933 and that of 1970.

34. The Baltic republics were denied external and internal self-determination. They were deprived both of their sovereignty and democratic choice. The countries of Eastern Europe lacked internal self-determination but clung to a tenuous external sovereignty. They at least remained nation-states albeit often in a physically skewed form such as was the case in Poland.

35. General Assembly Resolution 217A (III), 3 U.N.G.A.O.R. Pt I (1948), U.N. Doc A. 1811.

36. The British, Dutch, and the Spanish moved most rapidly. The French (in Algeria) and the Portuguese (in Angola, Mozambique, and East Timor) became involved in nasty colonial conflicts.

37. General Assembly Resolution 421 (V), 317th mtg., Dec 4th, (1950), at para. 6.

38. General Assembly Resolution 545 (VI), 375th mtg., Feb 5th (1952), at para. 1.

39. The International Covenant on Civil and Political Rights, 16 December 1966, U.N.G.A.O.R. 2200A (XXI), 999 U.N.T.S. 171 [hereafter I.C.C.P.R.] and the International Covenant on Economic, Social and Cultural Rights 1966, U.N.G.A.O.R. 2200A (XXI), 993 U.N.T.S. 3. [hereafter I.C.E.S.C.R.].

40. Article 1 (1) of both the I.C.C.P.R. and I.C.S.E.C.R. read: "All peoples have the right of self-determination. By virtue of that right they freely determine their political status and freely pursue their economic, social and cultural development."

41. Commission on Human Rights, 7th Session (1951). Most of the early objections to inclusion of the right came from the European powers, which advanced a number of different arguments to support their position. The British argued that self-determination remained a political principle incapable of being translated into a legal right or duty (E/CN.4/SR. 253, p.7 (G.B.), while the

Belgians pointed out that self-determination in the charter was conceived of as a principle of international organization rather than a legal right E/CN.4/SR. 243, p.11 (B). See statements of the Belgian delegate (E/CN.4/SR. 243 at p.11) and the British Delegate (E/CN.4/SR. 260 at p.5). See generally, M. Bossuyt, *Guide to the Travaux Preparatoires of the International Covenant on Civil and Political Rights* (1982), 20.

42. See ibid. at A/C.3/SR. 309, p.59 (Great Britain).

43. See ibid. at A/C.3/SR. 311, pp.21–23 (France) and A/C.3/SR. 647, p.19 (Australia).

44. See E/CN.4/SR. 254, p.8 (Chile) and E/CN.4/SR. 253, p.3 (Lebanon).

45. The Soviet representative did, however, rather surprisingly suggest the following proposal, "All peoples have the right to self-determination. This includes the right of every person to participate, with all members of a group inhabiting a compact territory, to which he belongs ethnically, culturally, historically or otherwise, in the free exercise of the right to self-determination, including the right to secede and to establish a politically and economically independent state." This avowal must be viewed, though, as either a diplomatic aberration or an exercise in Soviet formalism. Ibid. at E/CN.4/L.22.

46. See ibid., A/2929, Chapter IV, 9; A/3077, 39.

47. Gross argues that decolonization at this point was a matter of "political expedience" rather than legal approval. See Gross, "Self-Determination in International Law" in Mikelson (ed.), *New States in the Modern World* (1971).

48. If the Charter of the United Nations had been an attempt to give political significance to what had been a moral principle by making self-determination a political aspiration of the United Nations, then the Declaration on the Granting of Independence (1960) attempted to give the political winds of change some legal basis.

49. See, e.g., H. Gros Espiell, *The Right to Self-Determination*, (1980) at 8.

50. The contrast with Articles 73 and 76 of the U.N. Charter is remarkable. Trusteeship and colonial administrative authority are stigmatized as great evils in the declaration whereas in the Charter they were thought of as forms of benevolent authority.

51. See Cameron, *Nationalism, Self-Determination, and the Quebec Question*, 99. (1974).

52. General Assembly Resolution 1541 of 15 December 1960. Principles that should guide members in determining whether or

not an obligation exists to transmit the information called for under Article 73(e) of the charter. 15 U.N.G.A.O.R. Supp. (No.16), 29, U.N. Doc. A 4684 (1960).

53. See Principle VI. The alternatives offered are (a) emergence as a sovereign independent state, (b) free association with an independent state, (c) integration with an independent state. Note, however, that the threshold of participation in the latter two cases is much higher.

54. See A. Cassese "Political Self-Determination – Old Concepts and New Developments", in A. Cassese (ed.), *U.N. Law Fundamental Rights, Two Topics In International Law*, (1979), at 43 where he states, "The Declaration suffers from the same defects of ambiguity and vagueness that marred the Covenants."

55. See Gaetano Arangio-Ruiz, *The U.N. Declaration on Friendly Relations and the System of the Sources of International Law* (1979), 131.

56. It represents seven years work in committee and on the floor of the General Assembly. Brownlie claims that this contributes a normative character to the declaration. See I. Brownlie, *Principles of International Law*, 4th ed. (1990) 497.

57. See White, "Time for a Reassessment," 147 in *Netherlands Int'l L. Review* 28 (1981) 147–170.

58. For a fuller discussion of this see Part 3 of this Chapter.

59. See J.F. Engers, "From Sacred Trust to Self-determination", in H. Meijers and E.W. Vierdag (eds), *Essays on International Law and Relations*, (1977), 88.

60. See Ofuatey-Kodjoe, *The Principle of Self-Determination*, 111.

61. General Assembly Resolution 2131 (XX), 12 December 1965, N GAOR Supp (No.14) 11, N Doc A/6220 (1965). See also the General Assembly resolution of 1966 concerning strict observance of the prohibition of the threat or use of force in international relations which forbids action designed to deprive "peoples under foreign domination of their right to self-determination" and requests states to facilitate "the right of self-determination of peoples under colonial rule." General Assembly Resolution 2160 (XXI) of 30 November, 1966.

62. E.g., "every state has a duty to bring a speedy end to colonialism, having due regard to the freely expressed will of the people concerned and ... the subjection of people to alien ... constitutes a violation of the principle (of self-determination)."

63. See General Assembly Resolution 3314 XXIX of 14 December 1974: 29 U.N.G.A.O.R. Supp. (No.31) 142, U.N. Doc. A/9631 (1974).

64. See Article 7. See, too, the Bandung Conference communiqué of 1955 affirming that, "colonialism in all its manifestations . . . should especially be brought to an end," but noting in addition that, "the exercise of the right of self-determination is the prerequisite of . . . especially the eradication of racial discrimination." See Ofuatey-Kodjoe, *The Principle of Self-Determination*, 141.
65. *ICJ Reports*, 1975, 12. In his opinion, Judge Petren states, "inspired by a series of resolutions of the General Assembly, in particular resolution 1514 (XV), a veritable law of decolonization is taking shape. It derives from the principle of self-determination."
66. See Umozurike, *Self-Determination in International Law*, 190.
67. General Assembly Resolution 1541 makes it clear that Chapter XI of the Charter applies to non-self-governing territories "which were then known to be of the colonial type."
68. See, e.g., General Assembly Resolution 1541, supra n. 52, describing colonies as "geographically separate and . . . distinct ethnically and/or culturally from the country administrating it."
69. See R. Higgins, *The Development of International Law Through the Political Organs of the U.N.* (1963), 105.
70. Quoted in Neuberger, *Postcolonial Africa*, 83 (1986).
71. See Pomerance, "Self-Determination", 76.
72. Ibid. 44, 49–51.
73. Neuberger, *Postcolonial Africa*, 85.
74. Though the United Nations condemned the Indonesian invasion of East Timor at this time. See, e.g., Security Council Resolution 384, U.N. S.C.O.R., 30th Sess. at 10.
75. In virtually all cases this meant European.
76. This would account for the right to self-determination held by the South African and Rhodesian nonwhite majorities and the Palestinians in Israeli-occupied territories.
77. See Pomerance, "Self-Determination", 8.
78. See M. Pomerance, "Self-Determination Today: The Metamorphosis of an Ideal", *Israel Law Review* 9 (1984): 329.
79. This was noted as early as 1969 by the French delegate to the United Nations Sixth Committee, M. Deleau, when he argued that colonial self-determination was basically an unequal application of a universal principle. All peoples were entitled to exercise the right to self-determination according to the International Covenants but only a small number of these peoples were permitted to do so. 24 U.N.G.A.O.R. 1158th mtg., 6th Committee, 24 November (1969) at 284, para. 16–19, ((A/C.6/SR).

80. Consider the distinctions drawn between oppressive European colonial governments and their African and Asian counterparts.

81. It might be argued that the national and democratic types are really theories and practices of self-determination while devolution and secession are models and practices. For purposes of this discussion, they are being treated as if they were conceptually similar.

82. Even the Decolonization Committee at the United Nations seems to recognize this. See the Statement by the Assistant Secretary-General for Political Affairs, GA/COL/2933, 1441st mtg., 27 February (1995).

83. See Security Council Resolution 956 (1995) (on admitting Palau to membership of the United Nations) and also nn. 4 and 5 of this Chapter. For another view, see J. Hinck, "The Republic of Palau and the United States: Self-Determination Becomes the Price of Free Association," *California Law Review* 78: 913.

84. The classical colonial cases of the Western Sahara and East Timor are now viewed in terms of reconciliation and compromise and agreement, often against the wishes of the inhabitants of these territories, who would prefer to stigmatize their oppressors as "colonial." The right has become decidedly qualified by the requirements to negotiate and compromise.

85. See the Israeli-P.L.O. Declaration on Principles of Interim Self-Government Arrangements, 32 *International Law Magazine* 32 (1993); also Israel-P.L.O.: Agreement on the Gaza Strip and the Jericho Area, 33 *International Law Magazine* 621 (1994).

86. See T. Franck, "The Emerging Right to Democratic Governance" *American Journal of International Law* 86 (1992).

87. See Anderson's stylish contribution to the literature on nationalism, *Imagined Communities* (1991).

88. This view is put by Ignatief, *Blood and Belonging* (1993).

89. See E. Gellner, *Nations and Nationalism* (1982); T. Judt, "The New Old Nationalisms", *New York Review of Books*, 26 May 1994: 44.

90. For a powerful defence of this view, see G. Binder, "The Case for Self-Determination," *Stanford Journal of International Law* 29(2) (1993): 223. See also Y. Tamir, *Liberal Nationalism* (1993).

91. Witness the Croatian antagonism towards the secession of Serbian Krajina, the Serbian hostility to devolution for Albanian Kosovo, the Muslim Sandak region and Hungarian Vojvodina, and the general antipathy shown by all national movements toward multicultural forms of self-determination that once flourished in Sarajevo.

92. Eric Hobsbawm notes that, apart from rump Magyar Hungary and German Austria, each of the nation-states created at Versailles in 1919 was multiethnic in composition. See E. Hobsbawm, *The Age of Extremes* (1994), 33.

93. For a particularly poignant example of this, see the Meech Lake Accord, where Quebec's insistence on a single national identity in Quebec, opposable to the Canadian national identity, provoked a number of competing assertions of self-determination within Quebec from constitutional agitations of the English-speaking minority to the claims made by the indigenous minority. This contributed to the eventual scuppering of the agreement. Indeed, the Canadian experience would seem to indicate that sometimes the contradictions of self-determination cannot be resolved.

94. See S. P. Sinha, "Is Self-determination Passé?", *Columbia Journal Of Transnational Law*, 12 (1973): 260, 273.

95. See M. Beloff "Self-Determination Reconsidered, *Confluence: An International Forum* 15 (1956): 195–203.

96. See Security Council Resolution 948 of 15 October 1994, which talks of "returning Haiti to the community of nations." Security Council support for democracy in Mozambique should be noted. (See Security Council Resolution 957.) and in Tajikistan (Security Council Resolution 968 of 16 December 1994). See, also C.S.C.E. Copenhagen Document of 29 June 1990, *International Law Magazine* 29 (1990): 1305.

97. See Franck, "Right to Democratic Governance," Supra n.86 at 46.

98. See F. Téson, "The Kantian Theory of International Law" *Columbia Law Review* 92 (1992): 53.

99. A fairly comprehensive definition of "indigenous peoples" was drafted by the United Nations Indigenous Study in 1983. See U.N. Indigenous Study, E/CN.4/Sub.2/1983/21/Add.8. The common characteristics possessed by indigenous peoples according to the study are: (1) a historical or precolonial connection with the territory; (2) a sense of distinctive cultural identity; and (3) an experience of domination or oppression. Most of these characteristics are quite often shared by groups claiming self-determination though this is not always the case.

100. See U.N.P.O., Conference Report, supra note 2, at 31.

101. The feminist critique works with equal force against another form of self-determination – that is, colonial self-determination. The process of self-determination or nationalist struggle can have unfortunate implications for deeper feminist claims. The

creation or imagining of a national identity that is essential to the success of a national liberation struggle is often an exercise in myth-making in which the political institutions are changed but in which no comparable transformation in the modalities of power occurs. Indeed, the revolutionary nature of self-determination can work against the realization of feminist emancipation. Often, the claims of feminists within revolutionary movements will be regarded as trivial, diversionary, or decadent – in short, a product of Western or foreign feminism. Christine Chinkin also remarks on the effects of militarization, another inevitable by-product of anticolonial conflict. The link between men and power is made even more explicit in a military setting. Women tend to be increasingly diverted into domestic or caring roles during periods of war. Chinkin also notes that women and children are now the major victims of armed struggle and refugee crises. See C. Chinkin, "A Gendered Perspective to the Use of Force" *Australian Yearbook of International Law* 12 (1992): 279.

102. Feminists and democrats do at least share the premise that current formulations of the right to self-determination are fatally flawed to the extent that substantial proportions of the population are often denied participation in policy implementation and state-building even after a successful exercise of external self-determination.

103. See, e.g., the Tenth Amendment, U.S. Constitution; Article 30 of the Meech Lake Accord and *Australian Federalism*, ed., B. Galligan (1989).

104. For a number of other approaches to devolution, see an interesting essay by A. Eide, "In Search of Constructive Alternatives to Secession" *Modern Law of Self-Determination*, ed. C. Tomuschat (1993): 139–176, where he refers to consociational democracy and various schemes for minority protection.

105. See also the German Basic Law, Article 30, and the Spanish approach to regional autonomy (see H. Hannum, *Autonomy, Sovereignty and Self-Determination* (1989): 263–280).

106. See Treaty on European Union, Article 3(b). For general context, see V. Bogdonor, *Devolution* (1979).

107. For a discussion of self-determination and autonomy practices in the former U.S.S.R., see 3(1) P. Juviler (1994), *Transnational Law and Social Problems* 3(1) (1994): 72.

108. Ibid., 78, 80.

109. The Security Council was also careful to exclude the possibility of secession. See the Council's Resolution 939 of 29 July 1995.

110. Security Council Resolution 971 (1995), 12 January 1995.
111. See generally, H. Hannum, "Self-Determination, Yugoslavia and Europe: Old Wine in New Bottles," 3(1) *Transnational Law and Social Problems* (1993): 58.
112. Security Council Resolution 820 of 17 April (1993); Security Council Resolution 836 of 4 June 1993 (endorsing the Vance-Owen Plan, as contained in U.N. document S/25479).
113. There are arguably two distinct types of devolution, one based on territorial self-government and the other being more personal or group oriented.
114. See S. Wiessner, "Federalism: An Architecture for Freedom" *New Europe Law Review* 1(2) (1993): 129 (suggesting the compatibility of self-determination and federalism and calling for greater international involvement in the enforcement of these structures).
115. On this possibility, see R. Howse and K. Knop, "Federalism, Secession, and the Limits of Ethnic Accommodation: A Canadian Perspective," *New Europe Law Review* 1(2) (1993): 269, 272–274 (arguing for federalism as the process for reconstituting national expression into less exclusive forms).
116. Significantly, during a discussion of an amendment to the charter in Committee 1/1 it was stated : "the principle conformed to the purposes of the U.N. only insofar as it implied the right of self-government and not the right of secession." See U.N.C.I.O. VI, San Francisco (1946) 296.
117. See Article 2(4).
118. Attempts by nonstate actors to assert a right to devolution or self-determination has met with more success in national courts than at the international law level. The Human Rights Committee (established as a United Nations treaty body under the International Covenant on Civil and Political Rights) has compiled substantial jurisprudence on the right to self-determination. Unfortunately, its findings have not been favorable to groups seeking to bring communications based on the Article 1 right to self-determination. The committee has found in a number of cases that the right to self-determination for groups does not fall within its jurisdiction. In both the *Lubicon Band* and *Miqmaq Indian* cases, the committee found that the right of self-determination was not an individual human right but instead a collective right over which it could exercise jurisdiction. This is particularly the case when groups bring sovereignty claims – that is, a claim to secede or establish a new state. In such cases, the committee has deferred to principles of

territorial integrity and domestic jurisdiction and declined to rule in favor of indigenous groups or minorities.

119. See Umozurike, *Self-Determination in International Law*, 236.

120. V. Nanda, "Self-Determination under International law: Validity of Claims to Secede," *Case Western Reserve Journal of International Law* 13 (1981): 257.

121. This has been called "remedial secession." See Buchheit, *Secession: The Legitimacy of Self-Determination*, 220–223.

122. White, "Time for a Reassessment," 148. See, too, A. Cobban, *The Nation-State and National Self-Determination*, (1947): 74, where he states, "self-determination comes into play not as a panacea for all national dissatisfactions, but as the remedy, to be administered in extremis, when all else has failed."

123. Except on behalf of the governments.

124. See Security Council Resolution 688 of 5 April 1991. While the preamble spoke of reaffirming the territorial integrity of Iraq, the thrust of the resolution was for Iraq to cooperate with the secretary-general in creating what was to become an autonomous zone in northern Iraq.

125. This interpretation is not accepted by all commentators. For support, see Koskenniemi, "National Self-Determination Today," 43 I.C.L.Q.241 (1994); M. Boutin, "Somalia: The Legality of U.N. Forcible Humanitarian Intervention," *Suffolk Transnational International Law Review* 17 (1994): 138; and (more equivocally) R. Gordon, "U.N. Intervention in Internal Conflicts: Iraq, Somalia, and Beyond," *Michigan Journal of International Law* 15 (1994): 519. Others have taken the text of the resolution at face value. This argument focuses more on the tangible effects of the resolution.

126. See M. Weller, "Yugoslavia and Self-Determination: International Responses to the Dissolution of the Socialist Federal Republic of Yugoslavia," *American Journal of International Law* 86 (1993): 569.

# – 4 –

# Self-Determination in a Modern World: Conceptual Development and Practical Application

## Vladimir Rudnitsky

### Introduction

The concept of self-determination as formulated after World War II primarily reflected the parameters of the international struggle against colonialism. In the post-Cold War period, its practical application in this form to integrative and disintegrative processes in sovereign States and, in particular, to numerous conflicts arising from demands by various peoples and ethnic and other groups for autonomy and independence has revealed the urgent need for an adjustment of the concept to new realities and for the creation of effective mechanisms to deal with them. The United Nations, as a unique intergovernmental organization with broad competence in areas directly relevant to various issues of self-determination, should play a special role in this process.

A survey of conflicts and controversies related to claims of self-determination in parts of the former U.S.S.R. and in some of the East European states leads to the conclusion that lasting and workable solutions will be impossible without addressing fundamental questions about the nature and purpose of self-determination in the world of the late twentieth century, including the social functions of the concept and the correlation between self-determination, state sovereignty, and other principles of international law.

Clearly, the international community will have to develop consistent and coherent norms for the exercise of self-determination, respecting both fundamental individual human rights and the human rights of minorities and other established social groups.[1] Dealing effectively with the demands of such groups for self-determination will require a principled and coordinated approach, resting on the application of uniform criteria.

## Claims of Various Social Groups to Self-Determination: Questions to be Answered

The rapid disintegration of some of the East European states, following the breakup of the U.S.S.R. and the many conflicts that have erupted in the Commonwealth of Independent States are attributable to increasing self-assertiveness and claims of self-determination by peoples and national minorities. Ethnic, national, and religious groups often seek to have their own, separate states. Their claims to self-determination, statehood, and sovereignty usually invoke international law and practice, posing questions that the international community is finding it hard to avoid.[2]

In December 1992, the General Assembly of the United Nations adopted the Declaration on the Rights of Persons belonging to National or Ethnic, Religious and Linguistic Minorities.[3] Article 8 of the declaration emphasizes: "Nothing in this Declaration may be construed as permitting any activity contrary to the purposes and principles of the United Nations, including sovereign equality, territorial integrity and political independence of States."[4] While making a useful contribution to the protection of individual rights of minorities, the declaration did not attempt to define the various social groups whose rights must be protected in democratic societies. Instead of dealing with the "collective" rights of national or ethnic, religious, and linguistic minorities, it mainly addressed the rights of *persons* belonging to such groups,[5] leaving unanswered the question which social groups should be considered as holders of a right to self-determination.

Articles 1(2) and 55 of the Charter of the United Nations mention the principle of equal rights and self-determination of *peoples* without specifying or explaining the term "people." The 1960 Declaration on the Granting of Independence to Colonial Countries and Peoples proclaimed in 1960 clearly states, in its title and in its provisions, however, that it is dealing with the right to self-determination of *colonial* peoples in "territories which have not yet attained independence" (see Paragraph 5 and Principle I). Often an emphasis is put on *territories*, rather than on *peoples*.[6] International instruments referring to "all peoples" do not usually explain the term. Thus, Paragraph 1 of General Assembly Resolution 1514(XV) states that "the subjection of peoples to alien subjugation, domination and exploitation constitutes a denial of fundamental human rights," and Paragraph 2 provides that *"all peoples* have the right of self-determination" (emphasis mine) without specifying the substance or nature of this right. It was still unclear what are "peoples" and why only "peoples" were choosen among many other social groups as holders of this right.

Consideration of the principle of self-determination within the framework of the Special Committee on Principles of International Law concerning Friendly Relations and Co-operation among States set up by the General Assembly of the United Nations in 1966 was marked by attempts to clarify the principle in the broad context of a humanistic approach, with reference to values proclaimed by the French Revolution and precepts set forth in the Declaration of Independence of the United States.[7] It was clearly pointed out that though the principle was at that time primarily intended to deal with the elimination of colonialism, it nevertheless should not be applied *only* to colonial peoples and situations, being in essence a concept based upon *the right of every social group to collective expression.*[8]

The United Nations Declaration on Friendly Relations adopted in 1970 (General Assembly Resolution 2625) insisted that: "By virtue of the principles of equal rights and self-determination of peoples enshrined in the Charter of the United Nations, all peoples have the right freely to determine, without external interference, their political status and to pursue their economic, social, and cultural development, and every State has the duty to respect this right in accordance with the provisions of the Charter." Thus, *all peoples* were recognized as holders of the *right* freely to determine their *political status* and to pursue their economic, social and cultural *development* – a right that is at the core of self-determination. Similar formulations are contained in common Article 1 of the two international covenants of 1966 on human rights, referring to the right of self-determination of all peoples in the context of these rights, and in Chapter VIII of the Final Act of the Conference on Security and Cooperation in Europe (CSCE) promulgated in 1975.

Eastern Europe and the former U.S.S.R. provide the stage on which many contemporary issues of self-determination are playing out their most controversial and dangerous implications. That is why it is necessary to look again at some elements of the constitutional models that existed in these states in this part of the world as they relate to self-determination. The experience of these states underscores the need for uniform international and national standards and responses to the problem of self-determination. Such experience should be taken into consideration in the conduct of activities by the United

Nations aimed at strengthening the institutions of human rights and democracy, not only on the territory of the former U.S.S.R. but throughout the world.[9]

According to Article 70 of the Soviet Constitution of 1977 (as amended in 1981 and 1988), the U.S.S.R. was created on the basis of a "free self-determination of *nations*" (emphasis added). Article 72 provided that each republic or member of the Union had the right of secession from the U.S.S.R. Similar provisions can be found in the constitutions of the republics of the U.S.S.R. For instance, Article 68 of the Constitution of the Ukrainian Soviet Socialist Republic (1978) provided that Ukraine was a "sovereign Soviet Socialist State" and declared that it had joined the U.S.S.R. on the basis of self-determination of its people. According to Article 69 of the Ukrainian Constitution, the Ukrainian S.S.R. had the right of free secession from the U.S.S.R. At the same time, Article 70 of the Soviet Constitution stated that the U.S.S.R. was an embodiment of the *State unity* of the Soviet *people*[10] (emphasis mine). This raises several questions: What kind of democratic procedure would guarantee the right to self-determination? What is the correlation between the terms "people" and "nation" in the context of self-determination and secession in a multinational state? Who should be considered as a holder of this right to self-determination – the whole of the population of the multinational state, its indigenous populations, or its prevailing ethnic, national, linguistic, cultural or religious groups? Realization of self-determination even on the basis of a "traditional" democratic majority in states where, in some cases, as a result of a demographic policy and processes, the indigenous population does not constitute an absolute majority, may become a contradictory and painful process.[11]

Violent conflicts in Nagorno-Karabakh in Azerbaijan, in the Republic of Moldova, in Abkhazia and South Ossetia in Georgia, and in Chechnya in the Russian Federation, as well as the complicated situation in the Crimea in Ukraine, have already demonstrated all the complexities of self-determination in a multinational state, especially one in which large or considerable segments of nations and peoples that already had their statehood in eponymous republics lived on the territories of other republics. It becomes very difficult to distinguish which nations, groups, or indigenous populations of multinational States, can properly regard themselves as "peoples."

Another question that complicates questions of self-determination and related issues (such as State succession and continuation, international recognition of newly independent States, citizenship and protection of national, ethnic, linguistic, religious, cultural groups, and so forth) is the lack of clear and detailed constitutional, legal provisions that would establish proper procedures, mechanisms and guarantees of various modes of self-determination and the absence of corresponding effective national institutions.

The former U.S.S.R. lacked any effective federal judiciary body with the necessary competence to resolve controversies on the part of members of the Union concerning the provisions of the constitution dealing with self-determination or issues relevant to it. According to Professor Rousseau, for instance, "the structure of the U.S.S.R. remains very centralized and the federalism there is nothing but a facade."[12] In 1990, the U.S.S.R. adopted a Law on Procedures for Resolving Questions Related to the Secession of Union Republics from the U.S.S.R., but events quickly overtook these unwieldy procedures.[13] So the Soviet experience left a void concerning issues of national identity and self-determination for the international community to address.

In addition to these factors, which to a great extent were shared by other Eastern European States, there are also problems linked to citizenship in the context of state succession. Thus, Article 33 of the Constitution of the U.S.S.R. established citizenship of the Union and citizenship of the Union Republics, stating that every citizen of each Union Republic was also a citizen of the U.S.S.R. After the dissolution of the Soviet Union numerous questions arose in this connection in the context of state succession: What would be the legal basis for establishing the citizenship of various ethnic, national and other non–indigenous groups in the republics? Do such groups possess the right to choose the citizenship of the States where they are regarded as indigenous, while residing permanently on the territories of other States where they are not considered to be indigenous? Should they be granted dual citizenship? Is it acceptable to grant local citizenship to such groups on conditions different from the conditions of granting citizenship to local indigenous populations? What would be the status of individuals in cases of "mixed marriages" and of their children? These questions and various problems related to them are not just theoretical. They are at the core of concrete political, interstate debate and controversies demanding immediate practical solutions.[14]

# A Need for Conceptual Reevaluation and Adjustment of Self-Determination

Universal recognition of the principle of equal rights and self-determination of all peoples as a fundamental principle of international law means that it ought to be considered at least as important as other fundamental principles, including respect for sovereignty and the sovereign equality and territorial integrity of states. But, the reaction of the international community to claims for self-determination during the Congo crisis and in Bangladesh, Biafra, Sudan, Chad, Ethiopia, Tibet, Kurdistan, and other places implied a direct conflict between the principle of self-determination as currently formulated and other principles of international law and that there might be "a striking contradiction" between the right of all peoples to self-determination and the right of a state to its territorial integrity, which would seem to preclude secession.[15]

The establishment of a proper balance between self-determination and state sovereignty and the elimination of controversy in this area cannot be achieved in the framework of a purely formal legalistic approach. The concept of self-determination and the legal norms established for it should reflect and relate to real requirements in international life. The content of the concept is predetermined by the changing demands and necessities of the social life of mankind and should not be rigidly prescribed by the law once and forever. Thus, self-determination should be viewed as a broad sociological concept, giving rise to certain legal consequences. In order to deal successfully with the various legal elements and consequences of self-determination, it is necessary to clarify its social content, value, and functions.

In relevant international and national instruments, self-determination is regarded as one of the preconditions for the normal, peaceful functioning and development of the modern international community. It is also viewed as a prerequisite for ensuring and protecting individual human rights and the rights and identity of certain social groups – "peoples" or "nations" – through democratic mechanisms. Legal concepts of self-determination, however, focused primarily on statehood and sovereignty and their realization through the formation of independent sovereign states. In this narrow framework, practically all attention was devoted to legal aspects of the creation of such states in the context of decolonization or through secession, while only "peoples" were considered as holders of the right to self-determination.

Secession creates a new independent state, but creating a new independent state and attaining state sovereignty is only one of the modes of realizing self-determination. Self-determination is not always and not necessarily linked to statehood or sovereignty at all. Nor is self-determination applicable to "peoples" and "nations" alone. Self-determination, as a broad sociological concept, entails free choice of social status, through which the identity and development of every social actor can be realized, including individuals (as the most important subjects of social relations) and social groups (acting as "collective" social agents or parties). Such self-determination will be needed for individuals and societies to enjoy the broadest possible choice of social structures, relations, and life.

Broad variety in the forms of self-realization of individuals exercised and projected through various collective identities is crucially important – not only for the development of individual, human potential, but also for the development of as many alternative forms of social structures within the international community as possible. Diversity of social mechanisms within the international community enables it to respond in a quick and flexible way to new, often unexpected global and local problems. This social demand for freedom and diversity is reflected, in particular, in concepts of human rights, "individual" and "collective." The emergence of these concepts within the body of contemporary international law was a manifestation of international recognition of the need to move from the "superior" statist values embodied in the idea of "traditional," "absolute" sovereignty to human values[16] as vitally important for survival and the further development of civilization. This has affected the whole system of governance of the international community, encouraging an integrated approach to human rights and to all aspects of sociopolitical and economic security and development.[17]

If individuals and their identity are considered as a primary value of modern society and they find their identity not only in big social groups, such as nations, claims of other smaller groups to self-determination in a broad social context should be recognized as legitimate by the international community.

At the same time, realities of modern political and socioeconomic life[18] provide evidence that the unlimited fragmentation of states and societies (sometimes linked to the political ambitions of power-hungry groups and individuals)[19] may be counterproductive and dangerous. The collapse of tiny and nonviable states brought about by such processes may lead to the destruction of the identity and even the existence of previously stable social groups.

In this connection, it should be noted that democratic participation by the population,[20] which implies the involvement of a variety of stable social groups is itself a form of realization of self-determination. Self-determination is not limited to and need not be equated with such an extreme and radical mode of its realization as secession and the establishment of a sovereign state, especially a separate and totally independent state. States may, through a properly designed system of democratic institutions, guarantee to all groups appropriate forms of participation,[21] self-determination, and fundamental human rights, without discrimination. Individuals should not, however, be coerced into joining particular social groups for the purpose of protecting their rights. Fundamental human rights of individuals must be guaranteed to all on the basis of equality and non-discrimination even if they do not belong to some "subnational" or other social group. The international community should adopt a uniform approach to relevant issues of self-determination and elaborate proper international standards in this area. Protecting individual rights alone is not enough.[22]

The reason why the protection of individual rights does not provide a comprehensive solution is that collective self-identification is still a central feature of human life. International and national instruments and relevant studies[23] should place more emphasis on the protection of identity[24] and the collective rights of stable social groups, including the right of democratic representation and of a comprehensive (i.e., political, socioeconomic, and cultural) social participation[25] within the context of the right of democratic governance[26] and the right of development.[27] This would require a balanced set of mutual rights and duties for such groups and for individuals, states, and the international community, to be devised and put into effect at international and constitutional levels of setting standards, which would establish a proper "technology" for the legitimate exercise of self-determination in all its major forms.

Taking into consideration existing social realities and recognizing that it is not always possible to find constructive, peaceful solutions to conflicts arising in connection with the exercise of human rights and the right of self-determination in a given state, following the practice of "exhaustion of national and international remedies" presents an important alternative to conflict and the easy recourse to violence. The establishment of a new sovereign state as a mode of self-determination for smaller social groups should be a "last resort"[28] when: (1) all other means and social remedies within the state in question have been tried and proved ineffective for the purpose of protecting the existence and development of the identity of stable social groups and the human rights of their members on an equal basis; (2) it has been proved on the basis of international standards that such guarantees or mechanisms cannot be established in the given society and state in a reasonable time and without endangering either the identity of such groups or the fundamental rights of their members; and (3) the applicability of all the other modes of the realization of self-determination has been examined and tested without success.

## The Role of the United Nations

Against this background, it should be evident that the role of the international community and its various institutions, including the United Nations, is extremely important. First and foremost, they should develop appropriate conceptual approaches to the right of self-determination and establish relevant international standards for the exercise of that right.[29] Such international standards should be based on the vast body of existing international human rights instruments. They should emphasize "collective" human rights with special sensitivity to the situations of ethnic, religious, cultural, linguistic, or other social minorities and groups. To provide the basis for developing new conceptual approaches, further codification and progressive elaboration of international law would be needed. In this effort, sociological as well as legal research would have to be carried out, and suitable attention given to coordination at both the international and the national levels.

Difficulties in formulating definitions of various stable social groups[30] ("communities," "collectivities," "majorities," "minorities," "indigenous" and "nonindigenous populations," etc.), should not, however, become a stumbling block to protecting their status and self-determination (not reduced to secession) in various internationally recognized forms. In order to achieve such a result, the social value of such groups and of their identity should be explored, acknowledged, and protected. In this context, special attention should be paid to the concept of "identity."[31] The strong sense of a separate identity among cohesive groups has found some conceptual recognition even as a justification for their claims to territorial separation because of its fundamental importance for human dignity.[32] The protection, preservation, and development of the identities of stable social groups in the societies in which they find themselves should be considered crucially important to their self-realization through various forms of self-determination.

In each particular case of proposed self-determination the following considerations should be made: (1) the need to study the real causes of claims to self-determination and of the conflicts linked to them, including such factors as the socioeconomic, political, cultural, and psychological environment, and the historical background and traditions of the society involved and of related social groups; (2) the availability to the population and related social groups of professional and objective information about such causes and factors and about possible solutions to the problem, including the range of options or various modes of self-determination that would enable such groups to reach an effective solution; and (3) the availability of proper democratic procedures and the institutions necessary for the free expression of the democratic will of a properly educated population (sufficiently informed and politically advanced).

In the activities of the United Nations and other international and national institutions dealing with the issue of self-determination, the emphasis should be on conflict prevention rather than on postconflict response, in order to avoid violence, loss of human life, and the emergence of other factors that would make the peaceful settlement of a conflict more complicated. Full utilization should be made of already existing national, United Nations, and other international institutions and programs in dealing with self-determination, human rights, and related issues.[33] Coordination of activities,[34] rather than creation of new bodies should be the rule. A special role in this area could be played by the High Commissioner for Human Rights, whose post is suited for such responsibilities.[35]

Special emphasis should be placed on establishing an "early warning system" as a way of averting conflicts linked to self-determination.[36] Such a system should be based on the following major elements: (1) a complex sociopolitical, economic, cultural and legal study of the real causes of aspirations for self-determination; (2) the identification of possible ways and means of dealing with these causes and with potentially dangerous situations related to self-determination at both the national and the international levels; (3) research, training, and advisory assistance to affected societies and to relevant international institutions, including bodies of the United Nations; and (4) diplomatic and nongovernmental efforts to remove the sources of danger before conflict and violence result.[37] The possible role of regional and nongovernmental organizations should not be underestimated[38] since in some situations they may be better equipped to deal with specific local issues related to self-determination and human rights (individual and collective) than United Nations institutions.

For making preventive activities in this area effective, it might be necessary to establish a U.N. Center or a focal point for international research, monitoring, investigation, training and advisory assistance in the field of self-determination, which would use the expertise of an international pool of experts, or such functions might be performed by already existing international institutions dealing with human rights, self-determination, or the prevention and peaceful settlement of disputes under the supervision of the High Commissioner for Human Rights.[39]

When conflict does erupt, appropriate international mechanisms, coordinated by the United Nations, should be used to try to bring about a peaceful settlement. Whether of a peacemaking, peace-keeping, or peace-building nature, all efforts should be on the basis of a strict observance of international norms and principles and of neutrality and objectivity, with special sensitivity to local particularities and backgrounds.

The many-sided role the United Nations has played in connection with the formulation and implementation of the right to self-determination for colonial peoples, could be extended beyond the framework of decolonization. Drawing on the experience and institutions of the organization, the United Nations could conduct and coordinate a proper study of the issue of self-determination in relation to the realities of a changing world and formulate conceptual approaches and criteria necessary for adjusting the implementation of that right to a new international order. In this context it could adopt decisions, resolutions and declarations on the issue of self-determination, as well as contribute to the creation of relevant, legally binding international instruments through its system of codification and the progressive development of international law. It could thereby establish an appropriate, uniform international regime of self-determination, effectively balancing the mutual rights and duties of holders of this right and with those of sovereign states and international organizations.[40]

Regular system-wide consultations between the United Nations, specialized agencies, and nongovernmental organizations, and inter-agency meetings organized by the center for Human Rights take place to consider further measures of cooperation against racism and racial discrimination.[41] These consultations could also take up relevant issues relating to the right of self-determination. The knowledge and experience of human rights bodies dealing with racial discrimination and of the United Nations Committee on the Elimination of Racial Discrimination, as well as relevant United Nations programs in the area of human rights, could be useful in dealing with problems of self-determination and relevant rights of various social groups and of their members.

Self-determination, its conceptual development, and, its practical application should also be discussed in the framework of the United Nations Decade of International Law (1990–99),[42] following the Congress on Public International Law[43] held at United Nations Headquarters in New York from 13 to 17 March 1995 and through the United Nations Programme of Assistance in the Teaching, Study, Dissemination and Wider Appreciation of International Law;[44] and the long-term program of the International Law Commission. In this framework, however, legal matters ought to be discussed and addressed in conjunction with socioeconomic, political, cultural, and other issues related to self-determination,[45] – i.e., by taking a broad, integrated, multidisciplinary, and sociological conceptual approach.[46]

For the purpose of the codification and progressive development of international law, specific legal issues related to self-determination should be discussed not only in the framework of the Sixth Committee of the General Assembly of the United Nations, but also in the framework of the International Law Commission. Thus, such topics linked to the realization of self-determination as state succession and its impact on the nationality of natural and legal persons, and state succession with respect to membership in international organizations, and the law concerning international migrations, have already been suggested for inclusion in the long-term program of the work of the International Law Commission.[47] Other topics, more directly linked to the establishment of universal standards for self-determination, such as self-determination and state succession and continuation, or theoretical and practical aspects of the application of the concept of self-determination to federations could be also suggested for consideration by relevant international bodies.

Consideration of various issues of self-determination using such a broad, multifaceted approach would be of practical significance not only for the work of the legal bodies of the United Nations and their Secretariat, but also for other structures of the Organization dealing with various related conceptual and practical issues, including the prevention and peaceful settlement of disputes linked to self-determination; individual and collective rights; peacekeeping, and rendering consultative, training, and other forms of assistance.

## Conclusion

The international community faces nothing less than cataclysmic challenges linked to the rapid internationalization of social problems and the integration and disintegration of societies and states throughout the world.

Because of the close interrelation between these global trends and issues of self-determination, human rights, and development, relevant activities of the international community in these fields should be coordinated by the United Nations, drawing on its existing potential, experience, and programs in these areas. No other organization has the structure, support and world-wide connections necessary for the task.

### Notes

The views expressed in this chapter are solely those of the author and do not necessarily represent those of the United Nations.

1. In this connection see A/47/277, S/2411, paras. 17 and 18.
2. In connection with relevant issues of self-determination and state sovereignty, see, for instance, A/C.1/50/4, A/50/570, A/50/689–S/1995/890 and A/50/557.
3. See General Assembly Resolution 47/135 of 18 December 1992, Annex. See also A/50/514.
4. Ibid. See also in this connection paragraph 102 of the Report of the Secretary-General on the Work of the Organization, A/47/1.
5. The only exceptions are the provisions of the second preambular paragraph of the 1992 Declaration (Annex) in which the General Assembly reaffirms faith "in the equal rights . . . of *nations* (emphasis added) large and small" and of the Article 1(1), stating that "States shall protect the existence and the national or ethnic, cultural, religious and linguistic *identity* (emphasis added) of minorities within their respective territories and shall encourage conditions for the promotion of that identity."
6. In this connection see, for example, Article 73 (e) of the Charter of the United Nations; Principles IV and V of General Assembly Resolution 1541 (XV); General Assembly Resolution 742 (VIII), Annex, etc.
7. See Doc. A/6230, paragraph 463.
8. See Doc. A/6230, paragraphs 465 and 472.
9. In this connection see A/49/668.
10. In connection with the term "Soviet people", Soviet Academician

Julian V. Bromlei, for instance, stated: "A new ethnic entity with its own social parameters – the Soviet people has emerged". According to him "The milenia-long history of humankind has seen many such entities; take the present Indian and Indonesian peoples in the developing world, the people of Switzerland in the West and Yugoslav people in the Socialist countries". However, he indicated the most of the Soviet republics were multiethnic: ". . .alongside the nationality that gave the republic its name, there are other ethnic groups. All in all, ethnic groups which live beyond their national-territorial units or have no such units number 60 million people or 20 per cent of the country's population. (It totals more than the population of France.)" – See Julian V. Bromlei. Ethnic Relations and Perestroika. – in: Perestroika Annual. Vol.2. Editor-in-Chief: Prof. Abel G. Aganbegyan, English translation C 1989 Futura Publications, a Division of Macdonald & Co (Publishers) Ltd, London and Sydney, pp.104, 119 and 112. This raises some questions: Can we expect that in the future a unified "European nation" will emerge as a new social entity within the framework of a European integration? How would "traditional" peoples and nations exercise their self-determination within a new political and legal framework of a much closer regional integration?

11. Thus, as it was pointed out, for instance, by Julian V. Bromley: "Mass migration, which noticeably reduces the percentage of the indigenous population (for example, in Estonia and Latvia), also has an impact on ethnic relations in the republics". - Op.cit.,p.109. He also notes that "acute differences" concerning relevant legal issues between "the native population" and "new-comers" "breed armed conflicts" and indicates that "more progressive legislation on ethnic questions" is vitally needed.- Ibid., p.112. This clearly indicates that proper international legal standards in this field should be created in order to prevent such conflicts.

12. M. Charles Rousseau, Cours de droit international public, Licence 3 éme Année, Paris, 1953–1954, p.123.

13. See Hurst Hannum, Documents on Autonomy and Minority Rights, Martinus Nijhoff Publishers, Dordrecht/Boston/London, 1993, pp.742, 753–760.

14. See, for instance A/49/265, A/49/368 and A/50/483.

15. See, for instance, Chris N. Okeke, Controversial subjects of contemporary international law, Rotterdam University Press, 1974, pp.176–177. On issues of secession and self-determination see, for instance, also: L.C. Buchheit, Secession: The Legitimacy of

Self-Determination, New Haven and London: Yale University Press (1978): pp.xi, 260; R. Emerson, Self-Determination, 65 *American Journal of International Law* 459, 465 (1971); E. Suzuki, Self-Determination and World Public Order: Community Response to Territorial Separation, 16 *Virginia Journal of International Law* 779–862 (1976); L. Brinclayer, Secession and Self-Determination: A Territorial Interpretation, 16 *Yale Journal of International Law* 177 (1991); Debra A. Valentine, The Logic of Secession, *Yale Law Journal* volume 89, Number 4, March 1980; A. Buchanan, Secession: the Morality of Political Divorce from Fort Sumter to Lithuania and Quebec (1991); V. Nanda, Self-Determination Under International Law: Validity of Claims to Secede, 13 *Case Western Reserve Journal of International Law* 257 (1981); W. M. Reisman, Somali Self-Determination in the Horn, in Nationalism and Self-Determination in the Horn of Africa 151 (I.M. Lewis ed., 1983).

16. B. Boutros-Ghali, Democracy: A Newly Recognized Imperative, Global Governance. A Review of Multilateralism and International Organization vol.1, No.1, Winter 1995, Published by Lynne Rienner Publishers, 1995, p.3; David P. Forsythe, The U.N. and Human Rights at Fifty. An Incremental but Incomplete Revolution, Global Governance, Vol.1, No.3, September–December 1995, p.297.

17. See: The Vienna Declaration and Programme of Action, Adopted 25 June 1993 by the World Conference on Human Rights, U.N. DPI, New York, 1993, I(6), p.30.

18. See in this connection the List of Factors indicative of the attainment of independence or of other separate systems of self-government – in General Assembly Resolution 742(VIII), Annex. It should be also noted that the issue of self-determination is not only an issue of obtaining this legal right, but also an issue of material capacity to exercise it.

19. Ethnic conflicts as such are often linked to the struggle for political power resulting in mass violations of human rights – see in this regard, for instance, A/49/415, para. 102 and E/CN.4/1995/7.

20. Close interrelation between self-determination and democratic participation of the population may be illustrated, for instance, by para. 8(I) of the 1993 *Vienna* Declaration of the World Conference on Human Rights: "Democracy is based on the freely expressed will of the people to determine their own political, economic, social and cultural systems [which is, in fact, a core of realization of self-determination – V.R.] and their full participation in all aspects of their lives." Op. cit. pp.30, 31.

21. Democratic participation can be an alternative to conflicts between social groups seeking to protect their identities and to conflicts between individual and collective rights. In this connection, the Secretary-General of the United Nations, Boutros Boutros-Ghali pointed out: "The alternative is democracy. To have a voice in the arrangements that control on'e daily life is to act and be recognized as a human being." See Op. cit. Global Governance, Vol.1, No.1, winter 1995, p.8.

22. See General Assembly Resolution 47/135 of 18 December 1992, Annex.

23. For a detailed consideration of relevant issues see, for instance,: Hurst Hannum, Rethinking self-determination, *Virginia Journal of International Law*, Vol.34, No. 1, Fall 1993.

24. The importance of protection of identity of social groups may be illustrated, *inter alia*, by its role in the promotion and realization of the 1992 Declaration on the Rights of Persons belonging to National or Ethnic, Religious and Linguistic Minorities – see A/ 49/415, paras. 13–34, 68, 69; See also E/CN.4/Sub.2/1994/36, chapter V, para. 34; A/49/580, paras. 16–19, Appendix A (7), D (2); A/49/415, section B, para. 105, chapter IX, para. 147. See also: The General Comment N23 (50) adopted by the Human Rights Committee at its 1314th meeting (fiftieth session) on 6 April 1994, on article 27 of the International Covenant on Civil and Political Rights (Resolution 2200 A (XXI), annex), paras. 6.2 and 9. Thus the Committee emphasized the following:

> 6.2. Although the rights protected under article 27 are individual rights, they depend in turn on the ability of the minority group to maintain its culture, language or religion. Accordingly, positive measures by States may also be necessary to protect the identity of a minority and the rights of its members to enjoy and develop their culture and language and to practice their religion, in community with the other members of the group. In this connection, it has to be observed that such positive measures must respect the provisions of articles 2 (1) and 26 of the Covenant both as regards the treatment between different minorities and the treatment between the persons belonging to them and the remaining part of the population.

> . . .

> 9. The Committee concludes that article 27 relates to rights whose protection imposes specific obligations on States parties. The protection of these rights is directed to ensure the survival and continued

development of the cultural, religious and social identity of the minorities concerned, thus enriching the fabric of society as a whole. Accordingly, the Committee observes that these rights must be protected as such and should not be confused with other personal rights conferred on one and all under the Covenant.

See also in this connection A/49/36, paras. 111 and 112.

25. See, in this connection, A/49/415, sections E and F, paras. 57–67; A/49/36, para. 110; A/49/580, paras. 8, 9, 12, 15–19, 23, 25–28, 34, Appendix, C (4): A/49/713, Annex 1, para. 6; according to the Secretary-General of the United Nations. Boutros Boutros-Ghali: "With democratic participation, social advances are shared, economic freedoms are protected, and political rights are guaranteed by institutions," Democracy: A Newly Recognized Imperative, Op. cit., p.4.

26. In this connection, see, for example, Draft Declaration on the rights of indigenous peoples, as agreed upon by members of the Working Group on Indigenous Populations on its Eleventh Session, U.N. ECOSOC, Comm'n on Hum. Rts., 45th Sess., Agenda item 14, Annex I, U.N. Doc.E/CN.4/Sub.2/1993/29 (1993). See also U.N. Doc.E/CN.4/1985/10 (1984), pp.18, 36; Article 21 of the Universal Declaration of Human Rights; Articles 1, 25 and 27 of the Covenant on Civil and Political Rights; Human Rights Committee, General Comment No.23(50) (art. 27), U.N. G.A.O.R., Human Rights Comm., paras. 5.2, 6.1, 6.2, U.N. Doc. CCPR/C/21/Rev.1/Add.5 (1994); Thomas M. Frank, The Emerging Right to Democratic Governance, 86 Am.J.Int'l L. pp.46, 52, 58, 59; Managua Declaration adopted at the Second International Conference of New or Restored Democracies, held at Managua from 4 to 6 July 1994, paras. 1, 6, 8 and 10 U.N. Doc.A/49/713, Annex I, p.3; A/49/415, para. 157.

27. See, for instance, A/49/580, paras. 8, 9, 12, 15–19, 34. See also: World Conference on Human Rights. The Vienna Declaration and Programme of Action, June 1993, U.N. DPI, N.Y., August 1995, 30–32.

28. In connection with the recognition of self-determination of a minority in a form of its separation from the State and its population of which it forms a part as an "exceptional solution, a last resort when the State lacks either the will or the power to enact and apply just and effective guaranties" see, for instance, The Aaland Islands Question, p.28, League of Nations Doc. B 7.21/68/106 (1921) (English version) (Report submitted to the Council of the League of Nations by the Commission of

Rapporteurs). In connection with the practice in this area a note should be taken, however, of the cases within the United Nations framework when only "peoples"were recognized as holders of a right of self-determination – see, for instance, Communication No. 413/1990, *A.B. v. Italy*, Report of the Human Rights Committee, U.N. G.A.O.R., 46th Session, Supp. No. 40, p.320, U.N. Doc. A/46/40 (1991) (decision on admissibility of 2 November 1990), and Report of the Human Rights Committee, U.N. G.A.O.R., 42nd Session, Supp. No.40, p.106, paras. 401, 402, U.N. Doc. A/42/40 (1987). For doctrinal views supporting the right of secession as the "ultimate remedy" see, for example, Lee C. Buchheit, Secession (1978), pp.222, 227; Oneyeonoro Kamanu, Secession and the Right to Self-Determination: An OAU Dilemma, 12 J. Mod. Afr. Stud., pp.355, 359, 362 (1974); Benyamin Neuberger, National Self-Determination in Postcolonial Africa p.71, (1986); Conor C. O'Brien, Preface to 1 World Minorities, p.xv (Georgina Ashworth ed., 1977); W. Ofuatey-Kodjoe, The Principle of Self-Determination in Interational Law, p.188 (1977). In this connection, see also: Conor C. O'Brien, The Right to Secede, New York Times, 30 December 1971.

29. It should be noted that the formulation and application of such standards may benefit, *inter alia*, from the utilization of the relevant standards and factors listed in General Assembly Resolution 742(VIII), Annex entitled: "Factors which should be taken into account in deciding whether a Territory is or is not a Territory whose people have not yet attained a full measure of self-governing."

30. See, for example, *Official Records of the General Assembly, Third Session, Part I, Sixth Committee,* 74th and 75th meetings; E/CN. 4/sub.2/384/Add.1, paras. 3–8. See also A/48/147/Add.1,p.4.

31. In this connection, the Human Rights Committee, commenting on Article 27 of the 1966 Covenant on Civil and Political Rights, protecting the rights of minorities, pointed out that positive measures of States may be necessary "to protect the identity of a minority and the rights of its members to enjoy and develop their culture and language and to practice their religion, in community with other members of the group", see Human Rights Committee, General Comment No.23 (50), (art.27), U.N. G.A.O.R., Hmn. Rts. Comm., para. 6.2, U.N. Doc. CCPR/C/21/Rev.I/Add.5 (1994).

32. See, for instance, E. Suzuki, Self-Determination and World Public Order: Community Response to Territorial Separation, 16 VA.J.Int'l L. 779–862 (1976).

33. See, for instance, A/49/415, chapters III–IX, paras. 91–157, referring to relevant activities aimed at promotion of the 1992 Declaration on the Rights of Persons belonging to National or Ethnic, Religious and Linguistic Minorities; see also: A/49/444, A/49/12/Add.1, A/49/668 (esp. chapters II, III, V, VII–IX, XVI–XX, etc.) A/50/514 (esp. chapters 111–ix) and E/1995/51 (esp. paras. 7–29), dealing with the activities of the United Nations University addressing such issues as: "The United Nations System, Global Governance and Security," "Conflict Resolution and Ethnicity," "Governance, State and Society" and "Culture and Development".

34. In this connection see A/49/415 and, in particular, paras. 155, 156; see also A/49/L.20, A/50/514, paras. 75–78, etc.

35. See General Assembly Resolution 48/141 of 20 December 1993, para. 4. See also: A/49/537, paras. 21–23; A/49/36 and A/49/512.

36. As an example of regional efforts in this area may be considered a decision to entrust the High Commissioner on National Minorities within the C.S.C.E. with functions to receive and collect information in relevant areas, so as to enable him to warn the members of the C.S.C.E. of possible situations which could lead to conflicts – see U.S. Commission on Security and Cooperation in Europe, C.S.C.E. Helsinki Document 1992, The Challenges of Change, pp.24, 31 (1992). See also: A/49/537, paras. 26–29 and 33; A/49/415, section B (paras. 104–107), chapter IV (paras. 115–123), chapter V (paras. 124–126), chapter IX (paras. 143–146, 153).

37. It should be noted that the term "diplomacy" can not always be used to describe postconflict and preventive activities of States and international organizations. Thus, for instance, recent practice highlighted the need to deal directly with warring factions in a failed State, while "diplomacy" usually presupposes political involvement of at least two "traditional" subjects of international law, such as States, intergovernmental organizations, etc. Thus a proper vocabulary reflecting modern realities should be developed in this area.

38. In this connection see, for instance, A/49/537, paras. 41 and 42.

39. See, in this connection, A/49/415, para.154.

40. See, General Assembly resolution 48/130 of 20 December 1993.

41. In this connection the Programme of Action for the Third Decade to Combat Racism and Racial Discrimination (1993–2003) may be mentioned, see General Assembly Resolution 48/91 of 20 December 1993, Annex. See also A/50/514, paras. 75, 76.

42. See General Assembly Resolutions 44/23 of 17 November 1993, 48/30 of 9 December 1993 and 49/50 of 9 December 1994.
43. See General Assembly Resolutions 48/30 of 9 December 1993 and 49/50 of 9 December 1994; see also A/C.6/48/L.9. The issue of succession and continuation of states, linked to self-determination, was among major issues discussed during the Congress.
44. See General Assembly Resolution 48/29 of 9 December 1993.
45. As it is recognized in relevant reports of the Secretary-General of the United Nations: ". . . a fairly wide spectrum of economic, political and social policies" has "a considerable impact on ethnic relations." (A/50/514, para. 27 and E/CN.4/Sub.2/1993/34/Add. 1–4).
46. A complex, multidisciplinary approach to the issue of self-determination proved to be very productive, as it was demonstrated during the Workshop on International Organizations Studies at Brown University: "Internal Conflict and the World Community: Self-Determination, Security, and Human Rights," organized by the Academic Council on the United Nations System and the American Society of International Law (17–29 July 1994). Many issues highlighted by the author of this paper, who was among the participants to this workshop, have been raised and discussed during the workshop on the basis of such an integrated, multidisciplinary approach.
47. See A/CN.4/454, 9 November 1993, pp.27–47.

# – 5 –

# Sovereignty Without Nationalism? A Critical Assessment of Minority Rights Beyond the Sovereign Nation-State Model

Nergis Canefe

## Introduction

In the post–Cold War period legitimate humanitarian intervention has become a growing concern for both practitioners and observers of public international law. Faced with an increasing number of internal conflicts in countries where governments fail to guarantee the well-being of all sectors of society and with instances of armed clashes, ethnic segregation, the forced displacement of inhabitants, and similar social and political turmoil, people all over the world are demanding that nongovernmental and international organizations do more to prevent crimes against humanity committed by states within their own borders.[1] Expectations of this kind cannot be fully realized, however, without a clear understanding of what state sovereignty means, including possible alternative formulations of the basic normative principles underlying the concept.

Since 1945, international politics has, under the guidance of the United Nations, rested on a peculiar conceptual triplet: the sovereign nation-state. As the chain of catastrophic events in the Middle East, in Africa, in Eastern Europe and the former U.S.S.R., and particularly in what was once Yugoslavia has proved, though, there can be very disturbing repercussions from trying to create or protect a sovereign nation-state. The problem of the legitimacy of a nation-state becomes all the more difficult because of the context in which it commonly arises. The international community has long witnessed the same intricate scenario repeated in different settings. In multinational/

multiethnic states, ethnonationalist claims of separation and autonomy come into direct conflict with the legitimacy of the established sovereign nation.

My concern here is with neither the ethics of ethnonationalist secession nor with the value of sovereignty for already existing political units of the international system of states. Rather, it is with the issue of sovereignty as a concept containing two separate components that coexist in a peculiar condition of tension with one another: the sovereignty of a state, and the sovereignty of a people.[2] Except in the ideal or unproblematic case of a nation with its own state, devoid of any minorities, it is necessary to analyze the notion of sovereignty in this binary framework, because the main issue contested by minority-based ethnonationalist movements is the status of sovereignty attributed to their host state given their claim to sovereignty as a distinct people.

Although attention must be paid to the menacing characteristics of totalitarian/nondemocratic forms of nationalism (as opposed to liberal pluralistic nationalism), cautious consideration must also be given to the detrimental consequences of the ethnic essentialism that sometimes blossoms in the context of minority politics.[3] Secession, whether achieved through escalated internal conflict, constitutional negotiations, or intervention by an outside force, by no means guarantees that the nationalist appropriation of sovereignty will assume a more democratic character in the newly formed nation-state.

Thus, it will be argued that in light of the increasing number of contentious cases of minority separatism, postcolonial and postimperial reproductions of the European sovereign nation-state model do not provide the best beginning for the emergence of more flexible and accommodating forms of political authority. The desire of minority communities to have separate nation-states mostly stems from a mismatch between the implied legitimacy of existing central authority and that same authority's curtailment of democratic principles and human rights. This is not just an issue of finding a workable balance between the sanctity and the violability of a state's sovereignty. Debates about sovereignty should focus instead on the introduction of political mediation and arbitration in place of the totally closedand finalized authority of the nation-state. The mechanisms of constitutional negotiation may provide a counterpoise to totalitarian responses to ethnonationalist and minority-related conflicts.

In such a framework, active intervention might be replaced by regulatory monitoring of the provisions of the human rights conventions at times of heightened political conflict. Still, the starting point must be a plain understanding that the sanctified borders of many states recognized by the United Nations since 1945 are not necessarily symbols of protection for the populations residing within them.[4]

The inescapable reality that some nation-states contain potentially lethal internal divisions undermines the validity of the sovereign nation-state model of unified political community. Ethnic cleansing, forced migration, population exchanges and displacements, and related civil catastrophes often seem the natural product of the sovereign nation-state model. Perhaps these are only isolated episodes of abusive power relations, but they raise important questions about the value of nationalism, and the principle of sovereignty that is its natural corollary. Blaming the bureaucratic nature of the central state apparatus or a particular cadre of politicians provides too easy a solution for problems of this magnitude. For example, one could not analyze the breakup of the former Yugoslavia solely on the basis of the Milosevic government's maneuvers, without looking at the dynamics of ethnic conflict in the country and their roots in the Tito years' ideal of the "Yugoslav model."[5]

Solving the puzzles of sovereignty will require a new kind of scholarship, viewing the nationalist appropriation of sovereignty as hegemonic strategy rather than historical truth. This viewpoint alone may work to criticize the dead ends of nationalism without giving undue credit to the claims of ethnonationalist separatists.

In this context, the issue of membership in a political community has great significance. For the sovereign nation-state model with its primary referents in early-modern/modern European history, the best test for homogenizing tendencies would be the inclusiveness of membership criteria in the national community. The conditions for attribution or denial of membership reveal the extent of overlap between citizenship, individual and group rights, and the democratic content of national politics. The membership status of minorities can thus be discussed as a primary symptom of the structural workings of the nation-state model. Divergences in the ideological–institutional framework attending national minority problems afford a much more beneficial taxonomy of nationalism than the static and a historical nation-state model. Such a taxonomy will facilitate studies of nationalism in the context of state and civil society relations and provide new insights for debates on the ethics of subjecting national sovereignty to human rights considerations.

This approach requires some understanding of two important and interrelated subjects: (1) The European tradition of nationalism and the sovereign nation-state model; and (2) New forms of nationalism that emerged outside Europe from the late nineteenth century onwards, including present applications of the principle of sovereignty in multiethnic/multinational states.

To begin with, a brief introduction to the European sovereign nation-state model will be helpful. Nationalism is a unique socio-historical construct that has created unprecedented political formations on a global scale. This dispersion gave rise to a hierarchy of nationalisms, both in theory and practice. There are semi-Western, non-Western, colonial, postcolonial, authoritarian, totalitarian, revivalist, fundamentalist, and fascist forms of nationalism, all of which are judged against an original European blueprint. These comparisons suffer, however, from the illusion that the European model provides a pure and simple paradigm.

Like nationalism, sovereignty and autonomy have long been key terms in the rhetoric of international relations, whose current force has gradually declined. Even during the nineteenth century, only a small number of privileged polities could use such rhetoric to their benefit. Not all communities claiming national autonomy could obtain a sovereign nation-state of their own.

Neither nationalism nor the sovereign nation-state was a natural phenomenon outside Europe. Non-European attempts to create sovereign nation-states took place in a very different context. In general, European manifestations of nationalism were products of historical contingencies in the development of a world capitalist system in early-modern Europe.[6] Non-European manifestations, on the other hand, came into being initially in the context of anticolonial and anti-imperialist struggles. Different types of states emerged in these different social and historical circumstances, only a few of which conformed to the pure principles of the sovereign nation-state model.[7] This creates a conceptual problem. The discrepancy between actual nation-states and the nation-state model leads to the common phenomenon of multiethnic/multinational communities parading as unified nations. The resulting internal conflicts and systematic human rights violations often take the world by surprise.

The current definition of a nation-state implies both a sovereign central state apparatus and the institutional affirmation of the acclaimed nationality or dominant ethnic group/community in a bordered territory. Consequently, in situations where more than one national group exists without constitutionally binding recognition, the marginalized social and cultural communities confined within the nation-state are denigrated to the status of random "citizens."

When to ascribe the title of "nation" to a community and what criteria should be used to distinguish between minority nationhood and cultural distinctiveness have always been matters of dispute. Not every disadvantaged national minority is necessarily a nation. The present analysis will only apply to minority groups that have both a distinct cultural identity and a united political will, with a socio-cultural disposition conducive to autonomous institutional existence. Separation is, of course, not the only available solution for dealing with the sins of totalitarian nationalism. Minority nations might indeed choose to coexist with the larger polity if all the parties involved could reach agreement on the terms of their cohabitation. This cumbersome problem of when a separate national unit might be a feasible and desirable option for particular minority communities will be touched upon later.

Scholars of conflict resolution are repeatedly faced with the dilemma that even when there is a stated willingness for cohabitation in a multiethnic/multinational setting, there may not be a model in the nation-state tradition for the actualization of such an option. This dilemma arises in part from the narrow and rigid notion of sovereignty applied in international politics. The "national" component in "national sovereignty" reduces the general value of sovereignty itself as a beneficial political dictum. Indeed, it aggravates the already existing problems of every political community or nation-state. A look at some of the elements of intolerance embedded in the national appropriation of sovereignty will demonstrate the need for alternative formulations of political autonomy.

## Internal Dynamics of the European Sovereign Nation–State Model

A proper analysis of the concept of sovereignty must start with the contradictions in the European nation-state model. These contradictions become more apparent when the process of national identity formation is disassembled into separate moments. Among these moments, the focus will be placed here on the creation of the "other/outsider," to illustrate and clarify the elements of intolerance in the original nation-state model.

The economic, cultural, and political domination that came with imperialism and colonialism left an undeniable imprint on the construction of national identities outside Europe. The dispersion of the European nation-state model does not, however, mean that the nexus between Europe and "non-Europe" has been solely uni-directional, from Europe to the ex-colonies and collapsing empires. On the contrary, European forms of nationalism were historical constructs based on a clear identification of "insiders" and "outsiders," distinguishing political subjects from those without such a status. Admittedly, that the task of defining Europe's "other" is a very difficult one, especially since the image of the "other" is by no means impervious to history. At this point, it is important to make a distinction between the "other" that was visible or easily identifiable and a different kind of "other," kept at the margins or erased from dominant historical narratives. These two "others" have always been interdependent parts of the mechanism which dictated an exclusive European self-image, but their functions have been significantly different. The visible "others" of European civilization have been the colonized cultures, the Orient, the Far East, the distant landscapes whose history was forced to intersect with that of Europe. Or else these "others" referred to the enemies of Europe who were perceived as historical threats to cultural autonomy and superiority, such as the "Slavic tribes."

The unrecognized, invisible "others" were minority cultures and indigenous opposition to centralized political power. The intention in making this distinction is not to propose two unbreakable definitions of otherness. These two forms quite often overlap. Still, differentiation is necessary between enunciated and unrecognized instances of sociocultural otherness. This differentiation enables us to see what was deemed to be open for political negotiation in the tradition of plural democracy in Europe.

Early-modern European theories of nationalism facilitated the growth of a sharp ideological distinction between the insiders and outsiders of a political community through a very specific process. European concepts of statehood, nationhood, and national identity had a structural relationship with the global categorization of races and languages and the selective search for the distinct cultural roots of "European civilization" in antiquity. In particular, language became the defining characteristic. The language of a community was seen as the primordial phenomenon of nationhood. Consequently, during the eighteenth and early nineteenth centuries, the intellectual market for European consumers of nationalism was occupied by philologists, grammarians, and lexicographers who were studying obscure and unknown languages and classifying them into a hierarchy of language families. This linguistic categorization was supported by theories of ancient predecessors and "racial findings" that excluded the non-Aryan connection with Mediterranean civilizations and celebrated an isolated Greek heritage.

The protonationalist forms of racial and linguistic awareness reflected the circumstances of colonization, territorial expansion, and African slavery, which gradually crystallized into theories of European superiority. This process of rediscovering the roots of European civilizations produced two specific cultural exigencies. The first concerns the dismissal of certain communities residing in Europe – such as the Basques, the Hungarians, and the Finns – whose languages did not fall into the Indo-European classification, and the second concerns the exclusion of cultures and civilizations that did not fit into such a classification at all – i.e. those on the continent of Africa. The "other/outsider" distinction shut out recognition of differences within a given national polity. Smaller communities amalgamated into the newly formed European nation-states were mostly assumed to have linguistic and racial-cultural traits that were either mutations of or derivations from the primary/dominant pool of characteristics.

In this way, the revolutionary achievements of European nationalist discourse legitimized the political desire to purify the historicocultural heritage of the mythical "European" race.[8] At the end of the eighteenth century, a new genre of grand national narratives emerged that aimed at reconstructing and reanimating the ancient past with the help of the disciplines of orientalism and philology. Early-modern European studies of society and culture were already strongly influenced by theories of genetics and evolutionism based on scientific assumptions about the possible survival of a "pure" race. New theories of antiquity reinforced a static relationship between language, race, and civilization.

Under the auspices of the "centralizing" state, the territorial aspects of nationhood became coterminous with the sociocultural characteristics of the constructed image of a chosen community.[9] The term "nation" began to express not only a common historical heritage but also adherence to the appropriation of this heritage by absolute central authority. By the nineteenth century, the objectified description of national origins based on transhistorical linguistic and racial classifications gained considerable political prominence. Differences in physiognomy, manners, customs, pureness of blood, and endless details of everyday life, including ethnic and religious ceremonies, were blended into the criteria for national identification. The ultimate union of a nation with the central state apparatus meant a radical reterritorialization of communities. Overlapping boundary lines of cultural identities were replaced by absolute borders, and citizenship granted on the basis of one's nationality was institutionally cultivated as the sole criterion for membership in the political community.

In this new framework, the nation came to be defined as a territorially bounded political community protected by a centralized state apparatus. As the idiom of national identity established cultural and institutional hegemony, territorially defined patriotism became the primary political bond transforming early-modern European forms of cultural and political affinity. Under the rubric of the moral and ethical virtues of patriotism, earlier constructs of identity were replaced by the nationality-citizenship duo as the basis of the European nation-state system. It was this new meaning of nationality that led to the peculiar appropriation of the concept of sovereignty.

The vernacular usage of "nationality" originated in seventeenth-century England.[10] Earlier concepts of nationality signified basic differences in spoken languages, literature, and cultural products. As a simple device for mapping out the social geography of Europe, it allowed considerable flexibility. The nineteenth-century reformulation of nationality, on the other hand, was a new concept that triggered various forms of intolerance toward those who subscribed to other types of identification or to different nationalities. The primary form of intolerance was institutional. The new nationalist rhetoric legitimated organized violence instigated by the nation-state and justified by the principal of national sovereignty. Warfare was only one of the many kinds of confrontations engaged in by the early European nation-states. Permanent armies and regular police forces became more common in connection with efforts to consolidate the nation-state. There is a pronounced difference between interstate warfare and internal military surveillance and control of civilian populations. On the basis of this difference, the term "organized violence," as used here, refers to the specific relationship between a nation-state and the populace under its sovereign authority.

Marginalization, silencing, and the reordering of the civil society by the central state are integral to the construction of a national identity. Marginalization is a forgotten and invisible form of otherness. The enemies and outsiders of Europe were key actors in the construction of European superiority. The difference between the visible and invisible other/outsider is that the visible outsider is needed to create a unified image of "us," while the invisible other remains a challenge to the assumed homogeneity of any political community. One is emphasized, the other denied. The puzzle for nationalism has always been where to draw the boundary between real enemies who cannot be assimilated and others who are merely an "internal problem."[11] National sovereignty is the solid expression of how, at a certain time, this boundary has been established. Marginalization and the silencing of dissent result from an excess of power, and they can implicate race, gender, class, ethnicity, or religious identity. Thus, they target a whole array of social and political movements opposing existing structures of legitimacy.

Binary opposition between the erasure of differences and the accentuation of unity is endemic to the European model of the nation-state because of its individualistic conception of contractual membership in the political community. Consensual politics does not necessarily provide an entry for group identity or multiple alliances for individual members of the national polity. This commonly raises the problem of "minority historicity." Although the predominant mode of otherness in European nationalism was that of enunciation and naming, the ultimate consolidation of the nation-state apparatus has its, "other" in a systematically "unrecognized" form. Official narratives of national history do not include stories of resistance to the growing power of the central state.[12] Histories of conflict are replaced by victories attributed to national heroes. They are redeemed in the name of conquest, conversion, or reunification. For national politics, minority identity has always been a sore issue, seldom openly recognized. The European invention of the sovereign nation-state gave rise not only to democracy and liberalism but also to a new form of political identity marked by intolerance and exclusion in the name of consensus and unity. These two faces of nationalism, one pluralist and consensual, the other essentialist and exclusive, find various expressions in the replicas of the European nation-state model in different parts of the globe. The extent of the authoritarian replays of the original model is dependent on the strength of state and civil society relations and the degree of violence exercised by the central state apparatus in protecting the national ideal.

## The Dispersion of the European Nation-State Model: Form versus Content

The nation/nationalism/nationality trio is an historicocultural invention solidified by the institutional framework of the modern nation-state. The processes of establishing a nation-state are generally viewed as an evolutionary movement from nationhood to statehood, following the European nation-state model. This trajectory suggests that "Westernizing" or "developing" societies will become "national democracies" in an ideal situation. The non-European instances of the nation-state are assumed to be replicating the key aspects of the European construct of a nation – a homogeneous people bound by linguistic and cultural affinity, a common history, ethnoreligious sentiments, collective solidarity, and a shared concept of the common good.

In the postcolonial and postimperial cases of nationalism, however, the two separate moments (nationhood and statehood) of the trajectory of European nation-state formation usually converge into one "revolutionary leap" marked by the sanctioning of colonial geographical boundaries. Therefore, the term territorial state, rather than nation-state, better represents the processes of state formation outside Europe. Otherwise, the imposition of a European historical experience onto other forms of nationalism leads to the false homogenization of diverse political experiences. In fact, on this very issue, canonical theoretical debates on nationalism constitute a serious analytical obstacle. A critical look at some of the essential texts on nationalism will help us identify problems caused by the theoretical and historical assumptions operative in this field.

Nationalism plays a significant part in European civilization's conception of its own history. Theoretical studies of nationalism privileging the foundational status of European nationalism do not devote enough attention to analysis of the divergent forms of nationalism that have come into being either as a reaction to European colonialism or in close connection with European cultural and political domination. The two primary examples of such divergency in the first category are India and the continent of Africa. In the second category fall the historical example of the Ottoman Empire and the contemporary example of Eastern Europe and the former U.S.S.R. To define non-European forms of nationalism in the language of a Europe-centered historicity perpetuates the otherness of colonized and dominated cultures, with a twist: they are not European, but they are viewed as catching up with history as it has been defined by Europe.[13]

Elie Kedourie locates the philosophical underpinnings of European nationalism in the ideas that found expression in the period of the Enlightenment. For Kedourie, the actualization of the idea of a nation through the ideology of nationalism happened only with the French Revolution, after the Declaration of the Rights of Man and of the Citizen in 1789 provided the historical basis for the creation of a secular nation.[14]

Hans Kohn broadens this argument in asserting that the Declaration of Independence of the thirteen United States of America in 1776 and the independence of Latin American creole states at the turn of the century consummated Western egalitarian and rational ideals. It is not difficult to foresee the further extension of this consummation to identify possible post-French Revolution instances of nationalism as replicas of the original gesture. In any event, the ideals of the French Revolution are universalized as the necessary impetus for the conflation of a well-defined community with a central and secular political authority.

Ernest Gellner sought to determine whether the central state necessarily precedes the nation or the nation is the prerequisite for the state.[15] Gellner's choice put the state before the nation, making nationalism the cultural basis for an ever-growing state apparatus. So the state provides much more than a neutral arena for hosting negotiations. Since the French Revolution, the ideological vehicle for seizing political power has become the assertion of a nationalist utopia. The evolution of the central state into a nation-state also influenced social factors, including class conflict and ethnolinguistic superiority. In this context, Immanuel Wallerstein's work is useful in gaining an understanding of the dynamic of cohesion within set borders.[16]

Wallerstein sees nationalism as the primary social force behind the global structure of expanding capitalism. He dismisses ethnic, religious, and intrastate conflicts as lower-grade expressions of class conflict.[17] This supports a new theory of nationalism in the gray area between European and non-European circumstances. Wallerstein assesses nationalism without reference to culture. Benedict Anderson goes to the other extreme, putting the origins of both nationalism and capitalism almost entirely in the cultural sphere. Anderson's account treats nationalism as the locus for a dynamic interaction between capitalism and social life. For Anderson, a nation is an "imagined political community" that is inherently limited and sovereign.[18] Nations are limited, because they are defined by boundaries beyond which lie "other" nations, and nations are sovereign because the very concept of a nation was born in an age that destroyed the divine orders and dynasties.[19]

Finally, E.J. Hobsbawm's work is particularly relevant in the context of the sharp divide between "European" and "non-European" forms of nationalism. Hobsbawm's conception of nationalism designates a one-and-only phenomenon, the European nation-state that emerged by the end of the eighteenth century.[20] His criteria for distinguishing "genuine nationalism" discount ethnic, religious, or linguistic communities as hierarchically lower than nations. In other words, nationalism is to be regarded as above and beyond the communal identity claims that preceded or survived it.[21] Hobsbawm's conclusions concerning the uniqueness and nonreproducibility of European nationalism reflect a paradigm of "ethnocentric diffusionism" spreading "authentic forms of nationalism" from the core European world to a non-European global periphery.

Postcolonial critiques of the Eurocentric analyses of nationalism suggest a shift away from Europe and from the European "ruling classes."[22] For instance, Partha Chatterjee sees the problem of nationalism in the non-European world as a mirror image of

Eurocentrocism.[23] In this view, peripheral forms of nationalism simultaneously proclaim the authenticity of a non-European culture while adopting the moral-epistemic dogmas of the Enlightenment project. Elaborating on Chatterjee's views, R. Radhakrishnan states that nationalism outside Europe appropriates only selectively, to safeguard the "essential identity" of the colonized cultures. For both thinkers, nationalism in the postcolonial context articulates a negotiation between the "western blueprints of reason, progress and enlightenment" and self-identification of the national subject as a non-European cultural agent. At the same time, postcolonial national identification leads to a fundamental rupture in the psyche of the colonized.[24] The depth of this rupture is questioned by Homi Bhabha when he speaks of the colonial presence as "always ambivalent, split between its appearance as original and authoritative, and its articulation as repetition and difference."[25] Even mimicry contains a great potential for local reformulation of the descriptive narrative of the postcolonial subject.[26]

Despite the challenge of the postcolonial genre of critiques, the structural analysis developed by theories of European nationalism arguably has a certain validity owing to the repetitive pattern in which the sovereign state is the institutional setting for the emergence of a nation-state. The central state can help to create a national polity by facilitating the formation of national identity under its sovereign authority. This legitimation is reinforced by the larger body of nation-states.

Furthermore, the works of the postcolonial critics of nationalism preserve the core premise of the European nation-state in assuming that every nation must have its own nation-state. The postcolonial theory of nationalism starts with the old assumption that a unified national polity should have exclusive rights of self-determination and sovereignty within borders. So both European and postcolonial nationalism dismiss ethnicity, religion, and minority identity as obstacles to be overcome in creating a national polity. Identities outside the hegemonic nationalist idiom are seen as dangerous divisions, to be eroded.

Scholars must devote more attention to the peculiar sociopolitical dynamics of multiethnic and/or multinational states, instead of imposing the old ideal of national homogenization on every situation. The assumption of cultural homogeneity produces uncompromising utopian regimes at its best and gross human rights violations at its worst. To identify symptoms of political chaos, manifestations of constitutional deficiency and violations of human rights does not get at the fundamental problem of multiethnic states that claim a unified nationality. If the political community and the state do not show the level of convergence demanded by the model of the European nation-state, analysis should concentrate on the discontinuity between particular local, ethnic, or religious communities and the dominant nationalist ideologies.

## The Dilemmas of National Citizenship

Certain propositions seem to be held on all sides of the debate about nationalism. One is that a primary characteristic of the nation-state is its contractual nature as a political body. Another is that "common ideals" constitute an essential element of nationality politics. The assumption of commonality finds its most explicit expression in the language of citizenship and in membership rights. Thus, the origins of nationalism have a very close link with the origins of both liberalism and constitutionalism. The individual members of a national polity are assumed to share a communal and historical bond, and their togetherness is taken to justify the selective attribution of contractual rights under the authority of a central state.

There is a pronounced condition of tension embedded in the basic assumptions that are made. On the one hand, the institutional protection of membership rights and the contractual agreement among the citizens of a national polity suggest liberal democratic practices. On the other hand, the very reasons proposed for undertaking the national contract paradoxically impinge upon a common bonding, unitedness, or spirit of communitarian essentialism.[27]

As a result of this tension, nationalism as a doctrine suffers from blindness regarding the nature of the national polity. Simultaneously claiming and disclaiming its contractual and communal/essentialist characteristics, the nationalist discourse treats the alleged harmony and metaphoric historicity of a nation both as a given and as an achieved status. It is this very double-sidedness that allows nationalism to become a universalized idiom for culture, politics, and history. The construct of a nation is a negotiated finality.

Although the birth of a nation is always referred back to the history of a distinct people, the question of origins remains dangerously contentious, since in most cases it depends upon a highly selective political reading of the past. For example, in German National Socialist ideology, the origins of the "German people" became the philo-sophical basis upon which a genocidal military and bureaucratic Nazi agenda was built. Similarly, neofascist movements in contemporary Europe take issue with the already established citizenship rights of immigrants on the basis of the true origins and purity of the European nations.

In this regard, nationalism as a political practice depicts the nation not only as a contractual union, but also as a reinvention, a recovery of the past, and a remembrance of and extension of historical roots. The chosenness of a nation as a concept aims at the destruction of any signs of randomness attributable to the membership criteria of the national polity. From a different point of view, it might be said that the "other" of nationalism is forever captive to otherness, because it is this very "other" that makes the national "self" distinguishable. The "other" of nationalism always had to be there, from time immemorial, since it is the historicity of the "other/enemy" that makes the reinvention of a national past possible.

This transhistorical time dimension repeats itself in the nationalist construction of sovereignty. In twentieth-century international politics, rhetoric on the right of a nation to self-determination and sovereignty has become the primary expression of national identification. The ethics of national autonomy assumes for each nation the right to determine its own destiny. In theory, this right should be exercised regardless of temporal or spatial constraints. A nation will always have the right to sovereignty and self-determination, because it is a nation. Whether this right may be exercised by choice rather than necessity hardly enters the debate. Such an approach to self-determination inherently negates the possibility of negotiation with others who might have equally valid claims for sovereignty within a shared territory. Negation of the need to consider the context of autonomy is then formalized by the territorial imperative of nationalism.

At the moment of finalization of a nationalist movement geared towards self-determination and territorial sovereignty, the tension inherent in nationalism temporarily resolves itself, and the liberal idiom dominates the communitarian one. This dynamic can be easily observed in the framing of questions concerning membership or citizenship in the national polity. During the phase of establishing a central bureaucracy and the initiation of citizenship rights according to the European model, nationalist doctrines usually attend to the liberal philosophical premises of the contractual character of the national polity.[28] This contractual form may be totally devoid of an authentic content and unless the initial moment of welcoming translates itself into pluralism, the politics of nationalism quickly sours into what can be called a "totalitarian democracy."[29]

In the liberal pluralist model, the voluntary and involuntary characteristics of national identification are systematically absorbed by institutional democratic practices.[30] Still, a certain degree of differentiation is kept alive for the perpetuation of the myths surrounding national sovereignty. The voluntary aspect of national identification is basic to the continuous rearticulation of the will for national unity. Narratives of cultural roots, a common historical past, and linguistic and religious orthodoxy assert communal bonding as the primary mechanism of social cohesion. The forced aspect comes forward in the context of what the national will is supposed to be about. In both European and non-European forms of nationalism, the will to become a nation is founded on the premises of identity-based politics.[31] Class, race, ethnicity, religion, and gender constitute the underlying matrices of the nationalist will to power. The groups or communities that lack the desire to unite within a self-identifying national polity or that deny the legitimacy of a certain set of nationalist claims are thus to be "talked into" the nationalist discourse.

This is the point at which the contractual aspect of national politics reenters the discourse. Institutionally, citizenship is accessible to anyone and everyone residing within the borders of the territorial nation-state. Paradoxically, however, the credo of liberal pluralism also makes it possible to erase traces of marginalization. Even if someone does not want to become a member of a particular nation-state, that person is, by virtue of an assigned citizenship status, categorized under a particular nationality.[32] This noncongruity between the form and content of citizenship is directly observable in the realm of minority politics. In a myriad of non-European countries, national politics dictates that minorities and ethnoreligious communities are targets to be integrated into the national unity. At the same time, there is a much greater degree of variation in an ethnoreligious community than what the standard description ascribes to it. Groups that do not fit into the model of national politics can be majorities or minorities, dominant or subordinate, and their territorial base may or may not overlap with the territorial boundaries of their host state. Moreover, although these communities might be united by a vision of a common racial, cultural, or linguistic descent or by a shared system of beliefs and confessional practices, they are mostly divided by internal ties, familial linkages, religious heterodoxy, and regional attributes.

Still, the doctrines on political stability maintain that, regardless of their differences in communal and territorial organization, or of access to power, minorities and ethnoreligious conglomerations should primarily be judged as anomalous, anachronistic, and dysfunctional elements in the state.[33]

Based on these assumptions, ethnic or minority identity is perceived as a major problem for the political cohesion and legitimacy of nation-states. Cushioned with the principle of sovereignty, the non-European episodes of nationalism in multiethnic or multinational settings are paralyzed by the absence of an option for pluralist forms of legitimacy.

## The Fate of Minority Nations within a Sovereign Nation-State

Legitimacy is the central concern for any government that claims to have authority. Two forms of legitimacy can be delineated: (1) The mobilization of adequate mechanisms of consensus-building, such as genuine representative politics and practices of consociational democracy with respect to all issues of political decision-making; and (2) systematic prevention of opposition to the central authority through surveillance, censorship, organized political violence, and repression of human rights.

The list of methods of oppression and disprivileging that can be employed by military and administrative organs to ensure minority assimilation and integration into the ethos of a nation-state knows no limits. From this, it follows that minority-related problems can function as a theoretical means to decode the political nature of the kind of nationalism at work. In an institutional framework in which principles of constitutionalism and participatory democracy are observable, states can have either a pluralist model of sovereignty based on recognition of both human rights and group rights or a totalitarian model based on exclusive nationalist claims. The history of nation-states since 1945 suggests that the latter is the predominant form. But, the present reality does not necessarily negate the possibility that an open and tolerant form of sovereignty may emerge as the new norm in international politics.

At this point, it is important to clarify the causes of common adherence to the mononational appropriation of sovereignty. Four basic elements that have historically contributed to the problematic status of minority rights and the perpetual postponement of the recognition of minority communities as legitimate political conglomerates in national politics will be proposed.[34]

First and foremost, as long as the central state apparatus is perceived and functionalized as the basis for shifting coalitions between self-interested individuals and/or socioeconomic classes, there is no room left for the instrumental inclusion of minority communities as actors in state-building processes or state and civil society relations. In this regard, contested policies of the central state apparatus represent a very complex issue.[35] In the conduct of national politics, decisions that are open to choice and reflexive feedback often hide decisions that are unilaterally dictated by the institutional practices of the central state apparatus. The institutional mediation of power relations reflected in the "unquestioned policies" of the central state should be taken as the point of entry for understanding the democratic content of any given nationalism. For instance, the content of public education; the granting of civil and political rights, including the collective edge of minority rights; and the content of representative politics can be helpful in identifying the practice of pluralism, and the exercise of cultural and political tolerance. If national politics is perpetually based on the denial of group interests, there will usually be an observable paranoia against opening up decision-making processes conducted under the authority of bureaucratic offices. In response, the initial demands of minority politics usually concern the redistribution of central state power affecting the private lives of citizens. Unless the conception of group rights fundamentally changes, minority nationalism will remain a perpetual threat to state sovereignty.

A second cause of minority marginalization is related to the institutionalization of cultural and political practices of domination. The nation-state model is, above all, characterized by its absolute command over the life and well-being of its citizens; as such, the dialectic of control it employs constitutes an asymmetrical relationship between the central state and civil society. In the European nation-state model, homogeneity rather than heterogeneity of the social texture was the foundation for the legitimation of self-determination and sovereignty. This history discouraged the inclusion of minority communities into the image of a national polity. It also implied the impossibility of including minorities as a category in a nation-state's consideration of the well-being of its citizens. If there are no grounds for institutional negotiation between certain sectors of the civil society and the central state apparatus, minorities will seek changes in the mode of political representation. In a liberal democratic system, such changes provide individual members of a minority group with access to the decision-making mechanisms at the very top of the system, such as the parliament and the bureaucracy. Marginalized groups in the society can thus break apart the consolidated and homogeneous national "we" and bring forward new possibilities in social and political life.

Attempts to change the political system from within, however, call for a strong political will to preserve the structures of legitimation. If the central state apparatus has set precedents of injustice in state and civil society relations without there being a remedy for human rights violations, then victimized groups may not have the political will for further participation. They might rather seek partial, gradual, or total and immediate departure. Thus wrongdoings of nationalism spawn a universe of mininationalisms and particularly so-called ethno-nationalism.[36] Ethnonationalist separation does not necessarily lead to more democratic forms of nationalism. In fact, secessionism usually results not in the dispersion of centralized power but rather in new forms of focalization of power.

This phenomenon of repetition on a smaller scale is best exhibited in new forms of national historiography. In the official narratives of national history as well as in their particularistic negations based on the retrieval of excluded identity claims, historical knowledge becomes the new cultural battleground. In many mononationalist regimes established in the midst of multiethnic/multinational environments, the enhancement of selective historical claims is achieved by "reflexive monitoring" of the reproduction of nationalist history. Here the construction and maintenance of hegemony requires a single-handed mastery over territorial and spatial particulars. History becomes coterminous with territory, and historicity and cultural identity become endemic to territoriality. Consequently, what happens during the formation of counterhegemonic identity claims is that the same history is rewritten with a new cultural and territorial accent. The blueprint remains unchanged, and sovereignty is gained not on the basis of political negotiation, but as an attribute of the assumed natural dispositions of a given community.

The present paradigm of sovereignty in international politics and law makes the stakes very high when political mediation comes down to the constitutional recognition of minorities. There is an ultimate expectation of secession that leads to the understanding of minority rights as a fundamental threat to national unity. This is the third factor that inhibits the introduction of group rights as a legitimate part of international law. As for the fourth, as long as minority rights are feared as a camouflage for the much larger claim of secession, recognition of the distinctness of minority communities will seem very unappealing to existing nation-states.

Considering these four factors, which overshadow reconciliatory approaches to minority-related internal conflict, and also considering the problematic nature of the doctrines of national sovereignty and self-determination, the so-called minority question must be moved beyond the constraints of the sovereign nation-state model. One way to approach this issue from a new perspective would be to reformulate membership in the political community at two separate levels. At the first level, the common criteria for membership/citizenship in a sovereign state would be based on civil and political rights rather than national origin. At the second level, there would be protective mechanisms for the identity-based demands of individual citizens. While the first level would function to approve universal human rights of citizenship, the second level would guarantee the freedom of communal practices and group rights within the wider human rights framework. According to this two-tier structure, if an individual had a privileged or disprivileged ethnoreligious or cultural disposition, his or her situation would constitute a violation of human and collective rights. On this basis, the membership status of national minorities would be accommodated within the existing boundaries of sovereign states, so long as they are circumscribed by international rules and regulations.

## Conclusion

As the world spins toward the twenty-first century, internal political responses to totalitarian forms of nationalism constitute one of the most serious problems in international politics. Revolutionary ethnonationalism, violent ethnic insurgence, and large-scale ethnic conflict are, however, only a subset of minority politics. There are other viable options for protecting or asserting minority rights and self-expression. The threshold of acceptable costs to a nation–state seems to determine both the origins and development of internal political conflict. Ethnonationalism challenges the sovereign state's self-perception as a nation–state. Ultimately, denial policies of elimination, eradication, forcible repulsion, and entrenched dominance create the conditions for violent secessionism.

In studies of national politics, an undue emphasis on the European model of the sovereign nation–state leads to a profound misunderstanding of the postcolonial/postimperial proliferations of the prototypic "homogeneous national polity." The most common explanation offered for internal conflict is the "malfunctioning state." The argument put forth here has been that an alternative formulation of sovereignty is needed to provide a critical historical assessment of the nation–state. As an intermediary step, the peculiar dynamics of the geographical confinement of political power have been emphasized, and the term "territorial state" has been proposed to replace the expression of universalized political authority that resides in the concept of the "nation–state."

When the territorial state represents the interests of a hegemonic ethnoreligious community, either as a majority or as a minority, a large arsenal of measures to enforce the status quo becomes available to that specific segment of the total population. This is the point of convergence with the European nation-state model. Both systems of centralized power have direct command over party bureaucracies, the military, and the distribution of goods and services. In the territorial outgrowths of the European nation-state model, central power is frequently used to promote discrimination, segregation, expulsion, and the nonrecognition of the groups and communities that lie at the margins of national identity. In the European tradition, liberal democracy has taken care of these problems through consensus-building. On a global scale, though, unless the illusion of a monolithic national polity is undermined through a rearticulated norm of sovereignty as a political contract rather than a natural right, it is unrealistic to expect constitutional pluralism to blossom on the old terrain of patriotic nationalism.

## Bibliography

Abu-Lughod, Janet 1989. "Remaking History." in Barbara Kruger and Phil Mariani, eds. *On the Remaking of History: How to Reinvent the Past.* Seattle: Bay Press.

Adelman, Howard 1995. "Quebec: The Morality of Secession." in Joseph H. Carens, ed. *Is Quebec Nationalism Just?: Perspectives from Anglophone Canada,* Montreal : McGill-Queen's University Press.

Aijaz, Ahmad 1992. *In Theory: Class, Nation, Literatures* London and New York: Verso.

Amin, Samir 1989. *Eurocentricism.* New York: Monthly Review Press.

Anderson, Benedict 1983. *Imagined Communities. Reflection on the Origin and Spread of Nationalism.* London and New York: Verso.

Bebler, Anton 1993. "Yugoslavia's Society of Communist Federalism and Her Demise." *Communist and Post-Communist Studies,* 26.

Bhabha, Homi 1994. *The Location of Culture.* New York and London: Routledge.

Bhabha, Homi 1990. ed. *Nation and Narration.* London and New York: Routledge.

Blaut, James M. 1987. *The National Question. Decolonizing the Theory of Nationalism.* London: Zed Books.

Carens, Joseph 1985. *Migration, Morality and the Nation-State.* Toronto: Faculty of Law/University of Toronto Press.

Chatterjee, Partha 1986. *Nationalist Thought and the Colonial World. A Derivative Discourse?* London: Zed Books.

Chatterjee, Partha 1993. *The Nation and its Fragments: Colonial and Postcolonial Histories.* Princeton: Princeton University Press.

Forsythe, David 1992. *Human Rights and Peace: International and National Dimensions.* Lincoln and London: University of Nebraska Press.

Gellner, Ernest 1983. *Nations and Nationalism*. Ithaca: Cornell University Press.

Gibney, Mark, 1988. ed. *Open Borders? Closed Societies? The Ethical and Political Issues*. New York: Greenwood Press.

Giddens, Anthony 1985. *The Nation-State and Violence*. Cambridge: Polity Press.

Günlük, Nergis Canefe 1994. "The Yugoslavian Puzzle: Which Nation, Whose Nationalism and Other Unsettling Questions." *Refuge. Canadian Journal of Refugee Studies* (Special Issue on Yugoslavia).

Hall, John et al. 1988. *Europe and the Rise of Capitalism*. Oxford and Cambridge: Basil Blackwell.

Hannum, Hurst 1992. *Autonomy, Sovereignty, and Self-Determination. The Accommodation of Conflicting Rights*. Philadelphia: University of Pennsylvania Press.

Hobsbawm, E.J. 1990. *Nations and Nationalism since 1780, Programme, Myth, Realty*. Cambridge: Cambridge University Press.

Jusdanis, Gregory 1991. *Belated Modernity and Aesthetic Culture: Inventing National Literature*. Minneapolis and Oxford: University of Minneapolis Press.

Kedourie, Elie 1961. *Nationalism*. London: Hutchison.

Kohn, Hans 1946. *The Idea of Nationalism. A Study in Its Origin and Background*, New York: MacMillan Press.

Kymlicka, Will 1989. *Liberalism, Community, and Culture*. Oxford: Clarendon Press.

Lefebvre, Henri 1971. *Everyday Life in the Modern World*. New York: Harper & Row.

Lendvai, Paul 1991. "Yugoslavia Without Yugoslavs: The Roots of the Crisis." *International Affairs* 67(2).

Makolkin, Anna 1992. *Name, Hero, Icon: Semiotics of Nationalism Through Heroic Biography*. Berlin and New York: Mouton de Gruyter.

McLaurin, R.D. 1979. ed. *The Political Role of Minority Groups in the Middle East*. New York: Praeger.

Nairn, Tom 1975. "The Modern Janus." *New Left Review* 94.

Radhakrishnan, R. 1992. "Nationalism, Gender, and the Narrative of Identity." In Andrew Parker, Mary Russo, Doris Sommer and Patricia Yaeger, eds. *Nationalisms & Sexualities*. London and New York: Routledge.

Renan, Ernest 1990. "What is a Nation?" In Homi K. Bhabha, ed. *Nation and Narration*. London: Routledge.

Said, Edward 1979. *Orientalism*. New York: Vintage Books.

Smith, Anthony D. 1986. *The Ethnic Origins of Nations*. Oxford: Basil Blackwell.

Smith, Anthony D. 1981. *The Ethnic Revival*. Cambridge: Cambridge University Press.

Talmon, J.R. 1961. *The Origins of Totalitarian Democracy*. London: Secker & Warburg.

Talmon, J.R. 1981. *The Myth of the Nation and the Vision of Revolution: The Origins of Ideological Polarisation in the Twentieth Century.* London: Secker & Warburg.

Tilly, Charles 1975. ed. *The Formation of National States in Western Europe.* Princeton: Princeton University Press.

Vaziri, Mostafa 1993. *Iran as Imagined Nation: The Construction of National Identity.* New York: Paragon House.

Wallerstein, Immanuel 1991. *Geopolitics and Geoculture.* Cambridge: Cambridge University Press.

Wallerstein, Immanuel 1974. *The Modern World System.* New York: Academic Press.

Worsley, Peter 1984. *The Three Worlds. Culture and World Development.* Chicago: University of Chicago Press.

Zolberg, Aristide, A. Shurkre, and S. Aguayo, 1989. eds. *Escape from Violence: Conflict and the Refugee Crisis in the Developing World.* New York: Oxford University Press.

## Notes

1. Forsythe 1992.
2. Adelman 1995.
3. Talmon argues that the difference between these two forms is not that of denial or attribution of liberty, but rather is a matter of "their different attitudes to politics." (Talmon 1961, p.1). Talmon's proposition is of utmost importance in the context of the incongruity between universal applicability of human rights conventions within the institutional parameters, and the actual practices of human rights violations exercised by some of the subject states who have signed these conventions. In other words, the problem concerning the full-scale employment of democratic principles – as well as individual and groups rights entailed by those principles – does not seem to be about the lack of formal recognition of rules and regulations. The primary difference between liberal and totalitarian forms of democracy, or *de jure* and *de facto* recognition of human rights is that, totalitarianism, coercion and systematic political oppression are all based on a certain sense of self-righteousness and a vehement refusal to negotiate at times of political stress.

4. Zolberg 1989.
5. Lendvai 1991; Bebler 1993; Günlük 1994.
6. Wallerstein 1991.
7. Hall 1988.
8. Makolkin 1992; Smith 1986.
9. In the medieval period, for example, reference to *nation de France* would include Italians and Spaniards as speakers of the Romance languages (Vaziri 1993; Lefebvre 1971).
10. Vaziri 1993, p.37.
11. Gibney 1988; Carens 1985; Talmon 1981.
12. In the context of Greek nationalism, Jusdanis argues that "[n]arratives, once essential in the creation of collective identities, eventually become a means for orchestrating an ideological consensus." (Jusdanis 1991, p.xi).
13. For Ahmad Aijaz and Homi Bhabha, the changing characteristics of "otherness" attributed to the colonized and dominated cultures primarily resulted from the migration movements between colonies and Europe, which brought the subject who was once 'other' into the center of the European self-image. Europe was forced to remember its colonial history. However, this challenge was circumvented by denying the otherness of the 'other', and making what is different into something that is either unrecognizable, or something which fits into the contours of similitude (Bhabha 1994; Aijaz 1992).
14. "[T]he principle of sovereignty resides essentially in the Nation; no body of men, no individual, can exercise authority that does not emanate expressly from it." (Kedourie 1961, pp.12–13) For Kohn, on the other hand, "[t]he growth of nationalism is the process of integration of the masses of the people into a common political form. Nationalism therefore presupposes the existence, in fact or as an ideal, of a centralized form of government over a large and distinct territory." (Kohn 1946, p.4) Kohn sees the French Revolution as the first great manifestation of nationalism. In Kohn's discussion on the history of nationalism, even though the idea has existed in ancient Greeks, it was revived, revitalized and finally secularized with the French Revolution.
15. Addressing the same problem, Tom Nairn states that the roots of nationalism have to be sought "not in the folk, nor in the individual's repressed passion for some sort of wholeness of identity, but in the machinery of world political economy." (Nairn 1975, p.8) Wallerstein's world-system analysis achieves the systematic aggrandizement of such an approach with much firmer conclusions. In Wallerstein's writings on the nation-state system,

the actors of the accumulation of surplus need strong states to promote and protect them, both domestically and in foreign trade (Wallerstein 1987; 1974).

16. "Why should the establishment of any particular sovereign state within the interstate system create a corresponding 'nation,' a 'people'? States in this system have problems of cohesion. Once recognized as sovereign, the states frequently find themselves subsequently threatened by both internal disintegration and external aggression. To the extent that 'national' sentiment develops, these threats are lessened. The governments in power have an interest in promoting this sentiment, as do all sorts of subgroups within the state. Any group who sees advantage in using the state's legal powers to advance its interest against groups outside the state or in any sub-region of the state has an interest in promoting nationalist sentiments as a legitimation of its claims. States furthermore have an interest in administrative uniformity which increases the efficacy of their policies. Nationalism is the expression, the promoter, and the consequence of such state-level uniformities." (Wallerstein 1991a, pp.81–82).

17. A similar point is made by Worsley in his argument that "cultural traits are not absolutes or simply intellectual categories, but are invoked to provide identities which legitimize claims to rights. They are strategies or weapons in competitions over scarce social goods." (Worsley 1984, p.249).

18. "It is *imagined* because the members of even the smallest nation will never know most of their fellow-members, meet them, or even hear of them, yet in the minds of each lives the image of their communion." (Anderson 1983, p.15, emphasis as in the original).

19. For Anderson, in the aftermath of the assemblage of "related vernaculars" and the creation of "mechanically-reproduced print-languages, capable of dissemination through market," nationalism became the legitimate idiom for an unprecedented form of communal bondage (op. cit., pp.46–47).

20. "Those who strove for liberation [in the colonies] were 'nationalists' only because they adopted a western ideology excellently suited to the overthrow of foreign governments, and even so, they usually consisted of an exiguous minority of indigenous évolués... The unity imposed by conquest and administration might sometimes, in the long run, produce a people that saw itself as a 'nation', just as the existence of independent states has sometimes created a sense of citizens patriotism... However, this is not sufficient to call the

states which have emerged from decolonization, mainly after 1945, 'nation,' or the movements that led to their decolonization . . . 'nationalist' movements." (Hobsbawm 1990, pp.137–138).

21. In contradistinction, Worsley argues that "nationalism" is a special form of ethnicity in that it entails the institutionalization of a particular ethnic identity through the state apparatus. In Worsley's categorization, "ethnic groups" become "nationalities" when they desire to obtain a state of their own, and if they succeed, they become "nations." To put it slightly differently, the concept of nation is reserved for a particular mode of ethnicity that emerged with capitalism and the centralized state apparatus characteristic to European history (Worsley 1984, pp.247–248).

22. In Janet Abu-Lughod's words, "[t]here is no Archimedean point *outside* of the system from which to view historical 'reality.'" (Abu-Lughod 1989, p.112 – emphasis as in the original –) On the issue of Eurocentricism, Abu-Lughod argues that historical accounts are constructed backwards and therefore the beginning point is discretionary (Bhabha 1990; Amin 1989; Blaut 1987; Chatterjee 1986 and 1993; Said 1979).

23. "[T]he problem of the bourgeoisie-rational conception of knowledge established in the post-Enlightenment period of European intellectual history, as the moral and epistemic foundation for a supposedly universal framework of thought [is that it] perpetuates, in a real and not merely a metaphorical sense, a colonial domination. It is a framework of knowledge which proclaims its own universality; its validity, it pronounces, is independent of cultures. Nationalist thought, in agreeing to become 'modern,' accepts the claim to universality of this 'modern framework of knowledge.'" Yet it also asserts the autonomous identity of a national culture. It thus simultaneously rejects and accepts the dominance, both epistemic and moral, of an alien culture. (Chatterjee 1986, p.11)

24. Radhakrishnan, 1992.

25. Bhabha, 1986, p.169.

26. Bhabha's project also entails a re-writing of the European subject position: "[i]t is the historical certainty and settled nature of the term [nationalism] against which I am attempting to write the western nation as an obscure and ubiquitous form of living the *locality* of culture." (Bhabha 1990, p.292, emphasis as in the original).

27. This tension has been detected by Kymlicka in his critique of the historical debate between liberalism and communitarianism. Although Kymlicka does not contextualize his critique in terms

of nationalism, he chooses minority rights to be the venue for his theoretical explorations. Kymlicka 1989.

28. Adelman 1995; Giddens 1985.

29. Of course, here I am only referring to cases whereby the state apparatus assumes a formal constitutional character and the rituals of parliamentary democracy are followed with a certain degree of regularity. (Tilly 1975).

30. "[A nation] presupposes a past; it is summarized, however, in the present by a tangible fact, namely, consent, the clearly expressed desire to continue a common life. A nation's existence is, if you will pardon the metaphor, a daily plebiscite, just as an individual's existence is a perpetual affirmation of life." (Renan 1990, p.19)

31. According to Peter Worsley, a modern state "permits or insists upon certain identities and refuses others." (Worsley 1984, p.246) The suggested linkage by Worsley between nationality/ethnicity on the one hand, and state/civil society on the other, raises questions about the enforcement of the involuntary features of nationalism.

32. For Kedourie, the roots of the voluntary aspect of nationalism are even deeper, "[n]ational self-determination is, in the final analysis, a determination of the will; and 'nationalism' is, in the first place, a method of teaching the right determination of the will." (Kedourie 1960, p.83)

33. McLaurin, 1979, p.5.

34. Hannum 1992, pp.71–72.

35. Zolberg 1989; Giddens 1981.

36. Smith 1981; 1986.

# – 6 –

# Self-Determination and Secession in Islamic Thought

## Sohail H. Hashmi

### Introduction

In 1972 twenty-four countries established the Organization of the Islamic Conference (O.I.C.) in order to foster solidarity and cooperation among Muslim states on the basis of the "immortal teachings of Islam." Among the organization's more specific objectives was to strengthen the struggle of all Muslim peoples for their "dignity, independence, and national rights." Despite the rhetoric of the organization's charter, the member states of the O.I.C. have demonstrated in the years since its adoption that claims of independence and national rights – that is, of self-determination – are more legitimate for some Muslim peoples than for others. The charter has consistently been read to condone only the self-determination of Muslims living within states with a non-Muslim majority. Claims of self-determination advanced by Muslim minorities within existing Muslim states, especially when pressed to the point of secession, have been treated as illegitimate.

Since its founding the O.I.C. has hardly been free from controversy and serious challenges from a broad range of critics with respect to its "Islamic" credentials. But on the particular issue of self-determination and secession, O.I.C. policies have met with general support from Islamic theorists, activists, and movements. Public support for Muslim independence movements in non-Muslim states has ranged from local publicity and fund-raising to large-scale demonstrations and rallies and even the mounting of self-financed and self-armed volunteers for liberation struggles. The national aspirations of Palestinians, Kashmiris, Filipino Muslims, Turkish Cypriots, Bosnian Muslims, and Chechens, among others, have elicited public sympathy and sometimes concerted government action throughout the Muslim world. In stark contrast, however, are both public as well as official responses to claims of self-determination through secession advanced by Muslims in Muslim states. Secessionist movements in the Western Sahara, Bangladesh, and Kurdistan are three of the most prominent examples, all having been met with widespread apathy or opposition in the Muslim community generally.

The O.I.C.'s approach to self-determination and secession may of course be explained as deriving from considerations of realpolitik. Post-colonial Muslim states, like all states, have demonstrated little inclination to tolerate challenges to their sovereignty from groups claiming political autonomy, let alone territorial loss from groups seeking secession. Explanations based on realpolitik do not, however, account for the widespread public opposition to or lack of interest in self-determination and secession claims, especially from Islamic fundamentalist groups who so often find themselves at odds with state policies. Such explanations are insufficient because they neglect a crucial dimension of the issue, the ideological. Self-determination and particularly secession are problematic within Islamic political thought because they challenge certain core principles of Islamic ethics that promote a universal community of the faithful, transcending ethnic, tribal, racial, or national distinctions and territorial divisions.

What follows here is, first, an examination of the ethical sources of Islamic thought on this issue in the Qur'an and the *sunna* (practice of the Prophet Muhammad). Then, the classical political theory constructed by medieval theorists on the basis of these and other sources and the relevance of that theory to modern Muslim practice are considered. The application of the theory is discussed in the context of two modern cases, the Bangladeshi and Kurdish secessionist movements. Finally, an assessment is made of the prospects for a reinterpretation or reformulation of Islamic approaches toward self-determination and secession.

## The Religious and Historical Sources

Pre-Islamic Arabian society was built firmly upon tribal identities and unwavering loyalty. Although a hierarchy of tribes existed, determined by reputation for valor, nobility, or wealth, the intertribal political system was anarchical. Each tribe jealously guarded its sovereignty, which was equated not so much with territorial jurisdiction as with unrestrained exercise of its communal or commercial prerogatives. Consensus on the general principles of nonintervention appears to have kept this Arab system stable and on the whole free from large-scale warfare. Few instances are recorded of military campaigns aimed at eliminating a tribe's political autonomy or control over territory; much more common were internecine raids and reprisals arising from brigandage or affronts to tribal honor.

From its inception, Islam repre-sented a challenge not just to traditional Arab religions, but to the social and political ideas that they had sanctioned for centuries. It is no surprise, therefore, that the Qur'an's attack on tribalism commenced at an early date. The attack is aimed not so much at tribalism as a form of social or political organization, but at the chauvinism, parochialism, and injustice that tribal loyalties often promote. Since the most obdurate resistance to the Prophet came from within his own tribe, the Quraysh, several early Qur'anic verses explicitly or implicitly single out Qurayshi behavior as representative of the collective tribal mentality that rejects truth in favor of ancestral custom or group solidarity (43:22–24; 54:43–45, 51). This group inertia in maintaining false beliefs and practices, the Qur'an notes, typifies all communities to which prophets have been sent. Since the mission of each prophet was focused upon bringing God's universal message to his own particular community, he was rejected and abused by his own people for violating "sacred" tribal custom (Chapters 7 and 21 in particular deal with this topic).

The Qur'an's attack upon the "tribal mentality" was not limited to the Arab pagans who rejected Muhammad. Equally significant and extensive is its prolonged debate with believers in earlier revelation, the Jews and the Christians, who are charged with corrupting the true and identical message of all the prophets. Again, the Qur'an's condemnation is directed not so much at the existence of religious or moral diversity per se, which it views as a natural part of God's plan, but at the adverse psychological and social results that such diversity yields. The result of Jewish and Christian *bid'a* (innovation in religion) is not only theological disputations, but also and more importantly sectarian strife. Jews and Christians have transformed God's universal and inclusive message into communal and exclusionary ideologies. The Muslims are repeatedly enjoined not to imitate the behavior of these earlier communities (30:32; 42:13–14; 43:64–65; 45:17, 28).

In short, the Qur'an begins by assuming that human beings will naturally associate according to group loyalties. It does not attempt to eradicate such loyalties or social organizations based upon them, only to demonstrate their lack of moral worth. It attempts to supersede religious sects or moral communities restricted to tribes, ethnic, and racial groups and to replace them with a community of the righteous. This universalistic vision is clearly elaborated in the following verse: "O mankind! We created you from a single pair of male and female and made you into nations and tribes, that you may know one another. Truly the most honored of you in the sight of God is the one who is most righteous among you"(49:13). This verse is addressed to all human beings. By virtue of their acceptance of God's will (*islam*), however, Muslims have a special obligation to serve as exemplars of this universalistic social ethic. The question that immediately arises is what social or political organizations are legitimate expressions of Qur'anic ethics.

Some Muslim modernists have interpreted verse 49:13 as sanctioning the current fragmentation of the Muslim world into nearly fifty sovereign states. Their views have, however, been repeatedly assailed as a misreading of its actual import and as a decontextualization from numerous other verses that deal with this issue. Indeed, the thrust of the overall Qur'anic message seems quite opposed to the legitimacy of political divisions within Islam. Two verses speak of the Muslim community as a single community (*umma*) charged with the moral purpose of enjoining righteousness (2:143; 3:110). And, in addition to all the verses commanding Muslims to abjure Jewish and Christian sectarianism, two verses explicitly enjoin Muslim unity, advising Muslims not to be "divided against themselves" (3:103, 105). Terms denoting divisions within the umma, such as *hizb* or *shi'a* (party, faction, or clique), are invariably used with pejorative connotations (6:159; 23:53; 30:32). Their emergence, the Qur'an suggests, will inevitably foster *fitna*, a broad term evoking images of oppression, strife, and civil discord.

The Qur'an's unitary approach to the organization of the Muslim umma is strongly reinforced in the practice of the Prophet. Immediately after his migration from Mecca to Medina in 622 C.E., Muhammad took the first steps in loosening the hold of traditional tribal identities and loyalties and replacing them with a sense of Muslim community. Each Muslim immigrant from Mecca was paired off with a recent Muslim convert from Medina. They were henceforth to consider themselves as brothers.[1]

Two years after the migration, the Prophet expanded and formalized the initial steps toward Muslim unity by drafting what has come to be known as the Constitution of Medina.[2] This document was a contract between the tribes native to Medina that had recently converted to Islam and the Muslim immigrants from Mecca. It did not condemn or altogether eliminate the preexisting tribal structures; rather, it superseded them with the Muslim umma. Under the constitution, individual Muslims could still identify themselves as members of a particular tribe or clan, but the only relevant political or moral category was that of Islam. Within this arrangement, the Prophet played a central unifying role as the ultimate arbiter of disputes emerging between the tribes. Qur'anic revelations of the period establish the Prophet as a symbol of the Muslim community's unity and enjoins Muslims to obey him (3:132; 4:13, 59, 69; 5:95; 8:1, 20, 46; 9:71; 24:54).

The approach of the Prophet to issues of political organization is further elaborated in the extensive body of formalized sayings and actions ascribed to him known as the *hadith*. The authenticity of specific hadith has been debated among Muslim scholars from the earliest period. Some statements ascribed to the Prophet obviously smack of political convenience. In particular those hadith enjoining Muslim unity at all costs, even in the face of oppression by an illegitimate ruler, suggest fabrication by later Muslim generations seeking to legitimate obedience to a compromised caliphal institution. Other traditions were deployed by Sunni writers in opposition to schismatics, including the most famous: "My community shall never unite upon an error, so if you should see a disagreement, you must stay with the majority."[3]

Whether these and many similar traditions are authentic or not cannot be determined with precision. Their historical authenticity is, however, immaterial to the role they have played in shaping the orthodox approach to Muslim unity. They are authentic inasmuch as they are held by the majority to be an expression of the Islamic ideal. Moreover, despite the dubious veracity of specific hadith, the Prophet's general approach to this topic is clearly evident when the complete body of the hadith literature is read in context with other sources of his biography as well as the Qur'an. The Muslim community was for him a single collectivity (*jama'a*), functioning ideally as a single, living, and growing organism, as suggested in one hadith frequently quoted over the centuries: "The Muslims in their mutual affection and mercy should be as a single body: if one member is affected, the other members suffer fever and sleeplessness."[4] This metaphor leaves little scope for separation, withdrawal, or revolt. Another hadith narrated in the *Sahih al-Bukhari*, one of the two most important hadith compilations, suggests the Prophet's overriding concern with maintaining the communal solidarity of the umma:

Ibn Idris al-Khawlani said: "I said to the Messenger of God, 'What do you order me to do [if I should live until the time of troubles]?' He said, 'Cleave to the collectivity of the Muslims and their leader [*imam*].' I said, 'And what if they have neither collectivity nor leader?' He said, 'Then withdraw [*i'tazil*] from the factions altogether, even if you must gnaw the roots of trees until you die.'"[5]

Throughout the Prophet's lifetime, no serious attempt to challenge his authority or fragment the community from within is recorded. The Qur'an does allude in several verses to a party of hypocrites in Medina, people who had formally converted to Islam for the sake of security or conformity but continued to plot secretly for its overthrow (2:8, 11–12; 4:60–63, 88–89). Other verses mention the Bedouin tribes of the interior whose faith wavered according to their own interests (48:11; 49:14). But these groups are considered in the Qur'an to be outside the Muslim body politic, never having fully accepted Islam or the Prophet's authority.

Muslim unity, however, did not outlive the Prophet. The first serious internal split developed immediately upon Muhammad's death over the issue of succession. According to the tradition of the Sunni majority, the Prophet had died suddenly without designating any clear political heir. Upon receiving word of the Prophet's death, the native inhabitants of Medina gathered to select a new leader from within their old tribal leadership. The umma was apparently reverting at this point to its pre-Islamic social and political configurations. This reversion was checked only by the intercession of some of the earliest Muslim converts and closest companions of the Prophet, who, as Meccans, were outside of the Medinan tribal system. After lengthy discussion between the Meccan immigrants and the Medinan natives, the Prophet's close friend and father-in-law, Abu Bakr, emerged as the *imam* or the *khalifa* (caliph), the Prophet's "vicegerent," not fully his "successor," since according to Islamic tradition divine revelation ceased with the Prophet. But Abu Bakr's election did constitute in a profound sense a succession to the Prophet inasmuch as it affirmed the Prophet's organization of the umma as a distinct religious *and* political community.

News of Abu Bakr's election to the caliphate was received with dismay by 'Ali, the Prophet's son-in-law, who had been engaged in preparing for the funeral of the Prophet during the debate on the succession. 'Ali and a small group of his supporters had understood certain comments by the Prophet in the last few weeks of his life to be an unequivocal designation of 'Ali as the Prophet's successor. Realizing that Abu Bakr had obtained majority backing as the community's new leader, 'Ali did not challenge the consensus but withdrew from public life as an expression of grievances regarding the succession. He took this same position when he was twice afterward passed over for leadership of the community in favor of 'Umar and 'Uthman. During this time, his supporters began to coalesce into a distinct party (Shi'at 'Ali) that actively asserted his rights to the caliphate. This group, however, was forbidden by 'Ali from pressing his claims through either rebellion aimed at seizing leadership of the community or secession aimed at establishing a separate Islamic state.

In 656 C.E. 'Ali finally assumed leadership of the umma as the fourth caliph. With his election the still inchoate Sunni-Shi'i breach seemed to be mended. Yet the conditions under which 'Ali came to power – namely, the murder of his predecessor 'Uthman by disgruntled Muslims and the rival political ambitions of the murdered caliph's powerful clansmen, the Umayyads, forestalled any such mending. 'Ali's reign is characterized by Muslim historians as the first great fitna, or "trial." The trial pitted several key figures of the first Muslim generation against each other; in its wake many were dead, including 'Ali, and the Sunni-Shi'i breach was left unbridgeable.

The breach widened into an emotional chasm in 680 C.E. when the third Shi'i imam, 'Ali's son Husayn, was murdered along with many of his family on the plains of Kerbala by a force loyal to the Sunni caliph. Whether Husayn was preparing to lead a Shi'i rebellion against the Umayyads at the time of his death or not is still a point of great contention among Muslims. After his death, however, no subsequent Shi'i imam ever held political power. What had begun as a political dispute with little theological content evolved under the leadership of the nine imams who followed Husayn into a theological dispute with few political aspirations. Shi'i political theorists accommodated the realities of Muslim political life in which Shi'ism constituted a distinctly minor-itarian and, over most of its early history, powerless community. Although Shi'ism represented the "true" Islam and all Sunnis were therefore in error, the Shi'a, in keeping with the practice of 'Ali and his successors, were not expected to challenge the political authority of the state in which they lived. They could instead practice dissimulation (*taqiyya*) in the face of illegitimate government. The obligation to wage *jihad* (crusade or holy war) against Sunni Muslims or non-Muslims, had in particular, according to these theorists, lapsed with the end of the imamate, as only the legitimate ruler of the Muslim umma could authorize and lead it.[6]

Dissimulation was in fact the general policy of most Shi'i populations throughout the medieval period. Thus, despite the recurring anti-Shi'i polemics in the medieval Sunni literature, Shi'ism was quite clearly not perceived as a distinct and oppositional political force challenging the unity of the umma. Islamic thought on rebellion and political separateness would be shaped by other historical developments.

Two events – or rather, periods of rebellion – proved crucial: the *ridda* (apostasy) wars in the reign of Abu Bakr (632–634 C.E.) and the Kharijite revolt in the reign of 'Ali (656–661 C.E.). The first involved a number of Bedouin tribes spread throughout the Arabian peninsula. Most of these tribes had accepted Islam only in the last years of the Prophet's life, and only after a protracted period of tension and hostility. Within each tribe, it is unclear whether the majority or only the tribal leaders had converted. We have already seen that the Qur'an considered the faith of these tribes to be tenuous at best. As news of the Prophet's death spread throughout the peninsula, the majority of Bedouin tribes refused to acknowledge any allegiance to Abu Bakr as the head of the Islamic state. Their ties to the Islamic state under the Prophet had always been quite loose, but one tangible manifestation of their recognition of the Prophet's leadership was the payment of the alms-tax (*zakat*) to Medina. Some tribes now refused to pay the tax to Abu Bakr, while continuing to declare their faith in Islam. They were essentially seceding from the Islamic state. Other tribes refused to pay the tax as a demonstration of their reversion to their pre-Islamic religious attitudes. Whether the majority of tribes were apostates or seceders is not clear, but the former would provide the general title for the campaigns authorized by Abu Bakr to subdue them. In the end, the ridda wars had little to do with issues of belief or unbelief in the Islamic religion. They represented, rather, the first assertions of sovereignty and territoriality by the Islamic state centered at Medina. By the time they were over, the Islamic polity had expanded to include not only the recalcitrant Bedouins, but all the tribes of the Arabian peninsula.[7]

The second and more important revolt was that of the Kharijites beginning in the year 657 C.E. It was prompted by the decision of 'Ali to submit his dispute with Mu'awiya, the governor of Syria, to arbitration. Mu'awiya was a kinsmen of 'Ali's predecessor, the assassinated third caliph 'Uthman, and a leader of the party calling for vengeance to be taken for the murdered caliph. 'Ali was seen by this party as complicit in 'Uthman's murder for his failure to prosecute vigorously enough the caliph's assassins. When the majority of Medinans declared their allegiance to 'Ali as the fourth caliph, Mu'awiya and the Umayyad clan that he led withheld their support. With a strong political base in Syria and Palestine, the Umayyads soon launched hostilities aimed at overthrowing 'Ali's government. The fighting between 'Ali and Mu'awiya may accordingly be termed a civil war, not secession, since both claimed leadership of the same community and both had legitimacy in different regions of the empire.

In the midst of this civil war the insurrection of the Kharijites erupted. When 'Ali agreed to submit his dispute with Mu'awiya to arbitration, a number of his supporters withdrew from his camp, disgruntled that he had substituted human will for God's decision, to be realized presumably through war. This group became known as the *khawarij*, or those "outside" the community. They rejected the claims of both 'Ali and Mu'awiya to the caliphate and elected their own imam. When the results of the arbitration proved unfavorable to 'Ali, more of his party joined forces with the Kharijites. Within months, the dissenters had emerged as a powerful and militant force, bent more on disrupting what was to them a corrupted status quo than on promoting their own political or religious ideas. The core of these ideas, which always remained only vaguely defined, was belief in the strict equality of all believers. Thus the only legitimate credential for leadership of the community was piety, not lineage or race. Such ideas obviously appealed to non-Arab Muslims, who formed an important source of Khariji recruits. The converse of such egalitarian ideas was an intense fanaticism toward all Muslims who did not share them. These Muslims were in their view apostates and as such could be killed and their property seized.

As the Kharijites increased in numbers and stepped up their military activity – usually confined to raids against villages surrounding their base in central Iraq – 'Ali switched from his initial policy of avoiding contact with them to a policy of active engagement and suppression. On 17 July 658 C.E. 'Ali's forces destroyed the main Kharijite camp, killing a number of the founding members of the movement, including their leader. This action did not eliminate the Kharijite threat; it further radicalized the survivors, one of whom succeeded in assassinating 'Ali three years later.

The Kharijites continued to harass the government of 'Ali's successors, the Umayyads. Uprisings of individual groups occurred throughout the Umayyad period in the eastern portions of the empire, which remained the Kharijite base. These uprisings were seldom more than localized terrorist raids, but a number of more serious insurrections that led to the establishment of separate Kharijite rule in parts of the Umayyad empire are recorded. These Kharijite "states" were always short-lived, but the series of revolts ultimately weakened Umayyad control of the eastern provinces to the point where the Abbasid revolt in the eighth century that succeeded in toppling the Umayyads originated in Iraq.[8]

Under the Abbasids, Kharijite activity became less frequent and effective. The movement gradually lost its military and political dynamism and survived only as a separate school of interpretation on theological and political matters. The most profound legacy of the Kharijites was their impact on the juristic approach to rebellion and the issue of dissent within the community generally. The Kharijite rebellion and 'Ali's policies in suppressing it form the core of the medieval political and legal theory.

## The Medieval Theory and Modern Interpretations

Islamic political thought in the early medieval period (roughly the eighth through the twelfth centuries) was elaborated primarily by legal scholars. Thus discussions of political community, of challenges to it or separation from it, and of dissent occurred largely within the context of Islamic law (*shari'a*). The law was built upon Qur'anic interpretation, but not of a speculative type. In the field of administrative law, the Qur'an had already been interpreted, according to the medieval jurists, by the Prophet and the first four ("rightly guided") caliphs. The Medinan model of the Muslim community as an indivisible religio-political organization ruled by a just imam-caliph according to divine law became firmly established as a binding legal precedent from which all further codification and elaboration departed.

Because the institution of the imamate represented both the theoretical unity as well as the historical fragmentation of the Muslims, all discussion of political community and dissent concentrated on it. Within the four principal Sunni legal schools, the value of political order soon emerged as superior to that of justice. Despite the fact that Mu'awiya had risen in revolt against the legitimate caliph 'Ali, his seizure of power and his transformation of the caliphate into a dynastic institution were legitimated by the majority of Sunni jurists. Umayyad and Abbasid rule was acknowledged to be a departure and even a corruption of the Islamic ideal, but it was deemed legitimate nevertheless in order to maintain the cohesiveness and security of the umma. Qur'anic verses and Prophetic traditions enjoining obedience to the legitimate authority of the Muslims were applied diligently to sanction the rule of successive dynasts. One of the most frequently cited traditions has the Prophet saying:

> "Your best [leaders] are those whom you like and who like you, on whom you invoke blessings and who invoke blessings on you; and your worst [leaders] are those whom you hate and who hate you, whom you curse and who curse you." They [the Muslims] asked God's messenger whether in that event they should not depose them, but he replied, "No, as long as they observe the prayer among you; no, as long as they observe the prayer among you. If anyone has a governor whom he sees doing anything which is an act of disobedience to God, he must disapprove of the

disobedience to God which he commits, but must never withdraw from obedience."[9]

On the basis of this and similar hadith, the medieval jurists restricted the possibility of rebellion against the ruler to an extremely limited set of circumstances, namely, the ruler's renunciation of the basic tenets of Islam ("prayer among you"). If the ruler met that minimal test, no grounds for rebellion arose, even if the ruler was tyrannical. Specific "acts of disobedience to God" could be challenged, but the ruler's legitimacy itself could not be denied. Ibn Hanbal (d. 855), the last of the four great founders of Sunni jurisprudence, summarizes rather well the "classical" medieval view:

> Whoever secedes from the Imam of the Muslims – when the people have agreed on him and acknowledged his caliphate for any reason, either satisfaction with him or conquest – that rebel has broken the unity of the Muslims and opposed the tradition coming from God's messenger, God's blessing and peace be upon him.... It is not lawful for anyone to fight against the authority or to secede from it, and whoever does is an innovator, outside the tradition and the way.[10]

Given the importance of communal solidarity in the medieval approach, suppression of rebellion and civil strife invariably emerges as the chief obligation of the caliph. The medieval treatises generally deal with this topic under three categories: apostasy (ridda), rebellion (*bughat*), and brigandage or highway robbery (*hiraba*). The last category involves rather straightforward criminal behavior devoid of any political motives and is therefore irrelevant to the questions being addressed here. The regulations concerning apostasy raise far more complex theoretical issues. The Qur'anic passages dealing with Muslims changing their faith are consistent in deferring punishment, leaving it to be administered by God on the Day of Judgment (4:90; 5:59; 16:108; 47:25–28). Medieval jurists therefore relied on two traditions of the Prophet in establishing the death penalty for the apostate who refused to recant. It will not be necessary to go into a detailed treatment of the Prophetic precedents and the shari'a punishments adduced by the jurists.[11] What makes the laws of apostasy germane to the present discussion is the fact that one important source for the medieval law was Abu Bakr's actions toward the Bedouin tribes who had "turned their backs" (the literal root-meaning of *ridda*) upon the Islamic state. Many of the tribes, as previously indicated, did not renounce Islamic faith as such, only the obligation to pay zakat. Medieval jurists reasoned that Abu Bakr had fought the tribes because their withholding of zakat, one of the five core obligations of Islamic worship, constituted apostasy. But as many modern Muslim critics of the medieval law have pointed out, the actual significance of the ridda committed by the Bedouin Arabs was that it constituted political as well as religious defection.[12] The Bedouins had in essence sought to regain sovereignty after they had ceded it to the central Islamic state. Thus the penalties for ridda should be compared, according to these writers, to the penalties for treason, desertion, or secession, rather than apostasy strictly defined as change in religious belief. Such modernist views have been resisted by conservative interpreters, who frequently invoke the shari'a injunctions on ridda to prosecute a range of dissidents, including schismatics such as the Ahmadiyya in Pakistan and the Baha'is in Iran, political and social reformers such as Ustadh Mahmud Muhammad Taha in Sudan,[13] and secular critics such as Salman Rushdie.

The third category of internal warfare, rebellion or bughat, is most apposite to the question of self-determination and secession. The legal regulations on rebellion, labeled *ahkam al-bughat*, were derived largely from 'Ali's policies toward his opponents, principally the Kharijites. A number of important consequences relating to the treatment of rebels flowed from the precedents established by 'Ali: rebel prisoners, unlike apostates and criminals, could not be killed, nor could their property be confiscated. If rebel forces were fleeing without any expectation of regrouping, they could not be pursued by the Muslim army. Certain types of weapons that were permissible against other targets were to be avoided when fighting rebels. In general, these special prescriptions stemmed from the view that rebels remained Muslim in spite of their rebellion and that the Islamic state's policies should be aimed at their speedy rehabilitation into the umma, not their annihilation.[14] The ahkam al-bughat thus create the paradoxical situation that whereas the medieval theory virtually outlaws rebellion, rebels are given a remarkable degree of legal protection and immunity from punishment.

In order to separate rebels who enjoy special consideration as legitimate combatants from apostates/traitors or criminals, a clear definition of rebels was needed. The medieval jurists never differentiate clearly between rebel groups seeking to overthrow the regime and secessionist movements seeking to establish an independent state. Both goals were, of course, considered illegal by the vast majority. Nevertheless, the three defining characteristics of rebels discussed below clearly apply to seceders as much as they do to rebels.

(1) *Khuruj*, or "withdrawal," meant that the rebels had in some formal sense expressed their disloyalty to the Islamic state. Jurists

differed on whether khuruj necessarily involved violent resistance to the state, for example, capturing or killing the imam's agents, or whether acts of passive disobedience, such as refusal to pay taxes or serve in the army, were sufficient. The majority held that either kind of act satisfied the condition of khuruj.

Khuruj is achieved by a group that renounces its allegiance to the Islamic state and establishes a separate political community. This was in fact the initial policy of the Kharijites, who declared their political independence from both 'Ali and Mu'awiya and selected their own imam.

(2) *Ta'wil*, or legitimate grounds based upon interpretation of the Qur'an or sunna, sought to differentiate serious dissent from the "frivolous," such as that of the Bedouin tribes that refused to pay zakat to Abu Bakr out of stubbornness rather than any clear religious or political differences. Some jurists designated rebels as *mujtahidin*, or interpreters using their own reason to arrive at conclusions different from the majority opinion, which presumably was enforced by the imam. The majority of jurists held that the imam could not unilaterally pass judgment on the rightness or wrongness of the rebels' ta'wil.

Ta'wil raises more difficult issues for Muslim seceders than khuruj. Given the prime importance attached to communal solidarity in the Qur'an and sunna and the medieval view of the umma as a religio-political community, how could a group of Muslims seek to create a polity separate from the Islamic state and still remain Muslims? By advancing secessionist claims, did their ta'wil not become "frivolous"? Medieval jurists did not address these questions explicitly, believing perhaps that the answers were self-evident. Closer scrutiny of the legal texts, however, reveals ambiguity and even implicit acceptance of secession as a legitimate ta'wil, particularly among later jurists facing the reality of increasing political fragmentation. First, with regard to the ridda wars, some jurists declared that certain tribes were in fact rebels and not apostates because they interpreted one Qur'anic verse relating to zakat (9:103) as limited to the Prophet's lifetime. When they withheld zakat from Abu Bakr, they did so based on a serious point of difference in Qur'anic interpretation and therefore should have been treated as rebels, not apostates.[15] Since their act of rebellion consisted of withdrawing allegiance from the Islamic state, the logical conclusion of these jurists' views is that secession is a valid ta'wil.

Second, with reference to the Kharijites, most jurists acknowledged that these groups acted on the basis of legitimate ta'wil. Their challenge to 'Ali's rule was based on the claim that he had substituted human will for divine will when he agreed to arbitration in his dispute with Mu'awiya. This point of religious difference held profound political implications, as quickly became apparent in the evolution of Kharijite beliefs regarding the imamate. The Kharijites eventually developed distinct religio-political doctrines, which were applied intermittently during the short-lived reigns of various Kharijite rulers. By acknowledging the Kharijite rebellion against 'Ali as the most important precedent for ahkam al-bughat, medieval jurists were again implicitly acknowledging secession as a legitimate ta'wil. The Kharijite ta'wil became problematic when certain radical elements began indiscriminate killing of Muslim men, women, and children who fell within their wide definition of apostates. These actions had caused the Kharijites, according to some jurists, to forfeit their ta'wil, becoming apostates themselves.[16]

(3) *Shauka*, or the power to constitute an active rebellion, meant for many jurists that individuals or small groups opposing the imam could not claim the status of rebels. If such privileges were extended to every small band claiming khuruj and ta'wil, anarchy would be the inevitable result. The requirement of shauka also relates quite clearly to secessionist movements. Serious secessionist movements must demonstrate by their numbers, organization, and power the capacity to establish and maintain a separate state. Shauka may in modern terms be considered as a demonstration of political viability, of the potential to assume the obligations of both internal and external sovereignty. Groups unable to meet this requirement are not accorded rebel status by the medieval jurists. Again the precedent is 'Ali's behavior toward the Kharijites. He refrained from attacking or even incarcerating individuals or small groups expressing Kharijite sympathies. Only after the Kharijite opposition had assumed the proportions of an organized and violent rebellion did he authorize "police actions" aimed at containing it. At this point, the Kharijites already constituted in many important ways a separate state within a badly fractured Islamic community. They are certainly treated as such (by implication) in the important legal treatise composed by the Hanafi jurist al-Shaybani (d. 804). He writes for example that if the rebels gained so much control over a territory that they "dominated its people and collected from them the taxes," the people would be absolved of those particular tax payments once the territory reverted to the loyalists' control.[17]

Notwithstanding the wide latitude given by the jurists to the definition and treatment of rebels, the ahkam al-bughat must ultimately be seen as one part of a profoundly conservative theory of political power, grounded in an awareness of the historical schisms that had rent the community during its infancy and in an abiding fear that such turmoil lay only superficially below the surface of the medieval state. Indeed, the medieval jurists had strong reason to fear *fitna*, as all challenges to the imam in power were labeled, because by the beginning of the tenth century the Islamic empire was beginning to feel the initial onslaught by foreign invaders that would culminate in the Mongol sacking of Baghdad in 1258. But long before the destruction of the Abbasid caliphate, all the details of the medieval theory – those relating to the indivisibility of the umma, the unity of the imamate, and the illegitimacy of rebellion – had become anachronistic in the face of the actual political fragmentation of the Islamic world.

Political theory was slow to respond to political realities. One seminal work of Sunni political thought is al-Mawardi's (d. 1058) *al-Ahkam al-Sultaniyya* (Ordinances of government), written partly in response to the growing political irrelevance of the Abbasid caliphs in the face of their Buyid overlords. After describing the credentials of a candidate for the imamate, Mawardi considers the possibility of two similarly qualified rival candidates. He concludes that the final decision rests with the "electors" chosen to decide on the new caliph. Once they have reached a decision, however, it is irrevocable and unchallengeable, even if later a better qualified candidate emerges. Moreover, Mawardi rejects the possibility of there being two imams simultaneously in two different regions of the Islamic state. Such an occurrence would negate the *ratio juris* of the institution, namely to preserve the stability and unity of the community, which Mawardi lists as the imam's first obligation.[18]

Having reaffirmed theoretically the necessity and integrity of the caliphate, Mawardi concedes that political power may in fact be wielded by two types of agents for the caliph: the *wazir* (minister) and the *amir* (governor). For their part, amirs may accede to power either by delegation or by usurpation. Mawardi makes clear that his willingness to accept the latter eventuality stems from necessity and public welfare, "in order to induce him to obedience and to deter him from secession and opposition."[19]

The arguments put forth by Mawardi are generally followed by subsequent theorists, who add certain elements and emphasize certain aspects to fit their specific historical circumstances. Shortly after Mawardi, al-Ghazali (d. 1111), writing at a time of even greater challenges to the caliph's authority, continues to assert the importance of the imamate as a symbol of the unity of the umma and as a requirement of Islamic law. But Ghazali goes further than Mawardi in accommodating ideals of the imamate with political conditions. He concedes that the imam may be selected by the wielder of political power (*sultan*), who then gains legitimacy for himself and his princes and state officials through his protection of and obedience to the institution of the imamate. The argument for the sultan's legitimacy seems circular, but there is one important qualification: Ghazali insists that the sultan's choice must be "ratified" by spokesmen for the community, the *'ulama*.[20] In his later works, Ghazali accepts the division of the umma under a number of sultans, each one legitimate so long as he acknowledges the supreme authority of the caliph.

The legitimation of a corrupted caliphal institution is taken to its logical extreme by Ibn Jama'a (d. 1333), whose writings come after the destruction of Baghdad and the reduction of the Abbasid caliph to a pensioner of the Egyptian Mamluks. For Ibn Jama'a there was no question of a meaningful caliphal institution apart from effective political power. After mentioning the "traditional" methods of selecting the imam (i.e., election or designation), he makes quite clear that in his time the truly relevant means of acquiring the office was through gaining military power (i.e., usurpation). Quite simply, for Ibn Jama'a the imam was the sultan.[21] Sanctioning imamate by usurpation is necessary "so that the unity of the Muslims be assured and they speak with one voice."[22] Given this justification and in spite of the incontrovertible disunity of the umma in this late period, Ibn Jama'a continues to cling to the myth of the single imam at the head of an indivisible Muslim community. He does, however, make an important concession to reality, when he, like Mawardi and Ghazali, enjoins the caliph to accept the "agency" of governors who have seized power in one or another part of the Islamic empire.

The first truly "modern" Muslim political thinkers are Ibn Taymiyya (d. 1328) and Ibn Khaldun (d. 1406). Ibn Taymiyya accepts the division of the community into separate, autonomous states under the leadership of various rulers, whom he prefers to call *wali al-amr* (holder of authority) rather than imam. His work is motivated by the desire to protect the integrity of the umma from the ravages of foreign conquerors and internal dissension. But the means that he uses to accomplish this end is the championing of shari'a, not the universal caliphate, whose necessity he explicitly denies. So long as a ruler, regardless of how he comes to power, enforces Islamic law, he is the legitimate ruler entitled to the obedience of his people. Like earlier theorists, though, Ibn Taymiyya proposes no real means of challenging or deposing a tyrannical ruler.[23]

Ibn Khaldun, a North African writing in a milieu quite different from that of theorists in the central Islamic lands, approaches the political questions that had so agitated the others from a different perspective. With regard to the caliphate, he notes in the *Muqadimma* that scholars are divided on whether there could be two or more caliphs at the same time, but concludes that the majority forbid it on the authority of Prophetic hadith. A few scholars, however, particularly those from Spain and North Africa, permit the existence of multiple caliphs on the basis of the "general consensus."[24] By Ibn Khaldun's time, al-Andalus had in fact been ruled as an independent caliphate for well over 600 years.

The *Muqadimma*'s significance, however, lies not in its reiteration of the controversy on the caliphate and the disunity of the umma, but rather in its unique analysis of the sociological reasons for such disunity. Ibn Khaldun writes that loyalty to one's "group" defined by kinship or prolonged association is one of the most primal, universal, and powerful of human traits. He labels this force *'asabiyya*, or "group loyalty." 'Asabiyya is strongest among small kin groups forced by circumstances to rely upon each other for survival. Thus the 'asabiyya of the bedouin tribes is stronger than that of town dwellers. But this same group loyalty promotes strong xenophobia and resistance to authority, preventing nomads and desert dwellers from achieving civilization. A transcending force is necessary to supersede the parochial loyalties of tribal 'asabiyya and to forge a larger civilization. This broader 'asabiyya is created out of religion, which rearranges old loyalties and social organizations. Thus the Muslims of Medina under the Prophet were able to transcend the weak 'asabiyya of the settled tribes and to forge themselves into a political community that easily overran the decaying empires of the Byzantines and the Sassanians. The nomadic tribes, Ibn Khaldun observes, proved more difficult to conquer because of their stronger group loyalties:

> A dynasty rarely establishes itself firmly in lands with many different tribes and groups. The reason for this is the differences in opinions and desires. Behind each opinion and desire, there is a group feeling defending it. At any time, therefore, there is much opposition to dynasty and rebellion against it, even if the dynasty possesses group feeling, because each group feeling under the control of the ruling dynasty thinks that it has in itself (enough) strength and power.[25]

Africa in particular, Ibn Khaldun notes, has proven difficult to subordinate under Islamic hegemony. The Berber tribes and Christian communities resisted strongly the initial Arab conquests of the seventh century, and, even after Islamic rule had been established,

> they went on revolting and seceding, and then adopted dissident (kharijite) religious opinions many times. Ibn Abi Zayd said that the Berbers in the Maghrib revolted twelve times. . .This is what is meant by the statement

reported on the authority of Umar, that "Ifriqiyah 'divides' the hearts of its inhabitants" [a pun on the word *faraqa*, "to divide"].[26]

Ibn Khaldun notes that according to conventional opinion, the Prophet strongly opposed 'asabiyya and that Islam attempted to overthrow it. Such views, he avers, are a misinterpretation of the Prophet's position.[27] Since 'asabiyya is a natural feature of human existence, an aspect of God's will, it is neither possible nor desirable to eliminate it. The Prophet, writes Ibn Khaldun, castigated only the negative manifestations of group loyalty. At the same time, he sought to channel the constructive power of 'asabiyya into the creation of a new, divinely guided Muslim community. Under his rule and the rule of the first four caliphs, Islam did constitute the source of a new group identity, allowing the earliest Muslims to realize very nearly the Islamic vision of political community. Yet religion provides only an ideal for human striving, one that according to Ibn Khaldun's conception of human nature can be achieved only with great difficulty and maintained only briefly. Under 'Ali's tenure, the binding force of Islam loosened in the face of the old and more powerful tribal 'asabiyya. Mu'awiya, the leader of the Arab clan with the greatest 'asabiyya, triumphed in his struggle with 'Ali, converting the pure caliphate into a caliphate mixed with traditional aspects of kingship. Mu'awiya's actions are not condemned by Ibn Khaldun, who sees in the first fitna merely a natural unfolding of the laws of 'asabiyya. Likewise, the subsequent establishment of independent Muslim kingdoms throughout Asia and Africa was a departure from the Islamic ideals, but fully in keeping with the cyclical nature of human society.

Within a century after Ibn Khaldun's death, the Muslim world would be divided into three large empires, the Ottoman, the Safavid, and the Mughal, which came into existence almost simultaneously, and a number of smaller principalities along its periphery. Each of the new empires was ruled by dynasties theoretically and practically sovereign in their realms. The Ottomans, as protectors of Mecca, Medina, and Jerusalem, posed vaguely as successors to the caliphate, but their claims were never acknowledged by their Safavid and Mughal rivals.

The administrative organization of each of the empires was modeled theoretically on medieval Islamic practice. Non-Muslim communities defined by religious affiliation were recognized as *dhimmis* (protected peoples) and allowed to exercise autonomy in their communal affairs. The millet system, as it was known in Ottoman lands, always remained more an informal administrative approach than a formal bureaucratic arrangement. The important point about this system, though, is that it was understood to apply only to non-Muslims.[28] Theoretically, all Muslim subjects of an empire constituted a single community, despite the wide range of ethnic groups found within it. In practice, however, each empire prudently extended the autonomy of the millet system to various Muslim groups (such as the Kurds in Ottoman lands) or selected native elites to administer far-flung provinces (such as Bengal in the Mughal empire).

The progressive encroachment of European imperialism into the Muslim world and with it the dissemination of European political ideas had an obvious and profound impact on Islamic political discourse. Reform as well as independence movements were led by men who were imbued with the ideals of nationalism and self-determination stirring up much of Europe at the time. The Muslim activists were as little prepared to resolve the tensions and conflicts inherent in the two concepts as were their European counterparts. Unlike the secularized Europeans, however, the Muslims had to contend with an additional ideological factor, the religious appeals of Islam.

The relationship between Islam and nationalism is an extremely complex and ambivalent one. The debate on this modern issue nevertheless focuses on issues and employs terminology that are to a remarkable extent of medieval inspiration. Consider for example a well-known document in this debate: the *fatwa* of Egyptian jurist Rashid Rida (d. 1935).[29] Rida writes in response to a letter from an Indonesian Muslim asking for clarification of Islam's view on "group feeling" (i.e., 'asabiyya) and, by extension, Islam's view on modern nationalism. Rida's response largely follows Ibn Khaldun's argument for "'asabiyya rightly understood": Islam condemns only the adverse consequences of misguided group loyalty, not its positive aspects. Thus Islam is not opposed to nationalism or patriotism, writes Rida, so long as they are aimed at promoting the independence and welfare of the Muslims and their eventual solidarity. The exact form of this solidarity remains vaguely defined in Rida's statement, as it is in most Muslim statements.

Rida's Islamic sanction for national self-determination addressed Muslim anti-colonial struggles. But the application of the same arguments to Muslim revolts against Muslim empires has consistently aroused tremendous controversy. The most important case was that of the Hashemite-led Arab revolt against the Ottoman Turks in World War I. The revolt was strongly resisted by many Arabs and even more so by non-Arabs. It particularly agitated the largest Muslim population in the world at the time, that of British India. Indo-Muslim leaders castigated the Arab revolt as a European ploy to destroy the last remaining symbol of Muslim unity and power, the Ottoman caliphate, and later rejected the Hashemites' claim to the caliphate.

In short, Islam has been pressed into service by both nationalists (whether they are Turkish, Arab, Iranian, Indian, or others) as well as by their opponents. The most striking and significant aspect of this controversy, now well over a century old, is the fact that the Islamic opposition to nationalism has come almost entirely from pan-Islamists. In other words, the Islamic challenge to the sovereign "nation-state" has invariably been directed in an *upward* direction toward the formation of trans- or supranational Islamic groupings, of which the O.I.C. is merely the most prominent example. The pressure has never been in a downward direction, toward the breakup of the states into subnational ethnic groups. Arguments and attempts at such subnational fragmentation have been strongly resisted, as is clearly evident in the two cases considered below.

## Bangladesh

The seeds of the Pakistani civil war in 1971 from which emerged independent Bangladesh were sown in the partition of British India in 1947. Pakistan was created on the basis of the "two-nations theory" championed by leaders of the Muslim League. At a conference of the league in 1930, Muhammad Iqbal (d. 1938), the leading Indian modernist thinker of the early twentieth century, advocated the creation of an independent state in the Muslim-majority areas of northwest India. Iqbal did not live to articulate his vision fully, but within ten years of his address to the conference the Muslim League had formally embraced the idea of a separate Indian Muslim state as its central goal. The unified, independent India that leaders of the Congress Party sought was nothing but a chimera, argued the Muslim League's leader, Muhammad 'Ali Jinnah. India was a mosaic of various nationalities held together only by British rule. The fate of post-British India should be determined, he argued, through the self-determination of India's peoples, in particular the large Muslim minority of nearly 80 million.

Prior to 1940, neither Iqbal nor Jinnah envisioned a unitary Muslim state consisting of both the northwest provinces and the Muslim areas of Bengal. A number of plans were being floated in the late 1930s for the division of the subcontinent. But in the wake of the Lahore Resolution of 1940, whose ambiguous wording left much room for confusion, the Muslim League emerged as the champion of a single state for Indian Muslims, dubbed Pakistan.

The Muslim League's demand for Pakistan splintered the Indo-Muslim elites. Opposition came primarily from the leading religious organizations and activists on the subcontinent. The traditional 'ulama opposed partition because of deeply held suspicions about the modernist and secular orientations of those calling for the creation of Pakistan. They saw in Jinnah and his Muslim League supporters the hand of British imperialism attempting to divide and weaken the independence movement led by the Congress Party. Then there were Islamic revivalists such as Maulana Abu'l A'la Maududi, leader of the Jama'at-i Islami, a small but well-organized and active Islamic party, who both distrusted the Islamic credentials of the Muslim League and opposed its nationalist designs on ideological grounds. Maududi argued that the idea of Pakistan espoused by the Muslim League challenged the universality of the Islamic umma. Rather than trying to create a separate state for some Indian Muslims while leaving the rest to fend for themselves in a Hindu-dominated India, Maududi called for an "Islamic revolution," a revolution characterized by internal spiritual regeneration, education, and moral reform that would make Indian Muslims the vanguard for the universal Islamic revival. As Pakistan came close to becoming reality, however, some members of the traditional 'ulama, together with Maududi and his Jama'at party, decided to bow to political realities and settled in the country upon which they intended to impress their own visions of Islamic statehood.

The Pakistan that emerged from partition was a state fraught with ideological and practical dilemmas. It was a state divided into two "halves" by one thousand miles of hostile territory. Racially, linguistically, and culturally, West Pakistanis were quite different from their East Pakistani countrymen and women. The only unifying force was that of Islam, and even on this issue Pakistanis were intensely divided on the role of religion in politics.

All of the problems inherent in the country's curious configuration came to the fore during the nine-year process of drafting a constitution. The one possibility for continued national unity was the implementation of a democratic, federal system that provided autonomy for each of Pakistan's separate provinces. Such a system was, however, never implemented as Pakistan passed under the military rule of Ayub Khan after 1958. The national government, now firmly controlled by Punjabis and Sindhis, pursued policies aimed at keeping East Pakistan a largely agricultural, underdeveloped state while negating the Bengali cultural identity of its people. In March 1966 the Awami League led by Shaykh Mujib al-Rahman issued a Six-Point Proposal for East Pakistani autonomy within the Pakistani union. When Ayub Khan's reign finally ended in 1969 and the Pakistani generals announced the first national parliamentary elections in the country's history, the Awami League turned the elections into a referendum on its autonomy proposal. The elections in 1970 gave the Awami League a resounding victory in the East Pakistani provincial assembly and a clear majority in the national parliament. The Awami League should have formed the national government, and Mujib al-Rahman should have become the country's prime minister. Instead, the military leader General Yahya Khan, with the support of the West Pakistani political leader Zulfiqar 'Ali Bhutto, annulled the election results and jailed Mujib al-Rahman. The Awami League quickly proclaimed East Pakistan's secession and the creation of Bangladesh. At the same time, the Pakistani army was deployed to suppress the revolt.

The Pakistani civil war posed the first real test of the nascent Organization of the Islamic Conference. It was a test that the organization was woefully unprepared to handle. Not only was its charter still being drafted when the conflict began, but the organization's tentative declaration of principles clearly evinced a reluctance among its member states to endow it with any substantive political-military role. This was particularly true for a dispute considered to be essentially a domestic affair of a member state.

Throughout the early months of the crisis, the principal political organ of the O.I.C., the Council of Foreign Ministers, strongly supported Pakistan's position that the Bangladeshi secession was illegitimate and that Pakistan was within bounds in acting to quash it. No unequivocal demands for a cease-fire were issued, just as no calls had been made for implementation of the election results of 1970. When fighting escalated and Indian intervention appeared imminent, the council hastily designated the O.I.C. secretary-general, Tunku 'Abd al-Rahman of Malaysia, and representatives from Iran and Kuwait to arbitrate the dispute. The mission failed utterly when it was denied entry into India in order to meet with Bangladeshi leaders who had sought asylum there. India's snubbing of the O.I.C. was a result of the organization's earlier decision, prompted by Pakistan, to revoke India's membership.

The O.I.C. played a much more significant and constructive role in achieving Pakistani recognition of Bangladesh following the civil war. The secretary-general and a committee consisting of the foreign ministers of Algeria, Iran, Malaysia, Morocco, Somalia, and Tunisia were charged with bringing Bhutto and Mujib al-Rahman into direct talks on outstanding points of contention between the two countries. The secretary-general proposed that the two leaders meet in Mecca during the annual pilgrimage, but Mujib refused to attend the meeting until Pakistan had formally recognized Bangladeshi independence. Bhutto was under strong domestic pressure not to do so, particularly from the religious parties.

The O.I.C. summit in Lahore in 1974 provided Bhutto the pretext he needed to extend diplomatic relations to Bangladesh. In the course of planning the summit, Pakistan as the host country invited Mujib al-Rahman to attend as the leader of a Muslim country. Prodded by other O.I.C. states, the Bangladeshi leader accepted, and formal relations between the two states were established.[30]

The extent to which O.I.C. policies toward the Bangladeshi secession was determined or even influenced by "Islamic" considerations is open to question. What is indisputable, however, is that the resistance to Bangladeshi independence found within the official forums of the O.I.C. was mirrored by the general apathy and outright opposition found among Muslim peoples in general and Islamic activists in particular. The most intriguing as well as important case of such opposition on Islamic grounds was the response of the Jama'at-i Islami.

The Jama'at began its existence in independent Pakistan with virtually no presence in the eastern half of the country. At the time of partition, Maududi had only a single follower in all of East Pakistan. Even after a campaign to increase membership, the Jama'at could claim only thirty-eight members in 1954. The Jama'at's popularity in West Pakistan was also quite limited, but in the East, Maududi's views on a number of salient issues estranged the party from much of the middle class to which it appealed. In 1956 Maududi addressed Bengali grievances against the central government in a long speech delivered in Dacca. He began by conceding that Bengali should be accepted as an official state language alongside Urdu and that official discrimination against East Pakistanis in army and government service needed redressing. His speech concluded, however, with denunciations of Bengali leaders and groups who sought to capitalize on these grievances by fomenting strife and separatism. Maududi's overriding concern for Islamic (i.e., Pakistani) unity led ineluctably in his mind to the conclusion "that anyone who was championing the cause of Bengali nationalism and fighting for East Pakistani grievances was either a communist, a Hindu, or a political adventurer."[31] This view led Maududi to oppose strongly the Awami League's Six-Point Proposal as a secessionist manifesto.

The Jama'at saw in the elections of 1970 its long-awaited opportunity to prove its popular support and in the process to eliminate its principal political rivals, the two main leftist parties, the Pakistan People's Party (PPP) in the West and the Awami League in the East. Maududi and other Jama'at leaders plunged into the election campaign with great fervor, fielding candidates in both East and West Pakistan. The campaign in East Pakistan quickly turned violent. On 18 January 1970 a rally convened by the Jama'at in Dacca's main park was attacked by supporters of the Awami League minutes before Maududi was scheduled to appear. In the melee, two people were killed, who were subsequently claimed by the Jama'at as "martyrs of its cause."

After such intense campaigning, the election results created shock in the Jama'at ranks. The party won only four out of 151 seats in the National Assembly and only one out of 174 East Pakistan provincial assembly seats.[32] Maududi sought to make up for the election disaster by portraying the Jama'at as the "patriotic" party working to save Pakistani unity. In response to Bhutto's rejection of the election results, Maududi and the leader of the East Pakistani Jama'at, Ghulam A'zam, urged the military leader Yahya Khan to respect the results and thus avoid war between Muslims.[33] When Yahya Khan refused, the Jama'at attacked the government for undue bias towards the PPP. These attacks did not promote reconciliation between the Jama'at and the Awami League, however. Maududi remained convinced that the League was conspiring with Hindus and communists to dismember Pakistan. Thus when the Pakistani military launched its brutal campaign to suppress the East Pakistani uprising, the Jama'at fell in line behind the army.

The Jama'at's campaign to thwart the Bangladeshi secession was pursued along two fronts, one diplomatic, the other military. Throughout the spring of 1971, Maududi sent out several appeals to Islamic heads of state and organizations for support of the Pakistani position. In one telegram addressed to thirty-nine Muslim leaders, Maududi declared that the Bangladeshi separatist movement was not supported by the common Muslim Bengali, who favored union with Pakistan. In July 1971, Khurram Jah Murad, a leader of the East Pakistani Jama'at, toured several countries in Europe and Asia as a spokesman of the "true" Bengali position.[34]

Within East Pakistan itself, Jama'at policy during the civil war was charted largely by the Bengali leaders of the organization. It was these leaders who authorized the formation of two paramilitary groups consisting of young Jama'at workers drawn mainly from Indian Muslim immigrants to East Pakistan. These two groups, designated al-Badr and al-Shams, operated under the command of the Pakistani army as a counterinsurgency force fighting the Mukti Bahini guerrillas. The Jama'at's active participation in the fighting led to swift retribution by the Mukti Bahini following independence. Some 2,000

Jamaʿat members died, and 12,000 were imprisoned during the war.[35]

Why did the Jamaʿat-i Islami, including its East Pakistani cadres, align itself so solidly behind the Pakistani generals? Commentators have suggested a number of nonideological reasons, ranging from Maududi's quest for power after the devastating defeat in the national elections to a class-based alliance of conservative religious groups, West Pakistani capitalists, and the military attempting to contain a peasant rebellion in East Pakistan. But such explanations miss the crucial ideological motivation behind the Jamaʿat's policies. For Maududi the issues were sharply defined. Just as he had opposed the fragmentation of the Indo-Muslim community before partition, so afterward he consistently resisted the breakup of the Islamic community of Pakistan. He realized quite early that East Pakistani nationalism abnegated not only the two-nations theory, but also the one-Muslim-umma ideal that he cherished until his death. The creation of Bangladesh was one further regression from the Islamic ideal, and since no "true" Muslim could wish it, Bangladeshi nationalism had to be the creation of Hindus, imperialists, and their misguided Bengali agents.[36] Maududi's views were shared by many Muslims and Islamic groups around the world, who continue to view the Bangladeshi secession as a Muslim tragedy.

## Kurdistan

The Kurds were among the first non-Arab peoples to encounter Muslim armies in the mid-seventh century. But like the Arab Bedouins and the Berbers of North Africa, their assimilation into the Islamic empire proved to be a difficult and prolonged process. Well into the twelfth century, the Kurds were treated by medieval Muslim writers as generally a non-Muslim people.[37] Coupled with their reputation for religious nonconformity was a reputation for resisting central political authority. The Abbasids learned quickly not to challenge the power of Kurdish princes, the most powerful being the Ayyubids, whose founder Salah al-Din (d. 1193; known to the Crusaders as Saladin) overshadowed all other Muslim rulers of his time. Likewise, both the Ottomans and the Safavids extended a great deal of latitude to Kurdish princes (amirs), as each empire sought Kurdish support in their internecine border wars of the sixteenth and early seventeenth centuries. A scion of one of these princely families, Sharaf al-Din Bitlisi, responded to the devastation of Kurdistan resulting from the Ottoman-Safavid wars by composing the first pan-Kurdish history, the *Sharafnama*. Sharaf al-Din suggests in this work that Kurdish unity is disrupted by Islam and the "distracting idea" of the umma, which is nothing more than a curse on the Kurds imposed by the Prophet. "The Prophet Muhammad, disconcerted by the war-like and awesome looks of a Kurdish visitor asked the Almighty to place a curse of disunity on the Kurds, since in unity, the Prophet feared, they will overcome the world."[38]

The relatively autonomous position of the amirs began to change in the early nineteenth century when both the Ottomans and the Safavids launched belated efforts to centralize power in order to reverse their steady decline. The overthrow of the amirs left power in the hands of lower-level tribal leaders (aghas) who lacked the education and political sophistication of the amiri class. The relative political stability that the Kurdish regions had enjoyed for two centuries now gave way to open tribal rivalry and feuding.

By the mid-nineteenth century pan-Kurdish aspirations had re-surfaced in two quite different manifestations. The first was a secular, populist vision elaborated by Kurdish intellectuals schooled in Europe. Neither they nor their vision ever seem to have gained any sizable influence over the Kurdish masses. The second pan-Kurdish force was led by a new and rival source of authority to that of the aghas – namely, the leaders of Sufi religious orders that had rapidly grown in Kurdish areas during the early nineteenth century. The Sufi leaders (*shaykhs*) could claim the allegiance of a number of tribes and soon began to exert significant influence in political matters. One of these leaders, Shaykh 'Ubaydallah, organized the Kurdish League, a move-ment ostensibly aimed at pan-Kurdish unity but directed in reality at combating Armenian Christian and Shi'i Kurdish influence in Kurd-istan. Initially, the Ottoman government encouraged the activities of the Kurdish League, viewing it as a counter to the growing Armenian nationalist claims in the same region. When Shaykh 'Ubaydallah's Kurdish League threatened to become too independent, the Ottomans reversed their policy and exiled the Kurdish leader to the Hijaz.

The Young Turk revolution of 1908 stimulated the growth of secular, modernist nationalism among Kurdish intellectuals. Since most of them had by now congregated in Paris, Istanbul, or Beirut, the societies for Kurdish independence they created had little mass support within Kurdistan and, as a result, very little leverage among Turkish authorities. Power was still wielded by the shaykhs, who mixed religion – some of it quite heretical to Islamic doctrine – with politics to consolidate their own hold over different regions. Many of these leaders opted to support the Ottomans during World War I rather than follow the example of the Arab or Armenian revolts.

The nationalist propaganda of Kurdish intellectuals apparently did carry some political weight in the West, since the Allies convening in Versailles acknowledged the Kurdish right to self-determination alongside that of the Armenians and the Arabs. The Treaty of Sèvres (1920) provided for a referendum to be held within one year to decide the independence of the Ottoman Kurdish regions. The likely outcome of such a referendum and the likely character of an independent Kurdish state at that time raise some serious counter-factual issues. In 1920 the idea of pan-Kurdish unity, let alone modern statehood, was alien to the aghas and shaykhs who dominated local Kurdish politics. For many, their Kurdish identity was subsumed within a broader Sunni Muslim identity shaped by centuries of allegiance, however vaguely defined, to the Ottoman caliph.[39] Had an independent Kurdish state emerged, there is no reason to believe that it would have escaped all of the confusion and challenges over identity and legitimacy that have so complicated state-building in the modern Middle East. As it happened, of course, the referendum was never held as the Treaty of Sèvres gave way to the Treaty of Lausanne (1924), which laid the basis for the transformation of the Kurdish right of national self-determination into the Kurdish quest for civil and political rights as citizens of five sovereign states.

The history of the Kurdish movements and their nationalist demands in Turkey, Syria, Iraq, and Iran has been well studied in a number of recent works.[40] These works illuminate how Kurdish nationalism suffered at the hands of Arab, Turkish, and Iranian nation-alism. But what most studies neglect are the ways in which Kurdish nationalism has suffered at the hands of Islamic universalism. Indeed, the role of Islamic ideology within and in response to these movements has received scant attention. This may be due to the general absence of explicit appeals to Islam by Kurdish leaders after World War I. One notable exception is the revolt led by Shaykh Sa'id in 1925 against the heavy-handed secularization program of the Kemalist Turkish republic. The revolt was quickly crushed by the Turkish republican army, and Shaykh Sa'id was hanged before he could implement whatever specific religious agenda he had.

In the post-World War II period, the Kurdish leadership, like the elites of the states in which they operated, generally pursued secular goals. This was true even of men like the Iraqi Kurdish leader Mulla Mustafa Barzani who came from shaykhi backgrounds. Since the late 1970s, however, the Kurds — like all Muslim peoples — have experienced the impact of the "Islamic revival." In Iraq, Islamic symbolism and rhetoric have been frequently and perversely applied to Kurdish autonomy demands by the Ba'athists. For example, the genocidal campaign launched by the Iraqi regime in the late 1980s and culminating in the use of chemical weapons in Halabja was dubbed "al-Anfal." The term was carefully selected for its Islamic connotations it is the title of the eighth chapter of the Qur'an. The title comes from one of the main subjects in this chapter, namely, the dispensation of the "spoils of war" taken by Muslims fighting recalcitrant pagans. No Iraqi, nor indeed any Muslim, could mistake the import of the anti-Kurdish campaign's code name. The Kurds, by pressing their separatist demands, were beyond the pale of the Muslim community. Their rebellion could be suppressed as a jihad against infidels.

While the Ba'athists' self-serving application of the Qur'anic word anfal may have been transparent to most Muslims, very few condemned this gross distortion of Islamic rules regarding the treatment of rebel soldiers and the general proscription against targeting noncombatant populations, whether Muslim or non-Muslim. Kanan Makiya's voice is a plaintive exception: "Millions of Arabic words have been written about the more than 300 Palestinian villages destroyed in the creation of Israel. And justly so; would that I could add a million more words. But why is it that not one Arab intellectual has written about the elimination of more than 3,000 Kurdish villages by an Arab state?"[41]

Very few Muslim voices were raised in protest or condemnation when Iraqi President Saddam Hussein unleashed his Revolutionary Guards against the Kurdish population following the Gulf War. The O.I.C. foreign ministers, meeting for the first time since the end of the war, absolved themselves of any responsibility for the horrors unfolding in Iraq, blaming them all upon the Iraqi government. When the Europeans succeeded in prodding President George Bush of the United States to intervene on "humanitarian" grounds, the same states that had long opposed Saddam Hussein closed ranks to protest the threat to Iraqi sovereignty represented by the Kurdish "safe haven." The declaration of 4 October 1992 by Iraqi Kurdish leaders of a "regional parliament" for a federal state of Kurdistan within Iraq prompted the foreign ministers of Syria, Iran, and Turkey to voice their concerns over any possible partition of Iraq.[42] In response, Kurdish leaders Mas'ud Barzani and Jalal Talabani rushed to deny any Kurdish intention to secede from Iraq, contingent on the emergence of a democratic and pluralistic regime in Baghdad.[43]

As long as Saddam Hussein continues to reign in Baghdad, the de facto Kurdish secession in the north will become increasingly formalized. But the guarantee of Kurdish autonomy will continue to rest with the outside powers that brought it about, not with the regional powers and perhaps not even with some of the Iraqi Kurds themselves who remain politically and ideologically opposed to autonomy. Fighting erupted in December 1993 between the secular Patriotic Union of Kurdistan (P.U.K.) led by Talabani and the Islamic Movement of Iraqi Kurdistan led by Mulla 'Uthman 'Abd al-'Aziz. The Islamic Movement's goals were vaguely defined but believed to be pro-Iranian. The Islamic Movement's fighters were eventually killed or captured, yet the full extent of its ideological influence and potential for renewed challenges to the authorities in Iraqi Kurdistan remains uncertain.

For Iranian Kurds, the Islamic revolution led by Ayatollah Khomeini in 1979 held the prospect for a reversal of the centralizing and assimilative policies pursued by both Pahlavi shahs. The Kurdish Democratic Party of Iran (K.D.P.I.), which since 1945 had been the principal organization working for Kurdish autonomy in Iran, participated actively in the campaign to topple the shah's regime. Its leader was the leftist intellectual 'Abd al-Rahman Ghassemlou. Immediately after the revolution, another key figure, Shaykh 'Izz al-Din Husayni, joined the K.D.P.I. As a Sunni religious scholar, Shaykh Husayni was in an influential position to challenge Khomeini's views on Islamic government. Husayni and Ghassemlou became the Kurdish spokesmen before the new Islamic government.

In March 1979, one month after Khomeini's return to Tehran, the K.D.P.I. announced an eight-point program for Kurdish autonomy within the Islamic republic. The plan called for the recognition of a Kurdish province to be governed by a democratically elected parliament. The parliament would have jurisdiction over all "domestic" issues, but defense, foreign affairs, and economic planning would be the prerogatives of the central government. The K.D.P.I. proposals were not favorably received by Khomeini's government. Despite the Kurds' assurances that they wanted only "Democracy for Iran, Autonomy for Kurdistan," the new regime in Tehran adopted an approach very similar to that of the old: Kurdish demands, if granted, would herald the fragmentation of Iran by other ethnic groups. Khomeini provided an Islamic justification for rejection of Kurdish demands. Kurdish nationalism posed in his mind an anachronistic and insidious subversion of the emerging Islamic unity for which the Iranian revolution was merely the catalyst:

> There is no difference between Muslims who speak different languages. . .It is very probable that such problems have been created by those who do not wish the Muslim countries to be united. . .They create the issues of nationalism, of pan-Iranianism, pan-Turkism, and such isms, which are contrary to Islamic doctrines.[44]

Violent clashes erupted between Kurdish groups and Iranian government forces during the spring and summer of 1979. In August 1979 Khomeini designated the campaign to suppress the Kurdish revolt a religious obligation, banned all Kurdish political organizations, and denounced Ghassemlou and Husayni as enemies of the Islamic republic. After widespread fighting in the Kurdish region, the government called in November 1979 for a cease-fire and negotiations. Shaykh Husayni again put forth the Kurdish demands for autonomy, but the negotiations collapsed when the government responded with offers of limited cultural autonomy.

The outbreak of the Iran-Iraq war in September 1980 permitted both states – in a centuries-old pattern – to divide the Kurds among themselves and then crush any resistance while simultaneously waging their war with each other in Kurdistan itself. In 1981 Ghassemlou allied the K.D.P.I. with the National Resistance Council, which from its headquarters in Paris conducted anti-Iranian military campaigns from bases in Iraq provided by Saddam Hussein. The alliance ended in 1984, and Ghassemlou never lent much support to the Iraqi campaign against Iran. Iran, on the other hand, had much greater success in convincing the Iraqi Kurdish leader Mas'ud Barzani and Iranian Shi'i Kurds to aid government forces in suppressing the K.D.P.I.-led insurgency. In July 1989, while negotiating in Vienna yet another cease-fire with Iranian government representatives, Ghassemlou was assassinated, presumably by Iranian agents. The K.D.P.I. leadership today continues to oppose the Iranian government from exile and still espouses Kurdish autonomy, not independence.

## Conclusion

Since the turn of the twentieth century, Muslims have invoked the right of self-determination with as much fervor as any other people. They have also shared with other peoples the complex, sometimes intractable problems immediately arising from this principle. As should be evident from the foregoing analysis, claims of self-determination and secession in the Muslim world create problems unique to Islam. These problems stem from what has been called here "core" Islamic ethical principles elucidated in the Qur'an and the sunna. These principles provided the basis for endless interpretation and disputes among medieval political theorists. While many aspects of the classical theory are today anachronistic and in disuse, the theory's general approach to issues of Islamic political community still seems very much relevant to and influential in shaping present Muslim attitudes. One manifestation of this continuing influence is the strong Muslim resistance to the further political fragmentation of the "Muslim world."

What then can be said in conclusion about the possible contributions of Islamic thought to the ongoing debate on self-determination and secession? The following points represent one approach to this issue based on my own understanding of Islamic ethical requirements.

First, political community is defined according to religious profession, not tribe, ethnicity, or race. These latter categories are explicitly devalued by the Qur'an and sunna as sources of moral value. Because Islam incorporates politics into its moral vision, political communities based *solely* on tribal, ethnic, or racial appeals are deemed illegitimate. Non-Muslim minorities residing within a Muslim polity enjoy a broad sphere of communal autonomy in areas relating to their communal life. Such autonomy at the "national" level cannot be construed in ways detracting from their equal civil and political rights with the Muslim majority.

Second, the possibility of political communities based *partially* on ethnic or tribal loyalties is not foreclosed. Neither the Qur'an nor the Prophet attempted to overturn entirely the tribal system in which Islam emerged. The Qur'an describes human subdivisions as God's will, and the Prophet did not condemn tribal identities or attempt to eliminate tribal leadership. The Qur'an and sunna, in short, do not uphold a monolithic, antipluralistic conception of political community. At most, they establish the imperative of communal solidarity as the ultimate goal of Islamic political life. But this goal is not solidarity for solidarity's sake, as some medieval theoreticians interpreted it. Such an approach would negate the Qur'an's attack on the parochial mores of pre-Islamic Arab society which valued the tribe, right or wrong, for the tribe's sake. Rather, Muslim solidarity is essentially a *means* to further Islamic goals of peace, social justice, and individual welfare. For medieval theorists taking the Prophet and the earliest Muslim community as precedents, these goals required political unity under a single imam. They held to such a conception as the ideal long after it had ceased to exist in reality. The ideal is still alive today, as readily evinced in the continuing controversy over the Islamic legitimacy of nationalism and the territorial state. In my view, nationalism represents merely one modern manifestation of the particularistic human mind-set that Islam consistently challenges, and the sovereign territorial state represents a direct assault upon Islam's vision of a universal moral-political community. This is not to suggest that Islam calls for the overthrow of the current state system, only that states be seen as endowed with a derivative, functional legitimacy. States are merely the instruments for the realization of the welfare of the Muslim community as a whole. When they cease to promote that broad goal, as modern Muslim states have often done, and when they become obstacles to it, as modern Muslim states so often are, it is the duty of Muslims to seek alternative political arrangements.

The last point leads directly to the issue of secession. It is clear that the medieval theorists outlawed all rebellion against the imam – regardless of how he might come to power – unless he were to commit egregious violations of the shari'a. In that case revolution became not only a right, but a duty. Secession, or the complete renunciation of the community and the establishment of an independent state, was never held to be a legitimate option. An important aspect of the medieval law on rebellion as it relates to the modern debate is that ethnic or tribal self-determination is not a legitimate reason (ta'wil) for challenging the imam.

The Qur'an provides explicit guidelines for resolving intra-Muslim disputes:

> If two parties of the believers fall into quarrel, make peace between them; but if one of them transgresses beyond bounds against the other, then fight all of you together against the one that transgresses until it complies with the command of God. But if it complies, then make peace between them with justice, and be fair. For God loves those who are fair. (49:9)

The Muslim collectivity in its entirety is the subject of this verse. It has a clear right to intervene in disputes involving two or more Muslim parties. The goal of the intervention is reconciliation and the return of the disputing parties into the collectivity. If reconciliation fails, the collectivity is to fight against the party that has transgressed beyond the moral limits prescribed for Muslims. In other words, collective action is justified solely on the basis of the means employed by the transgressing party, not the merits of either party's case. If the transgressing party is the state oppressing its own people, as was the case in the genocidal campaigns waged by Pakistan and Iraq against the Bengalis and the Kurds respectively, an obligation of collective intervention exists in order to relieve the suffering of the people. If the regime desists from its oppression, then the obligation of the Muslim community is to seek reconciliation. Secession does not emerge anywhere in this scenario as a legitimate option, since it is seen as the complete failure of politics and collective intervention. It is noteworthy in this regard that both Bangladesh and Iraqi Kurdistan emerged in the face of strong Muslim opposition and after non-Muslim intervention that only compounded the Muslim resistance.

Ultimately, the issue of self-determination and secession resolves itself into the issue of democracy and human rights, in Islam as it does in other theoretical contexts. Unfortunately, it is in this very area that Islamic political theory has proven the most stagnant and opposed to Islamic ethical requirements. In their quest for political stability and conformity to the law, the medieval jurists subordinated the values of social justice and welfare. European colonialism disseminated democratic ideals in the Muslim world but did little to implement them. Muslim attempts to institute representative government have thus been fraught with insuperable obstacles originating from both inside and outside the Islamic tradition.

Islamic tradition may make the institution of liberal parliamentary democracy in the Western mold difficult, but there is certainly nothing within this tradition that forecloses representative government and the enforcement of human rights. Many Muslim advocates of democracy have long pointed out that the Qur'an itself describes the Muslims as those "who conduct their affairs by mutual consultation (*shura bainahum*)" (42:38), not as medieval theory would have it by the imam consulting his top advisors, nor as modern dictators would have it, with an autocratic regime dispensing largesse to its people. If Muslims are to continue to reject secession as a legitimate option under Islamic ethics, as I have done, then they must work assiduously for the realization of the full ethical context in which such a ban emerges. The Bengali and Kurdish secessions acquired legitimacy – limited though it was among Muslims – not just because of the violent means used to suppress them, but because of the long record of economic and political discrimination that both groups faced under successive authoritarian regimes. If Muslim politics continue to be conducted by means other than "mutual consultation" among all the constituent members of a political community, Muslims must be prepared to face other demands for self-determination and secession.

## Notes

1. Ibn Ishaq, *The Life of Muhammad*, trans. Alfred Guillaume (Karachi: Oxford University Press, 1967), 234–35.
2. Ibn Ishaq, *Life of Muhammad*, 231–33.

3. Narrated by Abu Da'wud, Tirmidhi, and Ibn Maja. See John Alden Williams, (ed.), *Themes of Islamic Civilization* (Berkeley: Uni-versity of California Press, 1971), 9.
4. Narrated by Muslim. See Williams, *Themes of Islamic Civilization*, 17.
5. Narrated by Bukhari. See Williams, *Themes of Islamic Civilization*, 10.
6. Ann K. S. Lambton, *State and Government in Medieval Islam* (Oxford: Oxford University Press, 1991), 229.
7. See Fred M. Donner, *The Early Islamic Conquests* (Princeton: Princeton University Press, 1981), 82–90.
8. See *Encyclopaedia of Islam*, 2nd ed., s.v. "Kharidjites."
9. Narrated by Muslim. See Williams, *Themes of Islamic Civilization*, 66.
10. Williams, *Themes of Islamic Civilization*, 31–32.
11. An analysis and critique of the medieval theory is available in Abdullahi Ahmed an-Na'im, *Toward an Islamic Reformation: Civil Liberties, Human Rights, and International Law* (Syracuse: Syracuse University Press, 1990), 86–87, 183–85; and Muhammad Salim al-Awa, *Punishment in Islamic Law: A Comparative Study* (Indian-apolis: American Trust Publications, 1982), 49–58, 61–64.
12. See Fazlur Rahman, "The Law of Rebellion in Islam" in Jill Raitt (ed.) *Islam in the Modern World*, (Columbia, Mo: University of Missouri, 1983), 1–2.
13. See Abdullahi Ahmed an-Na'im, "The Islamic Law of Apostasy and its Modern Applicability: A Case from the Sudan," *Religion* 16 (1986): 197–224.
14. Khaled Abou El Fadl, "*Ahkam al-Bughat*: Irregular Warfare and the Law of Rebellion in Islam'" in James Turner Johnson and John Kelsay (eds) *Cross, Crescent, and Sword: The Justification and Limitation of War in Western and Islamic Tradition*, (New York: Green-wood Press, 1990), 153.
15. Abou El Fadl, "Ahkam al-Bughat," 159.
16. Abou El Fadl, "Ahkam al-Bughat," 158–59.
17. Muhammad ibn al-Hasan al-Shaybani, *The Islamic Law of Nations: Shaybani's Siyar*, trans. Majid Khadduri (Baltimore: Johns Hopkins Press, 1966), 233.
18. Williams, *Themes of Islamic Civilization*, 86.
19. Cited in Lambton, *State and Government*, 101.
20. Lambton, *State and Government*, 114.
21. Lambton, *State and Government*, 140.
22. Williams, *Themes of Islamic Civilization*, 91.
23. Lambton, *State and Government*, 146.

24. Ibn Khaldun, *The Muqadimmah: An Introduction to History*, trans. Franz Rosenthal (New York: Pantheon Books, 1958), 1: 393.

25. Ibn Khaldun, *Muqadimmah*, 1: 332.

26. Ibn Khaldun, *Muqadimmah*, 1: 333.

27. Ibn Khaldun, *Muqadimmah*, 1: 414ff.

28. *Encyclopaedia of Islam*, 2nd. ed., s.v. "Millet."

29. Rashid Rida, "Patriotism, Nationalism, and Group Spirit in Islam," in John J. Donohue and John L. Esposito (eds), *Islam in Trans-ition: Muslim Perspectives* (Oxford: Oxford University Press, 1982), 57–59.

30. 'Abdallah al-Ahsan, *O.I.C.: The Organization of the Islamic Conference* (Herndon, V.A.: International Institute of Islamic Thought, 1988), 77–78.

31. Kalim Bahadur, *The Jama'at-i Islami of Pakistan* (New Delhi: Chetana Publications, 1977), 130.

32. See Seyyed Vali Reza Nasr, *The Vanguard of the Islamic Revolution: The Jama'at-i Islami of Pakistan* (Berkeley: University of California Press, 1994), 166–167.

33. Nasr, *Vanguard of Islamic Revolution*, 168.

34. Bahadur, *Jama'at-i Islami*, 133.

35. Nasr, *Vanguard of Islamic Revolution*, 169.

36. Maududi presents his own detailed account of the history and causes of the Bangladeshi secession in a pamphlet published by the Muslim Brotherhood in Cairo as a means of warning other Muslim countries of the dangers of political fragmentation. See Abu'l-A'la al-Maududi, *Nahnu wa banghladish* [*We and Bangladesh*], trans. Khalil Ahmad al-Hamadi (Cairo: Dar al-Ansar, 1977).

37. Ferhad R. Izady, *The Kurds: A Concise Handbook* (Washington, D.C.: Taylor and Francis, 1992), 135.

38. Izady, *Kurds: Concise Handbook*, 52.

39. David McDowall, "The Kurdish Question: A Historical Overview" in Philip G. Kreyenbroek and Stefen Sperl (eds), *The Kurds: A Contemporary Overview* (London: Routledge, 1992), 19.

40. See Izady, *Kurds: Concise Handbook*, 197–220, and Kreyenbroek and Sperl (eds), *Kurds: Contemporary Overview*.

41. Kanan Makiya, "The Anfal: Uncovering and Iraqi Campaign to Exterminate the Kurds," *Harper's*, May 1992, p. 61.

42. *New York Times*, 15 November 1992, p. A9.

43. See Micheal M. Gunter, "A de facto Kurdish State in Northern Iraq," *Third World Quarterly*, 14 (1993)2: 309–11.

44. Cited in Fereshteh Koohi-Kamali, "The Development of Nationalism in Iranian Kurdistan," in Kreyenbroek and Sperl (eds), *Kurds: Contemporary Overview*, 190.

# – 7 –

# Self-Determination as Ethnocracy: Perspectives from the South Pacific

## Stephanie Lawson

### Introduction

It is now a commonplace that ethnicity, in its ideological manifestation as a species of nationalism, has played a crucial role in most of the contemporary armed conflicts and in a great many less violent political struggles around the world. Figures on contemporary conflicts vary, but one important aspect of them is constant. They all point to a preponderance of "internal" conflict[1] – that is, conflicts taking place within the borders of an existing state or at least what was a state. In many such cases, conflicts seem to involve a struggle by an ethnically defined group to exercise the right of self-determination in order to gain either greater autonomy within an existing state or complete independence in the form of a new state. Conflicts of this kind have erupted in parts of the former U.S.S.R. and in ex-Yugoslavia, where numerous (apparently) ethnically driven armed clashes have devastated the lives of hundreds of thousands. The proliferation of conflicts, most would agree, has occurred partly in response to the disintegration of repressive regimes in the former Communist world, and it therefore seems reasonable to concur with John Keane's proposition that the virulent forms of nationalism thriving in these places are, in some sense, a toxic by-product of democratization.[2]

These problems are, however, scarcely confined to the former communist world or to the post-Cold War period. Indeed, most of the contemporary ethnically driven conflicts predate the end of the Cold War. David Brown notes that an "ethnic revival" has been evident at least since the 1960s, both in an increased incidence of ethnic conflict and in an increased awareness of the problem by social scientists.[3] Further evidence for the ubiquity of the phenomenon in this period is provided by the catalog of ethnic conflicts by Donald

Horowitz published in 1985. These range from secessionist warfare in Burma, Bangladesh, the Sudan, Nigeria, Iraq, and the Philippines to the "ethnoterrorism" of substate groups such as the Basques, the Corsicans, the Palestinians, the Tamils, and the Sikhs, and also include instances of continuing hostilities, ethnic rioting, or ethnic expulsions in Vietnam, Uganda, Northern Ireland, India, Malaysia, Zaire, Guyana, and many other countries.[4] A report in 1988 cited 111 instances of current armed conflict, of which 99 were classified as "internal conflicts" or "wars of state formation" involving issues of autonomy or secession.[5] Another study has identified 233 politicized communal groups as active during the period from 1945 to 1989, although not all of these have engaged in armed conflict. These include groups classified as ethnonationalist movements, militant sects, communal contenders, ethnoclasses, and indigenous peoples that have taken some sort of action in support of collective communal interests.[6]

The wide variety of types and locations of ethnic conflict is complemented by a range of strategies deployed by ethnic groups (or, perhaps more accurately, by their leaders) to secure their perceived needs and aspirations. Anthony Smith sets out six basic strategies that may be used by ethnic communities in polyethnic states to attain either recognition by the state of their political demands, which often include a measure of autonomy, or, in extremis, the formation of a new, completely independent territorial state in which they would enjoy a dominant status (and therefore "self-determination"). These strategies are: isolation, accommodation, communalism, autonomism, separatism, and irredentism. According to Smith, the first two are "defensive, solipsist stances" that were frequently resorted to in past eras but that have given way in contemporary times to the more aggressive and activist postures of the last four strategies. When linked to the powerful ideology of nationalism, these postures have produced a dynamic mobilization of identity that has contributed to the overall phenomenon of ethnic revival.[7] The principle of self-determination for all peoples, which has been described as the most vigorously promoted and widely accepted of contemporary international norms (despite its persistently vague and imprecise meaning),[8] has provided additional moral force to ethnonationalist claims.

The South Pacific region rarely makes international headlines, its problems being largely overshadowed by the enormity of disasters elsewhere. The region has, however, seen several outbreaks of violent conflict and one military coup during the past decade. Although the nature of these conflicts is admittedly complex, most of them have a distinctly ethnic dimension. One of the most obvious cases is Fiji, where much of the debate surrounding the military coup of 1987 and developments subsequent to it has been couched in terms of ethnic tensions between indigenous Fijians and Fiji Indians, and the political rights to which each of these groups is or is not entitled. In the still unresolved Bougainville crisis too, in which a violent secessionist struggle has been waged for over six years by a group of Bougain-villeans against the state of Papua New Guinea, ethnicity has been an important factor in the various arguments about political rights.

In places like Fiji and Papua New Guinea, political entities that were set up in connection with European colonization, usually in the form of centralized states, brought together people of very different ethnic or cultural backgrounds, often by very different processes. Papua New Guinea is a typical example of efforts, encouraged by the United Nations throughout the era of decolonization, to maximize the viability of a new unitary state rather than create boundaries based on ethnic or tribal ties.[9] Thus when Papua New Guinea became independent in 1975, approximately 750 language groups were integrated into the new state, including the 19 language groups of the North Solomons province (which is composed, geographically, of the islands of Bougainville and Buka plus a number of very small outliers). The indigenous population of Fiji at the time of colonization was also very diverse, although not to the same extent as Papua New Guinea's. Ethnic differences in Fiji's present "plural society" are however, usually resolved into those between indigenous Fijians and Fiji Indians, telescoping this diversity. The presence of Fiji Indians in the island group is due to the policy of the early British colonial administration, initiated in the late 1870s, to import cheap labor from India in order to build a strong plantation economy while at the same time protecting the "Fijian way of life" from the demands this kind of economy usually made on indigenous populations. By the time of independence in 1970 the population of Fiji Indians numbered just under half of the total population. There was no prospect of dividing territory between the two major ethnic groups. With the exception of the eastern island group and some of the other small adjacent islands, Fiji Indians and indigenous Fijians occupy more or less the same geographic space throughout the country.

There are many historical grievances associated with the legacy of colonialism, not just in Fiji and Papua New Guinea, but in most of the ex-colonial world, and the "ethnohistories" of postcolonial groups, especially those seeking greater autonomy, make much of these grievances. While doubtless there is often a case to be made for implementing programs designed to rectify inequities stemming from the colonial past, it should also be recognized that the collective social memory of some groups is sometimes fueled and fanned by political leaders who seek to gain advantage for themselves through purveying the kind of appealing nationalist rhetoric that flows so readily from recollections of past injustices – both real and imagined. There is also a point beyond which appeals to a historical reservoir of grievances offer little in the way of useful or practical guidance for the resolution of present problems. Furthermore, justice for one community may well be bought at the expense of injustice for another. More will be said about these matters shortly, as well as about the implications of ethnic or communal politics for democracy, but it is important first to explore briefly the meaning behind the words "ethnicity" and "nationalism," the significance of the hybrid term "ethnonationalism," and the problematic nature of the doctrine of self-determination and its manifestation as "ethnocracy."

## Ethnicity, Nationalism, and Ethnonationalism

Ethnicity is generally taken to denote a shared or common background with reference to certain "objective" factors such as language, religion, customs, social institutions, and so forth. Accordingly, ethnic conflict has been defined simply as "violent conflict between or among groups who differ from each other in terms of culture, religion, physical features, or language."[10] To be more explicit, it should be added that conflict is assumed to have erupted *because* of these differences. An important element in the construction of ethnicity is the idea of a common history, a shared body of tradition, which binds the group together. A corollary of this idea is the notion of common biological descent which is closely related to racialist thinking. In the logic of "descentism," the notion of biological inheritance is, further, often linked to political and social inheritance, "as if the latter follows, or ought to follow, inevitably or necessarily from the former."[11] In other words, the perception of common biological, social, and political bonds forges a sense of collective destiny on the basis of a collective past. It is often beside the point whether this past is real or invented as long as it serves its purpose in the present.

Another major element in the construction of ethnicity involves the twin ideas of inclusiveness and exclusiveness, for it makes no sense to speak of an ethnic group (or any other kind of group) unless it has an identity that distinguishes it from other groups. A cutoff point must be imposed at which others are excluded from membership. Ethnic identity is therefore both "self"-defining and "other"-defining, and ultimately it depends on demonstrating "difference." Manning Nash notes that the minimum-action aspect of ethnicity is the formal celebration of this difference, which may be nothing more than a national day of songs and costumes. At the opposite pole, however, the single-minded assertion of ethnic difference can overwhelm all other aspects of identity, resulting in the "total domination of social and cultural life."[12] To this should be added the total domination of political life as well, for wherever the salience of ethnic identity reaches the point where it subsumes all their forms of identity, a political program cannot be far behind. Taken to the extreme, such a program calls for self-determination through the establishment of an "ethnocratic state."

It follows that the question of ethnicity is hardly unproblematic, especially when vital issues of identity are at stake. This is one of the reasons why debates about culture, custom, and tradition, and the implications these have for identity are so prominent in the contemporary South Pacific region, particularly in relation to political authority and legitimacy.[13] It should also be noted that debates concerning the latter two concepts are taking place not only in ethnically heterogeneous countries such as Fiji and Papua New Guinea, but in more homogeneous countries as well. In Tonga, for example, the prodemocracy movement is challenging a political elite consisting of a monarchy and an aristocracy whose power and privilege are inextricably tied in with tradition and identity. The movement has the task of confronting a body of tradition that is held up as uniquely Tongan, as something that purportedly distinguishes the identity of Tongans from that of others, and that is embodied in the elite strata of society. The preservation of the status quo by Tonga's elite therefore rests on the assertion of a nationalistic identity vis-à-vis external "others."[14] A similar process has been at work in Fiji, where "Fijian tradition," which is closely connected to the chiefly elite, has been invoked by Fijian political leaders against a generalized conception of the West (especially Western democracy) and against the community of Fiji Indian citizens.

These brief illustrations suggest that the symbolic content of a community's culture, traditions, and ethnic identity can be manipulated instrumentally to serve a variety of political purposes – a proposition that is directly at odds with those analyses of ethnicity favoring the primordialist perspective. The position taken here is one that accords broadly with that put forward by Ted Robert Gurr – namely, that ethnically defined communal groups are not simply "primordial social entities based on biological, cultural, linguistic, and religious givens" and that the states that govern them are not "inherently artificial entities." Rather, Gurr proposes that all collective identities are to some extent situational and transitional, being shaped by complex forces and conditions.[15] On the other hand, he argues that the pure instrumentalist position "is a poor characterization of ethnonationalists who are fighting civil wars in Third World countries, or of defenders of indigenous rights of the First World."[16] The analysis here will seek to identify – and criticize – the instrumentalist aspects of ethnicity that are clearly evident in each of the cases. This should not, however, be taken to imply that all political expressions of ethnic identity and ethnically based movements for self-determination are driven simply by crude instrumental motives or that their causes are inherently selfish or unjust.[17]

Nationalism, like ethnicity, draws on a range of ideas and sentiments associated with cultural values, traditions, and practices. By itself, the English meaning of the term "nation" properly refers to "a people," which is usually defined in terms of more or less the same "objective" factors (outlined above) that generally attach to the contemporary understanding of *ethnos*.[18] In contemporary political/legal usage, however, nation is often equated with state – hence the ambiguous term "nation-state." The confusion is further exacerbated by some analyses of sovereignty in international politics. J. Samuel Barkin and Bruce Cronin, for example, point out that the idea of sovereignty in international relations has been associated with two conceptually separate entities. First, they say, it has been ascribed to states, which are defined as "the territories over which institutional authorities exercise legitimate control." Second, it has been ascribed to nations which are defined as "communities of sentiment" forming the political basis on which state authority rests.[19] If in all cases, a clearly discernible nation (understood as a people) fit neatly into the geographical borders of the state, there would be fewer conceptual and practical problems. These issues could be fruitfully discussed at greater length. For present purposes, however, suffice it to say that nation and state are not one and the same thing but that the normative desire to make them commensurate is a driving force behind contemporary forms of nationalism that take the ethnocratic state as the most desirable form of political community.[20]

As a product of the modern state system, the ideology of national*ism* links the nation or *ethnos* to a particular territory over which it is, by virtue of this link, the legitimate claimant to territorial sovereignty. In other words, the modern ideology of nationalism provides the essential basis for the normative claim that a particular geographic space is inextricably tied to a particular people or *ethnos and* that this space and the people inhabiting it should form a sovereign political unit. Again, the normative claims that are made by a group to a given geographic space are based on the idea that the members of the group possess a common heritage that is theirs and theirs alone. Clearly, these ideas operate not only to bind the group together with a sense of common interest and purpose but also to exclude "others" from a legitimate share of the territory in question – and of its resources. It follows that those outside the group who, for whatever reason, find themselves physically occupying part of the same geopolitical space may be regarded as "nonindigenous" or "alien" and treated as "guests," "immigrants," "refugees," and so forth.

The term "ethnonationalism" is best understood as an ideology that is grounded in the entire complex of ideas and concepts associated with ethnic identity and the modern territorial and political aspects of nationalism and sovereignty. It has been defined parsimoniously as "the sentiment of an ethnic minority living in a state (or living across state boundaries) that propels the group to unify and identify itself as having the capacity for self-government."[21] Self-government, of course, implies self-determination, which in turn is linked to the idea of sovereignty. But the question of the locus of sovereignty in relation to ethnonationalism is not a straightforward matter, and it will be helpful to digress briefly here to explain some of the various understandings of it. First, there is the territorial aspect of sovereignty – that is, the physical geographic realm over which sovereignty is exercised by the government of a state. The territorial aspect also defines the external dimension of sovereignty by which a state is identified vis-à-vis other states and through which the right to self-determination by a state excludes noninterference by external forces. Second, there is the question of "internal sovereignty," which concerns "who" is sovereign within the state. Democratic theories of self-determination, which deal largely with what goes on within the borders of a state (that is, the internal aspect),[22] posit "the people" as the legitimate source of sovereignty and conceptualize rightful political power as ascending from the body of citizens to empower those who, from one election to another, are granted temporary and conditional office as the government.[23] The democratic conception of the people is essentially pluralistic and inclusive in that it assumes, and in fact demands, recognition of the inherent political equality of each and every citizen regardless of his or her religious, linguistic, racial, occupational, or other kind of identity. The pluralistic and inclusionary conception of the people who are entitled to self-determination in democratic theory therefore stands in contrast to the (ethno)nationalist idea of "a people," by which is understood a singularity and separateness defined in terms of the *ethnos*.[24] It follows that the right to self-determination of a people, based as it is on the limiting and exclusionary notions outlined above, gives rise to ethnocracy rather than democracy. In sum, the distinction between the two notions of a "people" can be expressed as two distinct conceptual components of self-determination – the universalist and the nationalist. It has been suggested that the first component is satisfied wherever government is founded on demo-cratic, majoritarian principles. The second requires that government institutions be identified with a particular "community," a formulation that remains "quite disreputable in theory"[25] and with good reason.

The mix of ideas that constitutes ethnonationalism is a very volatile and, potentially, an exceptionally nasty one. This is especially so when biological descent is taken as a key element in the construction of contending identities. It is not necessary to look back very far in the twentieth century, to find its most hideous expression in the policies of Nazi Germany. The remains of extermination camps today stand as stark reminders of the supreme effort at ethnic cleansing embarked on during World War II. Yet, neofascists in France and Germany have been pressing for the expulsion of "others" who do not meet the cultural and biological criteria for authentic membership in the European political community. And in ex-Yugoslavia the effects of contemporary ethnic cleansing have been presented graphically every day in media reports. In these cases, the justification for the measures taken are ultimately grounded in the idea that a people rightfully belongs in one geographical space or another and that others do not. Put another way, the logic of ethnonationalism can operate not only to claim a particular space as one's own inalienable birthright, but also to deny a legitimate place within the same political-geographic space to those who are considered undesirable from a cultural-biological point of view.

The examples mentioned above make it seem an easy intellectual task to condemn the ideology of ethnonationalism and all that it stands for. But ethnonationalism is a more difficult phenomenon to deal with on an ethical level because it sometimes involves laudable principles relating to self-determination that are linked to indigenous rights. The latter rights are especially important to those belonging to the so-called Fourth World – the descendants of the people who first inhabited Australia, New Zealand, New Caledonia, North America, and South America and who are now grossly outnumbered by later European arrivals. In these cases, the concept of indigenous rights is closely associated with general principles of human rights, social justice, and attempts to provide a redress for past wrongs. Precisely how these problems should be treated is another question and beyond the scope of this discussion. The point that needs to be stressed is that when it comes to the Fourth World some of the principles that are brought forward in the exercise of self-determination are similar to those on which ethnonationalists almost everywhere stake their claims. On a general level, these involve a historical claim to a particular geographic space by a community defined in cultural-biological terms. The cases of both Fiji and Bougainville, which will now be examined more closely, bear out this similarity.

## The Case of Bougainville

Papua New Guinea has a population of some 3.5 million that is characterized by exceptional cultural diversity.[26] This diversity is best exemplified (although not exclusively so) by the fact that there are approximately 750 different languages spoken throughout the country, many of which are mutually incomprehensible. Each of the groups represented by these languages may plausibly argue that they have distinctive customs and practices that distinguish them "ethnically" from other groups around them. At the time of independence in 1975, a form of federalism was adopted in which the North Solomons (hereinafter referred to as Bougainville) became one of nineteen provinces. The system was meant to ease the difficulties of "nation-building" in a new state where attachments were – and remain – overwhelmingly local and particularistic. Separatist aspirations, however, continue to flourish in many parts of the country despite efforts to decentralize a range of governmental functions in order to satisfy calls for greater autonomy among local or regional groups. Apart from Bougainville, there have been separatist movements in Papua, the Gazelle Peninsula, and the Trobriand Islands. In each instance, some kind of distinctive ethnic identity has been emphasized, not without stereotyping on racial or other grounds.

Fundamental to a number of separatist claims have been issues concerning mineral resources, their exploitation, and the division of returns between landowners, provincial governments, the national government, mining companies, and investors. In this respect, Bougainville, with its enormous copper mine, is not unique. What does make Bougainville a special case is its remote location at the far eastern boundary of Papua New Guinea's territory, a circumstance of physical geography that gave the prospect of secession more feasibility than it would other provinces or regions.

The Bougainvillean secessionist crisis began in 1987 when a dispute erupted over compensation claims put forward by some of the landowners from the Panguna mine area in the southeastern region of Bougainville island. The failure of negotiations led to an initial campaign of sabotage by a number of younger and more radical landowners led by Francis Ona, who had formed a breakaway group in opposition to the traditional landowners' association. By 1989, the Bougainville Revolutionary Army (B.R.A.) was engaging in more extensive violence and advocating complete secession.[27]

In their quest for secession, the leaders and supporters of the B.R.A. also employed a strong line of argument based on ethnic differences. Although this was clearly not the only ground put forward, it became a prominent issue in the first few years of the secessionist war. In a letter published in the *Times of Papua New Guinea* in September 1989, Ona claimed that "our diverse customs will not let us live peacefully together as Papua New Guineans." Another of Ona's letters was signed "Mi, Father of Nation" (referring to himself as "father" of the "Bougainville nation"). Some of the most explicit ethnonationalist claims made by Ona appeared in his Declaration of Independence: Republic of Bougainville.

AND WHEREAS Bougainville is geographically apart and its people culturally distinct from Papua New Guinea. . . .

AND WHEREAS it has been a long standing wish and aspiration of the people of Bougainville to become a separate independent nation. . . .

AND WHEREAS it is the inalienable right of a people to be free and independent. . . .[28]

At a general level, this declaration invoked a number of normative ideals associated with the doctrine of self-determination.[29] These were underscored by recounting historical grievances both with respect to the incorporation of the North Solomons province in the state of Papua New Guinea at the time of independence and in relation to the copper mine at Panguna. Other grievances included inequitable treatment as compared with other provinces and what was perceived as poor returns from the proceeds of the mine. In the earlier stages of the crisis, Bougainvillean secessionists could also point to appalling abuses of human rights on the part of some members of the Papua New Guinea Defence Forces (P.N.G.D.F.) – abuses that seemed to strengthen the justification for secession.

Naturally, there were arguments on the other side too. For example, Bougainvilleans enjoyed a relatively high per capita income (before the crisis started), which indicated more – rather than less – favored treatment.[30] A detailed examination of the initial outbreak of unrest also shows that the troubles over the mine started as a dispute within the landowners association rather than between the landowners and the national government or the mining company, let alone between the province as a whole and the state of Papua New Guinea.[31] With respect to human rights abuses, it is also clear now that the B.R.A. turned on those fellow Bougainvilleans who did not support their cause and engaged in torture, beatings, and executions of them. In addition to detailing reports of abuses by members of the P.N.G.D.F., a report by Amnesty International released in November 1993 cited considerable evidence of similar abuses of Bougainvilleans by the B.R.A. itself:

> Serious human rights abuses by B.R.A. members have continued to be reported throughout the period from 1990 to 1993. They have included the deliberate and arbitrary killing of civilians, torture, rape and other forms of sexual abuse, and hostage-taking. The majority of victims have been people accused of being "spies" for the P.N.G.D.F., or of having betrayed the secessionist movement by negotiating with members of the central government. Residents of Bougainville have reported that after the withdrawal of P.N.G. troops in March 1990, armed B.R.A. members created a general atmosphere of fear and apprehension among the population. . . . Allegations of arbitrary killings, torture, beatings and harassment have continued since then.[32]

After the initial outbreak of violence, arguments advanced by the secessionists about inequitable treatment and environmental damage from the mine came to be overshadowed by the assertion of apparent ethnic differences between the people of Bougainville and the rest of the population of Papua New Guinea. One of the most common distinctions drawn between the two groups is the relative darkness of their skins. Bougainvilleans refer to themselves as "blackskins" and to mainlanders as "redskins" and vice-versa. Concern was expressed by some Bougainvilleans that the blood of their people had been "polluted" by redskins from other parts of Papua New Guinea who had settled on the island. In other words, part of the debate was reduced to establishing credentials on the basis of certain biological characteristics. In addition, the drawing of battlelines between "blackskins" and "redskins" detracted seriously from the importance of the original issues. As mentioned above, these concern resource development and the equitable distribution of the benefits that flow from such development, as well as the impact of environmental degradation and the implications this has for landowning communities. It should be emphasized again that these are problems that must be faced throughout Papua New Guinea and not just in Bougainville.

What has been said so far clearly favors maintaining the status quo as opposed to self-determination (in the form of secession) for

Bougainville. By implication, it favors retention of boundaries drawn by colonial powers with little regard for local identities and affiliations. While there may be many historical injustices associated with these boundaries and all that they imply, redrawing the boundaries now is unlikely to produce greater justice in the future. Although there is little prospect that the B.R.A. will succeed in its quest for secession, it is worth considering briefly the implications of such an outcome. First, the establishment of a new independent sovereign state would almost certainly have produced new injustices, created new minorities, and failed to solve problems of resource management and distribution, or of environmental degradation. Given that the indigenous people of Bougainville do not constitute a single, homogeneous, cultural or ethnic community, the scope for conflict between different groups would have remained. The eighteen or so different language groups that live in the province might well form the basis for new ethnic differences and claims. Second, resource exploitation and the distribution of benefits from this would almost certainly become an issue around which new inequities and conflicts would develop and become tied in with questions of ethnic identity within Bougainville. These assertions are speculative but, given the history of conflict involving such issues, they do not amount to a far-fetched scenario.

Finally, it seems that whatever support the B.R.A. and its quest for independence enjoyed in the early period of the crisis, this has declined significantly. While the behavior of the P.N.G.D.F. toward the local population has improved considerably since 1990, that of the B.R.A. seems to have become increasingly destructive. The following extract from a report by a visiting delegation of Australian parliamentarians illustrates the apparent turn of sympathies.

> The Delegation was informed, from a number of sources, that the strength of the B.R.A. had dissipated considerably from its high point of popular support in 1989–1990. Then, the longstanding sympathy of Bougainvilleans for secession and resentments over the high-handed reactions to compensation claims combined with the abusive and ill-disciplined behavior of some of the P.N.G.D.F. to ensure what some observers claimed to be a possible eighty percent support for the B.R.A.. Certainly many people the Delegation spoke to in the care centres openly stated that they were former members or supporters of the B.R.A.. All these people told a similar tale of disillusionment with a movement that was increasingly violent, unpredictable and dictatorial. They talked of increasingly primitive conditions and of political leaders who seemed to be making a virtue of this necessity. The B.R.A. philosophy, many said, had moved from claims to self-determination and independent statehood to an anti-Western, anti-

development and anti-intellectual attitude. It manifested itself in the turning back of the relief ship, Sankamap, the burning of the hospital and high school of Arawa and the shooting of intellectuals such as Tony Anugu.[33]

Nothing that has been said here excuses the behavior of some members of the P.N.G.D.F. or its record throughout the earlier years of the crisis, which was clearly abysmal. That record remains far short of exemplary. International condemnation of the P.N.G.D.F.'s activities and the government that is purported to be responsible for these forces is fully deserved. The behavior of the P.N.G.D.F., however, probably had a great deal more to do with the national government's limited capacity to control it than with a deliberate intent on the part of the government to perpetrate atrocities. But again, this does not excuse the government, nor does it make the government immune from external criticism for its handling of the crisis.

## The Case of Fiji

Ethnonationalism and racialism have also flourished under the banner of indigenous rights in Fiji.[34] More specifically, the idea of "Fiji for the Fijians" has been used to exclude nearly half the population from a meaningful share of political power and from equitable employment and educational opportunities. After Papua New Guinea, Fiji is the largest of the South Pacific island states. It comprises approximately 320 islands, of which Viti Levu and Vanua Levu form the largest land masses. The population of Fiji consists of about 720,000 people. Just over half of this number are indigenous Fijians, and Fiji Indians make up about 44 percent of the total. Small numbers of Europeans, part-Europeans, Chinese, and other Pacific Islanders (who for electoral and other legal purposes are called "General Voters") account for most of the remainder. Fiji became an independent state in 1970, at which time a constitution was adopted guaranteeing equal parliamentary representation (in the lower chamber) to indigenous Fijians and Fiji Indians. Indigenous Fijians effectively controlled the upper chamber, which had important veto rights over legislation affecting their interests. Other minority groups were also guaranteed a certain level of representation under a complex system of communal voting and representation.

A modified form of responsible government had been introduced in the 1960s, and elections in this period saw the rise to dominance of the Alliance Party. The leading figure in the party was Ratu Sir

Kamisese Mara, a high-ranking Fijian chief from the eastern region of the island group, a region from which most of Fiji's influential chiefs have been drawn since the earliest years of colonial rule. Mara became prime minister at the time of independence, thus heading the Alliance-controlled government, which remained in power under his leadership for the next seventeen years. The Alliance was defeated in the general elections of March–April 1987 by a coalition composed of the Fiji Labor Party (a multiracial party led by another indigenous Fijian, Dr. Timoci Bavadra), and the National Federation Party (a predominantly Fiji Indian party).

The election of the Bavadra government represented a significant break with a long tradition of eastern chiefly predominance in politics. As noted earlier, the idea of "Fijian tradition" is a primary element in the construction of Fijian ethnic identity, and it is tied very closely to the chiefly elite. The defeat of the Alliance was portrayed as undermining the very basis of Fijian tradition and therefore the identity and political status of Fijians themselves. It also meant that for the first time in Fiji's political history, Fiji Indians had a relatively significant voice in government, a factor that was seized on by antigovernment forces in the period immediately after the elections. A coup was staged less than six weeks after the new government assumed office. It was led by the then third-ranking member of the Royal Fiji Military Forces, Lieutenant-Colonel Sitiveni Rabuka (now prime minister).

Rabuka's intervention was largely explained as having been necessary to ensure the protection of indigenous rights, especially those relating to indigenous Fijian land ownership. Although many academic writers on the subject have pointed out that existing indigenous rights were fully protected via triple entrenchment in the constitution of 1970, and that the new government could not have interfered with these rights even if it had been so inclined, this basic point has been poorly understood. Certainly, most ordinary Fijians were unaware of the extent to which their lands were protected under the constitution of 1970. This is due partly to the circumstance that this constitution had never been translated into the Fijian language. Most important, it is testimony to the power of the ethnonationalist rhetoric propagated by Rabuka and many members of the Fijian establishment, especially those indigenous chiefs who had everything to gain by the staging of the coup. These included the president (and former governor-general), Ratu Sir Penaia Ganilau, as well as Mara and a number of other high-ranking eastern chiefs. Indeed, virtually every election campaign that had been held in Fiji since independence – that is, from 1972 to 1987 – featured ethnonationalist rhetoric purveyed by politicians intent on maintaining their based ethnic support. It should be added that many Fiji Indian politicians were not immune from using similar tactics when it suited their purpose.

Some of the more extreme Fijian nationalists had, in earlier periods, called for the "repatriation" (to India) of the Fiji Indian population in keeping with the slogan "Fiji for the Fijians." Similar calls were made in the wake of the coup by the nationalistic Taukei movement, a group formed immediately after the 1987 elections with the declared purpose of destabilizing the new government. For the vast majority of the Fiji Indian community, however, India is not their country, and they are citizens of Fiji by birth. Nor can Fijians claim a privileged position as the sole victims of enforced colonization and British colonial rule. Apart from the fact that British colonization was virtually invited by a number of leading (eastern-based) chiefs, most of the ancestors of the present population of Fiji Indians can also be depicted as victims because they were brought to the colony under the iniquitous indenture scheme instituted by Fiji's first substantive British governor. One irony of this is that, as mentioned earlier, the use of Indian labor rather than Fijian labor on the plantations in Fiji was part of a conscious paternalistic policy on the part of the colonial administration to preserve "the Fijian way of life." It was to protect Fijians from the social disintegration that so often followed when indigenous people were moved from their traditional villages to work for wages, while at the same time establishing a viable economic base for the colony through the use of alternative labor. The legacy of that policy remains today, not simply in an ethnically plural society, but in one with a relatively strong economy in which Fiji Indians have played a significant role.

To return to the question of ethnonationalism, it should be pointed out that some of the rhetoric used and the type of misinformation disseminated by Fijian nationalists during election campaigns and at other appropriate times was clearly designed to maintain a political division between indigenous Fijians and Fiji Indians. Given the security of indigenous rights afforded by the constitution of 1970, rhetoric implying that loss of land would inevitably follow loss of government office by the Fijian-dominated party was quite obviously politically motivated. It was also very successful. The result in Fiji has been the promulgation of a constitution that effectively enshrines a form of political apartheid by excluding some 46 percent of the population from a meaningful share of political power. But those who miss out on all the benefits associated with being an "authentic" indigenous Fijian are not just people of Indian ancestry. Also excluded are the small minorities that comprised "other races." These include part-Europeans (and part-Fijians) as well as the descendants of other

Pacific Islanders who previously enjoyed full citizenship rights. The composition of the House of Representatives under the Constitution of the Sovereign Democratic Republic of Fiji adopted in 1990 says it simply enough. Of a total of seventy seats, thirty-seven are allotted to Fijians; twenty-seven to Fiji Indians; five to general voters (other races); and one to Rotumans.

Although promises have been made from time to time by the current government to hold talks on constitutional reform with a view to restoring meaningful political rights of participation to non-indigenous Fiji citizens, it will be difficult to reverse the trend toward ethnic chauvinism, which was given an enormous boost by the coup in 1987. Nor is it certain that Prime Minister Rabuka's professed concern about restoring some of these rights is genuine. He was, after all, the leader of the military coup and one of the foremost proponents of a political position of paramountcy for indigenous Fijians.

## Conclusion

In the two cases described above, both indigenous rights and the doctrine of self-determination have been used in ways that are clearly incompatible with some of the basic principles of human rights and democratic government.[35] Indeed, they have been exploited to justify a form of ethnocratic rule. As for Bougainville, it seems that from an initial dispute over control and allocation of resources and a resurrection of certain historical grievances over the incorporation of Bougainville into the state of Papua New Guinea, the secessionist leaders have gone on to try to strengthen their bid for self-determination through appeals to ethnic differences, in cultural forms and racial characteristics, between Bougainvilleans as a whole and the rest of Papua New Guinea's population. But the claim to "ethnic" self-determination is obviously no straightforward matter. Except for biological criteria such as skin color (and even this does not hold in all cases), there are no clear criteria for differentiating the people of Bougainville from the people of other regions of Papua New Guinea. Moreover, cultural diversity is as much a feature of Bougainville as it is of the entire country. The weight given to ethnic arguments in attempting to devise an ethical approach to the general question of self-determination must also be balanced by a critical regard for the kind of principles on which these arguments are based. These are essentially ethnonationalist principles and, to that extent, are based on some of the most impoverished of political norms. The history of the crisis in Bougainville and especially the increasingly radical behavior of the B.R.A. suggests further that references to ethnic differences between Bougainvilleans as a whole and the rest of Papua New Guinea and depictions of rediscovered indigenous rights in the form of self-determination for Bougainvilleans, have served a largely rhetorical and instrumental purpose in rallying initial support for the secessionist cause.

In the case of Fiji, the elements of political apartheid entrenched in the new constitution of 1990 cannot possibly be regarded as consistent with basic rights to political equality. While South Africa remained a pariah state until the dismantling of its apartheid system, Rabuka and his fellow travelers have managed to secure external acceptance of the new regime. Australia, among others, has restored full ties with Fiji and has even seen fit to provide it with military aid. A point raised many times in this context is that Western liberal democratic ideas concerning political rights are simply out of place in Fiji and that European "outsiders" are not entitled to expect Fiji's political system to conform to Western standards of democratic practice. On many occasions postcoup Fijian leaders, in defending their version of ethnocracy, have emphatically denied that external critics have any right to apply (Western) democratic standards and values to Fiji. This has been portrayed as an attack on Fiji's "sovereignty" in the sense of interference in its internal affairs.

Attempts to evade democratic principles have also been made by relativizing the concept of democracy itself. In Fiji, Rabuka and others have asserted that Fiji has its own version of democracy which is reflected in its new constitution. Needless to say, it would hardly conform to what Fiji Indians take to be a democratic form of government. Nor can it be seen to conform to democratic principles in any substantive sense. To relativize democracy in the way proposed by Rabuka is clearly another way of saying that "anything goes." Democracy may be a highly contested concept, and there may be many different ways in which it can be expressed institutionally, but the elasticity of the concept is nonetheless limited. So too is the doctrine of cultural relativism when it is used to justify the abuse of human rights.

Taken together, these issues point to another irony. The doctrines of self-determination and indigenous rights (in their moral rather than technical sense) have been formulated and developed within the Western democratic tradition's general assertion of human rights, and they make little sense outside this tradition. Both the B.R.A. and Fijian nationalists have appealed to some of the principles within that tradition, but reject the rest. Furthermore, as one commentator has pointed out, Rabuka and others of his persuasion may well wish to reject the democratic tradition as Western in origin, alien to their cultures, and an unwelcome imposition on a "sovereign people." But in adopting this perspective, it is argued, they also implicitly deny themselves the moral ground from which the legacy of colonialism can be criticized. Nor can they claim the moral right to protection as members of a disadvantaged community, for these rights are grounded firmly in the Western democratic tradition. It is noted further that there are virtually no other codes of legitimation that peoples of different ethnic identities can appeal to except, perhaps, the application of superior force.[36] These and other points raised in the above discussion are no doubt controversial, but they need to be faced squarely in the quest for equitable solutions.

A further important point worth emphasizing in the context of ethnonationalist claims to self-determination is the nature of a democratic state. The ethnonationalist version of such a state is grounded in the idea of "ethnocracy" – that is, a state in which a particular community, defined in terms of ethnicity, may claim superior political legitimacy and authenticity, or sovereignty, over and above the claims of any other community within its geographical boundaries. A democratic state, however, is one in which a variety of identities and not simply an ethnic identity may find legitimate expression. This is especially important in a world where virtually all states are characterized by some degree of cultural pluralism. Furthermore, a democratic state is one in which ethnic identity (or any other form of identity except basic citizenship),[37] does not determine the extent to which political and other privileges may be enjoyed. It is also a state in which not just one aspect of identity is exalted at the expense of other actual or potential aspects. It follows that the conception of internal (popular) sovereignty in a democratic state is based essentially on a civic notion that is inclusive of "the" people, and not simply of "a" people. A civil conception of sovereignty therefore treats all citizens as politically worthy and entitled to equal consideration without regard to ethnicity, to racial, religious, linguistic, or cultural origin or background, or to gender or to or any other singular aspect of identity, and insists that none of these characteristics endow any person or group with a special status in relation to the state.

Finally, although some of the least attractive aspects of ethnonationalist ideology and its consequences have been highlighted in this discussion, the complete dismissal of ethnicity as a factor relevant to the organization of political life is untenable, especially with respect to the treatment of ethnic/indigenous minorities. In particular, it does not mean that there is no place for policies designed to rectify the consequences of past injustices for such minorities where they continue to suffer relative deprivation. Nonetheless, to afford this kind of identity primacy in justifying unqualified claims to self-determination is to endorse the normative nationalist claim that discrete ethnic communities comprise the "natural" foundations of a political community and to encourage intolerance, atavism, racism, prejudice, and cultural chauvinism. Self-determination in this sense, and as manifested in the ideology supporting ethnocracy, produces the very opposite of a pluralistic and tolerant democratic state.

## Notes

This chapter is based substantially on an earlier paper entitled 'Ethnicity and Democracy in the South Pacific" which was first presented to the Workshop on "Internal Conflict and the World Community: Self-Determination, Security and Human Rights," at the Watson Institute for International Studies, Brown University, Providence, RI, 17–29 July 1994, and subsequently presented at the XVIth World Congress of the International Political Science Association, Berlin, 21–26 August 1994. I am grateful to the Academic Council on the United Nations System and the American Society of International Law who jointly sponsored the Brown workshop, and to the Australian Research Council for funding a fellowship to enable the initial research to be carried out.

1. The term "internal conflict" needs to be treated with caution since in most cases where the phenomenon occurs it is clearly not just a domestic issue, but has far-reaching implications for regional security, international order, external intervention, refugee movements, and so forth.
2. See John Keane, "Democracy's Poisonous Fruit," *Times Literary Supplementary*, 21 August 1992, pp.10–12.
3. David Brown, "Ethnic Revival: Perspectives on State and Society," *Third World Quarterly*, Vol.11, No.4, October 1989, p.1.
4. Donald L. Horowitz, *Ethnic Groups in Conflict* (Berkeley, University of California Press, 1985), p.3.
5. See Rodolpho Stavenhagen, "Ethnic Conflicts and Their Impact on International Society," *International Social Science Journal*, Vol. xliii, No.1, p.117.

6. Ted Robert Gurr, *Minorities at Risk: A Global View of Ethnopolitical Conflicts* (Washington, D.C.: United States Institute of Peace, 1993), pp.5–7. Note that the term "communal group" is used to denote something more general than "ethnic group."

7. Anthony D. Smith, *The Ethnic Revival* (Cambridge: Cambridge University Press, 1981), pp.15–17.

8. Hurst Hannum, "Rethinking Self-Determination," *Virginia Journal of International Law*, Vol.34, No.1, Fall 1993, p.2.

9. See J. Samuel Barkin and Bruce Cronin, "The State and the Nation: Changing Norms and the Rules of Sovereignty in International Relations," *International Organization*, Vol.48, No.1, Winter 1994, p.125.

10. David Levinson, "Ethnic Conflict," *Peace Review*, Vol.6, No.1, Spring 1994, p.3. Such definitions are themselves problematic, but this point will not be pursued here.

11. Steven Thiele, "Taking a Sociological Approach to Europeaness (Whiteness) and Aboriginality (Blackness)" in Steven Thiele (ed.), *Reconsidering Aboriginality*, Special Issue of *Australian Journal of Anthropology*, Vol.2, No.2, 1991, p.180.

12. Manning Nash, *The Cauldron of Ethnicity in the Modern World* (Chicago: University of Chicago Press, 1989), p.15.

13. See Stephanie Lawson, "The Politics of Tradition: Problems for Political Legitimacy and Democracy in the South Pacific," *Pacific Studies*, Vol.16, No.2, 1993, pp.1–29.

14. See Stephanie Lawson, *Tradition versus Democracy in the Kingdom of Tonga*, Discussion Paper No. 13, Regime Change and Regime Maintenance Series, Department of Political and Social Change, Australian National University, Canberra, 1994.

15. Gurr, *Minorities at Risk*, p.4.

16. Gurr, *Minorities at Risk*, p.4.

17. The Indonesian government's treatment of Irian Jaya's indigenous Melanesians and the people of East Timor, for example, would justify a form of ethnonationalist resistance.

18. The words "nation" and "*ethnos*" are derived from Latin and ancient Greek respectively, and their contemporary literal meaning is very similar insofar as they both refer broadly to "a people," that is, a group which is assumed to share common cultural (and often biological) attributes and historical ties.

19. J. Samuel Barkin and Bruce Cronin, "The State and the Nation: Changing Norms and the Rules of Sovereignty in International Relations," *International Organization*, Vol.48, No.1, Winter 1994, pp.110–111.

20. For a detailed discussion of this point, see Stephanie Lawson,

"The Politics of Authenticity: Ethnonationalist Conflict and the State" in Kumar Rupesinghe (ed.), *Conflict Transformation* (London, Macmillan, 1995), pp.116–142.

21. Frederick L. Shiels (ed.), "Introduction" in *Ethnic Separatism and World Affairs* (Lanham, University Press of America, 1984), p.4. Although there is no logical reason why the definition should apply only to those ethnic groups that form a minority, it is nonetheless usually understood in these terms. Certainly in contemporary multiethnic Western states such as Australia and the United States, few members of the dominant Anglo-Saxon/ Celtic population would regard themselves as having an "ethnic" identity or belonging to an "ethnic" group – the term is commonly reserved for "minorities" within these states defined as such by virtue of their ethnic heritage. Nonetheless, since ethnicity is the concept around which both minority and majority communities are defined and demarcated in contemporary discourses about identity, it must logically apply to dominant communities as well.

22. None of this should be taken as endorsing the realist perspective on international relations which assumes the autonomy/ separation of the domestic and international spheres.

23. This accords with the "internal right" of self-determination, that is, "the rights of peoples within States to choose their political status, the extent of their political participation and the form of their government. . . . " See Robert McCorquodale, "Self-Determination: A Human Rights Approach," *International and Comparative Law Quarterly*, Vol.43, October 1994, p.864.

24. It can of course be argued that the body of citizens which comprises "the people" in a democratic polity is only inclusive to a point, and that "others" are in fact excluded in the process of defining entitlements to inclusion in the first place.

25. Guyora Binder, "The Case for Self-Determination," *Stanford Journal of International Law*, Vol.29, No.2, 1992–3, p.224. Binder, however, goes on to make a case for a limited defense of the nationalist component.

26. The material contained in this section draws partly on a previous work. See Stephanie Lawson, "Ethno-Nationalist Dimensions of Internal Conflict – The Case of Bougainville Secessionism" in Kevin P. Clements (ed.), *Peace and Security in the Asia-Pacific Region: Post-Cold War Problems and Prospects* (Tokyo and Palmerston North: United Nations University Press and Dunmore Press, 1993), pp.58–77.

27. For a recent chronology of events (up to April 1994), see Commonwealth of Australia, *Bougainville: A Pacific Solution (Report of the Visit of the Australian Parliamentary Delegation to Bougainville 18–22 April 1944)* (Canberra: Australian Government Publishing Service, 1994).

28. See Lawson, "Ethno-Nationalist Dimensions of Internal Conflict," p.68.

29. The doctrine of self-determination has been articulated in various instruments by the United Nations from 1960 onwards. As Lâm points out, however, its normative applicability has usually restricted the "right" of secession to the liberation of "bluewater" colonies from their colonial (usually European) masters. Nonetheless, as Lâm continues, "the earlier break-up of Pakistan, and now of the Soviet Union and Yugoslavia, unrolled, or is unrolling, in an atmosphere of great international anxiety but not prohibition." See Maivân Clech Lâm, "Making Room for Indigenous Peoples at the United Nations: Thoughts Provoked by Indigenous Claims to Self-Determination," *Cornell International Law Journal*, Vol.25, No.3, 1992, p.616.

30. See Peter Lamour, "Ethnicity and Decentralization in Melanesia: A Review of the 1980s," *Pacific Viewpoint*, Vol.31, No.2, October 1990.

31. See Henry Okole, "The Politics of the Panguna Landowners' Organization" and Colin Filer, "The Bougainville Rebellion, the Mining Industry and the Process of Social Disintegration in Papua New Guinea," both in R.J. May and Mathew Spriggs (eds), *The Bougainville Crisis* (Bathurst: Crawford House Press, 1990).

32. Amnesty International, *Papua New Guinea: Under the Barrel of a Gun: Bougainville 1991 to 1993*, p.24 (reproduced in full as Appendix VI, in Commonwealth of Australia, *Bougainville: A Pacific Solution*).

33. Commonwealth of Australia, *Bougainville: A Pacific Solution*, p.23.

34. The background material in this section is drawn partly from two previous publications. See Stephanie Lawson, *The Failure of Democratic Politics in Fiji* (Oxford: Clarendon Press, 1991), and Stephanie Lawson, "Ethnic Politics and the State in Fiji," Working Paper No. 135 (Canberra: Peace Research Centre, Australian National University, 1993).

35. It should be noted that in the guidelines set out by various United Nations instruments and other documents, neither the Bougainvilleans nor the indigenous Fijians are technically entitled to categorize their claims and justifications under the doctrines

of self-determination and indigenous rights. Nonetheless, this obviously does not prevent them using the rhetoric associated with such doctrines.

36. Richard Mulgan, "Should Indigenous People Have Special Rights?," *Orbis*, Vol.33, No.3, Summer 1989, p.380.

37. This has not, unfortunately, prevented some otherwise relatively democratic states from implementing discriminatory immigration and citizenship policies. Australia's historic record in this respect is quite tarnished given that the "White Australian Policy" was abandoned less than a generation ago.

# – 8 –

# Problems of Indeterminacy and Characterization in the Application of Humanitarian Law

René Provost*

## Introduction

Claims by a people to self-determination constitute a powerful force that sometimes results in the taking up of arms to challenge the yoke of racist, colonial, or alien oppression. Events in East Timor, Eritrea, Chiapas, and the Western Sahara indicate that national liberation armed conflicts are not just a quaint if interesting feature of decolonization in Africa but remain a reality in many parts of the world. International humanitarian law has come to recognize the special nature of this type of armed conflict, internal in its geography but international in its legal and political implications, and special rules have been devised to regulate them drawing on the same norms that are used to deal with other kinds of international armed conflicts. Because of the acrimonious environment in which these norms apply, disputes often arise over whether a situation is indeed an armed conflict and, if so, over what type of armed conflict it is.

For example, in Resolution 808 (1993) on the creation of an international criminal tribunal for former Yugoslavia, the Security Council of the United Nations makes reference only to norms applicable to international armed conflicts, leaving norms governing internal conflicts out of the tribunal's jurisdiction and opening a Pandora's

*I wish to thank Ian Brownlie and the participants in the 1994 A.C.U.N.S./ A.S.I.L. summer workshop for their helpful comments. Research for this article was made possible by financial assistance from the I.O.D.E., the Centennial Trust, the Fond pour la Formation de chercheurs et l'aide à la recherche, and the Boulton Trust (McGill).

box of characterization for each specific event that comes under examination by that body.[1] One of the tribunal's most difficult tasks is to characterize the various phases of the confrontations in the region as internal or international armed conflicts. In Bosnia-Herzegovina, this involves determining when Bosnia became an independent state, the nature and duration of the former Yugoslavia's involvement in the conflict, the intensity of combat between the government and Bosnian Serb rebels, the effect of the proclamation of an independent Serbian Republic of Bosnia-Herzegovina, the nature of the involvement of Croatian troops, the timing of Bosnia's succession to the Geneva Conventions and Protocols, and the applicability of Security Council Resolution 808. It seems likely that the conflict swung from internal to international several times after January 1991.[2] In this particular case an international body has been created to decide this and other questions, but it is likely that in most situations of this kind, no such body will be available, and other actors such as noninvolved or third-party states and international or specialized organizations will be faced with the need to proceed to their own characterizations of armed conflicts. Indeterminacies in humanitarian law as to the field of application *ratione materiae* threaten the applicability of the law in whole or in part. The nature, conditions and agent of the required act of characterization play a critical role in the effective realization of the standards contained in treaty and customary law.

Indeterminacy and the need for characterization are of course not peculiar to humanitarian law. The problem is inherent in to all legal norms. Such norms have a fluid content, or open texture, and an act of classification of the event, action, institution, or legal relationship is needed in every case in order to determine which legal regime is applicable.[3] The same is true of facts, which are often objectively determinable but require more than a passive assessment by an agent. Legally relevant facts are ascertainable only through the lens of an appropriate norm. Facts such as control over part of a national territory or the intensity of fighting in a conflict are by their nature somewhat fuzzy and call for an active act of characterization by an agent. The operation of characterization is very close to that of interpretation, the second seeking to clarify law in reference to a set of facts and the first to classify facts in reference to some legal norms. There is nothing automatic in characterization, even in cases where both facts and law are clear and undisputed. It is a creative "construction" of an undoubtedly political nature.[4] For example, the United Kingdom insisted that municipal law applied in Rhodesia, while the United Nations thought international law obtained, without any necessary disagreement between them over the facts or content of either set of rules.[5] Because of the tendency to manipulate facts and law in order to achieve a desired result, the identity, jurisdiction, and authority of the characterizing agent are of critical importance. In humanitarian law, initial characterization plays a key role, because the classification of a given situation as an armed conflict may render the legal system nearly or totally inapplicable.[6]

Indeterminacy in humanitarian law is by no means limited to broad issues of applicability. There is a sliding scale of indeterminacy from the very general to the very specific, from what may be easily ascertainable from abroad to what may be only perceptible through on-the-spot investigation. At one end, the scale calls for highly specific characterization — for instance, "is a particular individual a privileged belligerent" or "is incidental loss of civilian life disproportionate to the military advantage". A distinction may be drawn between procedures aiming at global characterization of a situation as an armed conflict and procedure aiming at enforcement of rules deemed applicable to a given set of facts, while conceding that initial characterization nevertheless forms part of the enforcement of humanitarian law. One important difference is that characterization having to do with the initial applicability of humanitarian law can be performed more easily from abroad, without on-site investigation, than characterization needed to bring about enforcement of specific rules.[7] As will be seen, this may imply that some bodies unsuited to perform enforcement tasks can properly characterize a situation as an armed conflict. More generally, when it comes to arguments of inapplicability, a facade of legitimacy may be erected, providing a blanket justification in a way that is dangerous for the integrity of the legal system created by humanitarian law, while the elaboration of enforcement procedures for the most part comes closer to a case-by-case evaluation of each action taken by belligerents.

This essay seeks to explore the nature of characterization by various agents as it relates to the applicability of humanitarian law in situations of armed conflict. The degree of indeterminacy of a norm conditions the need for procedural mechanisms aimed at the resolution of that indeterminacy, because indeterminate norms support a wider spectrum of apparently justified results. Clearer standards generate fewer debates.[8] Accordingly, standards applicable in armed conflicts are discussed, and an attempt is made to identify areas of indeterminacy. No systematic exposition of the law is intended. Attention is also given to the effect of characterization by various agents interested or involved in the application of humanitarian law.

## Areas of Indeterminacy

Even though norms might have an open texture, they nevertheless possess a core meaning and a penumbra that will not accommodate any and all possible applications. Some characterizations must be adjudged as unreasonable in order to uphold the normative nature of a rule.[9] Before considering the relative effect of characterization, the degree of indeterminacy of the relevant rules must be examined. An overview of applicable standards necessarily centers on the various categories of armed conflicts and their particular legal regimes. Five district situations are differentiated under humanitarian law relating to armed conflict, the last of which, internal disturbances and tensions, falls outside the reach of that law. The four others, which will be examined successively, consist of interstate armed conflicts, national-liberation armed conflicts, noninternational armed conflicts as defined under Additional Protocol II (1977) to the Geneva Conventions (1949),[10] and internal armed conflicts as defined under common Article 3 of the Geneva Conventions.[11]

### *Interstate Armed Conflicts*

The notion of "international armed conflict" evolved as a separate concept from "war" through the adoption after World War II of the Charter of the United Nations (1945) and, four years later, the Geneva Conventions. Previously, the law of war applied only in situations that have been defined by Oppenheim as "a contention between two or more states through their armed forces for the purpose of overpowering each other and imposing such conditions of peace as the victor pleases."[12] The notion of war was thus quite limited and excluded not only civil wars and measures short of war, such as peacetime reprisals, but also conflicts that belligerents did not view as war despite large-scale fighting between armed forces of several states. For example, the expeditionary forces sent by various Western states in 1900-1901 to quell the Boxer Rebellion in China which was threatening the lives of their nationals was never considered a war, although thousands of soldiers participated in combat operations resulting in a large number of dead and wounded. It does not seem that the law of war was considered applicable, and indeed there were reported to be episodes of pillage, rape, destruction, and refusals to give quarter by the expeditionary forces.[13]

The inadequacy of a unique definition of war in international law became progressively clearer as the number and sophistication of norms regulating the use of force grew during this century. The characterization of a situation as war has an impact on: (1) application of humanitarian law to armed conflict, or *jus in bello*; (2) nonhostile relations between belligerents, such as diplomatic relations and treaties in force; (3) relations with third states, by application of the law of neutrality; and (4) belligerents' obligations toward the international community under *jus ad bellum*, by effect of the Kellogg-Briand Pact (1928) and the Charter of the United Nations.[14] Each of these categories contains norms linked by their relation to war, but they nevertheless serve different purposes and call for distinct thresholds of applicability. There is thus a clear need for different criteria for the applicability of, on the one hand, humanitarian law and, on the other, rules governing the effect of war on treaties.[15] This in fact has been so for quite some time. For instance, in 1915 and 1916, Italy was at war only with Austria-Hungary, but some German divisions were fighting alongside Austro-Hungarian troops against Italy. Although neither Italy nor Germany considered itself in a state of war against the other, there was no disagreement over the applicability of the Geneva Convention of 1906 and the Hague Conventions of 1907.[16] With the prohibition of war under international law through the Kellogg-Briand Pact, the League of Nations Covenant (Article 12–16), and later the United Nations Charter (Article 2(4)), there was an even greater incentive not to admit to being in a state of war with another country. Thus, in the Sino-Japanese conflict from 1931 to 1933, despite widespread fighting, both belligerents denied that there was a war within the meaning of Article 16 of the League of Nations Covenant. The United States, France, and Germany agreed with this characterization for their own political reasons. Japan and China nevertheless considered that the Geneva and Hague Conventions were applicable.[17] Even prior to World War II, then, the notion of war with regard to the applicability of *jus in bello* was distinctly wider than a possible global definition of war in general international law.[18]

The adoption of the concept of armed conflict in the Geneva Conventions of 1949 was meant to reflect the growing obsolescence of the notion of war as the threshold of applicability of humanitarian law. The operative provision consists of the first two paragraphs of common Article 2:

Article **2.** In addition to the provisions which shall be implemented in peace-time, the present Convention shall apply to all cases of declared war or of any other armed conflict which may arise between two or more of the High Contracting Parties, even if the state of war is not recognized by one of them.

The Convention shall also apply to all cases of partial or total occupation of the territory of a High Contracting Party, even if the said occupation meets with no armed resistance.

Article 2 is completed by Articles 5/4/5/6, specifying that the Conventions apply from the outset of any conflict or from the date of capture of individuals until the general close of military operations, the end of occupation, or the final repatriation of protected persons. The threshold of applicability is clearly intended to be very low and to include all situations in which humanitarian law may provide some protection to victims of military operations. The most limited and brief border clashes, such as that between Mexico and the United States in 1916 involving 250 soldiers and lasting for thirty minutes, and measures constituting "resort to force short of war," such as reprisals or intervention, would probably constitute armed conflicts governed by humanitarian law.[19] Apart from rather vague statements that humanitarian law of armed conflict, including the customary rules embodied in the Hague Conventions of 1907, applies "in any case,"[20] there are no objective elements agreed upon as necessary to the existence of an international armed conflict.

One clarification brought about by the inception of the Geneva Convention of 1949 concerns belligerent occupation. The applicability of the laws of war to military occupation not preceded by any clash of arms was problematic until the adoption of Article 6.[21] Before and during World War II, there had been several instances in which German troops occupied foreign territory without the slightest resistance on the part of the occupied state. Cases include Austria in 1938, Czechoslovakia in 1938–9, and Denmark in 1940. In the *I.G. Farben Trial* and the *Ministries Trial*, two U.S. military tribunals took opposite views on the existence of a war between Germany and Austria and Czechoslovakia, the first finding that the fourth Hague Convention of 1907 did not apply,[22] the second that it did.[23] Under Article 6 of the fourth Geneva Convention of 1949, there is little doubt that these cases would be considered as constituting military occupation.[24] Adam Roberts suggests that four criteria can help identify military occupation of a territory: (1) a military presence not fully sanctioned by a valid agreement; (2) displacement of the local public order and government by a military force; (3) differences in nationality, allegiance, or interests between the occupier and the population; and (4) the need for emergency rules to protect the civilian population.[25]

Despite an apparent simplification and lowering of the threshold of applicability of humanitarian law, nagging indeterminacies still plague the characterization of a conflict as an interstate armed conflict. Added to the Geneva Conventions in 1977, Protocol I, apart from Article 1(4) dealing with national-liberation conflicts, did nothing to reduce the vagueness of the concept.[26] The illegality of the use of force in international relations since 1945 has meant that interstate armed conflicts, close to traditional international war, have become rarer. They have been replaced by other types of conflicts, in which states other than the one on whose territory the fighting is taking place are more or less directly involved. The conflicts in Vietnam and Afghanistan provide two examples of situations that proved difficult and controversial to characterize. In the case of Vietnam, the Republic of South Vietnam and the United States characterized the conflict as international, resulting from armed aggression from the North. North Vietnam viewed the conflict as an internal war in the South between Vietcong fighters and the Saigon government, in which it had no involvement except to defend itself from U.S. attacks in the North.[27] In the case of Afghanistan, the U.S.S.R.'s position was that it was assisting the government of Afghanistan in quelling a rebellion by bandits. The International Committee of the Red Cross (I.C.R.C.) was of the opinion that the hostilities were at least at the level of an internal armed conflict. Many other states and the United Nations considered that there existed an international armed conflict between Afghanistan and the U.S.S.R.[28] In a more current setting, the shifting nature of the various armed conflicts in the former Yugoslavia will demand characterization in order to decide which set of rules is applicable to each stage of the conflict.[29]

### National-Liberation Armed Conflicts

Throughout the decolonization period following World War II, the nature of struggles for national liberation was a matter of great debate. Under the impetus of developing and East bloc states, the United Nations General Assembly on several occasions during the 1960s and 1970s affirmed the legitimacy of struggles of this kind that were taking place in territories in Africa under the control of South Africa, Portugal, and the United Kingdom, and called for these powers to apply or ensure application of the Geneva Conventions of 1949 to these situations.[30] In December 1973, the General Assembly adopted Resolution 3103 (XXVIII), a more general, nearly legislative resolution on the legal status of combatants engaged in struggles for national liberation from colonial and alien domination and racist regimes. Its operative Paragraph 3 lays down the principle that such conflicts "are to be regarded as international armed conflicts in the sense of the Geneva Conventions of 1949."[31] The aim was to remove national-liberation armed conflicts from the ambit of common Article 3 of the Geneva Conventions, and create a new category of conflicts assimilable into interstate armed conflicts.

The Geneva Conference (1974–7) was convened in part to deal with the problem of classifying national-liberation armed conflicts. This way underscored by the fact that one of the first acts of the conference was to adopt Resolution 3(I), inviting national liberation movements recognized by the regional intergovernmental organizations concerned to participate in the conference.[32] After much acrimonious debate throughout the conference over the desirability and feasibility of classifying struggles for national liberation as international armed conflicts, Articles 1(4) and 96(3) were adopted with only Israel voting against, although the number of abstentions by Western states was significant:[33]

ARTICLE 1.

3. This Protocol, which supplements the Geneva Conventions of 12 August 1949 for the protection of war victims, shall apply in the situations referred to in Article 2 common to those Conventions.

4. The situations referred to in the preceding paragraph include armed conflicts in which peoples are fighting against colonial domination and alien occupation and against racist regimes in the exercise of their right of self-determination, as enshrined in the Charter of the United Nations and the Declaration on Principles of International Law concerning Friendly Relations and Co-operation among States in accordance with the Charter of the United Nations.

ARTICLE 96.

3. The authority representing a people engaged against a High Contracting Party in an armed conflict of the type referred to in Article 1, paragraph 4, may undertake to apply the Conventions and this Protocol in relation to that conflict by means of a unilateral declaration addressed to the depositary. Such declaration shall, upon its receipt by the depositary, have in relation to that conflict the following effects:

(a) the Conventions and this Protocol are brought into force for the said authority as a Party to the conflict with immediate effect;

(b) the said authority assumes the same rights and obligations as those which have been assumed by a High Contracting Party to the Conventions and this Protocol; and

(c) the Conventions and this Protocol are equally binding upon all Parties to the conflict.[34]

From the text of these provisions several criteria can be derived for the applicability of Protocol I and the Geneva Conventions of 1949 to national-liberation armed conflicts. These criteria relate to the type of struggle and the nature of the national-liberation movement.

Struggles for national liberation to which rules governing international armed conflicts are applicable must, first, involve a conflict by a people against colonial domination, alien occupation, or a racist regime and, second, be in furtherance of that people's right to self-determination. It should be noted at the outset that the notion of "alien occupation" corresponds to that of "alien domination" in the United Nations Declaration on Principles of International Law concerning Friendly Relations and Co-operation among States (1970). It is wider than belligerent occupation as understood in common Article 3 of the Geneva Conventions of 1949, and clearly covers cases such as Namibia, the Western Sahara, or the territories occupied by Israel, which constitute disputable or borderline situations under Article 3.[35]

There is no absolute identity between the notions of self-determination as understood in general international law and national-liberation armed conflicts under humanitarian law. In other words, not all peoples fighting to uphold their right to self-determination will be eligible for the status of national-liberation movements or benefit from the protections applicable to an international armed conflict. Only conflicts waged against colonial domination, alien occupation, and racist regimes, and not other wars of liberation fought against oppressive regimes on purely political, social, or religious grounds, are considered national-liberation armed conflicts. Struggles aiming at the partition of a state are generally not authorized by the Declaration on Friendly Relations, except when the state itself is a plural state and violates the right to self-determination by not according equal and nondiscriminatory participation or representation in the government.[36] In cases such as Eritrea, Biafra (1967–70), Bangladesh (1971), or Kurdistan, the struggles may meet the conditions of the Declaration on Friendly Relations because the state did trench on the right of equal access to government. Nevertheless, as the oppressive regimes cannot properly be labeled racist, alien, or colonial, liberation struggles such as these cannot constitute national-liberation armed conflicts as understood under Article 1(4) of Protocol I and do not qualify for the application of rules governing international armed conflicts.[37] Thus, the characterization of a state as colonial, alien, or racist is a key element of the applicability of humanitarian law to this type of conflict.

For the rules regulating international armed conflicts to come into force with respect to a national-liberation armed conflict, the authority representing a people in its struggle for self-determination must make a declaration under Article 96(3) of Protocol I, undertaking to apply the protocol and the Geneva Conventions of 1949. Apart from the mechanical and objectively ascertainable transmission of the undertaking to the depository (the Swiss government), the eligibility of the authority submitting the declaration is made conditional under the wording of Article 96(3) and other provisions of the protocol. First, the nature of the authority must be representative of the people. Some have suggested that the mere existence of an armed conflict over a prolonged period of time is probative testimony of the representative character of a national-liberation movement because such movements can only survive if supported by the population.[38] Past events have shown, however, that rebel groups have sometimes survived for many years by coercing the population into giving them support, for instance the Maoist guerrilla movement endero Luminoso, or Shining Path, in Peru – or by receiving substantial support from third states, such as the U.S.-backed Contras in Nicaragua. The possibility that several authorities seek to represent a people, as happened in Angola with the M.P.L.A., (the Popular Movement for the Liberation of Angola), U.N.I.T.A. (the National Union for the Total Independence of Angola), and the F.N.L.A. (the National Front for the Liberation of Angola), can also create problems with regard to representativeness.[39]

A second condition for the nature of the authority making a declaration under Article 96(3) is that a national-liberation movement undertaking to apply Protocol I and the Geneva Conventions must possess the characteristics of armed forces as described in Article 43 of the protocol.[40] The liberation movement must thus be an organized force under a responsible command, equipped with an internal disciplinary system that is charged with, *inter alia*, enforcing compliance with humanitarian law. In a national-liberation conflict, only a movement with the institutional capacity to carry out its undertaking to apply the protocol and the conventions will be recognized as having the standing to call for the application of rules governing international armed conflicts. The degree of organization and control exercised over the troops by the command of a liberation movement are likely to be highly subjective and controversial matters. In some cases, the lack of control of an authority is demonstrated by its inability to carry out effective enforcement of agreements signed with the enemy. Very often, however, there will be no such clear evidence of the degree of organization or disorganization of a national-liberation movement, and even a neutral and objective observer – to say nothing of the state itself – will often be hard pressed to make a determination on this ground of the eligibility of the movement.

A third condition affecting the eligibility of the authority making the declaration is the need for or effect of recognition of a national-liberation movement by a regional intergovernmental organization. Like many of the standards attaching to the legal regime governing national liberation armed conflicts, this consideration grows out of the practice of the United Nations with respect to participation by liberation movements in the activities of the organization. Since the early 1970s, various U.N. bodies have invited national-liberation movements to take part as observers in discussions touching on their interests. The issue of their participation was first raised in the U.N. Economic Committee for Africa, which resolved to invite movements recognized by the regional organizations in Africa – that is, the Organization of African Unity (OAU) and the League of Arab States (LAS). The practice gradually spread to the General Assembly and other U.N. bodies and specialized agencies.[41]

At the Geneva conference (1974–7), that developed and promulgated the additional protocols to the Conventions of 1949, Turkey presented an amendment reflecting U.N. practice, whereby Article 1(4) of Protocol I would apply only to liberation movements "recognized by the regional intergovernmental organization concerned."[42] The *travaux préparatoires* reveal little of the history of this amendment, but it was never adopted by the First Committee. Nevertheless, when Article 1(4) was voted on at the end of the conference, Turkey and several other states declared that its application was linked to recognition of the movements by regional organizations.[43] The United Kingdom, at signature, and South Korea, upon ratification, made declarations that recognition by regional organizations "is to be regarded as necessary" under Article 96(3) of Protocol I.[44] Many of those writing on the subject point, however, to the rejection of the Turkish amendment at the conference as evidence that such a condition cannot be read into the terms of Protocol I. They argue that recognition of national-liberation movements by regional organizations only creates a presumption or provides some indication of the eligibility of the movement under Articles 1(4) and 96(3).[45] This is the route taken recently by Canada, which in ratifying Protocol I declared in a statement of understanding about Article 96(3) that "the fact that such authority has or has not been recognized as such by an appropriate regional intergovernmental organization is relevant."[46] Another factor inconsistent with mandatory recognition by regional organizations is that there are many areas of the world that do not have such organizations.[47] For instance, there is no regional organization to grant recognition to the struggle of FRETILIN in East Timor.

Two further considerations have sometimes been presented as conditions for the applicability of Protocol I to national-liberation armed conflicts, the first being that a conflict should be of an intensity no less than that of internal conflicts as covered by Protocol II, and the second being that the liberation movement should exercise control over some part of national territory. The minimum-intensity require-ment finds its most serious support in a declaration made by the United Kingdom at signature.[48] But the requirement has been sharply criticized as lacking any foundation in the text of Protocol I and as introducing a concept of minimum intensity into the context of inter-national armed conflicts, something that had heretofore been clearly rejected by customary international law.[49] Territorial control is a condition found in Article 1 of Protocol II and one that formed part of the now obsolete practice of recognition of belligerency under the laws and customs of war. Writers have rejected this consideration as inappropriate in the context of modern guerrilla warfare, in which liberation movements may not, as a matter of tactical advantage, seek to hold a static position or occupy any specific area. Examples of liberation movements without any control over national territory include the A.N.C. and the P.L.O. It has been pointed out, further, that national-liberation struggles are grounded in the right of peoples to self-determination, thus deriving their status not from de facto control of territory but rather from their representativeness of the people as a whole.[50] In any case, the notions of minimum intensity and territorial control are extremely fuzzy concepts that must be applied to very fluid sets of circumstances underscoring the importance of the act of characterization.[51]

The norms defining the conditions for applicability of humanitarian law to national-liberation armed conflicts were the object of biting criticism, mostly from Western states, during and after the Geneva Conference (1974–7). The most serious and recurring criticism was that the norms were simply too vague to provide any real guid-ance for their application to real situations. The Federal Republic of Germany did not vote for Article 1(4) because in its opinion the provision contained no criteria of a fundamentally legal character. Italy commented that national liberation conflicts were "indefinable from the point of view of objective elements."[52] While these condem-nations seem overstated in light of the preceding discussion, it is nevertheless clear that a significant degree of indeterminacy exists in the criteria governing the applicability of humanitarian law to such armed conflicts. That these rules can become applicable "automatically" is out of the question. Intervention by an agent is required to characterize the factual and legal nature of the situation. The debate over the effect of recognition of national-liberation movements by regional organizations represents a partial recognition of the crucial role of characterization in this context, but the debate can be broadened to include all other aspects of the application of humanitarian law to this type of conflict.

### *Noninternational Armed Conflicts under Protocol II*

The regulation of noninternational armed conflicts by Protocol II is linked intimately to the regime set up by common Article 3 of the Geneva Conventions of 1949. Indeed, the initial goal of the International Committee of the Red Cross (I.C.R.C.) in its work leading to the Geneva Conference (1974–7) was to proceed to a revision of Article 3 rather than to create a wholly distinct set of rules. During the two conferences of government experts in 1971 and 1972, however, two contradictory tendencies emerged. Some thought that the scope of application for humanitarian rules governing noninternational armed conflicts should be expanded to cover more situations, or at least clarified in such a way as to increase the chances of application, even at the cost of giving up any amplification of the content of the rules. Others thought that a narrower scope of application would be deemed preferable because it would permit the elaboration of a more extensive regulation of noninternational armed conflicts. The solution eventually agreed upon was to create two regimes: one, Article 3, wider in scope but narrower in content; the other, Protocol II, of more limited applicability but containing detailed rules.[53] By definition, then, all conflicts to which Protocol II is applicable will also be governed by common Article 3.

The scope of application of Protocol II is set out in its first article:

ARTICLE 1.
*Material field of application*
    1. This Protocol, which develops and supplements Article 3 common to the Geneva Conventions of 12 August 1949 without modifying its existing conditions of application, shall apply to all armed conflicts which are not covered by Article 1 of the Protocol Additional to the Geneva Conventions of 12 August 1949, and relating to the Protection of Victims of International Armed Conflicts (Protocol I) and which take place in the territory of a High Contracting Party between its armed forces and dissident armed forces or other organized armed groups which, under responsible

command, exercise such control over a part of its territory as to enable them to carry out sustained and concerted military operations and to implement this Protocol.

2. This Protocol shall not apply to situations of internal disturbances and tensions, such as riots, isolated and sporadic acts of violence and other acts of a similar nature, as not being armed conflicts.

The second paragraph marks the threshold below which the protocol does not apply and is somewhat redundant in the sense that it essentially excludes those situations that do not meet the conditions of Paragraph 1 by stating the adverse of those conditions. Thus, "isolated and sporadic" stand in contrast to "sustained and concerted." By definition, situations not meeting the conditions listed in Paragraph 1 do not constitute noninternational armed conflicts but are internal disturbances and tensions and as such are not covered by Protocol II. The analysis here therefore need not be concerned with delineating the border between what are internal disturbances and tensions and what are noninternational armed conflicts but rather with the definition of the latter under Paragraph 1.[54]

From the text of Paragraph 1, four closely interrelated conditions for the applicability of Protocol II to a noninternational conflict can be distinguished. First, the conflict must involve a state and its armed forces on its territory. The involvement of a state and its armed forces does not in itself make an armed conflict, however, because the other conditions set forth in the article must also be present. Neither does the quelling of disturbances by a state without intervention by its armed forces constitute a conflict within the meaning of Article 1(1). Further, military operations involving several nonstate groups on the territory of a state but not involving the state's armed forces are not covered by Protocol II. The possibility that a conflict of sufficient intensity to warrant the application of humanitarian law might take place on the territory of a state without that state being militarily involved in it was thought to be academic at the Geneva Conference, despite the opinion of the I.C.R.C., which had direct experience in several such conflicts.[55] The conflict in Lebanon up to 1983, for example, involved the P.L.O. and various Lebanese armed groups but not the Lebanese state, conclusively showing that high-intensity conflicts can take place on the territory of a state without the state's involvement. This situation can arise where the state is either too weak or simply nonexistent.[56]

A second condition, for the applicability of Protocol II has to do with the disposition of the armed forces or armed groups in conflict with the state. They must be organized and under responsible command. Without a minimally organized structure, the group will not be in a position to carry out sustained and concerted military operations, exercise control over part of the state's territory, or implement the provisions of the protocol.

The requirement for organization and responsible leadership overlaps to a certain extent with the third condition requiring that the forces in conflict with the state be able to carry out sustained and concerted military operations. This condition underscores both the collective character of armed conflicts, as contrasted with the isolated and sporadic acts mentioned in Paragraph 2 of Article 1, and the fact that hostilities involving the use of weapons must be occurring in order for the conflict to be regulated by humanitarian law. The attributions "sustained" and "concerted" were adopted as criteria for military operations instead of designations of "intensity" and "duration," because it was thought that the latter were too specific and that a state could easily deny that such operations possessed these characteristics. It is notable that it was thought vaguer criteria on this score would dampen possible attempts by states to deny that armed forces opposing them met this condition. Indeterminacy was, in this instance, considered to be a desirable quality for a legal norm.[57]

Finally, the fourth condition under Protocol II's scope of application is that the armed forces or armed groups contending against a state must exercise control over part of the state's territory. This requirement, based on the recognition of belligerency under the laws and customs of war, had been abandoned during the preparatory expert conferences because of the perceived reluctance of states to admit to the loss of control over part of their territory during an internal conflict. For instance, France acknowledged in 1956 that common Article 3 of the Geneva Conventions was applicable to the Algerian war, but never conceded that it did not control the territory of Algeria in its entirety.[58] As mentioned earlier, territorial control is, in the context of national liberation conflicts, a slippery concept because armed forces opposed to the state may eschew holding static positions for the sake of gaining tactical advantage. The concept nevertheless resurfaced at the Geneva Conference (1974–7), and it was decided that control of part of state's territory was a necessary condition for national-liberation forces to carry out sustained and concerted military operations and also to implement humanitarian rules contained in Protocol II.[59]

The global effect of all these conditions is to severely curtail the scope of application of Protocol II. Upholding the idea of state sovereignty with respect to noninternational armed conflicts, governments have in effect required that the belligerent party possess the basic characteristics of a state – organization, population, and territory – before they will accept the applicability of international humanitarian law.[60] Only the rather rare "classical" civil war scenarios such as the Spanish civil war in 1936–9, the war in El Salvador during the 1980s, or perhaps the conflict in Bosnia-Herzegovina will meet these stringent conditions. Protocol II can be considered a regression in existing laws and customs of war given that it requires essentially the same conditions as did recognition of belligerency for bringing into effect the full application of all humanitarian rules for international armed conflicts. The key difference is that while recognition of belligerency depended on a state's characterization of a conflict, Protocol II presents the for criteria applicability as objectively ascertainable. In other words, the protocol leaves open the issue of who is to make the determinative characterization of the situation.

### Noninternational Armed Conflicts under Common Article 3

It has already been pointed out that the debate at the Geneva Conference (1974–7) over the most desirable way to expand humanitarian regulation of internal strife resulted in the creation of a regime distinct from common Article 3 of the Geneva Conventions of 1949, one of narrower applicability but broader content. It might be presumed from this that the scope of application of common Article 3 is broader than that of Protocol II and covers situations that would not be classified as armed conflicts under the protocol. In truth, the matter is far from certain, however, as the exact relation between the scope of Article 3 and that of Protocol II was not clearly spelled out at the Geneva Conference. There is only a general statement in Article 1(1) of the protocol to the effect that it "develops and supplements Article 3 without modifying its existing conditions of application." It is therefore necessary to turn to Article 3 itself for clues about the scope of its application.

Common Article 3 was one of the most heatedly debated provisions at the Geneva Conference of 1949. At the time of its inception it was far from being a simple codification of accepted international law, as there was no clear principle that all internal armed conflicts were matters of international concern.[61] The draft presented by the I.C.R.C. at the conference simply proposed that the Geneva Conventions be applicable to both sides in an armed conflict not of an international character, but no consensus could be found in support of that principle. A Working Party of the Special Committee of the

Joint Committee was created to prepare proposals defining and limiting the types of internal situations in which the conventions would be applicable.[62] No agreement could be reached and eventually an alternate solution was adopted, narrowing not the scope of application of Article 3 but rather its normative content, with the result that the rules applicable to noninternational armed conflicts are reduced to a bare minimum.

Although none of the proposals for defining noninternational armed conflict attracted sufficient consensus, the I.C.R.C. commentary on the conventions lists them as "convenient criteria" for determining whether a noninternational armed conflict exists.[63] They include: explicit or implicit recognition of belligerency or insurgency by the state or by the United Nations; organization of the insurgent forces under a responsible command exercising control over a specific part of national territory in which the group has the means to respect and ensure observance of the conventions; existence of a civil insurgent authority possessing the characteristics of a state, exercising de facto authority over a population and territory; acceptance by the insurgent of the rules of the Geneva Conventions; and use of military force by the state to try to quell the insurgency.[64]

However convenient, the criteria set forth by the I.C.R.C. in its commentary are seriously misleading. The criteria were elaborated in the context of an attempt to define armed conflict not of an international character in which the conventions as a whole would be applicable. A decision was made at the conference not to make the conventions applicable to a narrow type of internal conflicts, but rather to adopt a widely applicable but substantively limited regime. There is therefore no justification for the adoption of elements of a restrictive definition of noninternational armed conflict in the context of Article 3. Indeed, it seems illogical to list as being relevant criteria that the insurgent force should possess an organization enabling them to respect and ensure observance of the conventions and that the insurgent authority should agree to be bound by the conventions, when the conventions are not applicable to internal conflicts under Article 3. State recognition of belligerency or insurgency is also problematic, given that under the laws and customs of war it leads to the full application of rules regulating armed conflict, and not merely of the basic elements listed in Article 3.[65]

Tom J. Farer notes that the only assured thing about the notion of noninternational armed conflict in common Article 3 is that no one can say with assurance what it means.[66] Although the text of Article 3 is extremely open-textured, it does refer to "armed conflicts," so a minimum-intensity requirement was certainly intended.

Conflicts imply the conduct of military operations on the part of both sides. The nonapplicability of the provision to internal disturbances and tensions was one element agreed upon at the Geneva Conference of 1949.[67] Closely linked to the element of intensity is the requirement that the insurgent group be organized under responsible command. Without minimal organization and command structure, the group would not possess the ability to implement the basic humanitarian rules contained in Article 3. The need for the state to grant some form of recognition to the insurgent does not follow from the text or the spirit of the provision. Recognition is an essentially discretionary power of the state, hardly compatible with the obligatory application of humanitarian law.[68] Contrary to Protocol II, the state does not have to be involved in any way for Article 3 to apply. Internal strife in which nongovernmental factions are contending against one another, such as occurred in Lebanon and Somalia, are covered by Article 3.[69] Finally, control of a specific part of national territory by the insurgents is not a necessary condition for the application of Article 3. Territorial control was an element of the recognition of belligerency, built on the notion of a full application of the laws and customs of war when the insurgent side could be largely assimilated to a state-like entity.[70] Instances of internal armed conflict involving large-scale military operations but not a fixed territorial base – for example the first phase of the Algerian conflict or of the Vietnam war – reveal that there is not necessarily a correlation between intensity of fighting and control of territory.[71]

The vagueness of the conditions of applicability in Article 3 has meant that it has been applied in a rather discretionary way by states. Article 3 was deemed applicable in Guatemala (1954), Algeria (after 1956), Lebanon (1958), Yemen (1962–7), the Dominican Republic (1965), Vietnam (after 1965), Nigeria (1967-70), Uruguay (1972), Chile (1971), and the Portuguese territories in Africa (after 1974). On the other hand, in a few of many examples, the United Kingdom refused to apply it in Kenya (1954), Cyprus (1955), and Northern Ireland, Afghanistan rejected it in 1981 and 1985 and El Salvador in 1983.[72] The uncertain state of the law is partly due to the unsettled nature of the criteria governing the applicability of Article 3, but it also arises because of the absence of discussion of the effect of divergent characterizations by the state, the insurgent group, or other agents.

Despite efforts by writers and international bodies to develop sets of norms for defining armed conflict as precisely as possible, indeterminacies remain an important aspect of humanitarian law, leaving a wide margin of appreciation for assessment of facts and interpretation of law. The indeterminacy of these rules does not necessarily imply that the state or other agents are at liberty to block the application of humanitarian law. Indeterminacy means that, where a situation falls within the significant gray zone in the definition of armed conflicts, several conclusions about the nature of that situation can be lawfully derived from the norms. Disagreements may arise from these multiple characterizations. Ideally, there should then be a mechanism for intervention to resolve the indeterminacy and provide a definitive statement about the nature of the situation. Such mechanisms are commonly used in conjunction with extremely indeterminate norms. The Security Council, for example, has the power under Chapter VII of the United Nations Charter to determine the existence of a threat to international peace and security. In humanitarian law, however, few mechanisms are available that can lead to the designation of a situation as armed conflict. The relative effects of characterizations by various actors must be assessed, in order to determine whether there is a hierarchy among these divergent opinions, or whether another type of solution must be found.

## Legal Effect of Characterization

The whole edifice of international law is built on and around the state. Considerations of state sovereignty mean that the state will be the frontline agent performing characterizations of facts and law that are decisive to the actual application of humanitarian law. Application by the state of somewhat indeterminate norms to often ambiguous facts cannot be totally discretionary, as this would contradict the normative and mandatory nature of international law. There are necessarily some limits to the state's power of self-characterization. These can be found either in the norms themselves, or in concurrent or superior powers of characterization by other agents. Writers have noted that therein lies the key to the application of humanitarian law.[73] The occurrence of an armed conflict has legal implications under humanitarian law for nonbelligerent states, so that various international agents may perform acts of characterization that do not necessarily correspond to that of the belligerent state or of the national-liberation movement. It is clear that just who the characterizing agent is perforce becomes of critical importance.

Four different types of characterizations by agent can be singled out with respect to the applicability of humanitarian law, they being characterizations performed (1) by a state or by a national-liberation movement (self-characterization); (2) by other states as third parties;

(3) by political organs of international or regional organizations; and (4) by specialized bodies. The purpose of the analysis is not to fully explain the web of relations between the different characterizations but more modestly to contribute to a reflection on the legal nature and effect of each type of intervention in the context of humanitarian law.

## Self-Characterization

Self-characterization denotes characterization by one of the belligerents in a conflict, possibly including an insurgent or national-liberation movement. The term "self-characterization" is used here because the agent performing the act of characterization is not exterior to, but rather an active participant in, the situation under examination. Self-characterization of a situation as an armed conflict or as simple internal disturbances or tensions affects in a direct and important way the obligations of the agent.

Under traditional laws and customs of war, a state faced with insurgency on its territory was at liberty to grant the rebels recognition of belligerency or insurgency in cases in which the rebels met with certain conditions, close to those developed under Article 1 of Protocol II. The effect of recognition, which necessarily implied the characterization by the state of the situation as an internal armed conflict, was to make the laws and customs of war as a whole applicable to the conflict. Writers were generally of the opinion that the power of recognition of belligerency or insurgency was purely discretionary.[74] The same principle obtained with respect to international armed conflicts. War could only take place if one of the belligerent states deemed it so. Limited – and sometimes not so limited – incidents could take place involving the use of force by the state, without any state of war. For example, the Boxer expedition by several Western states in China in 1900–1 was not a war, despite fighting involving thousands of troops on both sides.[75]

Recognition of belligerency became obsolete over the course of the twentieth century, with no state practicing it after World War II and only limited instances prior to that war. The concept was superseded by the adoption of common Article 3 of the Geneva Conventions of 1949 and, more recently, the two Additional Protocols of 1977, in which recognition by the state in the classical sense plays no role. Likewise, the replacement of the notion of "war" by that of "armed conflict" in the Geneva Conventions of 1949 lowered the threshold of applicability so much that the humanitarian norms should apply as soon as an armed conflict factually takes place.[76] No mention is made under any of the relevant provisions of who is to be the judge, or characterizing agent, of the existence of one or the other type of armed conflict. Some have argued that since the state's power of appreciation is not curtailed, it subsists under the new under rules, so that the state is the sole agent empowered to assess whether the conditions of applicability of humanitarian law have been met. Thus, at the Geneva Conference of 1977, Colombia proposed an amendment specifying that only the state on whose territory a non-international armed conflict took place could determine whether the conditions listed in Article 1(1) of Protocol II had been met. The amendment was eventually withdrawn, but Colombia and other states maintained that the article as drafted left intact the state's exclusive power to assess whether its conditions were fulfilled in a given situation.[77] On the other hand, the fact that the amendment was not adopted at the Geneva Conference can be taken as an implicit rejection of the principle it embodies.[78]

Norms developed after World War II operated a fundamental change in the conditions for applicability of humanitarian law. Whereas norms under the older laws and customs of war depended at least in part on state recognition of belligerency or of the existence of a war, the Geneva Conventions and Protocols, and ensuing customary rules, contain norms that are intended to apply automatically. This is not to say that no act of characterization is required, but rather that the applicability of humanitarian law finds its source in the norms themselves and not in the intervening act of recognition or characterization. In other words, state characterization has a declaratory rather than a constitutive function.[79]

As for the state's having an exclusive right to assess whether the elements defining an armed conflict are present in a given situation, the state generally can proceed to a unilateral characterization only with respect to discretionary powers. These include recognition of governments, the establishment of diplomatic relations, or diplomatic protection of nationals abroad.[80] Application of humanitarian law to situations of armed conflict is, on the contrary, not a discretionary power. Customary norms, as well as the Geneva Conventions and Protocols, create a binding obligation for states to apply certain basic rules to all armed conflicts. A state cannot lawfully decide that, regardless of the fact that a conflict meeting the conditions of applicability of humanitarian law is occurring, it will not apply that body of law. This is consistent with the declaratory rather than the constitutive function of characterization. The International Court of Justice (I.C.J.) in the *Asylum* case noted with respect to the right of a state to qualify any offense committed by a refugee that "a unilateral competence to qualify involves a derogation from the equal rights of qualification that, in the absence of any contrary rule, must be attributed to each of the states concerned."[81] In the context of humanitarian law, the equal rights of other states to qualify or characterize a situation as an armed conflict is left untouched, so that the belligerent state's characterization "can only be, legally, *provisional and not definitive.*"[82]

The standing of national liberation movements under Protocol I and, to an even greater extent, of insurgent groups in noninternational armed conflicts is problematic insofar as proceeding to characterize a conflict is concerned. There have been a number of instances in the past in which rebel groups or national-liberation movements have declared their willingness to apply the Geneva Conventions of 1949 and have characterized their operations as armed conflicts, despite the fact that the states in question refused to acknowledge the existence of anything more than internal disturbances. Such situations have arisen in connection with hostilities in Algeria, Angola, Nicaragua, Nigeria, Western Sahara, Yemen, and Zimbabwe.[83] Rarely has any weight been given by the belligerent state or other states to such characterizations in the context of humanitarian law.[84] The burden of recognition of a national-liberation armed conflict rests, in a certain measure, on self-characterization by the liberation movement. The movement must seek to represent the people in its struggle and undertake to apply the conventions and protocol so that these can become applicable. As the characterization of a national-liberation armed conflict is based on the people's right to self-determination, an act of self-characterization by the liberation movement is required before the conflict can properly be said to fall under Article 1(4) of Protocol I. This act is evidenced by making a declaration under Article 96(3) of the Protocol. The same probably applies to noninternational armed conflicts, by insurgent groups, as a state is unlikely to agree that hostilities on its territory constitute an armed conflict if the insurgents do not at least make a claim to that effect. Conversely, because the characterization of a situation as an armed conflict constitutes an implicit acknowledgment for the insurgents of the success of their campaign, they will rarely oppose it.[85]

What effect do these statements from insurgent and national-liberation movements have on the legal nature of the situation? National-liberation movements and insurgent groups are not sovereign entities in international law, but they are recognized as a limited legal personality in the text of the Geneva Conventions and Protocols. The extent of this personality is a reflection of the rights and obligations of the movements under international law.[86] Under Protocol I, national-liberation movements are given the power to make humanitarian law applicable for both parties by way of a unilateral declaration (Article 96(3)), subject of course to the state's prior ratification of the treaty. Some have suggested that, by application of the principle of effectivity, movements in situations not covered by Protocol I could make unilateral declarations that have a binding legal effect, at least for themselves.[87] A power to determine the existence of an armed conflict can certainly be deduced from the power to render humanitarian law applicable to such a conflict, implying that characterization by insurgent and national-liberation movements will have some legal effect. Of course, this power of characterization is no more exclusive to the insurgent groups than it is to the states. Self-characterizations by insurgents are unlikely to suffice to authoritatively classify situations as one or the other type of armed conflict.[88] Nevertheless, statements by such movements should not be brushed aside as mere attempts to generate political support, without any genuine legal effect.

It is a critical problem of humanitarian law that its application hinges so much on self-characterization. More often than not, the state will simply disregard all relevant legal criteria and rely on strictly political considerations to make an official characterization of a situation as being or not being an armed conflict. The problem is particularly acute in situations of national liberation and other types of noninternational armed conflicts because there is only one international agent present to characterize the facts. For example, G.I.A.D. Draper notes that the refusal by France and the United Kingdom to apply common Article 3 to situations in Algeria, Kenya, Malaya, and Cyprus was "determined by political considerations and not by any objective assessment of the facts."[89] In international armed conflicts, the possibility of differing opinions by two agents about the nature of the hostilities naturally tends to internationalize the debate on characterization, with some chance that the most humanitarian interpretation of the situation will be favored. This occurred, for instance, during the Vietnam War, in which the United States initially applied the Geneva Conventions of 1949 to Vietcong fighters as well as North Vietnamese regulars, while the latter refused to consider the war an international armed conflict. Both characterizations reflected political considerations, the United States claiming the war to be an invasion of the South by the North, the Vietcong and North Vietnam considering it to be a struggle of the people of the South against an oppressive regime and its ally.[90] The Geneva Conventions were eventually applied by all sides, at least informally. Reliance on nonlegal criteria to characterize situations under humanitarian law owes much to the fact that internal judicial review of a characterization is rarely available while an armed conflict is still going on.[91]

Reluctance by states to admit to the applicability of humanitarian law does not necessarily imply that they can indeed prevent it. It is unwarranted to suggest that because the actual application of human-itarian law remains conditioned on the characterization of a situation by the state involved, it is in fact, if not in law, optional.[92] The Israeli representative at the Geneva Conference erred in much the same way when he criticized Article 1(4) of Protocol I, saying it "had within it a built-in nonapplicability clause, since a party would have to admit that it was either racist, alien, or colonial-definitions which no state would ever admit to."[93] It is undeniable that, when a state refuses to acknowledge the applicability of norms of humanitarian law, it is in a de facto position to prevent their enforcement. The previous discussion has shown, however, that the state does not have exclusive or ultimate powers of characterization, and that other agents may proceed to their own assessment of a situation. From the legal stand-point, the state cannot effectively prevent a situation from acquiring the status of an armed conflict. Thus, any characterization by the state will be at its own risk. Once the equal validity of characterization by other agents is recognized, there may be some pressure put on the state to revise its opinion, in addition to the effects of the existence of an armed conflict felt outside the jurisdiction of the state.

### Other States as Third Parties

Humanitarian law imposes on the state obligations *erga omnes* in the fulfillment of which all states have a legitimate interest in the name of the international community. As discussed earlier, the I.C.J. in the *Asylum* case stated the principle that all interested states have a con-current right to qualify facts unless an exclusive right is granted to one state by treaty or customary law. Humanitarian law, does not contain an exclusive devolution of the right to characterize situations as armed conflicts, opening the door to the possibility of concurrent characterizations by other states, especially given that all states have an interest in the application of humanitarian law.

The right of other states to make their own assessments of the facts and decide for themselves whether a situation amounts to an armed conflict warranting the application of humanitarian law follows naturally from the conclusion that a state principally involved does not have an exclusive right of characterization. Writers who, like Erik Castrén, find that a principal state does have an exclusive right naturally reject any foundation for a right of other states to characterize armed conflicts.[94] The rationale offered for this position is that a belligerent state is best positioned to evaluate the facts, and that characterization by other states may conflict with that of the belligerents and bring confusion to the applicable norms. The practice of other states in past armed conflicts indicates that they have not felt bound by the characterization of the belligerent parties, but rather have proceeded to their own evaluation of the facts.[95] In this respect, the position of the belligerents is not ignored but simply considered as one relevant probative element. To illustrate, many states considered that the hostilities in Afghanistan starting in 1979 constituted an international armed conflict between Afghanistan and the U.S.S.R., while Afghanistan maintained that it was simply quelling internal disturbances with the help of Soviet forces.[96]

Noninvolved states have proceeded to independent characterizations of facts even in situations of civil strife, in which the intrusion in the "internationalized" internal affairs of a state is greatest. During the Spanish civil war, for instance, the official Spanish administration formed by the Republicans never granted recognition of belligerency to the insurgent Nationalist forces under Franco. Nevertheless, the United Kingdom acknowledged that the Nationalist forces were the de facto government of a part of Spanish territory and granted them consequent belligerent rights.[97] A more recent example is provided by a note from the Swiss Legal Adviser with regard to the armed conflict in El Salvador. In his note, the legal adviser proceeds to an objective determination of the nature of the hostilities in El Salvador that in no way defers to the evaluation of the situation by the parties to the conflict but instead concludes that Protocol II is indeed applicable.[98] In national-liberation armed conflicts, as pointed out in 1977 by the Israeli delegate at the Geneva Conference, it is unlikely that the state concerned will admit to being racist, colonial, or alien or grant that the liberation movement is representative of the people and thus capable of making a declaration under Article 96(3) of Protocol I. Other states may proceed to these qualifications, however, and many have done so in the past. A considerable number of states have, for example, given recognition to the P.L.O. – including Austria, Greece, and the U.S.S.R., to mention only a few – as the representative of the Palestinian people in the territories occupied by Israel.[99]

In relation to humanitarian law, characterizations by other states share many of the same problems that mar self-characterizations. Most important, such characterizations are commonly made on the basis of purely political considerations, with only lip service paid to the legal criteria for characterizing situations as armed conflicts. In humanitarian law, High Contracting Parties have a duty to "ensure respect" of the Geneva Conventions of 1949. This may be construed as a duty for any High Contracting Party to call for the application of humanitarian norms in a state that is also a High Contracting Party if, in its opinion, hostilities in that state constitute an armed conflict. States have in fact made such calls in cases where they sought to support one or the other side in hostilities.[100] But the likelihood that an act of characterization would be considered interference in the internal affairs of a state has had a chilling effect on other states, often discouraging clear challenges to disputable self-characterizations.[101]

Characterization of hostilities by a state that is a third party binds only that state, and not a principally involved state or any other agent.[102] This is, of course, not to deny that the characterization can have significant effects at both national and international levels. A finding that an international armed conflict is taking place in the former Yugoslavia, for example, has given Austria, Denmark, and Switzerland jurisdiction under Article 49/50/129/146 of the Geneva Conventions and Article 86 of Protocol I to try individuals in their custody for serious violations of the Conventions and protocol committed in Yugoslavia.[103]

There have been some suggestions in favor of according greater importance in humanitarian law to characterizations by states as third parties. At the expert conference preceding the Geneva Conference in 1977, one proposed solution to the problem of self-characterization in internal strife was that recognition of belligerency by several other states would act as evidence that the hostilities warranted application of humanitarian law.[104] The proposition was not taken up by the conference. Some writers have argued that even under existing law, recognition of a national-liberation movement by a number of states would constitute evidence of the movement's capacity under Protocol I, on which the depositary could rely to accept a declaration under Article 96(3).[105] In all likelihood, as Article 1(4) has yet to be applied for the first time, the depositary state would adopt a neutral position similar to that which it took in the past when national-liberation movements or unrecognized governments tried to ratify the Geneva Conventions of 1949. When the Provisional Government of the Algerian Republic tried to ratify the conventions in 1960, the Swiss government simply transmitted the document to the High Contracting Parties with a note to the effect that it was thereby expressing no opinion about the capacity of the provisional government to ratify the conventions.[106]

Acts of characterization by states that are third parties are possible and can have legal effects both within and outside the jurisdiction of the characterizing state. This does not, however, solve the problem of reluctance on the part of a state directly involved in an armed conflict to accept these characterizations, because the principle of equality of states mandates that concurrent characterizations are equally authoritative, leaving the involved state considerable control over the application of humanitarian law in its territory. In a manner similar to directly involved states themselves in making self-characterizations, other states perform characterizations at their own risk, and may be held responsible for them, if their assessments are later proved wrong by a binding decision of an international or arbitrative body.

## Political Organs of International and Regional Organizations

*Characterization by Political Bodies.*    Political organs of international and regional organizations often express opinions amounting to characterizations of specific situations as armed conflicts. Among the bodies that have been want to do so, the most significant are the General Assembly of the United Nations, the Security Council of the United Nations, and the Organization of African Unity.

For its part, the General Assembly has been quite active since the latter part of the 1960s in designating certain situations as armed conflicts and calling for the application of the relevant norms of humanitarian law. The assembly has at one time or another managed to characterize every type of armed conflict, making use of the full range of humanitarian regimes available. In direct contradiction of characterizations by some of the principal states involved, it has labeled as interstate armed conflict or military occupation the hostilities in Afghanistan, the Iraq-Kuwait war, and the presence of Israel in the Golan Heights and other territories.[107]

The General Assembly has frequently given attention to national liberation struggles, deeming them to be international armed conflicts even before the adoption of Protocol I. Thus, it has called for the full application of the Geneva Conventions of 1949 in the conflicts in Southern Rhodesia, Angola, Mozambique, and Guinea-Bissau.[108] Since the adoption of Protocol I, it has designated several conflicts as falling within the definition of Article 1(4), involving a struggle by a people against a racist, colonial, or alien regime in furtherance of its right to self-determination. For example, the assembly has called repeatedly for the application of Protocol I in the national-liberation conflict in Namibia.[109] The General Assembly has adopted the practice

of relying on the recognition of liberation movements by the Organization of African Unity or the League of Arab States in order to grant
them observer status at the United Nations.[110] As mentioned earlier,
the practice originated in the Economic Commission for Africa in the
early 1970s, and there has never been a discussion in the General
Assembly of the wisdom or legal basis of such a delegation of powers
to regional organizations.[111] In the specific context of the application
of humanitarian law, the General Assembly has labeled as national-
liberation movements that are the "sole representative of the
people" not only the South West Africa People's Organization
(SWAPO) in Namibia, as recognized by the OAU, but also the
POLISARIO. Front in the Western Sahara and FRETILIN in
East Timor, two movements not recognized by any regional organizations.[112] The General Assembly has also expressed negative opinions
about the representative character of a national-liberation movement,
one example being the description of UNITA as "armed criminal
bandits."[113]

Finally, the General Assembly has characterized as noninternational
armed conflicts a number of situations in which a state did not consider hostilities on its territory to be more than internal tensions and
disturbances. Thus the assembly has called on the government of
Burma to apply common Article 3 of the Geneva Conventions
of 1949 to the civil strife in that country.[114] It has called for the
application of both common Article 3 and Protocol II in the noninternational armed conflicts in El Salvador and the Sudan.[115]

In comparison with the General Assembly, the U.N. Security
Council has been much more subdued in its characterization of
specific situations as armed conflicts calling for the application of
humanitarian law. It has limited its actions in this respect to interstate
armed conflicts, not dealing at all with armed struggles for national
liberation or noninternational conflict. The Security Council has
on several occasions reminded Israel that its presence in the Golan
Heights and other territories under its control since 1967 constitutes
military occupation governed by the fourth Geneva Convention of
1949, thus contradicting the Israeli position that the Geneva Conventions are not applicable.[116] Similarly, rejecting a claim made by Iraq
in August 1990 to the effect that it had annexed Kuwait, the Security
Council in Resolution 670 (1990) stated its opinion that the fourth
Geneva Convention applied fully to the Iraqi occupation of Kuwait.[117]
Finally, the council also affirmed the applicability of the Geneva Conventions of 1949 to the hostilities taking place on the territory of the
former Yugoslavia.[118]

The Organization of African Unity occupies a special place in any discussion of characterization in humanitarian law because it is the only organization to possess a permanent specialized agency whose work centers on the recognition and support of national-liberation movements. The Committee for the Coordination of the Liberation of Africa, or Liberation Committee, was established in 1963 by the OAU with the specific aim of funding and coordinating the struggles of national-liberation movements in Africa. It does not directly seek to contribute to the enforcement of humanitarian law, but, as pointed out earlier, the recognition of liberation movements by a regional organization can have an indirect effect on the applicability of Protocol I by establishing that a movement is representative of a people fighting for self-determination (Art. 96(3)). The Liberation Committee has granted recognition to thirteen different movements in Africa, relying on a set of criteria reflecting the purposes of its parent organization: the movement must be representative of an entire people, be militarily and politically organized, and carry out effective military operations.[119] The territorial integrity of members of the OAU is a primordial consideration, so that movements that have posed a threat of partition, such as those in Biafra, Katanga, Eritrea, or the Sudan, have not been given recognition. How rigidly these criteria are being applied by the Liberation Committee is a matter open to debate, as it has recognized several national-liberation movements not actively engaged in military operations – for instance, MOLINACO in the Comoros or SPUP in the Seychelles.[120] As for the League of Arab States, it does not have a body comparable to the Liberation Committee of the OAU, and has given recognition to only one national liberation movement, that being the P.L.O. as representative of the people of Palestine.[121]

Plainly, political bodies do express opinions – often with clear reference to applicable standards – on the legal character of a specific situation as an armed conflict, and they do call for the application of a set of humanitarian rules. The question thus arises: what are the nature and legal effect of this type of resolution in the context of humanitarian law.

*Nature and Effect of Characterization.*   Resolutions or other decisions of political organs of international organizations were occasionally considered as a possible remedy for the problems surrounding the requirement for an active act of characterization declaring humanitarian law fully applicable to a given situation. The potential sources of such power for political bodies have a bearing on the effect of this type of statement on the applicability of humanitarian law.

At the Geneva Conference of 1949, it was suggested in the discussions about common Article 3 that a situation could automatically be considered a noninternational armed conflict if it were labeled by the General Assembly or the Security Council as a threat to international peace and security under Chapter VII of the U.N. charter.[122] The need for characterization abated somewhat when the idea of a full application of the Geneva Conventions to internal conflicts was abandoned, and the suggested role of the United Nations in this regard was discarded. The same idea resurfaced at the two conferences of government experts preceding the Geneva Conference of 1977. There it was proposed that the problems surrounding the identification of noninternational and national liberation and other noninternational armed conflicts could be solved by using the General Assembly as a judge of whether hostilities were more than internal disturbances and tensions and, if so, whether they involved a struggle by a people against colonial domination, alien occupation, or a racist regime.[123] It was objected that the power of the United Nations, and primarily of the Security Council, is limited to determining the existence of a threat to or breach of international peace and security, and does not extend to declaring humanitarian law applicable to an armed conflict of any type.[124] The special representative of the Secretary-General pointed out that, quite apart from Chapter VII, the U.N. charter sets as one of the purposes of the organization the promotion of both peace and the self-determination of people (Article 1(3) & 55–56), leaving a way open for characterization of various situations as armed conflicts.[125] Despite recognition of the importance of the issue, a provision dealing specifically with characterization by the United Nations was rejected at the conference, owing mainly to the fear of long delays, the political nature of the U.N. process, and the factual complication of armed conflicts, particularly internal conflicts.[126]

Article 89 of Protocol I could perhaps be interpreted as furnishing a ground for U.N. intervention in the form of characterization. Initially proposed as a provision subjecting the taking of reprisals by belligerents to control by the Security Council, the article was diluted to the point of containing an exceedingly vague exhortation to states to cooperate with the United Nations in case of "serious violations" of the protocol or conventions.[127] The notion of "serious violations" is broader than that of "grave breaches" and, according to the I.C.R.C.'s commentary of the protocol, would include global violations of the protocol and conventions such as an unjustified refusal to admit that a situation constitutes an armed conflict. The I.C.R.C. suggested that one type of U.N. action possible with regard to a serious violation would be the adoption of resolutions requiring the application of the protocol or conventions to specific hostilities.[128] Several states abstained from voting in favor of Article 89 because of what they considered its overly vague and imprecise wording and also expressed serious misgivings about granting the United Nations the power to react in this way to serious violations of humanitarian law.[129] While it is possible to sympathize with the I.C.R.C.'s effort to make the most of a failed proposal to regulate reprisals, it is unjustified to include in a hortative call to cooperate with the United Nations the creation of a duty to submit to the organization's characterization of situations as armed conflicts. Even if it is admitted that the conference of 1977 could have granted additional powers to the Security Council or General Assembly, by a sort of *dédoublement fonctionnel*, it did not do so in adopting Article 89 of Protocol I.

In the end, no consensus could be found at the conference of 1977 in favor of a provision that would clarify the effect of the many resolutions adopted by various political organs of the United Nations characterizing hostilities as armed conflicts and declaring the applicability of the Geneva Conventions or Protocols. The conference discussions and treaty provisions touching on the relevance of characterization by political bodies of the United Nations to humanitarian law constitute the most extensive consideration of the role of such bodies in the classification of factual situations under humanitarian law. As mentioned earlier, recognition of national-liberation movements by regional organizations was contemplated as a possible condition for the application of Protocol I but, ultimately, no such provision was included.[130] Some writers, adducing the general powers of political bodies and their status as an embodiment of the community of states, nevertheless conclude that, despite the lack of a specific provision in most of the relevant instruments, characterization by these bodies does have a binding force on states.[131] Political, legal, and institutional elements combine to refute this position.

In addressing the issue of whether a given situation ought to be denominated an armed conflict for the purposes of the applicability of humanitarian law, political organs of international organizations such as the General Assembly of the United Nations are guided by essentially political considerations. The same is true of a declaration by the OAU that a national-liberation movement is representative of a people or that hostilities constitute an armed conflict.[132] This political factor explains the fact that recognition of states or governments by the United Nations does not imply or oblige recognition of them by individual member states of the organization.[133] Thus Arab states could cohabit with the state of Israel at the United Nations while not recognizing its existence. Similarly, recognition of a national-liberation movement as representative of a people by the General Assembly does not bind member states with respect to the application of Article 1(4) of Protocol I. For instance, the United Kingdom and Australia clearly rejected the General Assembly's repeated recognition of SWAPO as the movement representing the Namibian people.[134] The same obtains for characterization by the assembly of a situation as an armed conflict to which humanitarian law is applicable. In invoking humanitarian law, the assembly cannot determine whether that body of norms is legally applicable to the facts, but rather uses the Geneva Conventions and Protocols as sources of the most elementary considerations of humanity, to which all governments should feel morally bound in all situations.[135] Simply put, legal and political mechanisms at the international level have different, if sometimes overlapping or coincident, implications for different states.[136] The fact that the General Assembly held that Zionism is racism does not imply that Israel should legally be considered a racist regime for the purposes of Article 1(4) of Protocol I, as was called for by the P.L.O. representative at the Geneva Conference of 1977.[137] This is not to underestimate the value of a determination by the assembly that a state should feel compelled to apply the conventions or protocols, as it is by no means evident, considering the general underdevelopment of the international legal system, that political mechanisms are generally less effective than legal ones.

These remarks on the political character of the decisions of the General Assembly equally apply to the Security Council. The decisions of the council are also of an essentially political nature, as clearly shown by its voting procedures, which incorporate an unequal right of veto, and they should not be considered a legal opinion binding on all states when it comes to determining the existence of an armed conflict.[138] One element specific to the Security Council is its power under Article 39 of the Charter of the United Nations to determine the existence of a threat to or breach of international peace or an act of aggression. As noted at the Conference of Government Experts in 1971, the determination of the existence of such a threat and the characterization of a situation as an armed conflict do not necessarily coincide. Past threats to international peace have included severe violations of human rights that did not involve either international or intrastate armed hostilities, such as the events in Haiti leading to the adoption of Resolution 841 (1993). Two recent decisions by the I.C.J., *Lockerbie (Interim)* and *Application of the Genocide Convention (Provisional Measures)*, seem to suggest that there are few limits imposed on the Security Council's discretion to decide what constitutes a threat to international peace and security and to order whatever remedial measures it deems appropriate, including the application of the Geneva Conventions and Protocols.[139] For instance, the Security Council in Resolution 670 (1990), acting expressly under Chapter VII of the Charter of the United Nations, declared that the situation involving the Iraqi invasion and occupation of Kuwait was governed by the Geneva Conventions. The normative source of a decision of this kind lies entirely in the Charter, and not in international humanitarian law. Chapter VII is here the sword allowing the Security Council to cut right through the Gordian knot of characterization. Any decision by the Security Council based on provisions other than Chapter VII of the Charter will have no obligatory effect either on the state or state(s) involved or other states as third parties.

The I.C.J. discussed the nature of the decision-making process of both the General Assembly and the Security Council in its 1948 advisory opinion on the *Admission of a State to the United Nations*.[140] The question centered on whether member states, in voting for or against admission of a state to the United Nations, could take into consideration elements other than those listed in Article 4 of the Charter, including purely political elements. The court split sharply by a vote of nine to six. The majority found that, despite their nature as political bodies, the General Assembly and Security Council were entrusted with a quasi-judicial function by the Charter and thus were under an obligation to refrain from considering elements not included in the necessary and sufficient conditions listed in Article 4.[141] The dissenters strongly disagreed, stating that the Assembly and the Council were perfectly entitled to rely on political factors in making political decisions such as whether to admit new states as members.[142] Even if the validity of the more restrictive majority position is granted, it would apply strictly to functions specifically devolved to these bodies, and not to acts performed under their general powers. In other words, if in matters such as the admission of new members by the General Assembly or the declaration of the existence of a threat to peace by the Security Council, these bodies are limited in this way, they are not so limited when characterizing a situation as an armed conflict. In executing the latter function, political bodies of the United Nations are performing a political task to which should not attach effects similar to characterization by a judicial body. As noted by the I.C.J. in the *Nicaragua (Jurisdiction and Admissibility)* case, these two functions are "separate but complementary."[143] The question of the characterization of situations under humanitarian law thus does not raise problems similar to those posed by the *Lockerbie* and *Application of the Genocide Convention* cases.

At a very general level, the quasi-judicial and lawmaking functions of political organs of international organizations are intimately linked. Applications of an existing set of rules to particular facts inevitably result in the creation of a new, more specific rule, following the model of common-law development in Anglo-American municipal law.[144] As long as there is resistance to regarding the resolutions of political organs as creating positive law, and not merely aspirational "soft law," these resolutions cannot be accepted as being legally binding on states. Characterization by political organs is thus "soft characterization," not in itself imposing an obligation on member states.

*Independent Bodies*

Other types of supranational bodies concerned with the observance of humanitarian law have also been confronted with having to characterize situations as armed conflicts. These bodies differ greatly from one another in status and structure, but one feature they have in common is not being directly controlled by state interests. Among these specialized bodies two of the most likely candidates to take an active role in characterizing a situation as an armed conflict of one type or the other are the International Committee of the Red Cross (I.C.R.C.) and the International Fact-Finding Commission. While there are a few other specialized bodies that can be called on to give an opinion about the character of a conflict, the International Court of Justice being one of them, they are unlikely to play a significant role in the application of humanitarian law.

The I.C.R.C. is, of course, not an international organization but rather a hybrid body, formed by private individuals but given a measure of international personality by its recognition in the Geneva Convention and Protocols.[145] The role specifically envisaged for the I.C.R.C. by these instruments is one of protecting and assisting victims of armed conflicts.[146] Nowhere in the Geneva Conventions and Protocols is a provision expressly made for a role for the I.C.R.C. in the characterization of a situation as an armed conflict. Such a provision was under consideration at the Conferences of Government Experts in 1971 and 1972, during which suggestions were made to include in Protocol I an article giving the I.C.R.C. power or discretion to make a determination, which would be non-binding, of the existence of an armed conflict in a given territory.[147] In any event, the I.C.R.C. actually opposed these suggestions, which were never pursued further.[148]

Occasionally, the I.C.R.C. has expressed opinions about the legal basis of its intermediation. For instance, in response to the International Red Cross Conference, the I.C.R.C. opined that common Article 3 applied in Afghanistan, Ogaden, and the Western Sahara.[149] In speaking about other situations, such as the Iran-Iraq hostilities, the invasion of Kuwait by Iraq, and the fighting in Bosnia-Herzegovina, the I.C.R.C. has called for compliance with humanitarian norms, by implication qualifying these situations as armed conflicts.[150] Nevertheless, the general policy of the I.C.R.C. is to abstain from characterizing situations in which it intervenes. As put by its president, Alexandre Hay, "the primary interest of the I.C.R.C. is the protection of victims, and not to provide a legal definition of a conflict situation, or to specify the status of persons to be protected. Besides, the I.C.R.C. is perfectly aware that it has neither the competence nor the power to impose its views in these matters."[151] To take just two examples of how this policy is borne out by the record, the I.C.R.C. asked to visit prisoners in Kenya in 1957 and in Afghanistan in 1979 without specifically referring to their status as prisoners of war or to the nature of events occurring in these countries.[152] The I.C.R.C. visits political prisoners in peacetime as well as in wartime and provides relief in a wide variety of crisis situations, including natural disasters, so that its mere presence in a situation cannot in itself be taken as a characterization of that situation as an armed conflict. For the I.C.R.C., the fact that its intervention is not an implied or express act of characterization is seen as essential to its primary function of assistance, which it considers to be incompatible with one aiming to force the application of humanitarian law.[153] The I.C.R.C. is thus unlikely to fulfill any systematic role in the characterization of armed conflicts.

The International Fact-Finding Commission, the first permanent international body entrusted specifically with the implementation of humanitarian law, was established by Article 90 of Protocol I. The commission came into being in June 1991, a few months after Canada became the twentieth state to make a declaration accepting its competence.[154] Under the terms of Article 90(2)(c)(i), the commission is competent to inquire into any allegation of a "grave breach as defined in the Conventions and this Protocol or other serious violation of the Conventions or of this Protocol" committed by a state party having accepted the competence of the commission. While the concept of "grave breaches" is precisely defined in the Geneva Conventions (Article 50/51/130/147) and Protocol I (Article 11(4) & 85), that of "serious violations" appears for the first time in Protocol I, without any clear indication of what its content might be.[155] It is clear from the phrasing of the provision that serious violations are a broader concept than grave breaches. The I.C.R.C. in its commentary on

Protocol I suggests that serious violations include, *inter alia*, "global" violations of the conventions and the protocol, which can be described as improper characterizations of a situation to an extent that denies the applicability of humanitarian law.[156] Others have suggested that while grave breaches are offenses attributable both to the individual perpetrator and the state, incurring individual responsibility as envisaged in the conventions and the protocol, serious violations are actions exclusively imputable to the state, for which there would be no individual responsibility.[157] This is also consistent with an interpretation of serious violations as including improper characterization, given that this is an act of states rather than individuals.

Even admitting that serious violation should be read to include the question of characterization, three elements combine to undermine the potential contribution of the International Fact-Finding Commission in this respect. First, the commission's competence does not extend to cover violations of Protocol II (Article 90(2)(c)(i), Protocol I), nor does the narrowly defined notion of "grave breach" include the violation of common Article 3 of the Geneva Conventions of 1949. Thus, the application of humanitarian law in noninternational armed conflicts, in which disagreements over characterization are most frequent, seems excluded from the commission's general competence under Article 90(2)(c). Article 90(2)(d), however, in referring both to "other situations" – as opposed to "grave breach" and "serious violation" (in Article 90(2)(c)(i)) – and to "Parties to the conflict" – as opposed to "High Contracting Parties" (in Art. 90(2)(a)) – opens a door through which the commission could extend its competence to include noninternational armed conflicts.[158] The opening is quite narrow, however, in that it subjects the commission's competence to the consent of the other parties to the conflict. Alternatively, the concept of "serious violations" in Article 90(2)(c)(i) could be construed, in accordance with Security Council Resolution 955 (1994) on the establishment of an international criminal tribunal for Rwanda, to include violations of common Article 3 of the Geneva Conventions.[159] With the support of this bold innovation by the Security Council, the commission could expand its general competence to cover common Article 3 and, more generally, noninternational armed conflicts.[160]

The second element complicating the role of the International Fact-Finding Commission pertains to the power to initiate an inquiry. After protracted discussions at the Geneva Conference, the idea that the commission could initiate an inquiry *proprio motu* was rejected by a majority of states. Under the terms of Article 90(2), the procedure is necessarily inter-state. An inquiry can be started either at the request of any state, not necessarily a party to the conflict, having accepted the commission's competence with respect to a similarly obligated state (Article 90(2)(a)), or at the request of a party to the conflict if all other parties concerned agree (Article 90(2)(d)).[161] Given the marked reluctance of states to use inter-state complaint mechanisms where available, and especially with respect to the jurisdiction of human rights bodies,[162] it appears unlikely that states not involved in the conflict would present the necessary petition to the commission. This is especially problematic in noninternational armed conflicts and in national-liberation armed conflicts, where the concerned state would probably consider, albeit incorrectly, that the petition is an intrusion into its internal affairs. Only in the case of an international conflict in which the parties have already accepted the Commission's competence is it at all likely that that body will be given the chance to act.

The third element hindering a significant role for the Fact–Finding Commission in the characterization of armed conflict has to do with the nature of the commission's function. The commission is not a tribunal and does not adjudge the legality of the parties' conduct.[163] Its task is simply to assess the factual situation and report it to the parties involved with "such recommendation as it may deem appropriate" (Article 90(5)(a), Protocol I). Findings of facts cannot, of course, be completely detached from the law, if only in the evaluation of which facts are significant. What is more, the commission must determine whether there appears to be prima facie evidence of a grave breach or serious violation.[164] Nevertheless, the fact-finding function of the commission will probably limit its power to make firm recommendations about the legal character of a situation. Because the commission has never been called upon to perform its function, it would be rather speculative to say how strongly worded these recommendations can be. Much will depend on its interpretation of its own jurisdiction under Article 90 of Protocol I. Even a nonbinding recommendation by a neutral or impartial body such as the commission can be effective in drawing the attention of the world community to a situation of conflict and thus pressuring a state into recognizing the applicability of humanitarian law. The potential impact of the commission's findings and recommendations is hampered, however, by the fact that they cannot be made public by the commission unless so requested by all parties to the conflict (Article 90(5)(c), Protocol I). Parties to the conflict are, on the other hand, free to release the commission's report.[165]

It is still too early to predict the significance of the International Fact-Finding Commission's possible contribution to solving the problem of characterization of armed conflicts. Nevertheless, the low rate of acceptance of the commission's competence by state parties and the serious limitations imposed on that competence by Article 90 of Protocol I suggest that this contribution may well be rather limited.

Other international bodies have either proceeded to characterize armed conflicts on their own initiative or been presented as possible agents of characterization. The International Court of Justice in the *Nicaragua v. United States* case, for example, found that a non-international armed conflict was taking place on the territory of Nicaragua.[166] Such interventions by the I.C.J., however desirable because of their impartial and binding nature, are unlikely to be more than exceptions because of the limited acceptance of the court's jurisdiction. The problem is similar for ad hoc bodies such as the U.N. international criminal tribunals for Yugoslavia and Rwanda, whose powers are strictly limited to covering situations and acts within narrowly defined parameters.[167]

Some have suggested that human rights bodies might be used to control compliance with humanitarian law.[168] The competence of regional and universal human rights bodies is, however, limited to the enforcement of the human rights entrenched in the relevant conventions, and these bodies cannot simply expand their jurisdiction to cover the application of humanitarian law.[169] The European Convention for the Protection of Human Rights and Fundamental Freedoms does contain one window through which the European Commission on Human Rights and the European Court of Human Rights could examine the applicability of humanitarian law. Article 15(1) specifies that no derogation from the right to life (Art. 2) is permissible "except in respect of death resulting from lawful acts of war." This means that, in cases where the state concerned has declared a state of emergency, the European human rights organs may be called on to decide whether a killing was justified according to humanitarian law, and it necessarily implies a prior characterization by the European Commission or Court of the situation as an armed conflict. More broadly, the limitation found in the International Covenant on Civil and Political Rights (Article 4(1)), the American Convention on Human Rights (Article 27(1)) and the European Convention for the Protection of Human Rights and Fundamental Freedoms (Article 15(1)) whereby emergency measures must comply with "other obligations under international law" includes compliance with applicable humanitarian law.[170] Determining whether humanitarian law creates obligations applicable in the context of an emergency will likewise require the body monitoring human rights to characterize the situation either as armed conflict of one type or another or as disturbances not calling for the application of humanitarian law. It is thus possible that various human rights bodies could be called on to characterize armed conflicts.

In *Cyprus v. Turkey*, the majority of the European Commission addressed this point and concluded that, since Turkey had not declared a state of emergency, all norms were fully applicable, so that there was no need to examine the applicability of humanitarian law.[171] In dissenting opinions, two members of the Commission adopted a much broader position, holding that humanitarian law generally marks the limits of derogations "strictly required by the exigencies of the situations" (Article 15(1), European Convention), so that an action in compliance with humanitarian law will constitute a permissible derogation from human rights law.[172] This interpretation of humanitarian law as supplementary to human rights law is problematic, because the threshold of protection afforded by humanitarian law is not systematically lower than that of human rights law. Some rights are actually more fully protected under humanitarian law in wartime than under human rights law in peacetime (e.g., protection against medical experimentation), while some human rights have no equivalents at all in humanitarian law (e.g., prohibition of preventive detention).[173] Nevertheless, the significant parallels between the two legal systems suggest that in some respects humanitarian law could prove useful in determining which human rights derogations are strictly required by a state of emergency. There is clearly a need for a greater articulation of the relationship between human rights and humanitarian law in situations combining a state of emergency and an armed conflict.

Human rights bodies need to be cautious in labeling a situation an armed conflict, because it can be taken by the state concerned as a justification for any of its policies that violate human rights. For this reason, the Inter-American Commission on Human Rights has refrained from discussing the applicability of common Article 3 of the Geneva Conventions of 1949 to emergency situations, despite a call by the General Assembly of the Organization of American States to address the question of the violation of human rights by nongovernmental groups.[174]

Independent bodies active in the field of humanitarian law offer the most promising solution to the problem of characterization of situations as armed conflicts, because they are both impartial in their nature and legal in their approach. They suffer from serious limitations, however, related to the breadth of their powers and the extent of acceptance of their competence. Because of these limitations, characterization by specialized bodies does not provide a definite answer to the problem, but simply contributes one piece to the puzzle of the definition of armed conflicts.

## Conclusion

Principally involved states, national-liberation movements, other states as third parties, political organs of international organizations, and independent bodies all concurrently perform active acts of characterization. When recourse to independent bodies offering guarantees of neutrality and legality is impossible, a straightforward application of the doctrine of sovereignty would lead to the conclusion that each one of these characterizations remains valid within its respective sphere of authority. Thus, the concerned state could safely refuse to apply humanitarian law, and other states as third parties and political organs of international organizations could adopt measures within their competence to give effect to their own characterizations. Such a disjointed application of humanitarian law, subjecting it to the concerned state's whim, does not appear in conformity with the very nature of this legal system as imposing binding universal norms.

An alternative approach to characterization of situations as armed conflicts centres on consensus-building, in a manner similar to the process by which customary international law is created. Under such an approach, applicable when review by an specialized body is unavailable, the totality of opinions on the legal character of a situation would be taken into consideration; when a consensus has emerged among participants, taking account of their representativeness (for international organs), neutrality, and impartiality, that global opinion acquires an obligatory character for all agents.[175] Until that consensus is reached, any agent, state, or other party, may, at its own risk, proceed to characterize situations for its own purposes.

The solution to the problem of characterization proposed here is quite unsatisfactory, being both cumbersome and difficult to use. That, however, is symptomatic of international law generally at this stage of its development. The explosion of norms has not been accompanied by a corresponding evolution of mechanisms. The problem is mirrored in the context of the formation of customary international law, which is intimately tied to the question of the application of norms. Until the international community gives itself permanent bodies capable of guiding the development and application of international law, inconsistencies and shortcomings will have to be reckoned with.

## Notes

1. The Secretary General's *Report pursuant to Security Council Resolution 808 (1993)* notes with respect to para. 1 of the Resolution limiting the Tribunal's jurisdiction to events occurring after 1 January 1991 that "no judgment as to the international or internal character of the conflict is being exercised": U.N. Doc. S/25704 (3 May 1993), *reprinted in* 32 Int'l Legal Mat. 1159, para. 62.

2. See *The Prosecutor v. Duško Tadic a/k/a "Dule"* (Decision on the Defence Motion for Interlocutory Appeal on Jurisdiction), 2 October 1995, Case No. IT-94-1-AR72 (International Criminal Tribunal for Yugoslavia, Appeals Chamber) at 39–43 paras. 72–77; William Fenrick, *In the Field with U.N.C.O.E.: Investigating Atrocities in the Territory of the Former Yugoslavia* (1995), 7–13 (on file with the author); *Final Report of the Commission of Experts Established Pursuant to Security Council Resolution 780 (1992)*, U.N. Doc. S/1994/674 Annex (27 May 1994) paras. 42–54; Bosko Jakovljevic, *Agreements for the Implementation of International Humanitarian Law in the Armed Conflict in Former Yugoslavia*, in Sonja Biserko (ed.), Yugoslavia: Collapse, War, Crime (Belgrade: Center for Anti-War Action, 1993) 161, 182–184. See also Éric David, *Le Tribunal pénal international pour l'ex-Yougoslavie*, [1992] 2 Revue belge de droit international 565, 570–572; Karin Oellers-Frahm, *Das Statut des internationalen Strafgerichtshofs zur Verfolgung von Kriegsverbrechen im ehemaligen Jugoslawien*, (1994) 54 Zeitschrift für ausländisches öffentliches Recht und Völkerrecht 416, 422.

3. See generally Thomas Franck, The Power of Legitimacy Among Nations (New York: Oxford UP, 1990) 50–66; H.L.A. Hart, The Concept of Law (Oxford: Clarendon, 1961) 121–132; Martti Koskenniemi, From Apology to Utopia – The Structure of International Legal Argument (Helsinki: Lakimiesliiton Kustannus, 1989) 22–23; Jean J.A. Salmon, *Some Observations on Characterization in Public International Law*, in Antonio Cassese (ed.), U.N. Law/Fundamental Rights (Alphen a/d Rijn: Sijthoff & Nordhoff, 1979) 3–21; *id.*, *Les faits dans l'application du droit international*,' (1982–II) 175 Recueil des cours 257.

4. See Hans Kelsen, General Theory of Law and the State (Cambridge MA: Harvard U.P., 1946) 135–136 & 221–222; Salmon, *Les faits dans l'application, id.*, at 385–387.

5. Salmon, *Some Observations on Characterization, supra*, note 3, at 8–9.

6. For example, during the Vietnam War, both North and South Vietnam were party to the 1949 Geneva Conventions, but the

North considered the conflict an internal war while the South viewed it as a war of aggression waged by the North. See Dietrich Schindler, *The Different Types of Armed Conflicts According to the Geneva Conventions and Protocols* (1979–II) 163 Recueil des cours 117, 127.

7. See René-Jean Wilhelm, *Problèmes relatifs à la protection de la personne humaine par le droit international dans les conflits armés ne présentant pas un caractère international* (1972–III) 137 Recueil des cours 316, 341.

8. See Franck, *supra*, note 3, at 60.

9. See Franck, *id.*, at 55–57; Salmon, *Le fait dans l'application, supra*, note 3, at 277.

10. The two 1977 Protocols are: Protocol Additional to the Geneva Conventions of 12 August 1949, and Relating to the Protection of Victims of International Armed Conflicts (Protocol I), 8 June 1977, 1 *Official Records of the Diplomatic Conference on the Reaffirmation and Development of International Humanitarian Law Applicable in Armed Conflicts, Geneva (1974–1977)* (Bern: Federal Political Dept., 1977) 115; Protocol Additional to the Geneva Conventions of 12 August 1949, and Relating to the Protection of War Victims of Non-International Armed Conflicts (Protocol II), 8 June 1977, 1 *Official Records*, at 185, *reprinted in* Dietrich Schindler & Jiří Toman, The Laws of Armed Conflicts, 3rd ed. (Dordrecht: Nijhoff, 1988) 621 & 689.

11. Convention (I) for the Amelioration of the Condition of the Wounded and Sick in Armed Forces in the Field, 12 August 1949, *Final Record of the Diplomatic Conference of Geneva of 1949*, Federal Political Dept., Berne, at 205 (1949) 75 U.N.T.S. 31; Convention (II) for the Amelioration of the Condition of Wounded, Sick, and Shipwrecked Members of Armed Forces at Sea, 12 August 1949, *Final Record*, at 225 (1949) 75 U.N.T.S. 85; Convention (III) relative to the Treatment of Prisoners of Wars, 12 August 1949, *Final Record*, at 243 (1949) 75 U.N.T.S. 135; Convention (IV) relative to the Protection of Civilian Persons in Time of War, 12 August 1949, *Final Record*, at 297 (1949) 75 U.N.T.S. 287. *Reprinted in* Schindler & Toman, *id.*, at 373, 401, 423 & 495.

12. Lassa Oppenheim, 2 International Law, Hersch Lauterpacht ed., 7th ed. (London: Longmans, 1952) 202. See also Emmerich de Vattel, 3 Le droit des gens ou principes de la loi naturelle (1758), James Brown Scott ed. (Washington: Carnegie, 1916) Sec. 1–4 ("war is that state in which nations, under the authority of their respective government, prosecute their right by force"); Joseph

L. Kunz, Kriegsrecht und Neutrali tätsrecht (Vienna: Springer, 1935) 4–11; Louis Delbez, *La notion juridique de guerre*, (1953) 57 Revue générale de droit international public 177, 178–200 (defining war as "une lutte armée entre États, voulue par l'un d'entre eux au moins, et entreprise en vue de défendre un intérêt national" – at 178).

13. See Fritz Grob, The Reality of War and Peace (New Haven: Yale UP, 1949) 64–79.

14. See Christopher Greenwood, *The Concept of War in Modern International Law* (1987) 36 Int'l & Comp. L. Quart. 283, 294–295.

15. See Grob, *supra*, note 13, at 189. But see Werner Meng, *War*, in Rudolf Bernhardt (ed.), [Instalment] 4 Encyclopedia of Public International Law (Amsterdam: North-Holland, 1982) 282–290.

16. Grob, *id*. at 79–81 and 217–218.

17. Ian Brownlie, International Law and the Use of Force by States (Oxford: Clarendon, 1961) 386–388; Grob, *id*., at 140–161 and 208–216. Other examples could include the 1937–41 Sino-Japanese conflict, the 1935 Italo-Ethiopian conflict, the 1951–3 Korean War, the 1982 Falklands War, etc. See Julius Stone, Legal Control of international Conflict, 2nd ed. (London: Stevens and Sons, 1959) 311 n. 79; Greenwood, *supra*, note 14, at 293.

18. On the present (ir)relevance of the notion of war in other areas of international law, see Dietrich Schindler, *State of War, Belligerency, Armed Conflict*, in Antonio Cassese (ed.), The New Humanitarian Law of Armed Conflict (Naples: Ed. scientifica, 1979) 3–20.

19. See Grob, *supra*, note 13, at 217–218; Karl Joseph Partsch, *Armed Conflict*, in Rudolf Bernhardt (ed.), [Instalment] 3 Encyclopedia of Public International Law (Amsterdam: North-Holland, 1982) 25, 26. Note, however, the British declaration on signature of Protocol I, stating "in relation to Article 1, that the term 'armed conflict' of itself and in its context implies a certain level of intensity of military operations which must be present before the Conventions or the Protocol are to apply to any given situation": *reprinted in* Schindler & Toman, *supra*, note 10, at 717. If the declaration was meant to cover all armed conflicts mentioned in Article 1 of Protocol I, and not only national liberation conflicts in Article 1(4), it would raise the threshold of applicability of humanitarian law so as to exclude inter-state conflict of a low intensity.

20. Delbez, *supra*, note 12, at 207; Greenwood, *supra*, note 14, at 295.

21. The governing provision was Art. 42 of the 1907 Hague Regulation ("Territory is considered occupied when it is actually

placed under the authority of the hostile army. The occupation extends only to the territory where such authority has been established and can be exercised").

22. *U.S. v. Krauch et al. (I.G. Farben Trial)* (1948) 10 L. Rep. Trials War Crim. 1, 42 (U.S. Mil. Trib., Nuremberg).

23. *U.S. v. Weizsaecker et al. (Ministries Trial)* (1949) 16 Ann. Digest & Rep. Pub. Int'l L. Cases 344, 347 (U.S. Mil. Trib., Nuremberg).

24. See Jean Pictet, 4 Commentary of the 1949 Geneva Convention IV (Geneva: I.C.R.C., 1958) 59–60.

25. Adam Roberts, *What is Military Occupation?* (1984) 55 Brit. Y.B. Int'l L. 249–305.

26. Yves Sandoz, *La place des Protocoles additionnels aux Conventions de Genève du 12 août 1949 dans le droit humanitaire* (1979) 12 Revue des droits de l'homme 135, 140.

27. See Louis Henkin, How Nations Behave, 2nd ed. (New York: Columbia UP, 1979) 306–308; Katia Boustany, *La qualification des conflits en droit international public et le maintien de la paix* (1989–90) 6 Revue québécoise de droit international 38, 46–47; Tom J. Farer, *Humanitarian Law and Armed Conflict: Towards the Definition of "International Armed Conflict"* (1971) 71 Colum. L. Rev. 37, 57–60.

28. See Hans-Peter Gasser, *Internationalized Non-International Armed Conflicts: Case Studies of Afghanistan, Kampuchea and Lebanon* (1983) 33 Am. U.L. Rev. 145, 148–152; Michael Reisman & James Silk, *Which Law Applies to the Afghan Conflict?* (1988) 82 Am. J. Int'l L. 459–496.

29. See David, *supra*, note 2, at 570; Fenrick, *supra*, note 2, at 8–13.

30. See, e.g., General Assembly Resolutions 2383 (XXIII), 2395 (XXIII), 2508 (XXIV), 2547A (XXIV), 2621 (XXV), 2652 (XXV), 2678 (XXV), 2707 (XXV), 2795(XXVI), 2796 (XXVI), 2871 (XXVI). See Georges Abi-Saab, *Wars of National Liberation in the Geneva Conventions and Protocols* (1979–IV) 165 Recueil des cours 357, 373; Konrad Ginther, *Liberation Movements*, in 3 Bernhardt, *supra*, note 19, at 245, 248.

31. *Reprinted in* Schindler & Toman, *supra*, note 10, at 602–603. See Gérard Cahin & Demis Çarkaçi, *Les guerres de Libération nationale et le Droit International*, [1976] Annuaire du Tiers-Monde 34–56; Gérard Petit, *Les Mouvements de Libération nationale et le Droit*, [1976] Annuaire du Tiers-Monde 56–75.

32. C.D.D.H./SR.3 para. 48. Represented at the Conference were the A.N.C. (South Africa), A.N.C.Z. (Zimbabwe), F.N.L.A. (Angola), F.R.E.L.I.M.O. (Mozambique), P.L.O. (Palestine), PAC (South Africa), M.P.L.A. (Angola), S.P.U.P. (Seychelles),

S.W.A.P.O. (South West Africa), Z.A.N.U. and Z.A.P.U. (Zimbabwe).

33. Art. 1 was adopted in the plenary Conference by a vote of 87 in favour, 1 against, and 11 abstaining: C.D.D.H./SR.36, 6 *Off. Rec., supra,* note 10, at 40–41. Art. 96 was adopted by a vote of 93 in favour, 1 against and 2 abstaining: C.D.D.H./SR.46 para. 76, 6 *Off. Rec., id.,* at 354.

34. A similar provision is found in Art. 7(4) of the Convention on Prohibitions or Restrictions on the Use of Certain Conventional Weapons Which May be deemed to be Excessively Injurious or to Have Indiscriminate Effects, 10 October 1980, *reprinted in* Schindler & Toman, *supra,* note 10, at 179–184 [hereinafter 1980 U.N. Conventional Weapons Convention].

35. See Abi-Saab, *supra,* note 30, at 394–396; Schindler, *supra,* note 6, at 138.

36. "Nothing in the foregoing paragraph shall be construed as authorizing or encouraging any action which would dismember or impair, totally or in part, the territorial integrity or political unity of sovereign and independent States conducting themselves in compliance with the principle of equal rights and self-determination of peoples as described above and thus possessed of a government representing the whole people belonging to the territory without discrimination as to race, creed, or colour": 1970 Declaration on Principles of International Law Concerning Friendly Relations and Co-operation among States in Accordance with the Charter of the United Nations, General Assembly Res. 2625 (XXV), *reprinted in* David J. Harris, Cases and Materials on International Law, 4th ed. (London: Sweet & Maxwell, 1991) 1008.

37. See Abi-Saab, *supra,* note 30, at 396–398; Schindler, *supra,* note 6, at 136–138. The Australian delegation suggested at the Geneva Conference that the wording of Art. 1(4) ("The situations referred to in the preceding paragraph include armed conflicts which peoples are fighting. . .") is not exhaustive and could cover other types of liberation armed conflicts: C.D.D.H./I/SR.22 para.14. Although a wider application of more elaborate humanitarian norms is always desirable, it seems that the word "include" is used here because "armed conflict" under the Protocol and Conventions includes not only national liberation conflicts but also inter-state conflicts. In view of the difficulty and partial success in reaching consensus on the extension of Protocol I to national liberation wars, it seems unlikely that an open door to the applicability of Protocol I to unspecified types of armed

conflict was intended by the use of the word "include".

38. See Abi-Saab, *id.*, 413; Fatsah Ouguergouz, *Guerres de libér-ation nationale en droit humanitaire: quelques clarifications*, in Frits Kalshoven and Yves Sandoz (eds), Implementation of Inter-national Humanitarian Law (Dordrecht: Nijhoff, 1989) 333, 346.

39. Although not acting pursuant to Protocol I, it is interesting to note that the Organization of African Unity has in the past recognized several national liberation movements for one country, for example in Zimbabwe.

40. See Claude Pilloud et al., Commentary on the Additional Protocols of 8 June 1977 to the Geneva Conventions of 12 August 1949 (Dordrecht: Nijhoff, 1987) 55 [hereinafter I.C.R.C. Commentary].

41. See, e.g., General Assembly Resolution 47/29 (1992), *Observer Status of National Liberation Movements recognized by the Organization of African Unity and/or by the League of Arab States*, U.N. Doc. A/RES/47/29 (25 Nov. 1992). See generally Claude Lazarus, *Le statut des mouvements de libération nationale à l'Organisation des Nations Unies*, [1974] Annuaire français de droit international 173–200.

42. C.D.D.H./I/42, 14 March 1974.

43. Plenary Meeting, 23 May 1977, C.D.D.H./SR.36, para. 121 (Turkey); C.D.D.H./SR.36 Annex, Explanation of vote by Indonesia; Plenary Meeting, 31 May 1977, C.D.D.H./SR.46 Annex, 6 *Off. Records* 341, Explanation of vote by Mauritania and Turkey; Meeting of Committee I, 26 April 1977, C.D.D.H./I/SR.68, 9 *Off. Records* 369, paras. 5 (Indonesia), 15 (Turkey), and 30 (Zaire).

44. See para. 4 of the South Korean declaration and para. h of the British declaration, *reprinted in* Schindler & Toman, *supra*, note 10, at 713 and 717.

45. See Abi-Saab, *supra*, note 30, at 408–409; Schindler, *supra*, note 6, at 142; Ouguergouz, *supra*, note 38, at 343.

46. [1991] 2 Can. Treaty Ser. 182.

47. See Sandoz, *supra*, note 26, at 139.

48. See para. (a) of the U.K. declaration, *reprinted in* Schindler & Toman, *supra*, note 10, at 717.

49. See Abi-Saab, *supra*, note 30, at 413–414; Ouguergouz, *supra*, note 38, at 345; Schindler, *supra*, note 6, at 139–140.

50. See I.C.R.C. Commentary, *supra*, note 40, at 55; Abi-Saab, *id.*, at 410–412; Ouguergouz, *id.*, at 344; Schindler, *supra*, note 18, at 6–7.

51. See Salmon, *Some Observations on Characterization, supra*, note 3, at 5.
52. Plenary Meeting, 23 May 1977, C.D.D.H./SR.36, para. 77 (Italy); C.D.D.H./SR.36 Annex, Explanation of vote by the Federal Republic of Germany. See also Meeting of Committee I, 12 March 1974, C.D.D.H./I/SR.4, para. 10 (Ireland); *id.*, 25 March 1974, C.D.D.H./I/SR.14. Statements by Canada and the U.K. to the effect that Art. 96(3) applies only to a national-liberation movement "which is truly such a movement," or which "genuinely fulfills the criteria" do not do anything to resolve the indeterminacy: Plenary Meeting, 31 May 1977, C.D.D.H./SR.46 Annex, 6 *Off. Records* 361, Explanations of vote by Canada and the U.K.
53. See I.C.R.C., Report of the Work of the Conference of Government Experts on the Reaffirmation and Development of International Humanitarian Law of Armed Conflicts, Geneva, 24 May–12 June 1971 (Geneva: I.C.R.C., 1971) 34–36; *id.*, 1 Report of the Work of the Conference of Government Experts on the Reaffirmation and Development of International Humanitarian Law of Armed Conflicts – Second Session, Geneva, 3 May–3 June 1972 (Geneva: I.C.R.C., 1972) 68–69 paras. 2.54–.64; Wilhelm, *supra*, note 7, at 344–350. Similar tensions were also present at the 1949 Geneva Conference: 2B Final Rec., *supra*, note 11, at 76.
54. See Mohamed El Kouhene, Les garanties fondamentales de la personne en droit humanitaire et droits de l'homme (Dordrecht: Nijhoff, 1986) 78–81; I.C.R.C. Commentary, *supra*, note 40, at 1354–1355.
55. I.C.R.C. Commentary, *id.*, at 1351.
56. See Boustany, *supra*, note 27, at 42–43.
57. See I.C.R.C., 1972 Conference of Experts, *supra*, note 53, at 68 paras. 2.54–.59; I.C.R.C. Commentary, *id.*, at 1353; Wilhelm, *supra*, note 7, at 347–349; Charles Zorgbibe, *De la théorie classique de la reconnaissance de belligérance à l'Article 3 des Conventions de Genève*, in Droit humanitaire et conflits armés – Actes du colloque du 28 au 30 janvier 1970, Université libre de Bruxelles (Brussels: Éd. Univ. Bruxelles, 1976) 83, 91.
58. See Wilhelm, *id.*, at 338. Section 1808(2) Note 6 of the Canadian Forces Law of Armed Conflict Manual (Second Draft) (Ottawa: Dept. Nat'l Defense, 1984) goes so far as to demand that the insurgent organization be established in a fixed known place, or practically the establishment of the seat of a provisional government.

59. I.C.R.C. Commentary, *supra*, note 40, at 1352.
60. El Kouhene, *supra*, note 54, at 76.
61. The supranational dimension of the Spanish civil war certainly was the main influence on the internationalization of civil strife. See 2B *Final Record*, *supra*, note 11, at 9–15, 40–48, 75–79, 82–84, 90, 93–95 and 97–102; Farer, *supra*, note 27, at 43–48.
62. *Final Record, id.,* at 46–47.
63. 4 Pictet, *supra*, note 24, at 35–36.
64. See 2B *Final Record*, *supra*, note 11, at 121; Farer, *supra*, note 27, at 48.
65. The I.C.R.C. commentary does add that these conditions are not indispensable, given that few states would argue for a right to torture or mutilate bandits, and that states should observe these minimum rules at all times: 4 Pictet, *supra*, note 24, at 36.
66. Farer, *supra*, note 27, at 43.
67. See Schindler, *supra*, note 6, at 146; Wilhelm, *supra*, note 7, at 352; Charles Zorgbibe, *Le caractère armé des conflits*, in Droit humanitaire et conflits armés, *supra*, note 57, at 93, 94–99.
68. El Kouhene, *supra*, note 54, at 73; Victor Duculesco, *Effet de la reconnaissance de l'état de belligérance par les tiers, y compris les organisations internationales, sur le statut juridique des conflits armés à caractère non-international* (1975) 79 Revue générale de droit international public 125, 140; Partsch, *supra*, note 19, at 26. Lauterpacht argued for the development of a duty on the part of the state to grant belligerent or insurgent recognition: Hersch Lauterpacht, Recognition in International Law (Cambridge: Cambridge UP, 1948) 175–176 & 240–246; Wilhelm, *id.*, at 326.
69. See Michael B. Akehurst, *Civil War*, in Rudolf Bernhardt (ed.), [Instalment] 3 Encyclopedia of Public International Law (Amsterdam: North-Holland, 1982) 88; Michael Bothe, *Völkerrechtliche Aspekte des Angola Konflikts* (1977) 37 Zeitschrift für Ausländische Öffentliches Recht und Völkerrecht 572, 588–592.
70. See Wilhelm, *supra*, note 7, at 320.
71. See El Kouhene, *supra*, note 54, at 75 n. 165.
72. See El Kouhene, *id.*, at 74–79; Heather A. Wilson, International Law and the Use of Force by National Liberation Movements (Oxford: Clarendon, 1988) 124–125; Reisman & Silk, *supra*, note 28, at 479; Howard J. Taubenfeld, *The Applicability of the Laws of War in Civil War*, in John Norton Moore (ed.), Law and Civil War in the Modern World (Baltimore: Johns Hopkins Press, 1974) 499, 509–512; Examination by the U.N. Human Rights Committee of periodic reports by El Salvador and Afghanistan:

U.N. Doc. CCPR/C/SR.485 para. 5 (1983); CCPR/C/SR.608 para. 25 (1985).

73. See Theodor Meron, Human Rights in Internal Strife: Their International Protection (Cambridge: Grotius, 1987) 163.

74. See El Kouhene, *supra*, note 54, at 72; Lauterpacht, *supra*, note 68, at 240–246 (arguing that there is a duty to grant recognition); Akehurst, *supra*, note 69, at 92; Wilhelm, *supra*, note 7, at 326; Zorgbibe, *De la théorie, supra*, note 57, at 84.

75. See *supra*, notes 12–13, and accompanying text. See also Erik Castrén, The Present Law of War and Neutrality (Helsinki: Suomalaisen Tiedeakatemian Toimituksia, 1954) 33 ("the characterization of armed action as war is made by the conflicting parties themselves, or rather by one of them").

76. Schindler, *supra*, note 18, at 5–6.

77. *Plenary Meeting*, C.D.D.H./SR.49, 7 *Off. Records, supra*, note 10, at 66–83 (Colombia, Brazil, Saudi Arabia, Philippines); C.D.D.H./SR.56, at 239 (Chile); I.C.R.C., *1971 Conference of Experts, supra*, note 53, at 42 para. 203.

78. See El Kouhene, *supra*, note 54, at 75; Schindler, *supra*, note 6, at 148.

79. Wilhelm, *supra*, note 7, at 326 and 333.

80. Salmon, *Some Observations on Characterization, supra*, note 3, at 12; *id., Le fait dans l'application, supra*, note 3, at 369–370.

81. *The Asylum Case* (Colombia v. Peru), [1950] I.C.J. Rep. 274–275. See also Salmon, *id.*, at 12–13.

82. Salmon, *id.*, at 12 [emphasis in the original].

83. See Denise Plattner, *La portée juridique des déclarations de respect du droit international humanitaire qui émanent de mouvements en lutte dans un conflit armé* (1984–5) 18 Revue belge de droit international 298 n.2; Wilhelm, *supra*, note 7, at 330. For example, the 15 July 1981 declaration by S.W.A.P.O. read: "It intends to respect and be guided by the rules of the four Geneva Conventions of 12 August 1949 for the protection of the victims of armed conflicts and the 1977 Additional Protocol relating to the protection of victims of international armed conflicts (Protocol I)" (Plattner, *id.*, at 304).

84. Even in cases of partition and the creation of a separate state, which would internationalize the conflict, much seems to turn on the established state's response. Compare, for example, the reaction of Nigeria to the Biafran secession in 1967, refusing to recognize both the secession and the application of humanitarian law, and that of Yugoslavia to the partition of the state, implicitly recognizing partition in the new 1992 Constitution of "Yugoslavia" and accepting the application of the Geneva Conventions

and Protocol: David, *supra*, note 2, at 571; Duculesco, *supra*, note 68, at 149.

85. Even if both parties agree that the situation is an armed conflict, there can be disputes as to the specific nature of that conflict. Often, a government will label a conflict as an exterior invasion while the insurgents insist that it is actually a civil war. In Vietnam for example, South Vietnam and the United States viewed the conflict as an invasion from the North, while the National Liberation Front of Vietnam (Vietcong) insisted on the internal character of its struggle. The reversed occurred in Afghanistan, where the rebels considered the war an invasion from the U.S.S.R. while the Afghan government labeled the situation at most a noninternational armed conflict.

86. See *Reparation for Injuries Suffered in the Service of the United Nations Case*, [1949] I.C.J. Rep. 174, 178; Wilhelm Wengler, *La noción de sujeto de derecho internacional público examinada bajo el aspecto de algunos fenómenos políticos actuales* (1951) 3 Revista espanola de derecho internacional 831, 842–844.

87. See Plattner, *supra*, note 83, at 312–319. On the legal effects of unilateral acts, see *Nuclear Test Cases (Australia v. France; New Zealand v. France)*, [1974] I.C.J. Rep. 253 para. 43.

88. This is reflected in the Canadian declaration with respect to Article 96(3) upon ratification of Protocol II: "It is the understanding of the Government of Canada that the making of a unilateral declaration does not, in itself, validate the credentials of the person or persons making such a declaration and that States are entitled to satisfy themselves as to whether in fact the makers of such a declaration constitute an authority referred to in Article 96 [. . .]": [1991] 2 Can. Treaty Ser. 182.

89. GIAD Draper, The Red Cross Conventions (1958) 15 n.47. Fleiner-Gerster and Meyer go so far as to suggest that the decision to apply Article 3 usually rests on nonhumanitarian grounds: Thomas Fleiner-Gerster & Michael A. Meyer, *New Developments in Humanitarian Law: A Challenge to the Concept of Sovereignty* (1985) 34 Int'l & Comp. L. Quart. 267, 274.

90. See Wilson, *supra*, note 72, at 125; Farer, *supra*, note 27, at 58–59.

91. See Edward K. Kwakwa, The International Law of Armed Conflict: Personal and Material Field of Application (Dordrecht: Nijhoff, 1992) 74 & 80; Wilson, *supra*, note 72, at 126. Israel remains somewhat of an exception in this respect: *Tsemel v. Ministry of Defense (Israel)* (1983) 37:3 Piskei Din 365–380 (Israel Supreme Ct), *translated in* (1984) 1 Palestinian Y.B. Int'l L.

164–174 (reviewing the question of whether the territories are occupied within the meaning of the Hague and Geneva Conventions).

92. Aristidis Calogeropoulos-Stratis, Droit humanitaire et droits de l'homme: la protection de la personne en conflits armés (Geneva: Institut universitaire de hautes études internationales, 1980) 94.

93. Plenary Meeting, 23 May 1977, C.D.D.H./SR.36, para. 61.

94. Castrén, *supra*, note 75, at 35.

95. See Brownlie, *supra*, note 17, at 410; Zorgbibe, *De la théorie*, *supra*, note 57, at 87.

96. See Reisman & Silk, *supra*, note 28.

97. Among other things, the laws passed by the insurgents rather than by the official government were deemed to be in force in proceedings before British courts: Lauterpacht, *supra*, note 68, at 272–274. See also Grob, *supra*, note 13, at 204.

98. Lucius Caflisch, *Pratique suisse relative au droit international en 1986*, (1987) 43 Annuaire suisse de droit international 185–187.

99. See Lassa Oppenheim, 1 International Law, Robert Jennings and Arthur Watts eds., 9th ed. (Harlow, U.K.: Longman, 1992) 164.

100. Wilhelm, *supra*, note 7, at 337.

101. See Zorgbibe, *Le caractère armé,* supra, note 67, at 99.

102. See 2 Oppenheim (1952), *supra*, note 12, at 209; Duculesco, *supra*, note 68, at 130; Krzysztof Skubiszewski, *Peace and War*, in 4 Bernhardt, *supra*, note at 74, 75.

103. See Robert Block, *Serb Accused of Genocide at First War-Crimes Trial*, The Independent (London), 21 October 1994, at 12.

104. See El Kouhene, *supra*, note 54, at 74 n.162.

105. Duculesco, *supra*, note 68, at 130; Schindler, *supra*, note 6, at 144.

106. See Michel Veuthey, Guérilla et droit humanitaire (Geneva: Institut Henri-Dunant, 1976) 49. To the same effect with respect to the P.L.O. "ratification" of the Geneva Conventions and Protocols in 1989, see the Swiss government's letter of transmittal to High Contracting Parties: (1989) 5 Palestinian Y.B. Int'l L. 328–332.

107. On Afghanistan, see General Assembly Resolutions 40/137 (1986), 46/136 (17 Dec. 1991) and 47/141 (18 Dec. 1992) ("Noting with deep concern that a situation of armed conflict persists in Afghanistan. . ."). On Israel, see e.g., General Assembly Resolutions 36/147F (16 Dec. 1981), 26/226B (17 Dec. 1981), 47/63, 47/64, 47/70 (11 Dec. 1992). On Kuwait, see General Assembly Resolution 46/135 (17 Dec. 1991). See

generally David Weissbrodt, *The Role of International Organizations in the Implementation of Human Rights and Humanitarian Law in Situations of Armed Conflict* (1988) 21 Vanderbilt J. Int'l L. 313, 325–331.

108. See, e.g., General Assembly Res. 2383 (XXIII) para. 13 (Southern Rhodesia), 2395 (XXIII) para. 12 (Angola, Mozambique, Guinea-Bissau), 2508 (XXIV) para. 11 (Southern Rhodesia, Zimbabwe), 2547A (XXIV) (various terr.), 2652 (XXV) para. 11 (Southern Rhodesia), 2678 (XXV) para.11 (Namibia), 2707 (XXV) para. 6 (Angola, Mozambique, Guinea-Bissau), 2795 (XXVI) para. 7 (*id.*), 2796 (XXVI) para. 10 (Southern Rhodesia), 2871 (XXV) para. 8 (Namibia).

109. See General Assembly Res. 41/39A (20 Nov. 1986), where in para. 75 the Assembly "Declares that the liberation struggle in Namibia is a conflict of an international character in terms of article 1, paragraph 4, of Additional Protocol I to the Geneva Conventions of 12 August 1949, and, in this regard, demands that the Conventions and Additional Protocol be applied by South Africa." See also General Assembly Res. 41/35A (10 Nov. 1986) para. 8, 39/50A (12 Dec. 1984) para. 66.

110. See General Assembly Res. 35/167 (15 Dec. 1980), 37/104 (16 Dec. 1982), 41/71 (3 Dec. 1986), 43/160B (9 Dec. 1988), 45/37 (28 Nov. 1990), 47/29 (25 Nov. 1992). The practice has been adopted by other U.N. agencies and bodies, including the Committee Against Apartheid, I.C.A.O., I.L.O., U.N.E.S.C.O., U.N.D.P., U.N.I.D.O., and W.H.O.: (1981) 38 Y.B.U.N. 168–169; 1 Oppenheim (1992), *supra*, note 99, at 164 n. 12; *Legal Opinion Prepared for the Under-Secretary-General Office for Inter-Agency Affairs and Co-ordination*, [1974] U.N. Jur. Y.B. 149–156.

111. See Lazarus, *supra*, note 41, at 182. There was a debate in the U.N. Council for Namibia as to the desirability of relying on O.A.U. recognition of national-liberation movements for granting observer status, with some members seeking to admit as observer S.W.A.N.U. and S.W.A.N.U.F., in addition to S.W.A.P.O., the movement recognized by the OAU. The Council eventually recognized only S.W.A.P.O.: *id.*, at 183.

112. See, for S.W.A.P.O., General Assembly Res. 40/97A (13 Dec. 1985), 41/39A (20 Nov. 1986) para. 10, 41/101 (4 Dec. 1986) para. 27; for the Frente P.O.L.I.S.A.R.I.O., General Assembly Res. 34/37 (21 Nov. 1979), 35/19 (11 Nov. 1980); and for FRETILIN, General Assembly Res. 36/50 (24 Nov. 81).

113. General Assembly Res. 41/35A (10 Nov. 1986) para. 12. See

also General Assembly Res. 46/87 (16 Dec. 1991) para. 20, speaking of "externally supported armed terrorists" in Mozambique.

114. General Assembly Res. 47/144 (18 Dec. 1992) para. 10. Burma acceded to the 1949 Geneva Conventions only in 1992, being one of the last states not party to the conventions.

115. General Assembly Res. 36/155 (1982), 37/185 (1983) para. 2, 38/101 (16 Dec. 1984), 39/119 (1985) para. 9, 40/139 (13 Dec. 1986) ("**Considering** that there is an armed conflict of a non-international character in El Salvador in which the government of that country and the insurgent forces are under an obligation to apply the minimum standards of protection of human rights and humanitarian treatment provided for in article 3 common to the Geneva Conventions of 1949 and in Additional Protocol II thereto, of 1977"), 47/142 (18 Dec. 1992) para. 4 (calling for the application of the Additional Protocol despite the fact that Sudan is not a party thereto). See also General Assembly Res. 38/100 (1984), 39/120 (1985), 40/140 (1986), labeling hostilities in Guatemala as "an armed conflict not of an international character."

116. See Security Council Res. 465 (1980), 497 (1981), 672 (1990), 726 (1992), and 904 (1994) ("Reaffirming its relevant resolutions, which affirmed the applicability of the Fourth Geneva Convention of 12 August 1949 to the territories occupied by Israel in June 1967, including Jerusalem"). In 1951, the Security Council found that, contrary to claims by Arab neighbors of Israel, no state of war existed between these states (Res. S/2322, 1 Sept. 1951), but this was relevant more to *jus ad bellum* and neutrality laws than *jus in bello*. See Greenwood, *supra*, note 14, at 287–288.

117. Security Council Res. 670 (1990) para. 13. See also Security Council Res. 674 (1990).

118. Security Council Res. 764 (1992) para. 10.

119. See 1 Oppenheim (1992), *supra*, note 99, at 163 n. 6; Wilson, *supra*, note 72, at 145; Ginther, *supra*, note 30, at 246–247; Lazarus, *supra*, note 41, at 179–180. The OAU has recognized P.A.I.G.C., FRELIMO, M.P.L.A., F.N.L.A. & U.N.I.T.A. (in Portuguese territories), S.W.A.P.O. (Namibia), Z.A.P.U. & Z.A.N.U. (Southern Rhodesia), A.N.C. & P.A.C. (South Africa), MOLINACO (Comoros), S.P.U.P. (Seychelles) and F.L.C.S. (French Afars & Issas): Lazarus, *id.*, at 180 n.51.

120. Wilson, *id.*, at 143–144; Lazarus, *id.*, at 181.

121. See Ginther, *supra*, note 30, at 247. To this limited list of

examples could be added the recognition of the F.M.L.N. in El Salvador by the Andean Pact States: Julio A. Barberis, *Nouvelles questions concernant la personnalité juridique internationale* (1983–I) 179 Recueil des cours 145, 240.

122. IIB Final Record, *supra*, note 11, at 121; 4 Pictet, *supra*, note 24, at 35.

123. See El Kouhene, *supra*, note 54, at 74 n.162.

124. *1971 Conference of Experts*, *supra*, note 53, at 42 para. 201.

125. *Id.*, para. 207–208. Already in 1970 the Secretary-General had suggested the creation of a permanent U.N. body charged with the enforcement of international humanitarian law and, specifically, of the characterization of situations as armed conflicts of one type or another: U.N. Secretary-General, *Respect for Human Rights in Armed Conflicts*, U.N. Doc. A/8052 (1970) paras. 246–247.

126. See Wilhelm, *supra*, note 7, at 343 (referring to the 1971 Conference of experts).

127. "**Article 89 – Co-operation.** In situations of serious violations or the Conventions or of this Protocol, the High Contracting Parties undertake to act jointly or individually, in co-operation with the United Nations and in conformity with the United Nations Charter."

128. I.C.R.C. Commentary, *supra*, note 40, at 1033–1034.

129. Meeting of Committee I, 16 May 1977, C.D.D.H./I/SR.73, 9 *Off. Records*, *supra*, note 10, at 435 (remarks by Canada); Plenary Meeting, C.D.D.H./SR.46 and Annex, 6 *Off. Records* at 341 & 361 (remarks by Italy and others).

130. See *supra*, note 41 and accompanying text.

131. See David, *supra*, note 2, at 571; Duculesco, *supra*, note 68, at 144–145; Helmut Freudenschuss, *Legal and Political Aspect of the Recognition of National Liberation Movements* (1982) 11 Millennium: J. Int'l Stud. 115, 122; Zorgbibe, *Le caractère armé*, *supra*, note 67, at 100.

132. This is evidenced, for example, by the fact that the O.A.U. has not granted recognition to any national-liberation movement fighting against member states, despite the fact that it met all other conditions. See Wilson, *supra*, note 72, at 141–143; Abi-Saab, *supra*, note 30, at 408–409; Ginther, *supra*, note 30, at 247; Schindler, *supra*, note 6, at 143.

133. See Secretary General, *Memorandum on the Legal Aspects of the Problem of Representation in the United Nations*, U.N. Doc. S/1446 (8 March 1950), *reprinted in* (1950) 4 Int'l Org. 356, 359; 1 Oppenheim (1992), *supra*, note 99, at 177–178.

134. Parl. Deb. (Lords), vol.405, col. 564 (19 Feb. 1980); Parl. Deb. (Commons), vol.414, col. 749 (3 Nov. 1980); Sen. Deb. (Austral.) 1980, vol.84, at 168 (20 Feb. 1980). See Oppenheim, *id.*, at 164; Stefan Talmon, *Recognition of Governments: An Analysis of the New British Policy and Practice* (1992) 63 Brit. Y.B. Int'l L. 231, 253.

135. Theo van Boven, *Reliance on Norms of Humanitarian Law by United Nations Organs*, in Astrid Delissen and Gerrard Tanja eds, Humanitarian Law of Armed Conflict Challenges Ahead (Dordrecht: Nijhoff, 1991) 495, 502.

136. See Rusen Ergec, Les droits de l'homme à l'épreuve des circonstances exceptionnelles. Étude sur l'article 15 de la Convention européenne des droits de l'homme (Brussels: Bruylant/U. libre de Bruxelles, 1987) 343.

137. Plenary Meeting, 23 May 1977, C.D.D.H./SR.36, para. 114.

138. See Hans Kelsen, The Law of the United Nations (1950) 476–477; Monique Chemillier-Gendreau, *Rapport sur la fonction idéologique du droit international*, [1974] Annales de la Faculté de droit et de sciences économiques de Reims 221, 228.

139. *Questions of Interpretation and Application of the 1971 Montréal Convention arising from the Aerial Incident at Lockerbie (Libyan Arab Jamahiriya v. United Kingdom; Libyan Arab Jamahiriya v. United States of America), Provisional Measures, Order of 14 April 1992,* [1992] I.C.J. Rep. 3 and 114; *Application of the Convention on the Prevention and Punishment of the Crime of Genocide (Bosnia & Herzegovina v. Yugoslavia (Serbia & Montenegro)), Provisional Measures, Order of 13 September 1993,* [1993] I.C.J. Rep. 325; Vera Gowlland-Debbas, *The Relationship Between the International Court of Justice and the Security Council in Light of the Lockerbie Case* (1994) 88 Am. J. Int'l L. 643–677; Salmon, *Some Observations on Characterization, supra,* note 3, at 15; Skubiszewski, *supra,* note 102, at 75.

140. [1947–8] I.C.J. Rep. 57.

141. *Id.*, at 64 ("The political character of an organ cannot release it from the observance of the treaty provisions established by the Charter when they constitute limitations on its powers or criteria for its judgment [. . .]. There is therefore no conflict between the function of the political organs, on the one hand, and the exhaustive character of the prescribed conditions, on the other").

142. *Id.*, at 85 (Joint dissenting opinion by Basdevant, Winiarski, Sir Arnold McNair and Read) ("The main function of a political organ is to examine questions in their political aspects, which

means examining them from every point of view. It follows that the Members of such an organ who are responsible for forming its decisions must consider questions from every aspect, and, in consequence, are legally entitled to base their arguments and their vote upon political considerations"). See also Salmon, *Some Observations on Characterization, supra,* note 3, at 14.

143. *Military and Paramilitary Activities in and Against Nicaragua (Nicaragua v. U.S.), Jurisdiction and Admissibility,* [1984] I.C.J. Rep. 392, at 435 ("The [U.N. Security] Council has functions of a political nature assigned to it, whereas the Court exercises purely judicial functions with respect to the same events").

144. See Oscar Schachter, *The Quasi-Judicial Role of the Security Council and the General Assembly* (1965) 58 Am. J. Int'l L. 960–966; Salmon, *Le fait dans l'application, supra,* note 3, at 325–326. Castañeda is thus mistaken in his assertion that the General Assembly can make binding determination of "facts" which exist objectively as a condition to which the rule attaches legal consequences in the form of obligations for the state: Jorge Castañeda, Legal Effect of United Nations Resolutions (New York: Columbia U.P., 1969) 118–119 and 131–132. Facts become conditions because they are legally defined (Koskenniemi, *supra,* note 3, at 466–467). Every finding by an organ that a situation meets the legal definition of a fact constitutes a refinement of, and thus a change to, this legal definition. This is so despite the fact that the doctrine of *stare decisis* is inapplicable to this type of decision.

145. See Julio A. Barberis, Los sujetos de derecho internacional actual (Madrid: Ed. Tecnos, 1984) 150–157; Charles Dominicé, *La personnalité juridique du C.I.C.R.,* in Christophe Swinarski (ed.), Studies and Essays on International Humanitarian Law and Red Cross Principles in Honour of Jean Pictet (Geneva/The Hague: Nijhoff, 1984) 663–672; Paul Reuter, *La personnalité juridique du C.I.C.R.,* in *id.* 783–792.

146. See Art. 9–11 and 23, First Geneva Convention; Art. 3 and 9–11, Second Geneva Convention; Art. 3, 9–11, 56 and 72–81, Third Geneva Convention; Art. 3, 10–12, 14, 30, 59, 61, 63, 76, 96, 102, 104, 108–109, 111, 140, and 142–143, Fourth Geneva Convention; Art. 3, 5–6, 33, 78, 81 and 97, Protocol I.

147. Amendment CE/COM/II/61, 2 *1972 Conference of Experts, supra,* note 53, at 44; 1 *id.,* at 94 paras. 2.293–294; *1971 Conference of Experts, supra,* note 53, at 43 para. 215.

148. See *1971 Conference of Experts, id.,* at 42 para. 195; Wilhelm, *supra,* note 7, at 342.

149. See Weissbrodt, *supra*, note 107, at 343. But see Gasser, *supra*, note 28, at 151 and 156, where the author, head of the I.C.R.C. Legal Division, insists that the references to humanitarian law in Afghanistan and other conflicts were not a legal characterization by the I.C.R.C..

150. See Eric David, Principes de droit des conflits armés (Brussels: Bruylant, 1994) 499–500. Again, these are not clearly presented as legal opinions classifying the situations.

151. Alexander Hay, *The I.C.R.C. and the World Today* (1982) 226 Int'l Rev. Red Cross 12, 14. See also: Meron, *supra*, note 73, at 44 & 161–163; Donald Tansley, Final Report: An Agenda for Red Cross (Geneva: I.C.R.C., 1975) 70–71; David Forsythe, *Choices More Ethical than Legal: The International Committee of the Red Cross* (1993) 7 Ethics and Int'l Aff. 131, 137.

152. See David Forsythe, *Human Rights and the International Committee of the Red Cross* (1990) 12 Hum. Rts Quart. 265, 272; Zorgbibe, *supra*, note 67, at 91 and 101.

153. See *1971 Conference of Experts*, *supra*, note 53, at 43 para. 213; Wilhelm, *supra*, note 7, at 327.

154. See Erich Kussbach, *The International Humanitarian Fact-Finding Commission* (1994) 43 Int'l & Comp. L. Quart. 174, 175 (Dr. Kussbach is the current President of the Commission). See also: Dieter Fleck, *Die internationale Ermittlungskommission: Probleme und Perspektiven einer neuen Einrichtung des humanitären Völkerrecht*, in Schötter and Hoffman (eds), Die Genfer Zusatzprotokolle: Commentare und Analysen (1993) 258; Françoise Hampson, *Fact-Finding and the International Fact-Finding Commission*, in Hazel Fox and Michael Meyer (eds), 2 Armed Conflict and the New Law – Effecting Compliance (London: British Institute of International and Comparative law, 1993) 53.

155. The expression is also used in Art. 89 of Protocol I, again without definition. The *travaux préparatoires* of both Art. 89 and 90 do not shed any light in this respect.

156. I.C.R.C. Commentary, *supra*, note 40, at 1033; Kussbach, *supra*, note 154, at 178.

157. Meeting of Committee I, 14 May 1976, C.D.D.H./I/SR.58, 9 *Off. Records*, *supra*, note 10, at 223, para. 42 (New Zealand); Kussbach, *id.*, at 177.

158. The Commission already has stated its agreement with this position: David, *supra*, note 150, at 518.

159. Article 4 of the Statute of the International Criminal Tribunal for Rwanda provides that the latter has jurisdiction for "serious violations of Article 3 common to the Geneva Conventions

[. . .] and of Protocol II": U.N. Doc. S/RES/955 (1994) Annex. Compare with the Security Council's own Commission of Experts Final Report on War Crimes in the Former Yugoslavia, completed a few months before, where the experts clearly state that there is no concept of war crimes in noninternational armed conflicts: U.N.C.O.E., *Final Report, supra,* note 2, at 15–16.

160. Violations of Protocol II cannot, however, be successfully included in the general competence of the Commission even with this broad interpretation of the notion of "serious violations", because Art. 90(2)(c)(i) speaks of a "serious violation of the Conventions or of this Protocol" and not of Protocol II.

161. Nothing in the provision excludes national-liberation movements or insurgents groups from the definition of "Party to the conflict," allowing for the possibility of an investigation being initiated at the request of one of these nonstate actors, still with the consent of the state and all other parties concerned. See David, *supra,* note 150, at 516–517.

162. See Ergec, *supra,* note 136, at 381; Joan F. Hartman, *Working Paper for the Committee of Experts on the Article 4 Derogation Provision* (1985) 7 Hum. Rts Quart. 89, 122; Guy Tremblay, *Les situations d'urgence qui permettent en droit international de suspendre les droits de l'homme* (1977) 18 Cahiers de droit 3, 15.

163. See I.C.R.C. Commentary, *supra,* note 40, at 1045–1046; Kussbach, *supra,* note 154, at 176 and 183–184.

164. Kussbach, *id.,* at 177 (suggesting that the discretion of the Commission would be wider with respect to "serious violations" than with respect to grave beaches because the former are not defined in the Conventions and Protocol).

165. In case of petition by a High Contracting Party not involved in the conflict, the wording of the provision suggests that that state would not be entitled to publicize the Commission's findings without the agreement of all parties to the conflict.

166. *Military and Paramilitary Activities in and Against Nicaragua (Nicaragua v. U.S.A.),* [1986] I.C.J. Rep. 14, 114. See Meron, *supra,* note 73, at 162; 1 Oppenheim (1992), *supra,* note 99, at 167.

167. See for instance Art. 1 of Statute of the International Criminal Tribunal for Rwanda, giving the Tribunal power to prosecute persons for crimes committed between 1 January and 31 December 1994 in Rwanda or by Rwandans in neighboring states: U.N. Doc. S/RES/955 (1994) Annex.

168. See Christina M. Cerna, *Human Rights in Armed Conflict: Implementation of International Humanitarian Norms by Regional*

*Intergovernmental Human Rights Bodies*, in Frits Kalshoven and
Yves Sandoz (eds), Implementation of International Humanitarian Law (Dordrecht: Nijhoff, 1989) 31–68; Françoise
Hampson, *Using International Human Rights Machinery to Enforce
the International Law of Armed Conflict* (1992) 31 Revue de droit
pénal militaire et de droit de la guerre 119–142.

169. See Art. 40–41, International Covenant on Civil and Political
Rights; Art. 1, Optional Protocol to the International Covenant
on Civil and Political Rights; Art. 25–26, European Convention on Human Rights; Art. 44–45, American Convention on
Human Rights (but see Art. 41 which refers more widely to
"matters of human rights"); Art. 46–59, African Charter on
Human and Peoples' Rights.

170. See, e.g., Principle 67, *The Siracusa Principles on the Limitation
and Derogation Provisions in the International Covenant on Civil and
Political Rights* (1985) 7 Hum. Rts Quart. 3, 11.

171. *Cyprus v. Turkey* (Appl. 6780/74 & 6950/75), unrep. decision
of 10 July 1976, paras. 309 and 528.

172. *Id.*, diss. op. Sperduti & Trechsel, paras. 6–7 ("It follows that
respect for [the 1907 Hague Convention Regulations and the
1949 Fourth Geneva Convention] by a High Contracting Party
during the military occupation of the territory of another state
will in principle assure that High Contracting Party will not go
beyond the limits of the right of derogation conferred on it by
Art. 15 of the Convention"). This is explored by Hampson,
*supra*, note 168, at 123–135.

173. See Yoram Dinstein, *Human Rights in Armed Conflict: International
Humanitarian Law*, in Theodor Meron (ed.), 2 Human Rights
in International Law: Legal and Policy Issues (Oxford:
Clarendon, 1984) 345, 351–354.

174. General Assembly Resolution (XX–0/90); Inter-American
Commission on Human Rights, *Groups of Armed Irregulars and
Human Rights*, [1990–1] Ann. Rep. Inter-Am. Com'n Hum. Rts
504–514.

175. This builds on a phenomenon already in existence, whereby
actors rely on previous acts of characterization to support their
own conclusion. For instance the Swiss government, in support
of its characterization of the conflict in El Salvador as a noninternational armed conflict to which Protocol II was applicable,
relied on resolutions by the U.N. General Assembly, the
Economic and Social Council and the Human Rights Commission, in addition to the position of the government of El
Salvador: *Pratique suisse 1986, supra*, note 98, at 187. See Michel

Veuthey, *Assessing Humanitarian Law*, in Thomas Weiss and Larry Minear (eds), Humanitarianism Across Borders – Sustaining Civilians in times of War (Boulder: Lynne Rienner, 1993) 125, 131. The International Criminal Tribunal for Yugoslavia (Appeals Chamber) also proceeded in a similar fashion to characterize the situation in Bosnia-Herzegovina as an armed conflict, relying on express and implied acts of characterization by the warring parties, the ÍCRC, the Security Council and various states: The Pro-secutor v. Duško Tadic a/k/a "Dule" (Decision on the Defence Motion for Interlocutory Appeal on Jurisdiction), 2 October 1995, Case IT-94-1-AR72, at 39–42 paras. 73–75.

# – 9 –

# United Nations Peacekeeping Operations in Situations of Internal Conflict

## Gian Luca Burci

## Introduction

It has become almost platitudinous to say that the end of the Cold War has brought in its wake an increase in the number of particularly vicious civil wars, various kinds of ethnic strife, and even the disintegration or implosion of several states (including the U.S.S.R., Yugoslavia, Somalia, Liberia, Afghanistan, and Rwanda). At the same time, it perhaps gets forgotten that détente, as process and not event, had led to an appreciable loss of interest on the part of the two superpowers in fighting by proxy through assistance to opposing parties in civil wars and determined an opposite interest on their part in bringing an end to some embarrassing and costly confrontations. As a result, a substantial number of long-standing internal conflicts were or had become ripe for settlement as the Cold War ended.[1]

The United Nations has been called upon in most of these cases to deploy a field presence in order to assist in the containment and settlement of conflicts, bring humanitarian relief to civilian populations, monitor or supervise elections, and even try to rebuild political and administrative institutions. A United Nations unencumbered by reciprocal vetoes in the Security Council, commanding a wide political support, and finally free to use the powers entrusted to it in its founding charter suddenly seemed the most suitable organization for assuming complex security and humanitarian functions that hardly fit the concept of peacekeeping associated with previous practice. The sharp increase in requests for such operations is also to be explained by the failure of regional organizations to take over the effective peacemaking and peacekeeping role that it was hoped they would assume in the post-Cold War world.[2] The figures are revealing: out of sixteen ongoing or recently concluded peace-keeping operations, eleven are or were taking place in situations of current or recently settled civil wars or internal conflicts; this shows a reversal of the trend up to 1989, in which a United Nations military presence in noninternational conflicts was an absolute exception, mainly linked to decolonization.[3]

The involvement of the United Nations in a series of complex internal conflicts, at both a peacemaking and a peacekeeping level, has tested the capabilities of the organization and the political will of many of its members, and has precipitated an intense debate on its role in the post-Cold War era. From a legal point of view, the operations that will be examined here have challenged several assumptions and operative rules of traditional peacekeeping and led scholars to speak of second – and third – generation peacekeeping operations.

## The Expansion of Peacekeeping

The record shows the remarkable variety of conflict situations in which the United Nations has been mandated by the Security Council or the General Assembly to render assistance. Notwithstanding this variety, the functions discharged by the United Nations can be roughly assigned to five main categories. It should be noted, however, that the mandates of most operations involve a mixture or overlapping of the following categories and that the grouping of functions is not exhaustive.

1.    *Monitoring and supervisory functions*, which are carried out to ensure compliance with agreed standards or commitments by the parties involved. The United Nations has been discharging monitoring functions with respect to such different matters as: cease-fires (Georgia, the former Yugoslavia); elections (Angola, El Salvador, Liberia, Mozambique); human rights (El Salvador, Haiti); behavior of regional organizations (Liberia, Georgia/Abkhazia); police activities (El Salvador, Mozambique).

2.    *Humanitarian assistance to and protection of populations*, which are rapidly coming to represent the bulk of recent operations, either as a parallel activity within the framework of an operation (Liberia, Mozambique, Cambodia), or as the principal mandate of the operation (former Yugoslavia, Somalia, Rwanda after the events of 1994).

3.  *Disarmament of armed factions*, which takes either the form of assistance to an agreed-upon demobilization process (Mozambique, Cambodia) or the form of coercive disarmament with all the relevant implications (Somalia).

4.  *Institution-building*, which entails assisting local authorities in the training of personnel, and the restructuring or even outright establishment of civil and military institutions (Haiti, Somalia, Mozambique, Cambodia, El Salvador).

5.  *Organization of elections or referenda*, which may be destined to remain an exceptional function but has added an unprecedented dimension for U.N. involvement and raised special problems with regard to the scope and limits of U.N. authority (Cambodia, Western Sahara).

The exponential growth of U.N. operations between 1991 and 1993 led to the deployment of increasing numbers of military, police, and civilian personnel, peaking at almost 90,000 at one point in 1993 and holding at about 70,000 toward the end of 1994. It also led to a mushrooming of the financial contributions assessed on member states; to a burgeoning need for planning and coordinating the logistics of this deployment and the complex array of military, police, civil, regulatory and humanitarian functions associated with it; and to the breaking of new ground in terms of relations with regional organizations, the uses of military force, and requirements for protecting the personnel involved. The tide may already have turned after failures on the ground and internal divisions in the Security Council in connection with operations in Somalia, former Yugoslavia, and Rwanda. Whatever the case, growing reluctance to have the United Nations engage in other risky operations has become apparent.[4]

To a certain extent, it is misleading to label many of the activities being carried out recently by the United Nations as peacekeeping. The organization is now frequently involved in what U.N. Secretary-General Boutros Boutros-Ghali has defined "peacekeeping in the midst of war,"[5] with all its attendant difficulties and contradictions. Moreover, the Security Council has used its powers under Chapter VII of the Charter of the United Nations to place the operations in former Yugoslavia and Somalia on a nonconsensual or semiconsensual basis that is at variance with the traditional nature or understanding of peacekeeping. Finally, the expansion of the civilian and humanitarian components of several operations[6] has given new meanings to the concept of peace. As the Dutch Ambassador Johann Kaufman has noted, "Most of what is grouped together under peacekeeping is peace- or conflict-related, but not necessarily peacekeeping."[7]

## Peacekeeping Operations, Internal Strife and the Humanitarian Imperative

Unless the Security Council decides to exercise powers of enforcement, the United Nations should, pursuant to Article 2(7) of its Charter, abstain from intervening in an internal conflict, even if invited by a government concerned, Article 2(7) uses the parameter of "matters which are essentially within the domestic jurisdiction of any state" to delimit the scope of authority of the council. The concept of domestic jurisdiction and its scope, however, evolve in parallel with the perceptions of the international community and have changed to a notable extent since 1945. Therefore, it does not provide a rigid limit to the expanding authority of the Security Council. Does practice in the 1990s allow drawing some lines for the kinds of internal conflicts that are considered of international relevance for the purpose of authorizing a field operation?

An examination of the types of internal conflict for which the Security Council has authorized field operations shows the recurrence of certain situations: (a) particularly cruel and destructive civil wars that were left over from the period of the Cold War, and in which the superpowers had been actively involved; (b) internal conflicts involving acute humanitarian problems (starvation, mass displacement of populations) or widespread violations of basic human rights or both; and (c) conflicts threatening the stability and security of surrounding regions, either because of the possibility of a spillover of the fighting or because of the social and economic consequences of the hostilities (namely, mass migrations of destitute refugees, as in Rwanda and Liberia).

In each of these kinds of conflict, the decisive element seems to be humanitarian considerations: most internal conflicts in the 1990s have been accompanied by appalling violations of basic human rights and humanitarian law, on a massive scale and sometimes in situations made worse by natural causes that have endangered populations. Granted, some of these circumstances may hold true for practically all civil wars, but the ferociousness of most of these internal conflicts has been so extreme and unrestrained that it has gained high visibility and brought great pressure on the United Nations.[8] As a result, the provision of humanitarian assistance to civilian populations and, to a certain extent, also the protection of these populations have become principal objectives of U.N. operations and influenced the elaboration and the interpretation of their mandates. In some of the most complex and controversial of these operations, including UNPROFOR in Bosnia and Herzegovina and UNOSOM II in Somalia, humanitarian assistance was supposed to be the paramount and possibly the sole function to be carried out.

The growing humanitarian dimension of peacekeeping is undoubtedly part of a trend toward integrating humanitarian concerns into United Nations practice and has generated a revival of the long-standing debate on the right of humanitarian intervention and on the *droit d'assistance humanitaire*.[9] The trend is certainly not new, but it has probably been accelerated by a number of developments. The efforts of the General Assembly to spell out normative and operative principles for humanitarian assistance to victims of natural and other disasters are one example. The Assembly has passed a number of resolutions since its forty-third session that affirm a right of the population affected to humanitarian assistance but preserve in principle the requirement of state consent.[10]

Another landmark in this trend is Security Council Resolution 688 (1991) of 5 April 1991, in which the council made clear it had determined that gross violations of human rights in Iraq threatened international security and just as explicitly demanded that Iraq halt its repression and allow humanitarian assistance to the Kurdish and Shiite populations. For the first time, a government was requested by an international body to allow access to its population for humanitarian reasons as a matter affecting international security. The degree of discomfort of several nonaligned council members at this "invasion" of the sphere of human rights in a country by the Council is reflected in the narrow majority – 10 votes – with which the resolution was adopted.[11]

At the level of policy formulation, the statement issued at the Security Council summit meeting of 31 January 1992 contains two much-quoted passages that somehow codify this shift in emphasis:

The members of the Council note that United Nations peace-keeping tasks have increased and broadened considerably in recent years. Election monitoring, human rights verification and the repatriation of refugees have in the settlement of some regional conflicts, at the request or with the agreement of the parties concerned, been integral parts of the Security Council's efforts to maintain international peace and security. . . .

The absence of war and military conflicts amongst States does not in itself ensure international peace and security. The non-military sources of instability in the economic, social, humanitarian and ecological fields have become threats to international peace and security. The United Nations membership as a whole, working through the appropriate bodies, needs to give the highest priority to the solution of these matters.[12]

At the level of policy implementation, the Security Council has been extending its humanitarian "reach" in several directions, sometimes using its enforcement powers under Chapter VII in an unprecedented manner. The military deployments by the United States and other countries in Somalia and by France in Rwanda, for example, were authorized by the Security Council as exceptional measures to contain humanitarian catastrophes.

In the same vein, the Security Council has also shown its concern for the respect of humanitarian law and basic human rights in armed conflicts of an internal character by invoking on several occasions the principle of individual responsibility for war and particularly heinous crimes related to war. This approach has recently gathered momentum with the establishment of international tribunals for the punishment of grave violations of humanitarian law in the former Yugoslavia and Rwanda.[13] The council is increasingly concerned not only with respect of *jus ad bellum* but also with respect of the basic principles of *jus in bello*. In this connection, the council has requested the Special Rapporteurs of the Commission on Human Rights in Iraq, the former Yugoslavia, and Rwanda to communicate their findings to it and has taken these into account in reaching new decisions. This, of course, has brought strong criticism from Iraq and Yugoslavia, and has probably decreased their already very limited willingness to cooperate with the rapporteurs.

The foregoing considerations highlight a growing consensus within the United Nations that in situations of noninternational armed conflict gross violations of basic human rights or human catastrophes resulting from other than natural causes legitimate collective responses. The Security Council, in particular, is determining with increasing frequency: (a) that such situations are of international concern and affect or can affect international security; (b) that this legitimates collective involvement and possibly a United Nations field presence to assist in a settlement of the conflict upon a request by, or with the acceptance of, the parties involved; and (c) that in extreme cases, particularly when the central government has collapsed or is unable or unwilling to exercise its authority, enforcement measures are justified under Articles 2 (7) and 39 of the charter.

Of course, not all internal strife elicits a response from the Security Council. From a legal point of view, some internal conflicts have been considered as outside the threshold of applicability of Article 2 (7). Even though the practice of the council is far from consistent, the peacekeeping operations undertaken tend to make the "threshold" for intervention the existence of an armed conflict between identifiable and organized groups fighting for power or claiming self-determination. A review of such operations in the 1990s, both consensual and under Chapter VII, shows that the situations in which the Security Council has authorized the deployment of a field operation meet the definition of "noninternational armed conflicts" under Article 1 of Protocol II to the Geneva Conventions.[14] When the council has used its enforcement powers in connection with a field deployment – as in the former Yugoslavia and Somalia – it has established the existence of a threat to the peace on the basis of finding that a systematic and organized use of military force within a state has grave human consequences that could spill over into a surrounding region. The existence of such an armed conflict within a state provides a solid foundation for the involvement of the Security Council. The concept of a "threat" to the peace brings with it, in particular, an element of forecast that allows the Council to determine that a conflict affects international security even when it has not yet spilled over national boundaries.[15] By allowing the Council a political appreciation of the possible future consequences of an internal situation for international security, the concept of a threat to the peace dramatically increases the powers of that body and the margin of legitimacy for its action under the charter.

The foregoing seems to represent the lowest threshold for an intervention by the Security Council in an internal conflict. This is to say that a political regime may be violent and oppressive or deny human rights to its subjects, even in a blatant way, and still fall short of the threshold. As Rosalyn Higgins has noted, if the drafters of the Charter of the United Nations had wanted to give the Security Council the authority to enforce respect for human rights, the Charter would have said so. The fact that the sphere of human rights is undoubtedly no longer solely a matter "within the domestic jurisdiction of any state" under Article 2 (7) of the Charter does not necessarily mean that even grave violations of human rights affect international security per se and that they can be enforced by the Security Council.[16]

A remarkable exception is represented by the Security Council's involvement in the internal crisis in Haiti following the overthrow of President Jean-Bertrand Aristide in September 1991. The council took over the political management of the crisis, beginning with the imposition of an oil and financial embargo by Resolution 841 (1993) of 16 June 1993 and subsequently escalating this measure to a full economic embargo by Resolution 917 (1994) of 16 May 1994. On 31 July 1994, the council adopted Resolution 940 (1994), authorizing a military action by a multinational force in order to restore the legitimate president and government of Haiti and to establish "a secure and stable environment." In between, with Resolution 867 (1993) of 23

September 1993, the council authorized a peacekeeping mission (UNMIH) with the task of retraining the Haitian police and army; its mandate was expanded by Resolution 940 (1994) to assisting the government in a number of security matters. The situation in Haiti does not meet the threshold test proposed above, and the Haitian government was no worse than many other repressive and brutal regimes around the world. The opposition to General Cedras was not organized and certainly never coalesced into a force able to engage in an organized military struggle. There was virtually no risk of a military spillover into neighboring countries. What, then, threatened international peace and security in the view of the Council? Three themes that recur in the Council's resolutions and debates on Haiti are the violation of what has been called "the democratic entitle-ment,"[17] the brutal repression of the population by the state's security forces, and the social and economic impact of the outflow of refugees on third countries. In the preamble to Resolution 841 (1993), for example, the council recalls previous measures by the U.N. General Assembly and the Organization of American States (OAS); a request for sanctions by the legitimate government; the incidence of human-itarian crises "becoming or aggravating threats to international peace and security"; and the negative repercussion on the region of an out-flow of refugees. It concludes that these factors serve to define "a unique and exceptional situation warranting extraordinary measures." The resolution was adopted unanimously. Resolution 940 (1994) repeats the same determinations (in the voting in this instance China and Brazil abstained).

During the debate, several states stressed the weak legal basis of the action. Mexico, for example, argued that "the crisis in Haiti . . . is not a threat to peace . . . such as would warrant the use of force in accordance with Article 42 of the Charter."[18] Uruguay added that "the internal political situation in Haiti [does not project] externally in such a way as to represent a threat to international peace and security."[19] Nigeria, a member of the Council at that time, stressed that the Council's action was "country specific" and that it should not be seen "as a global license for external intervention through the use of force . . . in the internal affairs of Member States."[20] It can be argued that U.N. peacemaking in Haiti constitutes a case of collective mandatory measures to uphold basic civil and political rights. As such, it represents a substantial deviation from the practice of the Security Council and the spirit of the United Nations Charter. But, this may not be much of a precedent. Haiti indeed represents a special case because it lies in the Caribbean backyard of the United States, a special domain toward which the United States has always claimed an extended right of intervention to protect its security interests and, in more recent history, to stem possible refugee flows. It is unlikely that similar measures would be taken against a country in any other region.[21]

If the existence of a noninternational armed conflict within the purview of Protocol II seems to represent the lowest threshold for intervention in an internal conflict by the Security Council, what is its highest threshold? In which cases can the council determine that such conflicts threaten international security and act accordingly under Chapter VII? And, once again, can any consistency be discerned in the actions of the Council that might reveal a trend or the emergence of a customary practice?

Article 2 (7) of the Charter of the United Nations states that the limit of domestic jurisdiction "shall not prejudice the application of enforcement measures under Chapter VII." This means that a situation that, by its own nature, remains essentially domestic can nonetheless pose a threat to international security. The limits to the competence of the Security Council are thus removed on a basis of a determination under Article 39, the first article of Chapter VII. Under the pressure of the humanitarian imperative, though, how much has the Council been concerned with cross-boundary repercussions and how much with the purely human dimension of the various conflicts?

It is worth considering briefly the motivations for actions taken by the Security Council in a few cases other than that of Haiti to see whether the pattern holds. The Council imposed an arms embargo against Rwanda by Resolution 918 (1994) of 17 May 1994. In its preamble, this resolution focuses on the "death of many thousands of innocent civilians . . . internal displacement . . . and the massive exodus of refugees to neighboring countries . . . a humanitarian crisis of enormous proportions"; it also speaks of "systematic, widespread and flagrant violations of international humanitarian law." The Council declares itself "Deeply disturbed by the magnitude of the human suffering caused by the conflict and concerned that the continuation of the situation in Rwanda constitutes a threat to peace and security in the region." On 22 June 1994, the Council adopted Resolution 929 (1994), by which it authorized France to lead an emergency multinational operation of a humanitarian character in Rwanda, pending the reinforcement of UNAMIR. In its preamble, this resolution recognizes "that the current situation in Rwanda constitutes a unique case which demands an urgent response by the international community" and determines "that the magnitude of the humanitarian crisis in Rwanda constitutes a threat to peace and security in the region." Similar considerations are expressed in Resolution 955 (1994), which established the international tribunal for Rwanda. These determinations have, of course, to be viewed against the background of the total collapse of law and order that characterized the civil war of April–July 1994, the movement of almost three million Rwandans to neighboring countries, and the Council's finding of genocide, reached with considerable reluctance in Resolution 925 (1994) for the first time since World War II. In the case of Resolution 955 (1994), it is striking that the Council determined the persistence of a threat to international peace and security based on the fact that genocide and other grave breaches of humanitarian law had been committed months before and remained unpunished. From a factual standpoint, the civil war had come to an end in July 1994 and the internal situation no longer represented much of a threat to peace in the region. In this case, which seems to have somehow been overlooked by commentators, the Council made a kind of retrospective determination under Article 39 to provide a technical basis for establishing an international court with the legally binding authority of Chapter VII.

In the case of Somalia, the drastic state of affairs in the country led the Security Council to adopt Resolution 733 (1992) of 23 January, 1992, which noted "the rapid deterioration of the situation in Somalia . . . and . . . its consequences on the stability and peace in the region" and determined "that the continuation of this situation constitutes . . . a threat to international peace and security." The Council proceeded on the basis of this evaluation to impose an arms embargo against Somalia. In a letter of 30 November 1992,[22] the Secretary-General of the United Nations recommended a review of the basic premises of the organization's action with regard to Somalia in order to ensure access for humanitarian assistance to the population and the security of relief personnel in the face of the intractable anarchy and violence prevailing throughout the country. He stressed that "Somalia has become a country without a government or other political authorities with whom the basis for humanitarian activities can be negotiated" and that the Council would need to act under Chapter VII to address the immediate issue of humanitarian assistance. In the Secretary-General's opinion this would also indirectly support the wider goal of brokering a political settlement and the reconstitution of a government, and of police and armed forces. Guided by this assessment, the Council moved into the realm of enforcement procedures with Resolution 794 (1992) of 3 December 1992, which offers a complex scenario as justification for such a shift. The council underlined "the unique character of the present situation . . . requiring an immediate and exceptional response" and determined "that the magnitude of the human tragedy . . . exacerbated by the obstacles being created to the distribution of humanitarian assistance, constitutes a threat to international peace and security."

Acting therefore under Chapter VII on the basis of the foregoing premises, the Council authorized Member States "to use all necessary means to establish as soon as possible a secure environment for humanitarian relief operations in Somalia." The Secretary-General viewed the establishment of a secure environment as depending largely on disarmament, consensual or enforced, of the Somali factions. Consequently, when the United States insisted on the early withdrawal of the Unified Task Force (UNITAF) deployed in December 1992, the assumption of its functions by UNOSOM had to be based on Chapter VII owing to the unfinished job left behind by UNITAF. In his report of 3 March 1993[23] on the transition from UNITAF to UNOSOM II, the Secretary-General cogently states that "the situation in Somalia, though primarily of a domestic nature, could affect the peace and stability of the entire region of which Somalia forms an integral part, unless energetic and timely action is taken to avert a major humanitarian and security disaster." Resolution 814 (1993), which approved the mandate of UNOSOM II under Chapter VII, repeats most of the considerations found in Resolution 794 (1993), taking note also of the difficulties caused to neighboring states because of the influx of Somali refugees, but it does not reiterate the existence of a threat to regional security.

A third case that is instructive in assessing the motivations and approach of the Security Council is that of the former Yugoslavia. Faced with the secession of Croatia and Slovenia and a request for action by Yugoslavia, the council noted in Resolution 713 (1992) that the fighting in Yugoslavia, with its heavy toll in human lives, had consequences for the countries of the region and was threatening international peace and security. Paragraph 6 of this resolution imposed an arms embargo against the whole territory of the former Socialist Federal Republic of Yugoslavia. A laconic determination that the situation in Yugoslavia continued to constitute a threat to international peace and security was repeated in a number of subsequent resolutions.[24] The breakout of fighting in Bosnia and Herzegovina and the well-known atrocities against civilians, especially Muslims, accentuated the humanitarian dimension of the Balkan crisis and shaped the subsequent actions and determinations of the Council and UNPROFOR By Resolution 770 (1992), the Council authorized for the first time the use of force for the protection of humanitarian assistance throughout Bosnia and Herzegovina. In its preamble, the resolution declares that such assistance "is an important element in the Council's effort to restore international peace and security in the area" and expresses determination to establish as soon as possible the necessary conditions for providing it.

In Resolution 780 (1992) of 6 October 1992, the Council dealt squarely with the massive violations of humanitarian law being committed throughout the former Yugoslavia and established a Commission of Experts to collate information on such violations and their perpetrators; this course of action eventually led, in Resolutions 808 (1993) and 827 (1993), adopted under Chapter VII, to the establishment of the International Criminal Tribunal for the former Yugoslavia. In the preamble of Resolution 808 (1993), the Council unequivocally determined that widespread violations of international humanitarian law in the former Yugoslavia constituted "a threat to international peace and security." In the preamble of Resolution 827 (1993), the council added that "in the particular circumstances of the former Yugoslavia the establishment . . . of an international tribunal . . . would contribute to the restoration and maintenance of peace." In Resolution 836 (1993), the council gave UNPROFOR and NATO the authority to enforce the protection of the safe areas established in Bosnia and Herzegovina by Resolution 824 (1993), thus once again linking the use of military force to the achievement of humanitarian objectives. In the preamble of Resolution 836 (1993), the Council condemned, *inter alia*, obstructions to the delivery of humanitarian assistance and declared its resolve to ensure the protection of the civilian population in safe areas. Likewise, Resolution 913 (1994) concerning Serbian attacks against the town of Goradze puts emphasis on the loss of life and attacks against relief workers as grounds for the council's determination that a cease-fire should be brought into effect in that area.

Clearly, then, in the enforcement measures adopted by the Security Council, the humanitarian imperative looms very large and is at the heart of each of these determinations of a threat to the peace. It is equally clear that crises such as those reviewed in the preceding paragraphs have serious repercussions for the regions in which they take place, particularly when it comes to the Balkans. The threat to regional stability is, however, almost an afterthought in the various resolutions. The principal purposes of the Council expressed in these resolutions are to ensure humanitarian assistance; to protect civilian populations in safe areas in Bosnia and Herzegovina; to reestablish law and order, facilitate political processes, and restore democratic government; and to control and prosecute violations of humanitarian law. A further element that looms large in the three cases described above is the "failure" of a state – that is, a situation in which central governmental authority has collapsed and the authorities controlling a certain territory are unable or unwilling to assume responsibility for the protection of basic human rights or even the survival of civilians. Insofar as Haiti can be considered a meaningful precedent, the failure of a state can be equated with situations in which the existing government is not "legitimate", – it oppresses its own subjects and has forcefully interrupted a democratic process supported by the international community.

The Security Council has thus been willing to determine the existence of a threat to the peace under Article 39 of the Charter of the United Nations in situations of acute humanitarian crisis within a state, in which the normal mechanisms of peacekeeping and humanitarian relief have been unusable or ineffective and the structures of government have collapsed or been turned against the population. What is more, the powers of the council under Chapter VII have been used for the first time to pursue a vision of "democracy" or "justice" in such situations. The forcible disarming of the Somali factions was intended to facilitate a democratic and peaceful settlement of internal strife; the military intervention in Haiti was intended to bring about the removal of "illegitimate" and brutally repressive authorities and thereby to facilitate the return of the democratically elected president; the establishment of international tribunals for Rwanda and the former Yugoslavia was based on the belief that an impartial administration of justice for wartime atrocities could facilitate internal reconciliation and contribute to the restoration of a lasting peace.

The relevance of the collapse of a state, or of the "illegitimacy" of its government for a determination by the Security Council of a threat to the peace under Article 39 of the Charter of the United Nations, is particularly interesting. It takes to the extreme the functional concept of state sovereignty that finds its foundation in the Charter. This concept has slowly grown with the development of international law and international cooperation in such apparently disparate areas as human rights, environmental protection, economic cooperation, and the use of common resources, and it was somehow codified in the General Assembly's Declaration on Principles of International Law, in 1970.[25] Viewed from an external perspective, sovereignty is a political and legal framework that allows states to exercise rights but also requires them to discharge duties and functions crucial for maintaining order in the international community of an increasingly interdependent world in which human entitlements have acquired growing recognition and importance. The international community has progressively set up monitoring and supervisory mechanisms to verify the correct discharge of such duties and functions by states, thus attesting to a legally relevant interest on the part of the international community in the protection and fostering of certain basic values. The systematic failure or persistent unwillingness of a state to carry out its responsibilities in protecting its subjects, coupled with the existence of an internal armed conflict and gross violations of humanitarian law and basic human rights, has come to be seen by the international community as justifying intrusive forms of intervention to bring emergency assistance and help reestablish normal and "legitimate" government. This form of intervention is less and less exercised unilaterally; intervening states seek multilateral legitimacy, mainly through international agencies that reach determinations on the basis of multilateral decision-making processes.

It would be going too far to aver that sovereignty is altogether forfeited in such cases; it would be more realistic to say that certain sovereign rights are temporarily attenuated by the exercise of other, collective rights vested in the international community. It is unfortunate, however, that the Council has entered this sensitive area of convergence between sovereignty and international responsibility without developing a more coherent approach to the kind of situations that might probably have been anticipated. It is remarkable that the interventions in Somalia, Rwanda, and Haiti have been justified on the basis of, among other considerations, their all being "unique" cases. But this succession of "unique" cases has taken on significance as a precedent and is raising expectations that might remain unfulfilled in view of the lack of consistency of the Council.

## Consensual Operations

Most of the peacekeeping operations undertaken by the United Nations in the 1990s have been formally based on the fundamental principle that the force or mission should be deployed only at the request and with the acceptance of the parties to a conflict. This principle is, of course, consistent with the essential nature of peacekeeping as the introduction of an impartial international presence into a conflict situation to assist the involved parties in avoiding recourse to armed force and in finding a way of settling their disputes through peaceful means. It also projects a vision of the role of the United Nations that has continued to have political importance in contemporary peacekeeping operations, the functions of which have become multidimensional and increasingly affect areas of responsibility normally falling within the jurisdiction of state sovereignty.

Adherence to the principle of consent by the parties concerned has opened a whole range of legal problems for the peacekeeping operations to be considered here, in view of the need to deal with nongovernmental factions that control part or parts of the territory in which the operations are to be carried out and, sometimes, in view of the dispersion or dissolution of governmental authority in the countries involved. Groups that claim the right of self-determination and a sovereign status, such as of the Bosnians and the Croatians, pose delicate problems of recognition and political standing for the United Nations. Moreover, not being formally established or responsible at the international level, they do not have a strong legal incentive to respect any commitments they might make with the United Nations.

In most cases, assistance from the United Nations is requested by the parties to a civil war or similar conflict in an agreement with which they settle their dispute or by which they accept interim confidence-building measures to facilitate progress toward a political settlement. Obviously, these agreements are not international in nature, being concluded between a government and an opposition movement or between rival factions. Only in the case of Cambodia was the request for assistance from the United Nations, including the terms of U.N. involvement, set down in a proper intergovernmental instrument, the Paris Agreement of 23 October 1991.[26] Often, however, the agreements concluded by the parties to a conflict are given a dimension of international significance by being countersigned or witnessed by agents that helped to facilitate them, such as the Secretary-General, on behalf of the United Nations, or ranking government officials, on behalf of other states, usually donor countries. Even though the United Nations does not normally participate in such settlement agreements, a request by the parties for a U.N. presence, their acceptance of its functions and tasks, and their commitment to respect them constitute an essential legal precondition for the organization.[27] Thus, the mandate and authority of the United Nations in these situations are based on three legal sources: the agreement between the parties requesting U.N. assistance, the resolution of the Security Council establishing the operation, and the bilateral agreement between the United Nations and the host government.[28] This cumulation of legal instruments is a remarkable feature of United Nations peacekeeping operations. On the one hand, the organization is called on to assist in the implementation of a settlement agreement to which it is not a party. On the other hand, the ultimate source of authority for the peacekeeping operation is a decision of the Security Council that somehow insulates the operation from any modifications that may have to be made in or any legal defects that may turn out to exist in the settlement agreement.

From a legal point of view, and with particular reference to U.N.

peacekeeping operations in internal conflicts, a number of questions arise. Is the full and unconditional consent of the parties sufficient and necessary for the deployment and permanence of a U.N. force or mission? Is the operative and political imperative also a legal one? And how much do humanitarian considerations, which exert considerable pressure on the decision-making process of the United Nations, weigh upon the behavior of the organization?

To begin with the question of sufficiency of consent, a request by the parties to an internal conflict is not by itself sufficient under the Charter of the United Nations to provide an adequate legal basis for the Security Council to authorize the establishment of a peacekeeping operation. It is also necessary that the situation in question meet the requirements stipulated in the charter for the exercise by the Council of its authority. In other words, the fact that such a request has been made is not enough for the Council to act *intra vires*. The situation in question must be one that requires action "for the maintenance of international peace and security" or measures "to maintain or restore international peace and security" pursuant to Articles 24 or 39 respectively of the charter. If it were not so and the Council were, from a legal point of view, absolutely free to accede to requests for assistance by parties to internal conflicts that are devoid of any perceivable effects on international peace and security, the United Nations would not be very different from a contractor of peacekeeping and security services. It can be argued that the importance given to consent as a consideration in the decision to launch a peacekeeping operation has somehow been overstated for the sake of overriding objections based on the state-jurisdiction provision laid down in Article 2 (7) of the charter.[29] The United Nations is an intergovernmental organization bound by the terms of its charter. Flexible and adaptable to changing circumstances as these may be, they do have limits and conditions. Even though the Security Council is a political organ that acts on a case-by-case basis, a legal analysis of its actions cannot ignore the limits and conditions established by the Charter, which is the instrument on which the authority of the council is based. The crucial issue, therefore, is not only whether the parties to an internal conflict have given their consent to a U.N. presence, but the determination of the circumstances that make that conflict a threat to international peace and security. The example of Haiti shows the extent to which this threshold of applicability can be lowered when the geopolitical interests of a superpower are involved.

The issue of necessity of consent by the parties to an internal conflict can be equally elusive from a legal point of view. Some scholars have suggested that the consent of the host state is not a legal requirement for a peacekeeping operation because member states of the United Nations have already undertaken, pursuant to Article 25 of the Charter, to accept the decisions of the Security Council. They argue further that peacekeeping operations fall within the concept of collective measures and that in any case the principle of estoppel would bar a state from withdrawing its consent after having accepted the presence of a United Nations mission.[30] The Secretariat of the United Nations has instead always taken the position that the consent of the parties is an absolute condition for the establishment of an operation, even though it is not always clear whether the necessity is a political and operative rather than a strictly legal one.[31]

When emerging practice with regard to U.N. peacekeeping operations in internal conflicts is considered, however, it becomes clear that the principle of consent by the parties involved is not in fact looked upon by the United Nations as so fundamental as it is declared to be in official documents and policy positions. The humanitarian dimension of most such operations often makes it necessary for the United Nations to be deployed in conflict situations in which genuine and reliable consent by the parties cannot be expected. It is easy for a party to give consent only in order to exploit the U.N. presence to partisan advantage. This creates an inherent paradox: the Security Council, troop-contributing states, and the Secretary-General and his representatives in the field all continue to attach great importance to satisfying at least the fiction when not the reality, of acting at the request and with the genuine consent of the parties concerned. At the same time, the necessity of a legally relevant and genuine consent is increasingly challenged by the United Nations itself for the sake of being able to take action in completely new and unprecedented situations or to react to human disasters calling for humanitarian tragedies.

Several examples will illustrate the practice and the problems. As already noted, intervening in an internal conflict makes it unavoidably necessary for the United Nations to deal with nongovernmental entities party to the conflict: liberation or insurgency movements (RENAMO in Mozambique; UNITA in Angola; FMLN in El Salvador, RPF in Rwanda); armed factions without a clear status (such as those pillaging Liberia); ethnic or religious groups (the various peoples in the former Yugoslavia); clans (such as those in Somalia); or de facto authorities without international legitimacy (such as General Cedras in Haiti). The United Nations must gain their acceptance and cooperation. Sometimes the nongovernmental groups actually have more secure control over the area of the peacekeeping operation than the formally responsible government (the situations in Liberia and Bosnia and Herzegovina are exemplary in this respect).

The case of Somalia constitutes an extreme example of this phenomenon. In view of the incontrovertible evidence that there was no effective government in power, the Secretary-General recommended in April 1992 the initial deployment of UNOSOM on the basis of unilateral (but not identically phrased) commitments obtained from the two factions that were controlling Mogadishu.[32] The force was established on this basis by Resolution 751 (1992). This case, from a legal point of view, is particularly interesting, since the United Nations had to abandon even the pretense of dealing with a government and base its presence instead on often informal arrangements with nongovernmental entities. The political pressure to respond to a growing human catastrophe, compounded by the breakdown of law and order in the country, forced the Security Council and the Secretary-General to stretch to the limits the concept of governmental consent in order to authorize the deployment of a protection force without invoking Chapter VII of the charter.

As an intergovernmental organization, the United Nations finds itself in a delicate position when dealing with entities of dubious standing, especially when they claim sovereign status or compete to be considered the only lawful government. In practice, status of force and status of mission agreements (SOMAs and SOFAs) are only concluded with the host government, while the Secretariat adopts a number of special arrangements for nongovernmental parties in order to avoid raising issues of recognition. The degree of recognition that can in practice be extended to nongovernmental parties is also determined by the manner in which the Security Council has defined the situation and elaborated the mandate of the operation. In Mozambique and Cambodia, for example, the focus of the operations was the monitoring or organization of an electoral process that involved all parties to the conflict and recognized them as political parties. For both Somalia and Bosnia and Herzegovina, the initial mandate was of a humanitarian nature, and assistance was directed to people in need rather than to this or that group as such; hence, the limited recognition initially offered to the Bosnian Serbs and Croats.

In other cases, the lack of agreement by or between the conflicting parties has forced the United Nations to rely on acquiescence rather than a formal expression of consent. In the case of the initial deployment of UNPROFOR, for example, after having unsuccessfully negotiated for a full acceptance of the Vance Plan by the Croatian Government and the Krajina Serbs, the Secretary-General, on 16 February 1992, recommended the establishment of UNPROFOR while acknowledging that there remained a number of unanswered questions about the level of cooperation that the force could expect. He concluded that "the danger that a United Nations peacekeeping operation will fail because of lack of co-operation from the parties is less grievous than the danger . . ." of a breakdown of the ceasefire.[33] In the case of Bosnia and Herzegovina, the United Nations was overtaken by the situation without yet having legal arrangements in place. The presence of UNPROFOR's Headquarters in Sarajevo at the outbreak of hostilities and the decision of the Security Council to provide humanitarian assistance to that city precipitated UNPROFOR involvement. Even though the United Nations subsequently concluded a status of force agreement with the government of President Alija Izetbegovic, the other two parties never formally recognized or accepted the presence or functions of the force on the territories under their control. UNPROFOR, from a legal point of view, discharged its functions in Bosnia and Herzegovina on the basis of the informal acquiescence of the Bosnian Croats and Serbs. The UNPROFOR Command for Bosnia and Herzegovina, however, concluded a number of specific agreements with the Bosnian Serbs and Croats concerning, for example, freedom of movement and access for United Nations forces or humanitarian convoys.

In yet other cases it has been clear that a request for U.N. intervention by the state in which a conflict is taking place was really a legal formality for justifying action by the Security Council in view of the dubious legitimacy of the government or the lack of an effective central authority in the country. In the case of UNOSOM, for example, Resolution 751 (1992) recalls in its preamble "the request by Somalia for the Security Council to consider the situation in Somalia." It is known, though, that in April 1992 there was no government in Somalia, and the reports of the Secretary-General of that period confirm this. The same formula was repeated in the subsequent resolutions concerning UNOSOM, until the council decided to apply Chapter VII in Resolution 794 of 3 December 1992.

Finally, in several instances the basis of consent on which a United Nations presence was premised had probably ceased to exist at some point during the operation. Still, largely for humanitarian purposes, the Secretary-General and the Security Council decided in favor of maintaining the operation deployed. Bosnia and Herzegovina once again provide an example. Even though relations between UNPROFOR and the various parties were always rather tense and cooperation was at best erratic, the unprecedented level of harassment and premeditated violence by Bosnian Serbs against U.N. troops and humanitarian personnel reached such a point during December 1994 and May 1995 that it amounted to a denial of consent, even in the loosest sense of the word.[34] This led France, the main contributor of troops to UNPROFOR, to request in December 1994 contingency plans for an evacuation.[35] Other examples of U.N. operations kept in place despite the collapse of a consensual basis for them are those in Rwanda (UNAMIR) and Liberia (UNOMIL). Both operations were requested by the warring parties in these countries, to assist them in implementing settlement agreements, the Arusha Agreement in Rwanda and the Cotonou Agreement, which aimed at implementing the previous Yamoussoukro Accords, in Liberia.[36] These agreements contain broad provisions of a military, political, and constitutional nature that embody a comprehensive settlement of the previous conflict and render them analogous to a peace treaty at the international level. It seems clear that the subsequent relapse into civil war, particularly in the case of Rwanda, constituted a repudiation by the parties of the commitments assumed in these agreements and, from a legal point of view, rendered them null and void because of the fundamental change in circumstances. As a consequence, one of the legal bases for the U.N. presence had lapsed. All the same, the Security Council decided to maintain these operations in place, once again with the stated purpose of guaranteeing at least some limited humanitarian assistance and protection to the population. In the case of Rwanda, this unfortunately took place in an atmosphere of such uncertainty and lack of political will on the part of the Security Council that it led France to deploy an emergency military force pursuant to an authorization of the council.[37]

From the foregoing, it should be evident how much United Nations peacekeeping practice has been shaped by the need to respond to immediate humanitarian imperatives and to adapt concepts and practice to the changing nature of the crises that the organization is called upon to contain in the post-Cold War world. Even if, for political, operative, and administrative reasons the principle of consent by the parties involved had to be upheld, such consent was, in legal terms, of dubious relevance in view of the circumstances in the countries concerned. Nevertheless, the United Nations deployed its forces – or kept them deployed – in a number of cases. In other cases, the realization of a lack or unraveling of consent and of the inapplicability of the principle of peacekeeping and its operative assumptions led the organization to resort to its enforcement powers.

## Enforcement Actions

It has become another platitude of the post-Cold War period to note that the Security Council has finally discovered the full potential of the powers granted to it by Chapter VII of the Charter of the United Nations, and made use of them.[38]

Practice shows that in connection with the deployment of field operations the Council has utilized Chapter VII in a variety of ways in the 1990s:

1.   In the cases of Somalia, Rwanda, and Haiti, it has authorized a group of states to deploy temporary military forces outside United Nations control. The justification given for this deployment was the gravity of the humanitarian situation and the inability of the United Nations to perform certain tasks. These military forces over-lapped with United Nations missions – respectively, UNOSOM, UNAMIR and UNMIH – and withdrew or partly merged with the missions once the initial emergency was over.[39]

2.   In other cases, the power to take enforcement actions was en-trusted to the Secretary-General, or to third organizations, for the support and at the request of the United Nations. This was obviously the case in Somalia, where UNOSOM II was fielded under Chapter VII by Resolution 814 of 26 March 1993, with an ambitious mandate that will be discussed later. UNOSOM II took over the functions of the multinational force authorized by Resolution 794 (1992). As for the segments of UNPROFOR deployed in Croatia and Bosnia and Herzegovina, the Security Council has in some instances attributed enforcement powers directly to the force.[40] In other instances, it has authorized member states, "acting nationally or through regional organizations," to use air power for the support and protection of United Nations forces.[41]

3.   Finally, in a number of cases the Security Council has imposed military embargoes (prohibitions on providing military equipment and assistance) against countries or territories in which a peacekeeping operation was or would be deployed. The paramount consideration for imposing such restrictions was limiting the influx of weapons in the area of fighting to facilitate the task of the peacekeeping force and increase its security.[42]

When it comes to internal conflicts, the use of force by third parties, either by the United Nations or by other organizations or states, is obviously one of the most fiercely debated contemporary issues in political and legal discourse. The legal issues raised by the enforcement mandates entrusted to the United Nations or for its support are numerous and touch upon the essence of the role and capabilities of the organization in the post-Cold War era. Questions naturally arise about how United Nations "peace-enforcement" relates to the concept of peacekeeping. Even though the operation in the former Yugoslavia raises a number of delicate legal issues in this regard, the discussion here will be limited to considering UNOSOM II and identifying some of the key issues at stake in that operation by way of suggesting the contours of the ongoing debate.

UNOSOM II is the only operation in which the United Nations itself has been entrusted with full enforcement powers by the Security Council. Thus the issues and problems related to the exercise of such powers within a peacekeeping context have been experienced directly by the organization. The spectacle of United Nations peacekeepers saving human lives by protecting relief activities, while at the same time killing scores of Somali civilians under the banner of an essentially humanitarian operation, has provoked much soul-searching and reflection.

The Secretary-General has addressed these issues in his Supplement to *An Agenda for Peace*,[43] a position paper that he prepared for the occasion of the fiftieth anniversary of the United Nations. The tone of the Supplement contrasts dramatically with that of the parent agenda, which was issued in 1992. In the supplement, the Secretary-General emphasizes the changes that have occurred since the end of the 1980s, leading the United Nations to concentrate its peacekeeping and peacemaking efforts on intrastate conflicts fought within the framework of "failed" states, and on military protection of humanitarian operations. This "peacekeeping in the midst of war" is characterized, according to the Secretary-General, by "an emotional environment in which effective decision-making can be far more difficult." And indeed, he regrets that the emotional circumstances surrounding the situations in Somalia and Bosnia and Herzegovina led the Security Council both to abandon certain prerequisites of classical peacekeeping operations, including consent of the parties involved, impartiality, and use of force solely for self-defense, and to endow the operations with enforcement mandates unaccompanied by sufficient military capabilities. In his view, this approach has resulted in conspicuous failures and blurred the boundaries between peace-keeping and peace-enforcement. The Secretary-General advocates the maintenance of a clear and rational distinction between the two concepts, which have to be seen as alternatives based on different political premises rather than "as adjacent points on a continuum, permitting easy transition from one to the other." The general tone of the document is clearly unenthusiastic about peace-enforcement by the United Nations.

Taking the ideas presented in the supplement a step further, Giandomenico Picco, a special assistant to the former secretary-general Javier Pérez de Cuéllar,[44] has maintained that it is always a mistake to entrust the use of force to the Secretary-General, since he, positioned as a nongovernmental institution, does not have the necessary tools (money and troops at his complete disposal) to perform enforcement functions efficiently, and is thus condemned to failure. Moreover, even if he did have such tools, the Secretary-General would be perceived by the parties to a conflict as representing the vested interests and the agenda of the Security Council – i.e., of its most influential members – and would lose the image of impartiality crucial to the discharge of his genuine institutional role. Picco concludes that the Council and the Secretary-General should have complementary roles; the Secretary-General should play the function of negotiator and peace-keeper and distance himself from the use of force.

These considerations, which are well-founded, find their reflexes in the legal aspects of the U.N. operation in Somalia, in which the use of force coexisted with peacekeeping, humanitarian, and peace-making functions. Two interrelated aspects of the legal framework for this conjoining of functions need to be emphasized: (1) the conceptual difficulty in defining the scope of a mandate under Chapter VII; (2) the contradiction and tension between the peacekeeping function, in which the United Nations must be perceived as impartial, and an enforcement authority in support of the peacekeeping function.

It is useful to recall that the mandate of the multinational force in Somalia (UNITAF) authorized by Resolution 794 (1992) was essentially humanitarian and consisted in the establishment of "a secure environment for humanitarian relief operations." UNITAF, which was deployed alongside UNOSOM I, did not interpret its functions as including a forcible disarmament of the Somali factions, while the Secretary-General insisted that a secure environment could not be established until the various factions were disarmed.[45] This was one of the factors that led the Secretary-General to recommend that the mandate of UNOSOM II be placed in part under Chapter VII. This mandate, spelled out by the Secretary-General in his report of 3 March 1993[46] and approved by the Security Council with Resolution 814 (1993), consisted of two segments: the first segment, not approved under Chapter VII, requested the Secretary-General to provide humanitarian assistance to the people of Somalia; to assist in the rehabilitation of the Somali economy; to seek political reconciliation of parties at variance through broad participation of all sectors of Somali society; to help bring about the reestablishment of the Somali police and judiciary; and to facilitate the return of refugees. The emphasis is on assistance to a Somali political process. The second segment, adopted under Chapter VII, was devoted to security of the U.N. and relief operations and to disarmament. It contained a disarmament and demobilization plan that was to be discussed in detail with the various factions but that was directly enforceable upon them, with or without their cooperation. It also provided for the enforcement of the cease-fire negotiated by the factions in January 1993. The U.N. mandate in Somalia was thus divided along a rather clear line.

The actual implementation by UNOSOM of its mandate considerably blurred the distinctions, however. Deployed in the middle of a difficult and anarchic environment on the basis of an unprecedented mandate, UNOSOM II attempted to pilot the course of the political settlement and the reestablishment of civil institutions. There is no doubt that the United Nations attempted to impose a form of trusteeship on Somalia, based on a mandate adopted under Chapter VII for well-defined purposes that did not include the direction in which political reconciliation was supposed to move. In this sense, the absence of a formally constituted government created a power vacuum that led the United Nations to use an essentially humanitarian operation for partly different purposes not clearly falling within its mandate. Needless to say, this led to charges of partiality from the Somali National Alliance (SNA) of General Aidid, which had emerged as the leading force throughout most of Somalia and saw its power jeopardized by UNOSOM's attitude. The escalation of violence between June and October 1993 and the offensive military role played by UNOSOM and the U.S. Quick Reaction Force assisting it created a climate of warfare that contradicted the humanitarian mandate of the operation.

These contradictions have been cogently summarized in the report of the Commission of Experts established pursuant to Security Council Resolution 885 (1993) to investigate armed attacks against United Nations troops.[47] Some episodes mentioned in the report are worth recalling:

1. The basic document for Somalia's transition toward an elected government was an agreement concluded by most factions in Addis Ababa in March 1993. This agreement was strongly influenced by the United Nations's approach calling for a political reconstruction "bottom up"[48] with guarantees for popular participation in the trans-

itional government (TNC) outside the influence of the factions. Immediately after the conclusion of this agreement, the Somali political leaders concluded a separate agreement outside United Nations auspices, which contradicted the first and put the composition of the TNC entirely in their hands. UNOSOM. refused to recognize the validity of this second agreement, even though it had been unanimously adopted by the Somali leaders. In this case, a role was certainly played by the ideological preference of UNOSOM for a democratic process representative of the various segments of the Somali society, a rather alien concept, however, for Somali political leaders. This political stand by the United Nations laid the ground for the subsequent tensions, and its conformity with UNOSOM's mandate can be questioned.[49]

2.   In its efforts to reconstruct a viable judiciary, UNOSOM agreed with a group of Somali lawyers on a procedure for the election of judges and retained the right to nominate some of them, even though the Addis Ababa agreement gave this power to the TNC, and neither it nor Resolution 814 (1993) mentioned a U.N. authority in the choice of the judges.[50]

3.   The special representative of the Secretary-General unilaterally declared, in May 1993, that the Somali Penal Code would be the applicable criminal law in Somalia, even though nothing in UNOSOM's mandate provided for law-making powers.[51]

4.   UNOSOM heavily interfered with the organization by the SNA of a regional peace conference for central Somalia, which would have sanctioned the leading role of General Aidid. UNOSOM tried to control participation in the conference, its chairmanship and agenda, to the great displeasure of the SNA. The conference was never held as initially planned, and the Commission of Experts regards this episode as decisive in initiating a pattern of open confrontation between UNOSOM and the SNA.[52]

It is significant that UNOSOM occasionally justified the exercise of its powers or a particular course of action on the basis of the agreements concluded by the Somali parties, which would have conferred to the United Nations the power to enforce its provisions upon recalcitrant factions. It is legally quite remarkable that an international operation, deployed pursuant to a decision by an inter-governmental organization, would come to perceive political agreements concluded by the parties in an internal conflict as an autonomous source of legitimacy for its powers. In other words, the mandate conferred by Resolution 814 (1993) had become blurred and was seen indistinctly as the basis for a general assumption of quasi-governmental powers by the United Nations. Chapter VII has been used in this case well beyond the parameters of security or humanitarian considerations discussed above. Beyond the possible political motivations or the cultural bias of certain individuals or participating states, the foregoing overreach of the mandate's intent is also the result of the need to adapt peacekeeping parameters and practice to a completely different legal, military, and "mental" setting without a clear precedent.

Similar considerations can be made concerning the military strategy pursued by UNOSOM. The force decided to follow an aggressive and confrontational approach in enforcing its disarmament mandate, unlike the negotiating approach chosen by UNOSOM I and UNITAF. This previous "softer" tactic conformed more to the operating procedures used in previous peacekeeping operations with a disarmament component, such as that in Cambodia, which privileged agreement and negotiations and relied on the right of self-defense of U.N. troops as an enforcement tool of last resort. According to the Commission of Experts, UNOSOM decided to use its enforcement authority to its fullest extent when an inspection of a weapons storage site controlled by the SNA culminated in its first major armed clash with a Somali faction.[53] UNOSOM did not propose negotiations on standard operating procedures, on that or following occasions, and did not pursue the incremental steps normally observed in classical peacekeeping operations when a suspicion arises of possible violations by a party of its commitments. UNOSOM took instead the position that its mandate under Resolution 814 (1993) authorized it and even required it simply to inform the Somali factions of its decisions and to require compliance. In other words, UNOSOM did not try to exhaust peaceful remedies before taking a more aggressive stand. The course of the whole operation illustrates the difficulty of transforming a peacekeeping culture into an enforcement culture, both from an operative and a legal point of view.

This interpretation of UNOSOM's mandate hardened after the adoption of Security Council Resolution 837 (1993), in which the Secretary-General was authorized "to take all necessary measures against all those responsible for the armed attacks [against the Pakistani contingent] . . . including to secure the investigation of their actions and their arrest and detention for prosecution, trial and punishment." Senior UNOSOM military officers and even the Secretary-General interpreted this as an unqualified request, one that tied their hands, to capture General Aidid and his aides and to subject them to a judicial process. It will be recalled that a number of Somalis were indeed arrested and detained, with a view to handing them over to a recontituted Somali court. Once again, however, this procedure was alien to previous peacekeeping procedures and could hardly be accommodated by the mandate of UNOSOM without stepping into a legal vacuum. Without the realistic prospect of rehabilitating the local judiciary, such detentions came to be seen as arbitrary and hardly in keeping with standards of due process, and they were terminated after the adoption of Security Council Resolution 886 (1993).[54]

This "maximalist" interpretation of a Chapter VII mandate prevailed also in the conduct of subsequent military operations, both by UNOSOM II and by the U.S. Quick Reaction Force, whose status under Resolution 814 (1993) was quite obscure. What is meant, in particular, are operations such as the bombing by the Quick Reaction Force of Abdi House in July 1993, which was carried out without warning to eliminate the military leadership of the SNA and which caused a substantial number of civilian casualties. Such occurrences increased doubts and misgivings about the implementation of the United Nations mandate as well as the application of principles of humanitarian law in the choice of legitimate military targets.

## Conclusions

This review of some aspects of peacekeeping operations in situations of internal conflict shows how many United Nations activities that apparently rest on consolidated and widely accepted principles and procedures are suffering growing pains in adapting to completely different realities and assumptions. As noted above, the high tide of ambitious operations, breaking new ground in their mandates and legal foundations, may be finished, and the operations in the former Yugoslavia may become a model for the type of situation most unfit for the kind of aggressive humanitarian peacekeeping attempted by UNPROFOR.

The practice of the United Nations that has been examined here shows the paramount humanitarian dimension of most of these operations. Their legal basis rests solely or predominantly in the perception by the Security Council that internal armed conflicts, characterized by widespread violations of humanitarian law and massive human suffering, threaten or may threaten international peace and security. We have seen how the need to respond somehow to this humanitarian imperative, and in particular the pressure to ensure a military presence to help relief operations and somehow protect populations in danger, has been shaping the legal and operative assumptions under which the United Nations acts.

A definitely new element is the democratic concern that has crept into the treatment by the Security Council and its forces of situations such as those in Haiti and Somalia. It points to the emerging relevance of the democratic entitlement as a community value the repression of which can be seen as endangering international security. This is a very delicate development in the policy of the Council; moreover, the exceptional nature of the Somali situation and the strong interest of the United States in an early resolution of the crisis in Haiti decrease the value of these operations as precedents. More generally, however, the relevance of violations of human rights or of a "Western" concept of representative democracy for purposes of international security does not clearly fall within the spirit, let alone the letter, of the Charter of the United Nations.

Another new element that has crept into United Nations operations in the 1990s is the need to deal with "failed" states. The political experiment attempted in Somalia has been a failure and shows that the procedure, assumptions, and legal concepts of peacekeeping operations are not easily adaptable to more ambitious scenarios involving the use of force and the assumption of quasi-governmental powers not falling within the clear mandate of an operation. Still, the underlying principle has positive aspects that might be replicated in the future, using the experience accumulated in Somalia, Rwanda, and Bosnia and Herzegovina.

The evolution of peacekeeping and its meaning within the framework of the functions and the policies of the United Nations is still under way. Moreover, until now United Nations operations (with the possible exceptions of UNPROFOR/UNPREDEP in Macedonia) have been reactions to ongoing crises, adapted to the peculiarities of each such crisis, and have evolved in parallel to the changing pattern of conflicts around the world. The main lesson that emerges from practice to date is the importance of returning to the primary function of peacekeeping to ensure that the Secretary-General and the forces under his command be left to do what they are naturally more inclined and best suited to do: negotiate, assist, persuade, and try to draw conflicting parties into a political process that can be assisted, but not coerced, by a peacekeeping and humanitarian presence.

## Notes

Gian Luca Burci is a Legal Officer in the office of the Legal Counsel in the office of Legal Affairs at the United Nations. The views expressed here are those of the author and do not necessarily represent the views of the office of Legal Affairs or of the United Nations.

1. The only available legal definition of internal conflict is contained in Article 1 of Protocol II to the 1949 Geneva Conventions on the law applicable to armed conflicts. The Protocol is applicable to all armed conflicts not covered by Protocol I "and which take place in the territory of a High Contracting Party between its armed forces and dissident armed forces or other organized armed groups which, under responsible command, exercise such control over a part of its territory as to enable them to carry out sustained and concerted military operations and to implement this Protocol." Paragraph 2 of this Article adds that the Protocol "shall not apply to situations of internal disturbances and tensions, such as riots, isolated and sporadic acts of violence and other acts of a similar nature, as not being armed conflicts." The "internal" quality of the conflicts in question, of course, is largely relative since the most recent such conflicts were fueled or kept alive by third States, neighbors and/or superpowers, which sometimes became directly involved in them.

2. See B. Rivlin, *Regional Arrangements and the U.N. system for Collective Security and Conflict Resolution: A New Road Ahead?*, The Ralph Bunche Institute of the United Nations, Occasional Paper XII, May 1992.

3. One can recall the ONUC in Congo, UNFICYP in Cyprus (still ongoing), and UNTEA in West Irian. The United Nations field operations currently deployed by the Security Council in connection with a noninternational conflict, together with the establishing resolutions (besides UNFICYP) are the following: UNAVEM III in Angola (Resolution 976 (1995) of 8 February 1995); ONUSAL in El Salvador, terminated in April 1995 (Resolution 693 (1991) of 20 May 1991); UNPROFOR in Croatia, Bosnia and Herzegovina and Macedonia (Resolution 743 (1992) of 21 February 1992, 758 (1992) of 8 June 1992, and 795 (1992) of 11 December 1992) subsequently transformed into UNCRO in Croatia (Resolution 981 (1995) of 31 March 1995) and UNPREDEP in Macedonia (Resolution 983 (1995) of 31 March 1995); ONUMOZ in Mozambique, withdrawn in November 1994 (Resolution 797 (1992) of 16 December 1992); UNOSOMII

in Somalia, withdrawn in March 1995 (Resolutions 751 (1992) of 24 April 1992 and 814 (1993) of 26 March 1993); UNOMIG in Georgia (Resolution 858 (1993) of 24 August 1993); UNOMIL in Liberia (Resolution 866 (1993) of 22 September 1993); UNMIH in Haiti (Resolution 867 (1993) of 23 September 1993); and UNAMIR in Rwanda, which has absorbed the previously established UNOMUR deployed on the border between Rwanda and Uganda (Resolution 872 (1993) of 5 October 1993) withdrawn in March, 1996.

The term "peacekeeping operation" is used in this article in a comprehensive manner to indicate field operations established by the Security Council and carried out under the command and control of the Secretary-General, including those wholly or partly endowed with enforcement powers under Chapter VII of the Charter, which are commonly defined "peace-enforcement operations."

For a recent compilation of bibliography on peacekeeping, see G. Fermann, *Bibliography on International Peacekeeping* (1992).

4. The scope of the changes already introduced or planned by the Secretariat, and the requests presented to member States, for meeting the new demands of peacekeeping, are reflected in two reports of the Secretary-General: *Improving the capacity of the United Nations for peace-keeping*, S/26450, 14 March 1994; *Effective planning, budgeting and administration of peace-keeping operations*, A/48/945, 25 May 1994. The President of the Council issued a statement on 3 May 1994 (S/PRST/1994/22) in response to the first report.

5. *Building Peace and Development. Report of the Secretary-General on the Work of the Organization*, A/49/1, 2 September 1994, p.57.

6. The UNTAC operation in Cambodia is the best example, combining border monitoring, disarmament of factions, human rights monitoring, supervision and control of the civil administration, repatriation of refugees, demining and organization of elections.

7. J. Kaufman, *The Evolving United Nations: Principles and Realities*, The John W. Holmes Memorial Lecture (1994), at 4.

8. As the Secretary-General commented in opening the summit meeting of the Security Council of 31 January 1992, "Civil wars are no longer civil, and the carnage they inflict will not let the world remain indifferent", U.N. Doc. S/PV.3046 (1992), at 9.

9. J.A. Carrillo Salcedo, *Le Rôle du Conseil de Sécurité dans l'organisation et la réglementation du "droit d'assistance humanitaire"*, in The Development of the Role of the Security Council, Hague Colloquium 164 (1992).

10. The most relevant is GA Res 46/182, 46 GAOR Supp. (No. 49), at 49, which has reorganized the operative principles for the coordination of U.N. humanitarian activities. See also GA Res. 43/131, 43 GAOR Supp. (No.49), at 207.

11. The strong reservations by several nonaligned States on that occasion were, to a certain extent, disingenuous. It is indeed well-known that, during the Cold War period, the only two sanctions regimes established by the Council were those against Southern Rhodesia and South Africa, and that the nonaligned actively promoted those actions. Even though the language of the relevant resolutions uses the threat to regional stability in order to justify a determination under Article 39, still the central reason for both actions was the denial of basic human rights elevated to State policy by the Apartheid system. Even considering the exceptional character of those cases, still the relevance of human rights for the maintenance of international security finds its roots well before Resolution 688 (1991).

12. U.N. Doc. S/23500 (1992), at 2 and 3.

It seems clear from the context of this statement that the expression "threat to the peace" is not used in the same way as in Article 39 of the Charter, and is not necessarily linked with the adoption of enforcement measures. It rather indicates the concern of the United Nations with a series of indicators revealing areas of instability that may lead to an actual threat to international security. In this sense, the statement blurs the boundary between Chapters VI and VII of the Charter and fits the emphasis given by the Secretary-General to the concepts of early warning and preventive diplomacy for the management of potential crises. Examples of this use of the element of forecast implicit in the general notion of "threat to the peace" are found in some recent resolutions relating precisely to internal conflicts. Besides resolution 688 (1991), one could consider Resolutions 721 (1991) and 751 (1992), in which the Council considered that the "continuation of the situation" in Yugoslavia and Somalia, respectively, constituted a threat to the peace. It is hardly necessary to underline the weight of the humanitarian crises in those countries on such determinations by the Council.

The Security Council, during the Cold War, had used similar expressions in a number of resolutions concerning the situations in South Africa and Southern Rhodesia. In those cases, their use was evidently a compromise solution to give more gravity to the pronouncement of the Council while avoiding the recourse to Chapter VII, on which there was no agreement. See for example

Resolution 217 (1965), in which the Council determined that the unilateral declaration of independence by Southern Rhodesia was extremely grave and that "its continuance in time constitutes a threat to international peace and security."

13. This was accomplished, in the case of Yugoslavia, by Resolutions 780 (1992), which established a Commission of experts to investigate grave violations of international humanitarian law in the former Yugoslavia; as well as Resolutions 808 (1993) and 827 (1993). The statute of the Tribunal is reproduced in U.N. Doc. S/25704 of 3 May 1993. The international tribunal for Rwanda was established by Resolution 955 (1994), which annexes the Statute of the Tribunal. The Council, by Resolution 935 (1994), had already established a commission of experts with the same mandate as the "780 Commission." The Commission, in its interim report, had concluded rather straightforwardly that the Hutu ethnic element had been engaged in genocidal activities within the term of the 1948 Genocide Convention.

14. See *supra*, note 1.

15. It has recently been argued that there can be no allegations that the Council is acting *ultra vires* when it "intervenes" in an internal conflict marked by such use of military force. See B. Conforti, *Le pouvoir discrétionnaire du Conseil de Sécurité en matière de constatation d'une menace contre la paix, d'une rupture de la paix or d'un acte d'aggression*, in The Development of the Role of the Security Council, *supra*, note 10, at 51.

16. R. Higgins, *Problems and Process* 254 (1992).

17. T. Franck, *The Emerging Right to Democratic Governance*, 86 AJIL 46 (1992).

18. U.N. Doc. S/PV.3413 (1994), at 4.

19. *Id*. at 7.

20. *Id*. at 11.

21. Another apparent deviation from the "minimum threshold" argument exposed in the text is the deployment of a part of UNPROFOR within Macedonia, even though no armed conflict was underway in that country. However, the exception is clearly only apparent: the situation of Macedonia cannot be considered in isolation from the ferocious conflict raging at that time in Bosnia and Herzegovina and Croatia. The deployment of a United Nations force, which represents the first application of the concept of "preventive deployment" advocated by the Secretary-General in "An Agenda for Peace" (B. Boutros-Ghali, *An Agenda for Peace* 16–18 (1992)), was aiming at preventing the conflict from spreading into Macedonia.

22. U.N. Doc. S/24868.
23. U.N. Doc. S/25354, at 22.
24. See, for example, the fifth preambular paragraph of Resolution 743 (1992) of 21 February 1992, which established UNPROFOR, and the last preambular paragraph of Resolution 757 (1992) establishing economic sanctions against the Federal Republic of Yugoslavia.
25. General Assembly Declaration on Principles of International Law concerning Friendly Relations and Cooperation among States in Accordance with the Charter of the United Nations, GA res. 2625 (XXV), 24 October 1970. See also the interesting comments contained in *Changing Concepts of Sovereignty: Can the United Nations Keep Pace?*, 27th U.N. of the Next Decade Conference, The Stanley Foundation (1992).
26. See the "Agreement on a Comprehensive Political Settlement of the Cambodia Conflict", concluded in Paris on 23 October 1991. This exceptional legal format was due in part to the peculiarity of the settlement process, in part to the fact that the "package" included the neutralization of Cambodia as guaranteed by the other signatories, and in part to the sweeping transfer of sovereign powers from the *pro forma* "Supreme National Council" of Cambodia to the United Nations mission.
27. In the case of Mozambique, for example, the General Peace Agreement concluded on 4 October 1992 in Rome between the Government of President Chissano and Renamo, was witnessed by the representatives of a number of Governments and countersigned by the Italian Government, the Bishop of Beira and the representatives of an Italian religious community which had been instrumental in the negotiations. The agreement spelled out in considerable details the functions of the United Nations for the monitoring of the cease-fire and the electoral process, the provision of humanitarian assistance and the chairmanship of several of the organs established to oversee the transition process. See U.N. Doc. S/24642 (1992).

    A similar legal basis is provided by various other settlement agreements: for example, the Arusha Agreement of 4 August 1993 in the case of Rwanda, the Cotonou Agreement of 25 July 1993 for Liberia, and the agreements concluded in 1992 and 1994 in Moscow for the settlement of the conflict between the Government of Georgia and the separatist Abkhaz movement.
28. These bilateral agreements are called Status of Force/Mission Agreements (SOFAs and SOMAs, respectively) and aim at spelling out the reciprocal rights and duties of the United Nations

and the host country. Their conclusion sometimes proves particularly difficult in view of the reluctance of many Governments to undertake a binding commitment *vis-à-vis* the United Nations, either for broader political reasons or in connection with a number of rights and facilities requested by the Secretariat for the regular discharge of the operation's mandate.

29. Views of this nature had been expressed in connection with the Congo crisis. The somehow legally ambiguous mandate of ONUC, and the need to justify the substantial amount of military force used within that State to support the central Government against the secession of Katanga, had led some to give absolute importance to the request for assistance by the Leopoldville authorities. See, on a critical vein, R. Higgins, *The Development of International Law through the Political Organs of the United Nations* 106 (1963).

30. D. Bowett, *United Nations Forces* (1964); T. Weiss, J. Chopra, *United Nations Peacekeeping* 31–36 (1992).

31. It will certainly be recalled that the decision of U Thant to withdraw UNEF from the Sinai in 1967 after Egypt so requested has been one of the most criticized moves by a Secretary-General, and that several scholars have argued that the United Nations was not legally obliged to comply with the Egyptian request. See T.G. Weiss, J. Chopra, *supra* at 34.

32. They are reproduced in U.N. Doc. S/23289 (1992).

33. U.N. Doc. S/23592 (1992), at 7.

34. *Rebel Serbs Trick U.N. on Captive Troops*, New York Times, 7 December 1994, at A12.

35. *France Seeks Plans for a Bosnia Pullout*, New York Times, 8 December 1994, at A1.

36. The agreements are reproduced in U.N. doc. S/26915 (1993) and U.N. Doc. S/26272 (1993), respectively.

37. The Council, in Resolution 929 (1994) of 22 June 1994, determined that "the magnitude of the humanitarian crisis in Rwanda constitutes a threat to peace and security in the region" and authorized member states (in practice France with the support of a limited African contingent) to conduct a temporary military operation to protect civilians in Rwanda.

38. On the general issues of the use by the Council of its enforcement powers, see Burci, *The Maintenance of International Peace and Security by the United Nations: Actions by the Security Council under Chapter VII of the Charter*, in Prospects for Reform of the United Nations System 123–157 (1992).

39. In the case of Somalia, the United States and other countries

deployed a United Transitional Assistance Force (UNITAF) pursuant to Resolution 794 (1992) of 3 December 1992. UNOSOM had already been deployed since the previous August, but fighting in Mogadishu had largely confined it to defensive positions within the port and airport.

In the case of Rwanda, France launched "Operation Turquoise" in June 1994, pursuant to Resolution 929 (1994). The French troops were assisted by a few small contingents from African countries to give the operation a multinational character; they established a "safe humanitarian zone" in southwest Rwanda which certainly saved innumerable lives and somehow stabilized a displaced population of approximately 1.4 million. The final report on the operation is in U.N. Doc. S/1994/1100. The operation was concluded on 21 August 1994 and its functions (short of enforcement) taken over by UNAMIR, which had been expanded by Resolution 925 (1994) of 8 June 1994 but had been redeployed only in August due to the unwillingness of many States to provide troops or matériel.

In the case of Haiti, the United States led a multinational force authorized by Resolution 940 (1994) of 31 July 1994 with the purpose of removing the *de facto* authorities, facilitating the return of President Aristide and developing a "secure and stable environment." The Multinational Force also facilitated the redeployment of UNMIH, which had been evacuated in October 1993 and which took over the functions of the Force (once again, short of enforcement) at the end of March 1995.

40. For example, for the enforcement of safe areas under Resolution 836 (1993) and to guarantee its security and freedom of movement in some resolutions extending its mandate.

41. See, for example, Resolution 816 (1993) on the enforcement of the flight ban over Bosnia and Herzegovina; the aforementioned Resolution 836 (1993) on the safe areas; and Resolution 958 (1994), extending to the territory of Croatia the authority of the United Nations to request "close air support" for its protection. This has led to the selection of NATO as the supporting military arm of UNPROFOR, with all the well-known problems of coordination and difference of mandates between the two organizations.

In still other cases, the Council and the Secretary-General have "stretched" the right of self-defense of UNPROFOR as a substitute for enforcement powers due to a lack of consensus within the Council. This is the case of Resolution 776 (1992) of 14 September 1992, adopted on the basis of the report of the

Secretary-General of 10 September 1992 (U.N. doc. S/24540), which requests UNPROFOR to escort humanitarian convoys and to react to armed attacks against them in exercise of the right of self-defense. The resolution was not adopted under Chapter VII.

42. An arms embargo was initially imposed against Yugoslavia by Resolution 713 (1991). Subsequently, Resolution 727 (1992) confirmed its continued applicability against the whole territory of the former Socialist Republic – i.e., Croatia, Slovenia, Bosnia and Herzegovina, Macedonia and the Federal Republic of Yugoslavia (Serbia and Montenegro). Arms embargoes were also imposed against Haiti, Somalia, Liberia, Rwanda and the part of Angola controlled by UNITA.

43. *Supplement to an Agenda for Peace: Position Paper of the Secretary-General on the Occasion of the Fiftieth Anniversary of the United Nations*, S/1995/1, 3 January 1995, particularly at 5 and 9.

44. G. Picco, *The U.N. and the Use of Force – Leave the Secretary-General Out of It*, 73 Foreign Affairs 14 (1994).

45. See U.N. Doc. S/5354, *supra*, note 24, at 13.

46. Id.

47. U.N. Doc. S/1994/653, especially at 17–34.

48. That is, through the election of district councils, regional councils and, at the end of the process, a Transitional National Council as a repository of Somali sovereignty.

49. U.N. Doc. S/1994/653, *supra*, note 48, at 16–17.

50. *Id.*

51. *Id.*

52. *Id.* at 18–19.

53. It will be recalled that SNA militias ambushed the Pakistani troops engaged in the inspection and provoked 24 fatalities among them.

54. In paragraph 8 of this resolution, the Council requested the Secretary-General to "... suspend arrest actions against those individuals who might be implicated but are not currently detained pursuant to resolution 837 (1993), and make appropriate provision to deal with the situation of those already detained under the provision of resolution 837 (1993)."

# Human Rights, Democracy, and the Multidimensional Peace Operations of the United Nations

Philippe Ch. A. Guillot

## Introduction

Since the Peace of Westphalia put an end to the Thirty Years' War in 1648, international society has been based on the principle of sovereign statehood.[1] One corollary of sovereignty is the prohibition of interference by states in other states' internal affairs. The Thirty Years' War arose when Roman Catholic countries refused to accept the Protestant challenge to the emperor's secular power and the pope's spiritual power. From Pomerania to Sicily and from Portugal to Transylvania, Europe was set ablaze. It was a Catholic country, France, which was allied with Lutheran Sweden and the German Protestant principalities, that first invented and developed the concept of sovereignty in order to be fully independent from both the emperor and the pope. This changed the international order: from 1648 onwards, European states were for the most part free to choose their own religion, their own moral principles and somewhat later, their own political systems too.[2]

The order of Westphalia was first challenged in 1792, when revolutionary France declared war on the European monarchies.[3] Then, in the name of self-determination, republican and Napoleonic armies invaded neighboring countries in order to "free" people from tyrants. The Congress of Vienna (1814–15) reshaped the map of Europe according to the balance of power, and the Holy Alliance (Austria, Prussia, and Russia) emerged to crush any further attempts at "democratic destabilization."[4] Other countries joined the club, making it a great-powers directorate that came to be known as the Concert of Europe. Europe's great powers intervened, on political grounds, to preserve the monarchical order worldwide[5] or, for humanitarian reasons, to protect fellow Christians[6] or Jews.[7]

In 1919 and again in 1945, the principle of state sovereignty and its corollary of noninterference were reaffirmed as the basis of international society. The League of Nations and, later, the United Nations were created to prevent interstate conflict through collective security. In the Charter of the United Nations, Article 2(7) prohibits intervention "in matters which are essentially within the domestic jurisdiction of any state."[8]

Nowadays most armed conflicts are intrastate conflicts, and the United Nations is increasingly involved in internal conflict-resolution through "multidimensional" operations in support of peace.[9] In countries affected by internationalized civil wars, peacekeeping operations seek to promote the peace and rebuild states by assisting in a democratic process toward independence or political renewal. These multidimensional operations reflect U.N. Secretary-General Boutros Boutros-Ghali's *Agenda for Peace*. They are the expression of "a new requirement for technical assistance which the United Nations has an obligation to develop and provide when requested: support for the transformation of deficient national structures and capabilities, and for the strengthening of new democratic institutions."[10]

Multidimensional operations are missions of "assistance to democratic transition," implementing comprehensive peace plans that are endorsed (or even drafted) by the U.N. Security Council and that tend to universalize Western liberal standards of democracy. These peace plans, which often owe more to the five permanent members of the Security Council than to the Council as a whole, foster a process of national reconciliation in countries torn by internal strife, or set up a "conservatorship" in a U.N.-assisted "failed" state.[11] A conservatorship is nothing more than a transitional trusteeship granted to a U.N. member state.

A common feature of these operations is recourse to liberal democratic formulas to resolve conflicts. For years, U.N. members have paid lip service to democracy, but with the end of the Cold War these comprehensive peace plans foster liberal democratic solutions, even though the U.S.S.R. was and the People's Republic of China still is part of the group of five permanent members of the Security Council. Thus, multidimensional operations promote worldwide Western standards of government: hence, one may wonder if the U.N. Security Council is turning into a world directorate.

In what follows, it will be argued that the multidimensional approach to internal conflict is not really new. Precedents for assistance-to-transition operations can be found throughout the history of peacekeeping. The second part of the discussion will show that the New World Order represents an increase in "prodemocracy" operations, which include a sort of "constitutional engineering."

## Precedents for Assistance-to-Transition Operations

Precedents for multidimensional operations can be found in the peace-keeping operations by the League of Nations and in early monitoring by the United Nations of plebiscites in divided countries, decolonized states, and trust or non-self-governing territories. Some other aspects of peacekeeping, such as civilian and humanitarian assistance, can be found in the work of the Organisation des Nations Unies au Congo (ONUC);" of the U.N. force in Cyprus (UNFICYP); and, to a lesser extent, of the U.N. interim force in Lebanon (UNIFIL). The U.N. peacekeeping operation that provides the most relevant precedent for multidimensional operations is undoubtedly the U.N. temporary executive authority for West Irian/West New Guinea (UNTEA); which was assisted by a security force (UNSF). The operation that paved the way for multidimensional operations involving assistance to "Western-style democratic" transition was, however, not organized by the United Nations, but by the Commonwealth, in dealing with Rhodesia-Zimbabwe.

### *Earlier Monitoring of Plebiscites*

The first instance of a referendum on self-determination dates back to 1552 with the French annexation of Toul, Metz, and Verdun. Asking people to choose their fate was not usual before the unification of Italy and the annexation of Savoy and Nice by France in 1860. A few other international referendums were held prior to 1914, but no international supervisory body emerged to supervise them.[12] After World War I, internationally monitored referendums were used, or planned, but only to resolve minor border disputes involving self-determination. After 1945, the United Nations monitored some plebiscites in connection with decolonization or in the context of the Cold War.

*Internationally Monitored Plebiscites Between the Wars.* The treaties growing out of the Paris Peace Conference (1919–20) and ending World War I provided that the disposition of certain territories be determined by plebiscites. The first plebiscites were held in 1920–1: in Schleswig, to fix the Danish-German border; in Allenstein,

Marienwerder, and Upper Silesia, to delimit Germany and Poland; in the Klagenfurt Basin, to set the boundary between Austria and the Kingdom of the Serbs, Croatians and Slovenians (the future Yugoslavia); and in Sopron, to tidy up the division of Hungary and Austria. These plebiscites were monitored by international or interallied commissions, which had temporary general powers of administration.[13]

In 1920, a referendum to be monitored by the League of Nations was contemplated for Aaland islanders, but in 1921 the Council of the League, a body devoted to the settlement of international disputes and made up of larger states, announced that the Aaland Islands should remain a Finnish territory provided that the rights of Swedish speakers were protected.[14]

On 28 October 1920, the Council of the League proposed that a plebiscite should be held in the city and surrounding territory of Vilna (now Vilnius) to settle the dispute over sovereignty between Lithuania and Poland. An international plebiscite commission was appointed by the Council of the League. In addition, an international police force was set up. But in March 1921, the council refused to organize a plebiscite because of renewed fighting between Poles and Lithuanians.[15]

From 1919 to 1935, the Saarland (a rich industrial German territory on the French border) was placed under the administration of the League of Nations in a trusteeship arrangement. A five-member international commission ruled the territory. In 1934, a plebiscite commission and a supreme plebiscite tribunal were set up for the area. Some 1,000 officials staffed these international bodies and supervised the referendum. Security was guaranteed by the deployment of a 3,300-man international force of the League of Nations. The plebiscite took place on 13 January 1935. In all, 90 percent of the electorate voted for reunion with Germany, while a small minority voted for maintaining the trusteeship and an even smaller group favored union with France.[16]

*First-Generation U.N. Monitoring of Elections.* At the end of World War II, Soviet and U.S. controlled separate zones of occupation in Korea north and south of the 38th parallel respectively. In December 1945, the Allied Council of Foreign Ministers (representing the United States, the U.S.S.R., and Great Britain) met in Moscow and agreed on a plan for a four-power trusteeship of up to five years for Korea, with a view toward settling the issue of unification and withdrawing both the U.S. and the Soviet occupying forces. But the idea of a trusteeship met with resistance on the part of all Koreans, particularly those in the South of the country. When the U.S.S.R. insisted that those Korean political groups that had opposed the trusteeship be excluded from further consultations, the United States refused. Further joint U.S.-U.S.S.R. discussions on the matter were stymied, and the United States submitted the entire question of Korea's unification to the United Nations. On 14 November 1947, the U.N. General Assembly adopted Resolution 112(II), which had been proposed by the United States. The resolution established a U.N. Temporary Commission on Korea, UNTCOK, and called for the general election, under the observation of the commission, of a Korean National Assembly. But UNTCOK was denied access to North Korea by the U.S.S.R. So on 10 May 1948, elections were held only in the South, which became the Republic of Korea (claiming to represent the entire Korean nation) under the leadership of Synghman Rhee. Although UNTCOK had observed only 2 percent of the polling stations, the elections were reported to have been "free and fair." In 1949, the U.N. General Assembly created the U.N. Commission on Korea, UNCOK, to continue UNTCOK's work. UNCOK observed the South Korean elections of 30 May 1950, with a staff of only eighteen. The Korean War broke out some weeks later.[17]

On 20 December 1951, the General Assembly created the U.N. Commission to Investigate Conditions for Free Elections in Germany. Given communist reluctance to support international bodies, its task would not be carried out. The commission adjourned indefinitely in August 1952.[18]

Through the Trusteeship Council, the United Nations supervised or organized thirty plebiscites, referendums, and elections between 1956 and 1990: in the British and French Zones of Togoland; the British and French trust territories of the Cameroons; Western Samoa; Rwanda-Urundi; the British colonies of Sabah and Sarawak (Malaysia); the Cook Islands; Aden (but the mission was not allowed to fulfill its mandate); Equatorial Guinea; West Irian; Bahrain; Papua New Guinea; Niue; Gilbert and Ellice Islands; the Trust Territory of the Pacific Islands (several operations from 1975 to 1990); French Somaliland (Djibouti); New Hebrides; Turks and Caicos Islands; Cocos (Keeling) Islands; and Namibia.[19]

The Trusteeship Council[20] fulfilled its mandate under the Charter of the United Nations to promote self-determination in non-independent territories by observing or supervising elections carried out by the "administering authority," which was usually the government entrusted with the territory under a U.N. mandate. From this period dates the distinction in U.N. vocabulary between "supervision" (i.e., direct involvement in establishing the mechanisms of elections) and "observation" (i.e., less direct involvement deemed necessary to ensure "free and fair" elections).[21]

## ONUC in the Congo

U.N. Security Council Resolution 143 (1960) established ONUC to assist the government of the newly independent Congo (now Zaire) which was facing anarchy and secession.[22]

ONUC was an operation that included a peacekeeping force, which performed a "de facto mandatory enforcement action"[23] pursuant to Security Council Resolution 161 (1961), and a U.N. civilian administration, which carried out a de facto management of the Congo and helped the government to restore its effective authority throughout the country.[24]

General Assembly Resolution 1474 (ES–IV) established a U.N. Fund for the Congo, and economic assistance was deployed through ONUC's civilian component which dealt with matters regarding agriculture, communications, state education, public finances, external trade, natural resources, employment, public administration, and social affairs. U.N. civilian personnel were in charge of all the posts previously occupied by Belgians, while training programs were organized for local people.[25]

Secretary-General U Thant proposed a plan for national reconciliation to the Congolese parties and U.N. experts drafted a federal constitution, but these proposals were rejected by the parties.[26]

## UNFICYP on Cyprus

In December 1963, a civil war broke out between the Turkish Cypriot and the Greek Cypriot communities. For the second time, the United Nations had to face an internal armed conflict.[27] U.N. Security Council Resolution 186 (1964) established UNFICYP in order to prevent further escalation of the conflict, restore law and order, and contribute to a return to normal conditions.[28]

The first goal was to create a climate of security. UNFICYP was deployed all over the island because the two communities were intermingled. A U.N. civilian police force, UNCIVPOL, was given the task of monitoring the activities of the local police force.[29] With little success, UNFICYP tried to help the Turkish Cypriots, who suffered from various forms of discrimination. U.N. pressures forced the government to halt economic sanctions against the Turkish community and to proclaim a general amnesty.[30] UNFICYP was also in charge of humanitarian assistance and of helping displaced persons in cooperation with the Red Cross and the Cyprus Joint Relief Commission.[31]

A mediator, Galo Plaza Lasso, was appointed by the secretary-general to work with the parties at variance in order to reach a political settlement of the conflict. Distrusted on the Turkish side, the mediator, had to resign. After 1966, special representatives were entrusted with a good-offices mission.[32]

In 1974, Turkey intervened in response to a coup d'état on the Greek Cypriot side. Ethnic cleansing took place: Turkish Cypriots now live in the Turkish-occupied northern third of the island; Greek Cypriots live in the southern part. UNFICYP's presence is reduced to policing a buffer zone along the cease-fire line. A humanitarian mandate was given to UNFICYP by Security Council Resolution 361 (1974).[33] Secretaries-General Pérez de Cuéllar and Boutros-Ghali have both unsuccessfully proposed constitutional arrangements to resolve the conflict.[34]

### UNTEA/UNSF in West Irian

A Dutch colony, West New Guinea (or West Irian) was claimed by newly independent Indonesia. On 15 August 1962, both the Netherlands and Indonesia agreed that the territory would be temporarily administered by the United Nations, pending the transfer of sovereignty to Indonesia, which had to organize a plebiscite on self-determination.[35] The U.N. General Assembly Resolution 1752 (XVII) created a temporary executive administration, later to be assisted by a security force. It was the first time that a U.N. peacekeeping operation was established as a result of a prior settlement between the parties.[36]

UNTEA had to adapt Dutch institutions to the change of sovereignty: high-ranking positions in the police, justice, and administration could no longer be occupied by Dutchmen, nor could they yet be taken over by Indonesians, and few Papuans were qualified to hold them. Consequently, an international team ruled the country, but it was criticized for insufficient respect of the Papuan party's right to freedom of speech.[37] For its part, UNSF immediately restored order in West Irian and organized a local police force able to relieve it.[38] On 1 May 1963, West Irian was incorporated into Indonesia.[39]

In 1968, a representative of the Secretary-General was sent to West Irian. He reported that local consultative assemblies had decided that West Irian should remain an Indonesian territory. U Thant considered that it was an act of free choice and did not organize a plebiscite as had been stipulated in the agreement of 15 August 1962.[40] Given the fact that Indonesia subsequently recolonized West Irian, U Thant's decision was later said to have been a tragic mistake.[41]

## UNIFIL in Lebanon

Following an invasion of Lebanon by Israeli forces in March 1978 in retaliation for P.L.O. terrorist raids on Israel, UNIFIL was created by the Security Council under Resolution 425 (1978). The peace-keeping force was, *inter alia*, to help the Lebanese government reestablish its authority over southern Lebanon. The Israeli forces had withdrawn by June. UNIFIL was able to provide the local authorities and population in the South with civilian and humanitarian assistance, but it had only limited success in separating the Palestinian commandos and their Lebanese leftist allies from the Christian militia. During the Israeli occupation, Resolution 511 (1982) authorized UNIFIL to protect the local population and to deliver humanitarian assistance to displaced Lebanese citizens and Palestinian refugees. UNIFIL in many ways replaced the local authorities until the Lebanese army's deployment in southern Lebanon and performed many of the local authorities' duties.[42]

## Commonwealth Monitoring Force in Rhodesia-Zimbabwe

In August 1979, Commonwealth heads of government meeting in Lusaka, Zambia, decided to put an end to the long-standing Rhodesian question,[43] agreeing to hold all-party talks in London the following month. At the talks, negotiations were held between the Patriotic Front (Shona-dominated Robert Mugabe's Zimbabwe African National Union, ZANU, and Ndebele-dominated Joshua Nkomo's Zimbabwe African People's Union, ZAPU) and the Salisbury government. Implementing "divide and rule" and "coercive chairmanship," British Foreign Secretary, Lord Carrington was able to force concessions from all parties, who eventually agreed to what in the long run was a decolonization process: a cease-fire, the gathering of ZANU and ZAPU guerrillas at designated assembly points, the international monitoring of Rhodesian police, the end of white minority rule, a liberal constitution providing for twenty seats for whites in the parliament for a seven-year period,[44] and international supervision of elections. The United Kingdom did not want the United Nations to be involved, and a Commonwealth peacekeeping operation was organized.[45]

Alongside a large British contingent, some troops from Australia, the Fiji Islands, Kenya, and New Zealand were deployed to monitor the cease-fire.[46] A civilian Commonwealth observer group, headed by Ambassador Rajeshwar Dayal (a former special representative of the secretary-general in ONUC), was sent to monitor elections that were afterwards declared to have been "free and fair."[47]

Thus, assistance to a process of democratic transition or the international administration of a territory cannot be said to be novelties in the 1990s, but U.N. exercises in world government are now performed more systematically and on a scale that was not usual before.

## The Second Wave of U.N. Prodemocracy Operations

The second wave of U.N. prodemocracy operations shows a reliance on large-scale peace-building measures, that include a new concern for human rights. Then, the supervision or observation of elections follows. Some of these operations promote Western standards of liberal democracy, with U.N. assistance in drafting the host state's constitution.[48]

### Peace-Building Measures

To build peace, multidimensional operations are given the task of working out preparatory and confidence-building measures, which are seen as the prerequisite for a just, comprehensive, and sustainable resolution of a conflict. The most important of these measures are repatriation and resettlement of displaced persons and refugees, amnesty of political prisoners, disarmament and demobilization, and monitoring of human rights.

*Peace-Building Through Assisting Refugees and Displaced Persons.* UN peacekeepers, in cooperation with the U.N. High Commissioner for Refugees (UNHCR), are charged with assisting displaced persons and refugees in returning. In Cambodia, the repatriation process was one of UNTAC's greatest successes, although the timetable of the Security Council was not met. Nevertheless, UNHCR's initial promise to give each returnee two hectares of land was not realistic. Eventually, most of the returnees were given cash to facilitate reintegration.[49] To a lesser extent, ONUSAL's repatriation and resettlement programs were quite successful in El Salvador.[50] The same cannot be said, however, of UNAMIR's program to repatriate Rwandan refugees from Zairian or Tanzanian camps, given that most of them fear their homes will be occupied by Tutsi returnees from Burundi or Uganda. They are also frightened by rumors of reprisals. UNPROFOR II has clearly been a failure in Bosnia and Herzegovina, because it not only cannot stop "ethnic cleansing" but also unwillingly participates in the creation of ethnically homogeneous areas.[51]

*Peace-Building through General Amnesty.*   A general amnesty is the first step toward national reconciliation. Indeed, this is the first mark of the involved parties' willingness to make peace. In Namibia, UNTAG abrogated discriminatory or restrictive laws imposed by the South African Administration. A general amnesty was proclaimed, thus permitting implementation of the voluntary repatriation program. Prisoners and detainees were released. UNTAG refused to distinguish political prisoners from common law ones. It was feared that the South African Administration would use this distinction to retain political opponents in its jails.[52]

### Confidence-Building through Disarmament and Demobilization

The success of classical peacekeeping operations largely depends on the trust that can be developed among all the parties concerned. The Blue Helmets are deployed when two fighting parties want to put an end to hostilities but do not trust each other and, as a consequence, need an impartial presence in a buffer zone between them. In multidimensional operations, U.N. soldiers have to deal with two (or more) parties that may have been fighting each other for years in internationalized internal conflict. While certainly not redundant, classical peacekeeping techniques are clearly not sufficient to bring together the parties at variance. Hence, U.N. peacekeepers must begin by guaranteeing disarmament and the demobilization of warring factions. Then, civilian observer units can be sent in to monitor human rights.

To assist peaceful transition to a democratic resolution of a conflict, multidimensional operations organize the disarmament and demobilization of warring factions: guerrillas and government troops are gathered in separate U.N.-monitored camps to lay down their arms and (for the most part) eventually return to a civilian life. Later, a new national army will be planned and put together, composed of the remaining soldiers from the different factions.

Such measures were successful in Namibia, in Nicaragua, and in El Salvador. So far, they seem to have also worked in Mozambique. They partially failed in Cambodia because the Khmer Rouge refused to be disarmed. In Angola, national reconciliation was a complete failure because neither the government troops of the Popular Movement for the Liberalation of Angola (MPLA), nor the rebels of the National

Union for the Total Independence of Angola (UNITA) were disarmed, and hostilities resumed.[53]

### Confidence-Building through Monitoring Human Rights

Confirming a trend that began in Cyprus, the link between humanitarian norms or human rights and international peace and security is
increasingly to be found in Security Council resolutions. It also seems
that democratic government is perceived as a guarantee for a peaceful
world order, based on Kant's belief that democracies do
not fight each other.[54] ONUSAL in El Salvador was the first U.N.
peacekeeping operation to have an *expressis verbis* mandate to monitor
human rights. Human rights monitoring and human rights education
were part of UNTAC's mandate in Cambodia, because of evidence
of previous mass murders. For the same reason, U.N. human rights
monitors have been assigned to Rwanda, through their brief is separate
from the mandate of UNAMIR.

*ONUSAL in El Salvador.* Urging the Salvadoran government and the
Farabundo Marti National Liberation Front, or FMLN, to agree to a
cease-fire and a final pacific solution to the conflict in El Salvador,
Security Council Resolution 693 (1991) established ONUSAL to
verify the cease-fire and to oversee the conciliation. The parties
formally ended the civil war by agreements signed on 31 December
1991, and on 16 January 1992.[55] In consequence, Security Council
Resolution 729 (1992) expanded the peacekeeping operation's
mandate: a U.N. military force was given the task of verifying the
cease-fire, and a civilian police unit (which also included lawyers,
magistrates, and human rights specialists) was created to monitor
public order and human rights.[56] Human rights violations by the army
and the government, on the one hand, and by the FMLN, on the
other, were investigated by a truth commission. A second commission was given the task of identifying military personnel who had
committed major human rights violations.[57]

*UNTAC in Cambodia.* In order to prevent "past atrocities" (i.e.,
genocide) in Cambodia, the Paris peace agreements set up a mechanism for monitoring human rights. UNTAC was in charge of: (1)
supervising, in consultation with the Supreme National Council, the
implementation of laws to ensure impartial public order and respect
for human rights; and (2) investigating alleged violations of human
rights and taking appropriate corrective measures.[58] Monitoring of
human rights was accepted by all parties, save the Khmer Rouge. The

state of Cambodia was a reluctant partner.[59] Nevertheless, the prison
system was rationalized, and prison conditions were improved. Cambodian police, lawyers, judges, and magistrates were instructed in
human rights. An interim judiciary, a criminal code, and criminal
procedures were established according to a set of conditions drafted
by UNTAC.[60] UNTAC's Human Rights Component also developed
various programs of human rights education that were able to nurture
local human rights movements.[61] The component benefited considerably from the help of local Buddhist monks.[62]

*U.N. Human Rights Monitors in Rwanda.* The genocide in Rwanda
began on 6 April 1994. On 21 April, Security Council Resolution 912
reduced the number of the U.N. peacekeepers in Kigali. In May,
Resolution 918 reshaped UNAMIR's mission. The peacekeeping
operation was given the mandate to support humanitarian assistance,
and a group of human rights monitors was entrusted with a fact-
finding mission on human rights violations. Although not a part of
UNAMIR, these human rights monitors in fact depend on the U.N.
peacekeeping operation for logistics. The main problem they face is
that in such small numbers their effectiveness is questionable.[63]

### Monitoring Elections

The end of the Cold War initiated a second wave of U.N. prodemocracy operations. Significantly, the first such operation had been
established de jure for Namibia by Security Council Resolution 435
(1978) but could not be deployed owing among other considerations to the end of détente. With the end of Soviet-American rivalry,
UNTAG eventually could fulfill its mandate. While UNTAG was,
more or less, a UNTEA/UNSF-type of decolonization case as in West
New Guinea, U.N. supervision operations in Central America and
Haiti were the first to take place in sovereign states. UNAVEM II
supervised the elections in Angola, but the losing faction did not
accept the result. It was feared that ONUMOZ in Mozambique
would face the same kind of situation, but civil war has not resumed
in that state. UNTAC in Cambodia has been the most ambitious, the
most complex, and the most expensive multidimensional operation;
it also represented the first time that the United Nations had organized
the elections. MINURSO is supposed to supervise the plebiscite in
Western Sahara on self-determination, but it does not seem likely that
this referendum will take place.

*UNTAG in Namibia.* UNTAG began to deploy on 1 April 1989. Despite the fact that the Blue Helmets were not numerous enough to stop cross-border attacks by the external wing of the South West Africa People's Organization (SWAPO), UNTAG succeeded in creating the political conditions for "free and fair" elections. The electoral process was under the responsibility of the South African administrator-general, but the U.N. special representative had veto power at each step in the process, and UNTAG officials and UNTAG civilian police kept a close eye on South African administration. The elections took place from 7 to 11 November. More than 97 percent of the registered voters expressed themselves in peaceful self-determination. On 14 November, the U.N. special representative certified that the electoral process had, at every stage, been "free and fair." A week later, the newly elected Constituent Assembly convened. The week after that SWAPO leader Sam Nujoma was elected president. The Republic of Namibia became independent on 21 March 1994. Having brought a democratic nation into the world, UNTAG withdrew.[64]

*ONUVEN in Nicaragua.* To end the Nicaraguan conflict peacefully, the United Nations did not mount a multidimensional operation as such but rather established two distinct operations: an observer mission to verify the electoral process in Nicaragua, ONUVEN, and an observation group in Central America, ONUCA. These two operations were complementary.

Following a summit meeting of the heads of state of five Central American countries at Costa del Sol on 14 February 1989,[65] Nicaraguan President Daniel Ortega Saavedra agreed to hold elections in Nicaragua. The U.N. Secretary-General was requested to establish a group of international observers, who would verify that the electoral process was genuine at every stage. For the first time ever, an independent state requested an international verification of its electoral process. In July, the Secretary-General announced that ONUVEN would be established to supervise the elections,[66] and the operation was endorsed by Security Council Resolution 637 (1989) and by General Assembly Resolution 44 (10). ONUVEN became operational on 25 August, and its observers were granted complete freedom of movement. Elections took place on 25 February 1990. The opposition candidate, Violeta Chamorro, won the presidency, and her party became the new majority. ONUVEN reported that the electoral process had been "free and fair" throughout.[67]

ONUVEN might not have been so successful without ONUCA's presence. As a matter of fact, the peace was maintained during the electoral process by the peacekeeping operation, which had been authorized by Security Council Resolution 644 (1989). After the elections, ONUCA was redeployed by Security Council Resolution 650 (1990) to demobilize the Contras.[68] It should be noted that ONUCA was not operating only in Nicaragua, but also in neighboring countries, while ONUVEN was deployed only on Nicaraguan territory. Thus, the two operations could not be merged, because Nicaragua would certainly have objected.

*ONUSAL in El Salvador.* Initially, ONUSAL was set up in El Salvador to verify compliance by both the government and FMLN with the human rights accord they had signed at San José in July 1990.[69] Then, ONUSAL was to supervise FMLN's dismantlement and its metamorphosis into a political party. Officially, the civil war in El Salvador ended on 15 December 1992. In January 1993, the Salvadoran government requested the United Nations to verify forthcoming elections. A Security Council presidential statement made clear that the government had not fully complied with its obligations regarding its armed forces, nor had FMLN fulfilled its duty to destroy its weapons under ONUSAL supervision. Nonetheless, Security Council Resolution 832 (1993) included in ONUSAL's mandate an electoral component to monitor and verify the elections.[70] Elections were held in 1994, and the electoral process was declared to have been "free and fair."

*ONUVEH in Haiti.* Although the Haitian government's request for U.N. electoral assistance and for verification and supervision of elections could not easily be related to any concern for international peace and security, a U.N. operation was launched to support Haiti's consolidation of democratic institutions. With the Security Council's blessing and despite the reluctance of some Latin American countries, the General Assembly adopted Resolution 45/2 and requested the secretary-general to provide the "broadest possible support" to Haiti. A U.N. Observer Group for the Verification of the Elections in Haiti, ONUVEH, was established to help create a climate conducive to the holding of democratic elections. The electoral campaign and voter registration took place almost entirely without intimidation or violence. The first round of elections was held on 16 December 1990. Voters had to choose, by separate ballots, their president, legislative representatives, and local officials. Over 70 percent of the registered citizens voted. Jean-Bertrand Aristide was announced the winner with 67 percent of the vote. The second round of legislative elections was held on 20 January 1991. On 7 February the newly elected president was inaugurated.[71]

Aristide was overthrown by a military takeover on 30 September 1990. The "coup d'État" was condemned by a Security Council presidential statement on 4 October and by General Assembly Resolution 46/7 on 11 October. For four years, negotiated solutions were sought with the Haitian junta. Eventually, a U.S. operation, "Restore Democracy," was launched to return Aristide to power.

*UNAVEM II in Angola.* One of the two U.N. operations conducted in African states that were formerly overseas dependencies of Portugal, UNAVEM II came to represent the second failure of U.N.-monitored elections. On 31 May 1991, an accord designed to end sixteen years of internal conflict in Angola was signed in Lisbon between the ruling Popular Movement, or MPLA, and the rebel National Union or UNITA. This peace agreement provided for a cease-fire, the creation of a pluralist democracy, respect for human rights and basic freedoms, and internationally supervised elections. A U.N. observer mission, UNAVEM I, was already on the spot to verify the withdrawal of Cuban troops from Angola, pursuant to the Angolan-Cuban accord of 12 December 1988,[72] which was linked to a tripartite accord between Angola, Cuba, and South Africa concerning the withdrawal of South African troops from Namibia and signed the same day.[73] The Security Council unanimously adopted Resolution 696 (1991), which gave UNAVEM II a mandate to monitor the cease-fire, supervise the Angolan police force, and monitor elections. On 29 and 30 November 1992, the elections were held under UNAVEM II's supervision and were declared "free and fair" by the U.N. Secretary-General's special representative. MPLA won. UNITA did not accept this result. Despite the intervention of an ad hoc investigation commission appointed by the Security Council, UNITA launched a nationwide offensive. Civil war started again.[74] In autumn of 1994, a new peace treaty was signed by President José Eduardo dos Santos and a high-ranking UNITA official, but the fighting continued.

*ONUMOZ in Mozambique.* Like UNAVEM II, ONUMOZ. was an operation launched in a former Portuguese colony torn by an internationalized civil war. On 4 October 1992, a general peace agreement was signed in Rome between the president of the People's Republic of Mozambique, Joaquin Alberto Chissano, and Afonso Dhlakama, leader of the Mozambique National Resistance (RENAMO). This agreement ended fourteen years of civil war, and called for U.N. monitoring of its implementation and for technical assistance with, and supervision of, elections. Security Council Resolution 797 (1992) established ONUMOZ to demobilize and disarm the two sides' forces, and to provide assistance in the holding of democratic elections. Humanitarian assistance was also included in the mandate. The deployment of ONUMOZ was slow, and the two parties did not trust each other. The result was that elections were postponed until the end of October 1994.[75] Chissano was democratically elected as president, and his party, FRELIMO, or the National Front for the Liberation of Mozambique, won control of the legislature. RENAMO eventually accepted this decision of the people and renounced its claim for a national union government.

*UNTAC in Cambodia.* With UNTAC, the United Nations for the first time directly organized an election from the planning stage through the writing of an electoral law to registration and conduct of the poll. To ensure a neutral political environment conducive to democratic elections, administrative agencies and other bodies that could directly influence the outcome of the elections were placed under the direct control of UNTAC. But UNTAC was not able to create a neutral political environment, both because of opposition from the Khmer Rouge and because of lack of support from the government. Nevertheless, by March 1993, UNTAC's electoral component had registered 4.7 million voters (i.e., over 96 percent of the total eligible population). During the voting period, nearly 90 percent of the registered voters cast ballots. The elections, which ended on 28 May, were declared to have been "free and fair." Prince Ranaridh's FUNCINPEC won the largest number of votes. At first, the ruling Cambodian People's Party (CPP), did not accept the outcome. The U.N. secretary-general's special representative tried to mediate, but, eventually Prince Norodom Sihanouk found a balanced formula: FUNCINPEC accepted self-restraint, CPP was offered attractive concessions, and a relatively small third party provided the presidency of the National Assembly.[76]

*MINURSO in the Western Sahara.* Wrangling over the Western Sahara, a former colony and later an overseas province of Spain, involved Morocco, Mauritania, Algeria, and the movement for self-determination of the peoples of the Western Sahara known as the Popular Front for the Liberation of Saguia el-Hamra and Rio de Oro (POLISARIO). King Hassan II of Morocco, claiming that the Western Sahara was historically part of his country, was opposed to a U.N.-sponsored referendum on self-determination for the territory. The U.N. General Assembly requested the International Court of

Justice to give an advisory opinion on the legal status of the territory. The court did not find any basis for a claim of territorial sovereignty over Western Sahara by Morocco. In 1975, some of 350,000 Moroccans crossed the border into Western Sahara to support their government's claim that the territory was historically part of Morocco. When Spain relinquished the territory in 1976, Morocco and Mauritania divided it between themselves, and POLISARIO proclaimed the founding of the Saharawi Arab Democratic Republic. POLISARIO, openly backed by Algeria, managed to secure the withdrawal of Mauritania in 1979, after which Morocco occupied the whole of the Western Sahara. Fighting between Moroccan forces and POLISARIO guerillas based in Algeria went on for years. Then, in 1990, a settlement plan was drafted jointly by the United Nations and the Organization of African Unity. Security Council Resolution 690 (1990) approved the creation of MINURSO, an integrated support group of U.N. civilian, military, and civil personnel, to supervise a cease-fire and monitor a referendum on self-determination in the Western Sahara.[77]

Determining the identity of the West Saharan "self" was the first of MINURSO's problems: POLISARIO and the United Nations rely on the Spanish census of 1974, while Morocco would like to add a list of more than 120,000 additional potential voters. By encouraging the defection of POLISARIO leaders through pardons, jobs, and financial rewards and doing what he can to hamper the deployment and the functions of U.N. military and civilian contingents, King Hassan II seemed to be trying to delay or undermine the referendum. Furthermore, it has been said that France played the Moroccan card, and was doing everything possible to slow down the process and induce a deadlock.[78]

U.N.-monitored elections have proved to be a useful device for conflict-resolution, provided that the parties really desire to make peace. Obviously, lack of a genuine commitment to a pacific solution leads to failure, as in Haiti, Angola, or the Western Sahara.

## Constitutional Engineering

The ultimate aim of multidimensional U.N. operations has been to promote Western standards of liberal democracy. Undertaken in the name of "assistance to democratic transition," such operations not only draft electoral laws but also become involved in improving criminal codes and procedures. In a few cases, they have imposed a constitutional framework on an assisted country, including declarations of political rights and sophisticated checks and balances. Thus, the price of U.N. assistance and protection seems to be a limitation of sovereignty, for the making of a constitution (i.e., the choice of a political and legal system) is undoubtedly the most significant expression of a country's independence.

U.N. constitutional engineering does not just provide technical assistance for the drafting of legal texts; it imposes Western legal norms and political values on non-Western states. Constitutional engineering goes further than simply facilitating peace. It universalizes a model that is not necessarily suited or adapted to the economic, social, and cultural context of the assisted country. Provisions such as those that were proposed to the Nicaraguan and Salvadoran warring parties and finally agreed upon were not, strictly speaking "constitutional engineering." These proposals had no direct U.N. origin but were put forward by a regional grouping as technical adjustments, and the role of the local lawmaker was not altogether superseded. These examples confirm the trend toward universalization of liberal democracy, but their relevance is limited because both Nicaragua and El Salvador are Western countries. Clearer examples of U.N. constitutional engineering can be found in the cases of Namibia and Cambodia.

### The Namibian Constitution

In February 1977, five Western members of the Security Council (Canada, the Federal Republic of Germany, France, the United Kingdom, and the United States) set up a working diplomatic committee on Namibia known as the Western Contact Group (WCG).[79] On 12 July 1982, the WCG presented a set of "Principles concerning the Constituent Assembly and the Constitution for an Independent Namibia."[80] These principles sketched out a Western-style parliamentary regime. Eventually, the Namibian Constituent Assembly gave birth to the most liberal African constitution.

*The Constitutional Principles of 1982.* In accordance with Security Council Resolution 435 (1978), Part A of the constitutional principles for Nambia concerned the Constituent Assembly: eligibility of every adult Namibian; vote by secret ballot (with special provisions for illiterate people); full freedom of speech, assembly, movement, and the press; proportional representation; and the requirement of a two-thirds majority for the adoption of a constitution. Principles for a constitution for an independent Namibia are detailed in Part B: a unitary, sovereign, and democratic state; possibility of amendment by the legislature or by a popular referendum; a periodically elected executive branch (responsible to the legislative branch); a legislative branch periodically elected by universal and equal suffrage; an independent judicial branch (responsible for the interpretation of the constitution); a declaration of fundamental rights (mainly from the so-called first-generation human rights); freedom from ex post fact criminal laws; a balanced structuring of public service, police, and defense forces; and establishment of elected local or regional councils.[81]

Security Council Resolution 632 (1989) unanimously approved the U.N. secretary-general's report endorsing the constitutional principles of 1982. Thus, the WCG's proposals officially became a part of the U.N. settlement plan.[82]

The South West Africa People's Organization (SWAPO), which was recognized as the sole and authentic representative of the Namibian people by General Assembly Resolution 31/146, was a Marxist movement, and it was clear that these principles would conflict with SWAPO's constitutional ideas. The WCG wanted a liberal regime for Namibia in order to reconcile Western moral imperatives (end the illegal occupation, end racial discrimination) with Western geopolitical interests (make the communist states' support of SWAPO redundant and remove the Soviet threat to this part of the world). The "two-thirds majority" rule was included in the principles to preclude SWAPO from imposing a single-party dictatorship. Had SWAPO obtained a two-thirds majority, the binding nature of the principles of 1982 would have been questionable. The constitutional principles of 1982 have, however, become a sacred cow for nearly all members of the Constituent Assembly.[83]

Consequently, the principles are mirrored in the constitution,[84] and, because of their integration into the international settlement plan, which is the basis of the Namibian *Rechtsstaat*, these principles have achieved a quasi-supraconstitutional value and cannot be amended.[85]

*A Presidentialist Parliamentary Democracy.* The Namibian Constitution[86] begins with a brief preamble that emphasizes national unity: "We, the people of Namibia . . . desire to promote amongst all of us the dignity of the individual and the unity and integrity of the Namibian nation among and in association with the nations of the world." Then follows the description of the Republic of Namibia as "a sovereign, secular, democratic and unitary state founded upon the principle of democracy, the rule of law and justice for all."

The preamble is not a bill of rights. Fundamental human rights and freedoms are incorporated into Chapter III of the constitution – notably, protection of life (Article 6); protection of liberty (Article 7); respect of human dignity (Article 8); prohibition of slavery and forced labor (Article 9); equality before law and freedom from discrimination (Article 10); *habeas corpus* (Article 11); right of property (Article 16); right of every citizen to participate in political activity (Article 17); and fundamental freedoms (Article 21). The provisions in Chapter III can only be amended to extend human rights protection (Article 131).

Sam Nujoma, the leader of SWAPO, was elected president of the Constituent Assembly and became president of the republic, pursuant to transitional provisions (Article 134). His successor will be elected directly by the people for a five-year period. The Namibian form of government creates a semipresidential political system.[87] The president is both head of state and head of government and must act in consultation with the cabinet (headed by a prime minister). But, according to Article 36, the role of the cabinet is to advise and assist the president, acting as the head of government. Most of the powers are concentrated in the office of the president, but the president can be impeached and all of her or his decisions based on Article 32 (which enumerates the presidential powers) can be reviewed, reversed, or corrected by the National Assembly.

The National Assembly is the lower and most powerful house, being composed of seventy-two elected representatives chosen by proportional representation and of six persons who are appointed by the president but have no right to vote. The National Council is the upper house and cannot exert any kind of political control over the executive branch.

The judiciary is organized according to the tradition of the common law (Chapter IX).

Chapter XI spells out the principles of state policy. These include sovereignty over natural resources below and above the surface of the land of the republic and sovereign rights over its continental shelf and within its territorial waters and exclusive economic zone (Article 100). Namibia is a unitary but territorially decentralized state (Articles 102 to 111).

From all this it follows that the constitution gives Namibia a classical liberal democratic system, in keeping with constitutional principles of 1982. SWAPO's influence is reflected in Chapter XI, but private property is protected, and foreign investment encouraged in Article 99.

Given that South African constitutions were inspired by British liberalism (applied to whites only) and that South Africa is a common-law country, the Namibian constitution cannot really be said to be an imported legal or political regime. Similarities with the Zimbabwean constitution are striking, and explain some of the changes that the Namibian Constituent Assembly made in the Westminster model.

Nevertheless, it is surprising how little the Constitution's framers altered their basic British legacy.

It is beyond dispute that Western liberal democratic regimes have reached a more or less satisfying balance between individual freedoms and governmental efficiency. It also stands to reason that the drafters of the Namibian Constitution were aware of the failure of socialist or "third-way" regimes. Yet, it is also reasonable to think that the constitutional principles of 1982 reduced the possibility of creating indigenous norms that would have been more closely adapted to the country.

While the U.N.'s universalization of Western standards was quite easy to bring about in a newborn state, it would be less so in an older nation.

### The Cambodian Constitution

Since the recovery of total independence in 1953,[88] Cambodia has experienced five different constitutions: the Kingdom of Cambodia, a constitutional Asian monarchy (revised once in 1957, twice in 1958, three times in 1959, twice in 1960, and once in 1964); the Khmer Republic, a presidentialist regime in 1970; Democratic Kampuchea, a Khmer Rouge regime in 1975 (or rather a Maoist assembly regime, but the constitution was of little importance at that time); the People's Republic of Kampuchea, a Soviet-style assembly regime in 1979; and the State of Cambodia, a liberalized socialist assembly regime in 1989.[89] So, changing the constitution to start from a new basis was almost a Cambodian tradition.

Notwithstanding lip service to the inalienable right of states to choose freely their own political system according to the wishes of their peoples and without any interference, the Paris peace accords included "principles for a new constitution"[90] and proposals for a liberal democratic system based on pluralism, an independent judiciary, and a "two-thirds majority rule" for the new constitution's approval by the Constituent Assembly.[91]

Western standards of democracy are dominant in the new Cambodian Constitution, but traditions and the Marxist legacy are also present.

*Constitutional Monarchy and U.N. Influence.* According to Article 1 of the new Cambodian Constitution, the Kingdom of Cambodia is a constitutional monarchy that will observe pluralist liberal democratic principles. It is clear that this choice of regime was made under U.N. influence. As a matter of fact, before the constitution was adopted

Prince Norodom Sihanouk declared that Cambodia was neither a kingdom, nor a republic, but an independent, neutral and nonaligned state.[92]

Title IV, a division of the constitution, defines the political regime as a pluralist liberal democracy and Cambodian external policy as one of nonalliance and perpetual neutrality.

Article 92 forbids the assembly to pass bills that could be contrary to the maintenance of independence, sovereignty, the territorial integrity of the kingdom, or to political unity. In all other matters, the assembly (Cambodia has a single house of parliament) is the only institution that has legislative power (Article 90). The Royal Government is the Council of Ministers, headed by a prime minister who is nominated by the king, but is invested through a vote of confidence by the assembly. The government can be overthrown by the assembly, but if two governments have to resign within a year owing to a vote of the Assembly, the king must dissolve the assembly at the prime minister's request, provided that the president of the assembly agrees (Article 78). The judiciary is independent. Contrary to a proposal of 1993 by UNDP, there is only one legal order (and not two legal orders, as in most civil-law or civil-law-inspired countries). Consequently there is a Supreme Court, but there is also a Constitutional Council established by Title X. This French-inspired institution (it is not a court) controls the conformity of the bills before or after their promulgation.[93]

UNTAC's concern for human rights is reflected in Title III on "the rights and duties of Khmer citizens." Article 31 asserts that Cambodia respects human rights "as defined" in the Universal Declaration of Human Rights and in U.N. treaties and conventions and stipulates that Khmer citizens are equal. Article 32 is directly inspired by Article 3 of the Universal Declaration. Article 38 establishes a sort of *habeas corpus*. Other human rights and fundamental freedoms are included in Articles 33 to 46. Articles 47 to 49 deal with a citizen's duties, which are of the common-sense kind (e.g., parents have the duty to educate their children and every Khmer citizen must abide by the constitution and the laws).

U.N. influence can also be seen in Article 63, which provides that Cambodia has chosen a market economic system.

*Traditional Heritage and Marxist Legacy.*    Monarchy plays a special role in Cambodian culture. For most of the peasants (90 percent of the population), Sihanouk is the legitimate leader. Significantly, Title II concerning the king is placed in the constitution before "rights & duties of citizens." While the word "Assembly" is quoted 122 times in the constitution, the word "king" comes up 59 times (as many times as "law(s)"), the word "rights" appears 55 times, "state" 51 times, and "citizen(s)" 38 times. The words "liberty," "individual," and "social" are found ten, six, and five times respectively.[94]

Cambodian monarchy is not hereditary, but elective. Several articles deal with succession to the throne.

The constitution tends to foster national unity. Provisions for human rights are reserved for citizens alone. Traditions also dictate provisions on family and land tenures.

Although reference is made to a market economy, the state owns almost everything: soil and subsoil, mountains, sea, continental shelf, maritime coasts, channels, rivers and lakes, woods, natural resources, economic and cultural centers, and national defense bases and other sites (Article 58). The state is also in charge of planning management and allocation of natural resources, including air, wind and wild animals (Article 59). Finally, the state may control the market to ensure decent standards of living (Article 63).

The Cambodian Constitution is only apparently liberal, with deep cultural and historical trends playing an important role. The king is the key factor in the evolution of the regime. At the beginning of 1993, Sihanouk forecast that when Cambodia ceased to be a U.N. protectorate, the Khmers' internal affairs would have to be settled by Cambodians themselves. He added that it would be possible to form, under his presidency, a national provisional government of reconciliation.[95] This is exactly what happened, despite the elections' clear results.

Namibia respected the letter and the spirit of Western constitutional engineering, but Cambodia superimposed the U.N. constitutional framework on its own culture. This should be a signal for the U.N. Security Council not to act as a world directorate.


## Conclusion

The new multidimensional operations of the United Nations give conflicting parties the opportunity to settle their problems with ballots rather than bullets. If peace-building measures are required,[96] the surest way to build peace is to rely on the choice made by the people, and comprehensive peace plans inevitably resort to plebiscites to secure either external or internal self-determination.[97] These peace plans, which are endorsed or even drafted by the U.N. Security Council, or by the permanent members sometimes working together with other powers, are eventually ratified by the concerned people. Therefore, international law tends to acknowledge a right to "free and fair" elections,[98] and the embryonic world directorate seems to promote an emerging right to democratic government.[99]

United Nations multidimensional operations promote human rights, but most of the relevant treaties were also signed by Third-World states, which cannot protest against the enforcement of conventions they have ratified. Yet when Western standards of democracy are similarly imposed on assisted states, there are no treaties that oblige them to restrict their choice to only one (democratic) form of political system. Westerners generally deny the existence of a problem, claiming that Western democratic values are universal. They are not. From a legal viewpoint, a norm becomes universal when a significant number of countries from all cultural areas genuinely agree to it.[100] If a rule is perceived as being imposed on a country, local people will reject it. In the case of multidimensional operations, this means that the solution to conflicts should be adapted to the local situation and to people's cultural values. Otherwise, not only will the operation risk being rejected, but so will the United Nations as a whole.

## Notes

1. See: A. James, *Sovereign Statehood. The Basis of International Society* (London: Allen & Unwin, 1986); B.B. Ferencz, *New Legal Foundations for Global Survival. Security through the Security Council* (New York: Oceana, 1994), pp.163–170; M. Koskenniemi, *From Apology to Utopia. The Structure of Legal Argument* (Helsinki: Finnish Lawyers' Publishing Co., 1989), pp.192–263; J. Charpentier "Le phénomène étatique à travers les grandes mutations politiques contemporaines" in Société Française pour le Droit International (ed.) *L'Etat Souverain à l'Aube du XXIe Siècle. Colloque de Nancy* (Paris: Pédone, 1994), pp.11–38; J.-D. Mouton "L'Etat selon le droit international: diversité et unité", ibid., pp.79–106; H. Thierry "L'Etat et l'organisation de la société internationale", ibid., pp.189–211.

2. See: L.H. Miller, *Global Order. Values and Power in International Politics* (Boulder, Colorado: Westview Press, 2nd edition, 1990), pp.19–41.

3. see: F. Attar, *1792: la Révolution française déclare la guerre à l'Europe* (Brussels: Complexe, 1992).

4. The Monroe doctrine was an American response to the Holy Alliance's wish to quel the revolt of the Latin American colonies against Spain. See: L. Oppenheim, *International Law: A Treatise* Vol.I *Peace* (London: 8th edition revised by H. Lauterpacht, 1955), pp.313–316; M.A. Kaplan & N. de B. Katzenbach, *The Political Foundations of International Law* (New York: John Wiley & Sons, 1961), pp.62–63; Ch. Rousseau, *Droit International Public* Vol.IV *Les relations internationales* (Paris: Sirey, 1980), p.57.

5. It is the reason why Second Empire France intervened in Mexico to establish the Austrian Prince Maximilian as an emperor.

6. It was notably the case of the French intervention in (then) Syria to save the Maronite Christians from mass murder perpetrated by the Druzes, and to impose an home rule status for Mount Lebanon. See: S. Kloepfer, "The Syrian crisis, 1860–1: A Case Study in Classic Humanitarian Intervention" *Canadian Yearbook of International Law* XXXIII, 1985, pp.246–260.

7. 1905 humanitarian intervention in Macedonia; on humanitarian intervention, see: L.F. Damrosch & D.J. Scheffer (eds), *Law and Force in the New International Order* (Boulder, Colorado: Westview Press, 1991), pp.143–184; A. d'Amato, "The Relation of the Individual to the State in the Era of Human Rights" *Texas International Law Review* Vol.XXIV, 1989, pp.1–12; F.R. Téson, *Humanitarian Intervention: an Inquiry into Law and Morality* (New York: Transnational Publishers, 1988); R.B. Lillich (ed.), *Humanitarian Intervention and the United Nations* (Charlottesville: University Press of Virginia, 1973); L.-A. Sicilianos, *Les réactions décentralisées à l'illicite. Des contre-mesures à la légitime défense* (Paris: L.G.D.J., 1990), pp.464–494; A. Rougier, "La théorie de l'intervention d'humanité" *Revue Générale de Droit International Public* 1910, pp.468–526.

8. See: B.B.Ferencz, op. cit., pp.170–177; B. Conforti, "The Principle of Non-Intervention" in M. Bedjaoui (ed.), *International Law: Achievements & Prospects* (Paris/ Dordrecht–Boston–London: U.N.E.S.C.O./ Martinus Nijhoff, 1991), pp.477–480; I. Brownlie, *Principles of Public International Law* (Oxford/ New York: Clarendon Press/ O.U.P., 4th edition, 1990), pp.293–295; J.S. Watson, "Auto-Interpretation, Competence and the Continuing Validity of Article 2(7) of the U.N. Charter" *American Journal of International Law* 1977, pp.60–83; L.M. Goodrich, "The United Nations and Domestic Jurisdiction" *International Organization* Feb. 1949, pp.60–83; L. Preuss, "Article 2(7) of the Charter of the U.N. and Matters of Domestic Jurisdiction" *Collected Courses of The Hague Academy of International Law* LXXIV, 1949–1, pp.553–653; G. Guillaume, "Article 2, paragraphe 7" in J.-P. Cot & A. Pellet (eds), *La Charte*

*des Nations Unies. Commentaire Article par Article* (Paris: Economica, 2nd edition, 1991), pp.141–159.

9. See: A.B. Fetherston, "Putting the Peace Back into Peace-keeping: Theory must Inform Practice" *International Peacekeeping* Vol.I, No.1, 1994, p.4; these U.N. operations are also called "second gener-ation peacekeeping operations", see: Netherlands Institute of International Relations (ed.), *Case-Studies in Second Generation U.N. Peacekeeping* (Clingendael: N.I.I.S., 1994); G. Abi-Saab, "La deuxième génération des opérations de maintien de la paix" *Le Trimestre du Monde* Vol.IV, No.20, 1994, pp.87–97; J.Mackinlay & J. Chopra, *A Draft Concept of Second Generation Multinational Operations 1993* (Providence, Rhode Island: Thomas J. Watson Jr Institute for International Studies, Brown University, 1994), p.4, this chapter deals only with what they call "Level II operations"; R. Dreyer, "State Building and Democracy in Second Generation Peacekeeping Operations" in D. Warner (ed.), *New Dimensions of Peacekeeping* (Dordrecht/Baton/London Martinus Nijhoff 1995) pp.147–155.

10. *An Agenda for Peace*, § 59.

11. S.R. Ratner, "The United Nations in Cambodia: A Model for Resolution of Internal Conflicts?" in L.F. Damrosch (ed.), *Enforcing Restraint: Collective Intervention in Internal Conflicts* (New York: Council on Foreign Relations Press, 1993), pp.260–269. S.R. Ratner, *The New U.N. Peacekeeping: Building Peace in Lands of Conflict after the Cold War* (New York: Council of Foreign Relations/St. Martin's Press, 1995), p.239.

12. See: M. Suksi, *Bringing in the People. A Comparison of Constitutional Forms & Practices of the Referendum* (Dordrecht-Boston-Paris: Martinus Nijhoff, 1993), pp.238–241.

13. See: ibid., pp.242–243; Y. Beigbeder, *International Monitoring of Plebiscites, Referenda & National Elections. Self-Determination & Transition to Democracy* (Dordrecht-Boston-Paris: Martinus Nijhoff, 1994), pp.80–83.

14. See: ibid., pp.83–84; on Aaland Islands, see: B. Driessen, *A Concept of Nation in International Law* (The Hague: T.M.C. Asser Instituut, 1992), pp.154–160; L. Hannikainen, "Cultural, Linguistics & Educational Rights in the Aaland Islands" *Publications of the Advisory Board on International Human Rights* No.5, 1992, p.8–12; H. Hannum, *Autonomy, Sovereignty & Self-Determination* (Philadelphia: University of Pennsylvania Press, 1990), pp.370–375.

15. See: Y. Beigbeder, op. cit., p.84.

16. Ibid., pp.84–87. See also S.R. Ratner, *The New U.N. Peace-*

*keeping*, op. cit, pp.91–94.

17. Ibid., pp.120–125; J.M. Ebersole, "The United Nations' Reponse to Requests for Assistance in Electoral Matters" *Virginia Journal of International Law* XXXIII, 1992, pp.92–93.

18. See: Y. Beigbeder, op. cit., p.125.

19. See: U.N. Doc. A/46/609/ Annex; Y. Beigbeder, op. cit., pp. 94–99.

20. See: commentaries of relevant U.N. Charter Articles in J.-P. Cot & A. Pellet (eds), op. cit., pp.1101–1247; I. Brownlie, op. cit., pp.172–176. See also G. Chand, "The United States and the Origins of the Trusteeship System" *Review* XIV, 1991, pp.171–229.

21. J.M. Ebersole, op. cit., pp.93–94.

22. See: R. Higgins, *United Nations Peacekeeping, 1946–1967, Documents and Commentary, Vol.III: Africa* (London: Oxford University Press, 1980), pp.14–16; W.J. Durch (ed.), *The Evolution of U.N. Peacekeeping. Cases Studies & Comparative Analysis* (London: Macmillan, 1993), pp.319–320; on the Council's debates, see: T.J. Kahng, *Law, Politics and the Security Council: An Inquiry into the Handling of Legal Questions involved in international disputes and situations* (The Hague: Martinus Nijhoff, 1964), pp. 83–88.

23. N.D. White, *The United Nations & the Maintenance of International Peace and Security* (Manchester: M.U.P., 1990), p.201.

24. See: A. James, *Peacekeeping in International Politics* (London/New York: Macmillan/St. Martin's Press, 1990), pp.296–297.

25. See: U.N. Dept. of Public Information, *The Blue Helmets. A Review of United Nations Peace-Keeping* (New York, 2nd edition, 1990, hereinafter *Blue Helmets*), pp.253–256; "L'ONU et le Congo" *Chroniques de Politique Etrangère* (Brussels) XV, 1962, pp.486–543; more generally on ONUC, see: T.O. Elias, *New Horizons in International Law* (Dordrecht–Boston–London: UNITAR/ Martinus Nijhoff, 2nd edition revised and edited by F.M. Ssekandi, 1992), pp.165–171.

26. See: U.N. Doc. S/5053 to S/5053/Add.15; Constitution draft in S/5053/Add.13/Annex 11.

27. See: Z.M. Necatigil, *The Cyprus Question & the Turkish Position in International Law* (Oxford: O.U.P., 1989); A.R. Norton, "The Roots of the Conflict in Cyprus" in K. Skjelsbaek (ed.), *The Cyprus Conflict & the Role of the United Nations* (Oslo: Norwegian Institute of International Affairs, N.U.P.I. Report 122, Nov. 1988); S.G. Xydis, *Cyprus. Reluctant Republic* (The Hague: Mouton, 1973); S. Kyriakides, *Cyprus. Constitutionalism and*

*Crisis Government* (Philadelphia: University of Pennsylvania Press, 1968).

28. See: J.A. Stegenga, *The United Nations Force in Cyprus* (Columbus: Ohio State University Press, 1968), pp.49–52; A. Boyd, *Fifteen Men on a Powder Keg. A History of the U.N. Security Council* (London: Methuen & Co, 1971), pp.278–279.

29. See: R. Higgins, *United Nations Peacekeeping. 1946–1979.* `Documents and Commentary Vol.IV: Europe* (London: Oxford University Press, 1981), pp.131–132; *Blue Helmets*, pp.291–292.

30. See: R. Higgins, op. cit., pp.235–236 and 311–315.

31. See: *Blue Helmets*, pp.295–296.

32. See: R. Higgins, op. cit., pp.142–147; on the Turkish viewpoint, see: N.M. Ertekün, *The Cyprus Dispute & the Birth of the Turkish Republic of Northern Cyprus* (Nicosia: Rustem, 2nd edition, 1984), p.21.

33. See: *Blue Helmets*, p.306; R. Higgins, pp.142–143.

34. See: B.G. Ramcharan, "Ethnic conflicts & Minority problems" in D. Gomien (ed.), *Broadening the Frontiers of Human Rights* (Oslo: Scandinavian University Press, 1993), pp.33–34.

35. See: U.N. Doc. A/5170; R. Higgins, *United Nations Peacekeeping, 1946–1967, Documents & Commentary, Vol.II: Asia* (London: Oxford University Press, 1970), pp.101–106; F. Monconduit, "L'Accord du 15 août 1962 entre la République d'Indonésie et le Royaume des Pays-Bas relatif à la Nouvelle-Guinée Occidentale (Irian occidental)" *Annuaire Français de Droit International* Vol.VIII, 1967, pp.491–516.

36. R.E. Riggs and J.C. Plano, *The United Nations. International Organization and World Politics* (Chicago, Illinois: Dorsey Press, 1988), pp.139.

37. See: *Blue Helmets*, pp.270–276; R. Higgins, op. cit, pp.141–142.

38. See: R. Higgins, op. cit., pp.139–140.

39. It was an "Anschluss" according to F.Ch. Iklé, *How Nations Negotiate* (New York: Harper & Row, 1964), p.85.

40. See: U.N. Doc. A/7723, Annexes I & II.

41. R. Nassif, *U Thant in New York 1961–1971. A Portrait of the Third U.N. Secretary-General* (London: Hurst, 1988), p.97.

42. See: B. Skogmo, *UNIFIL. International Peacekeeping in Lebanon, 1978–1988* (Boulder, Colorado: Lynne Rienner, 1989); E. Erskine, *Mission with UNIFIL. An African Soldier's Refections* (New York: St. Martin's Press, 1989); M. Heiberg, "Observation on U.N. Peacekeeping in Lebanon" *N.U.P.I. Note* No.305, Sept. 1984; K. Skjelsbaek & A. McDermott (eds), *A Thankless Task: The Role of UNIFIL in Southern Lebanon* (Oslo: Norwegian

Institute of International Affairs, N.U.P.I. Report 122, December 1988).

43. See: J. Davidow's comments in D.B. Bendahame and J.W. McDonald (eds), *Perspectives on Negotiation. Four Case Studies and Interpretations* (Washington, D.C.: U.S. Dept. of State, 1986), pp.171–175; M.E.K. Neuhaus, "A useful CHOGM: Lusaka 1979" *Australian Outlook* Vol.XLII, 1988, pp.161–166.

44. Abrogated by *Constitution of Zimbabwe (No.7) Act* of September 21st, 1987 – see: D.L. Horowitz, *A Democratic South Africa? Constitutional Engineering in a Divided Society* (Berkeley: University of California Press, 1991), pp.134–136.

45. See: J. Sedman, *Peacemaking in Civil Wars. International Mediation in Zimbabwe, 1974–1980* (Boulder, Colorado: Lynne Reiner, 1991), pp.169–172; J. Davidow's comments in D.B. Bendahame & J.W. McDonald (eds.), op. cit., pp.176–178.

46. I.J. Rikhye, *The Theory & Practice of Peacekeeping* (London: Hurst, 1984), pp.174–175; A. James, op. cit., pp.107–110.

47. See: S. Chan, *The Commonwealth Observer Group in Zimbabwe* (London: Lester Crooks, 1985).

48. See: Y. Beigbeder, op. cit., pp.148–149.

49. See: J. Chopra, *The United Nations Authority in Cambodia* (Providence, Rhode Island: Thomas J. Watson Jr Institute for International Studies, Brown University, Occasional Paper #15, 1994), pp.61–67.

50. See: F.M. Deng, *Protecting the Dispossessed: A Challenge for the International Community* (Washington, D.C.: Brookings Institution, 1993), pp.88 and 104–105.

51. See: F.M. Deng, op. cit., pp.29–36; M. Mercier, *Crimes Sans Châtiment. L'Action Humanitaire en Ex-Yougoslavie* (Brussels/ Paris: Bruylant, L.G.D.J., 1994).

52. See: *Blue Helmets*, pp.376–377.

53. See: C. Messiant, "Le coût de l'Angola" *Panoramiques* Vol.IV, No. 15, 1994, pp.77–83; C. Alden, "Swords into Ploughshares? The United Nations and Demilitarization in Mozambique" *International Peacekeeping* Vol.II, No.2, 1995, pp. 175–193.

54. See: D.P. Forsythe, *Human Rights & Peace. International and National Dimensions* (Lincoln: University of Nebraska Press, 1993); F.H. Hinsley, *Power & the Pursuit of Peace. Theory and Practice in the History of Relations between States* (Cambridge: C.U.P., 1963), pp.62–80.

55. See: U.N. Doc. S/23999.

56. See: N.D. White, "U.N. Peacekeeping – Development or

Destruction?" *International Relations* (London) Vol.XII, No.1, 1994, pp.141–142.

57. See: T.G. Weiss, D.P. Forsythe and R.A. Coate, *The United Nations and Changing World Politics* (Boulder, Colorado: Westview Press, 1994), pp.67–68.

58. See: U.N. Doc. S/22059; J. Chopra, op. cit., pp.38–40.

59. See: J. Chopra, op. cit., pp.40–43.

60. See: T. Duffy, "Toward a Culture of Human Rights in Cambodia" *Human Rights Quarterly* Vol.XVI, 1994, pp.92–95.

61. See: ibid., pp.99–100.

62. S.P. Marks, ACUNS/ASIL Summer Workshop, Providence, July 20th, 1994.

63. Based on interviews of humanitarian agencies personnel, who have worked in refugees/displaced persons camps. See L. Minear and Ph. Guillot, *Soldiers to the Rescue: Humanitarian Lessons from Rwanda* (Paris: OECD Development Centre, forthcoming).

64. See: Y. Beigbeder, op. cit., pp.157–162.

65. On the Central American peace process, see: J. Tacsan, *The Dynamics of International Law in Conflict Resolution* (Dordrecht-Boston-Paris: Martinus Nijhoff, 1992), pp.168–180.

66. See: U.N. Doc. S/20699.

67. See: N.D. White, op. cit., pp.139–141; Y. Beigbeder, op. cit., pp.164–169; J.M. Ebersole, op. cit., p.95.

68. See: N.D. White, op. cit., pp.140–141.

69. See: U.N. Doc. S/21541.

70. See: N.D. White, op. cit., pp.141–142.

71. See: Y. Beigbeder, op. cit., pp.169–176.

72. U.N. Doc. S/20345.

73. U.N. Doc. S/20346.

74. See: Y. Beigbeder, op. cit., pp.180–184; N.D. White, op. cit., pp.142–144.

75. See: Y. Beigbeder, op. cit., pp.213–217; S. Samkange, "L'ONU et le processus de paix au Mozambique" *Le Trimestre du Monde* 1993, pp.154–173. For a critical assessment, see: S. Willett, "Ostriches Wise Old Elephants and Economic Reconstruction in Mozambique" *International Peacekeeping* Vol.II, No.1, 1995, pp.34–55.

76. See: Y. Akashi, "The Challenge of Peacekeeping in Cambodia" *International Peacekeeping* Vol.I, No.2, 1994, pp.206–207; M. Doyle and N. Suntharalingam, "The U.N. in Cambodia: Lessons for Complex Peacekeeping" *International Peacekeeping* Vol.I, No.1, 1994, p.124; Y. Beigbeder, op. cit., pp.197–212; M. Hong, "The Paris Agreement on Cambodia: In Retrospect" *International*

*Peacekeeping* Vol.II, No.1, 1995, pp.93–98.

77. See: Y. Beigbeder, op.cit., pp.190–197.
78. Conversation with French contingent members; see: J. Chopra, *United Nations Determination of the Western Saharan Self* (Oslo: Norwegian Institute of International Affairs, N.U.P.I. No.1, March 1994).
79. On the WCG and the negotiation on Namibia, see: V. Jabri, *Mediating conflict: Decision-Making & Western Intervention in Namibia* (Manchester: M.U.P., 1990).
80. U.N. Doc. S/15287.
81. See: *South African Yearbook of International Law* Vol.XV, 1989–90, pp.7–8.
82. Ch. Cadoux "La République de Namibie. Un modèle constitutionnel pour l'Afrique australe?" *Revue de Droit Public* Vol. CVIII, 1992, p.13.
83. Ibid.
84. See: M. Wiechers "Namibia: The 1982 Constitutional Principles & their Legal Significance" *South African Yearbook of International Law* Vol.XV, 1989–90, p.14.
85. Ibid., pp.20–21; Ch. Cadoux, op. cit., p.14.
86. Constitution in U.N. Doc. S/20927/Add.2; see also: T.O. Elias, op. cit., pp.175–177; Ch. Cadoux, op. cit., pp.14–35.
87. See: B. Chantebout "La Constitution namibienne du 9 février 1990: enfin un vrai régime semi-présidentiel" *Revue Française de Droit Constitutionnel* No3, 1990, pp.339–349. In French, "semi-presidential regime" and "presidentialist parliamentary regime" are almost synonymous: they are both used to described the French Fifth Republic.
88. Cambodia became a French protectorate in 1863. Her independence was *de jure* recognized by France in 1949, but Cambodia was then an associated state within the French Union (sort of Commonwealth between France and her former colonies during the Fourth Republic).
89. See: R.M. Jennar (ed.) *Les Constitutions du Cambodge, 1953–1993* (Paris: La Documentation française, 1994).
90. U.N. Doc. S/23177/Annex III.
91. U.N. Doc. S/23177/Annex V.
92. See: M. Gaillard *Démocratie cambodgienne. La Constitution du 24 septembre 1993* (Paris: L'Harmattan, 1994), pp.16–18.
93. Ibid., pp.125–133.
94. Ibid., pp.171–173.
95. P. Isoart 'Le Cambodge' in Société Française pour le Droit International (ed.), op. cit., p.232.

96. See: G. Evans *Cooperating for Peace. The Global Agenda for the 1990s and Beyond* (St Leonards, Australia: Allen & Unwin Pty Ltd, 1993), pp.52–58; J.S. Sutterlin *The United Nations and the Maintenance of International Security: A Challenge to be Met* (Westport CT & London: Praeger, 1995) pp.75–80.

97. On self-determination, see: F.L. Kirgis Jr "The Degrees of Self-Determination in the United nations era" *American Journal of International Law* Vol.LXXXVIII, 1994, pp.304–310; H. Hannum 'Rethinking Self-determination' *Virginia Journal of International Law* Vol.XXXIV, 1993, pp.1–69; K. Markoukadis "The Relationship between minority rights and self-determination" *European Law Students' Association (E.L.S.A.) Law Review* Vol.IV, 1994, pp.38–53.

98. See: P. Klein "Le droit aux élections libres en droit international: mythes et réalités" in Association Droit des Gens (ed.) *A la Recherche du Nouvel Ordre Mondial. Vol.I: Droit international à l'épreuve* (Brussels: Complexe, 1993), pp.106–111.

99. T.M. Franck "The Emerging Right to Democratic Governance" *American Journal of International Law* Vol.LXXXVI, 1992, p.46.

100. See for instance on the Muslim viewpoint: D.A. Westbrook "Islamic International Law & Public International Law: Separate Expressions of World Order" *Virginia Journal of International Law* Vol.XXXIII, 1993, pp.219; B. Tibi "Islamic Law/ Shari'a, Human Rights, Universal Morality & International Relations" *Human Rights Quarterly* Vol.XVI,1994, pp.277–299; R. Afshari "An Essay on Islamic Cultural Relativism in the Discourse of Human Rights" *Human Rights Quarterly* Vol.XVI, 1994, pp.235–276.

# – 11 –

# From Human Rights to Good Governance: The Aid Regime in the 1990s

## Nira Wickramasinghe

### Introduction

When nineteenth-century ideas of "imperial power" gave way after the collapse of colonial rule to the notion of international responsibility and the birth of the United Nations, the "white man's burden" needed a new justification[1] – and the aid regime was born. South Asia today is part of the interdependent world that emerged after World War II from the Bretton Woods agreements of 1944 providing for the establishment of the World Bank and the International Monetary Fund. For example, the industrialization of Pakistan since independence has largely depended on foreign aid and private foreign investment. The economy of Bangladesh also rests on handouts of foreign aid, which have failed significantly to improve that nation's abysmal standard of living. Sri Lanka relies on export revenues from the sale of primary products – garments have replaced tea as the prime export – displaying a similar network of external economic ties and dependence.[2] The movement of capital, ideas, technologies, and persons has reduced the real importance of statehood and dramatically eroded the significance of nominal state sovereignty.

The volume of aid to the Less Developed Countries (LDCs) has grown at a phenomenal rate. In the early 1950s, aid from all sources was less than $11.8 million. Supported by a U.N. campaign urging member states to give at least 0.7 percent of G.N.P. as aid, today's total disbursements amount to $60 billion.[3] As the volume of aid increased, taxpayers in developed countries began to demand that their contributions should not support regimes that failed to respect the human rights of their citizens. They also learned that in many instances aid was not trickling down to the people.[4]

This has led in recent decades to an increasing concern for human rights issues in the principal donor countries. By "human rights" is meant those civil, political, economic, social, and cultural rights embodied in the Universal Declaration of Human Rights and the International Covenants that were promulgated by the United Nations and to which most countries of the world have subscribed. In signing these covenants states accept that human rights are an international responsibility and that governments are accountable not only to their own citizens but to the world community as well. They willingly concede a share of their state sovereignty. Many now recognize that consideration of human rights should and does affect the provision of aid and development assistance.[5] As will be shown, the human rights discourse is itself subject to national security interests, and is in the process of being displaced and supplanted by another and more perverse ideological discourse, that of "good governance," which is fast becoming a new orthodoxy in official Western aid policy and on Third World thinking about development.[6]

The issue of human rights and foreign policy will be examined briefly before considering the linkages that existed between aid and human rights in the context of bilateral and multilateral aid relationships until the end of the 1980s. Consideration will then be given to the shift that has occurred from a total lack of concern for human rights on the part of multilateral aid agencies and from a primary concern for individual human rights on the part of donor countries to a more complex and interventionist approach embodied in the notion of "good governance" and "political conditionality." In this new approach the aim is nothing less than to change the world-system by reforming the fundamental institutions of the recipient state.

## Human Rights and Aid: Negative Linkages in the 1980s

### Human Rights and Foreign Policy

Kautiliya, the ancient Indian political theorist, conceptualized six different categories of policies for handling interstate relations: peace, war, indifference, strengthening one's position, subordinating an ally or vassal, and duplicity. Concern whether development assistance should be linked to a country's observance of human rights stems from perplexity among the public in aid-dispensing countries over the duplicity of their government's aid policies, which at certain times seem indifferent to the plight of starving masses and at other times spell a readiness to intervene for hardly commendable reasons. This debate reflects apprehension that repressive regimes may maintain their power through foreign aid, using it as an instrument of legitimation to strengthen and perpetuate their position. Clearly, ideological or geo-political considerations on the part of donor countries have often overridden moral concerns, as in the case of the support given by the United States to Pakistan during the period of martial law in that country or in U.S. dealings with Central American dictatorships.

The experience of the United States as a large donor country serves to illustrate the linkage between aid and foreign policy. As Stansfield Turner has pointedly observed, "the most obvious specific impact of the new world order is that except for Soviet nuclear weaponry, the preeminent threat to U.S. national security now lies in the economic sphere."[7] The end of the Cold War loosed U.S. foreign policy from its moorings, requiring a thorough reorientation of aid strategy. Indeed, as James C. Clad recently wrote, "after 45 years America's foreign bilateral assistance program lies dead in the water."[8] Without communism to contain, the United States has had to reassess and readjust its aid programs.

Since the end of World War II, there has been a series of ideo-logically inspired shifts in aid policy. Throughout the Cold War, U.S. priorities in foreign aid were conditioned by national security concerns, creating an important linkage between foreign policy and foreign aid. The first subsumed the second. Before the collapse of the U.S.S.R., aid was given to friendly non-Communist countries, particularly those forming a political buffer against the Soviet Empire. Even strategically insignificant countries were affected. Sri Lanka was at this time ruled by the left-wing government of Sirimavo Band-aranaike, which nationalized Western oil and other business facilities. The United States reacted immediately by cutting its aid program to Sri Lanka, including the provision of milk and buns to school children. An important shift occurred under President Jimmy Carter who, building on efforts of the U.S. Congress, established the legiti-macy of human rights as a distinct concern, although the success of this upgrading was not apparent until after Carter had left office. Human rights became a factor in his administration's decisions about providing economic aid, and legislation was adopted to reflect this. But the belief that human rights must yield to national security interests imposed limitations on the policy. Carter's approach was (in the words of a State Department official) "imperfect but honest."[9]

The second shift in U.S. aid orientation occurred when President Ronald Reagan appropriated human rights (viewed as the embodiment of Western values) for his ideological crusade against communism. Reagan's successor, President George Bush, also linked aid and human rights selectively, but with less impunity than Reagan.[10] A comparison of the per capita O.D.A. received by democratic and authoritarian regimes points to the gulf between rhetoric and reality. The relationship between aid and human rights in the 1980s has been quite rightly described as "perverse."[11] U.S. President Bill Clinton's China policy also illustrates how foreign policy considerations and economic motives often override human rights concerns.

It can be argued that during the Cold War the linkage between aid and human rights was only a single element in a multipronged foreign policy in which covert international war was practiced on many occasions against elected governments deemed unsupportive of U.S. interests, and, therefore, outside the circle of democratic communities. Iran in 1953, Guatemala in 1954, Indonesia in 1957, Brazil from 1961, Chile in 1973, and Nicaragua from 1984 are the most striking examples.[12] In these cases, the United States organized or aided covert interventions involving violence because it was felt that American national security was at stake. In countries where intervention was not possible or not crucial, aid linked to human rights was deemed sufficient as a foreign policy instrument.

Most Western European donor countries (with the exception of Nordic states) have followed the pattern of the United States, turning a blind eye to human rights abuses when committed by friendly countries, as in France's acquiescence in Emperor Bokassa's murderous reign in Central Africa. French protégé Mobutu Sese Seko in Zaire owned 51 Mercedes-Benz cars when he dismissed 7,000 school teachers from the Zairian school system on the grounds that there was no money to pay their salaries. Despite such outrages, his government remained for many years one of the most favored recipients of Western aid in Africa. The degree and nature of the distortion varies from donor state to donor state. The influx of refugees from the south into Europe has added a twist to the human rights issue. European countries seeking to rid themselves of refugees, such as Switzerland, must refrain from even mentioning the human rights situation in the country of return. This contributes to the cynical application of human rights standards for reasons of political expediency.

### Negative Linkages and Aid

Among the instruments available within the framework of development cooperation for the purpose of influencing, promoting, and maintaining human rights, it is possible to differentiate between "positive measures" geared to improving the human rights situation and "negative measures" as a response to gross and systematic violations of human rights.

Negative measures consist of using aid as a political weapon. There are many gradations: funding can be conditioned on certain improvements in observance of human rights, a cutoff may be threatened, and finally aid may be withheld. Sanctions have worked in South Africa but not in war-ridden Bosnia. The effectiveness of the policy depends on the credibility of the threat; the relative size of the donor's aid package; and, most important, on the nature of the recipient regime and its susceptibility to this form of manipulation. There is also the danger that the withdrawal of development assistance might lead to worse hardships for the population. One illustration of this is what happened in Ethiopia. Following the establishment of a Marxist regime and a brutal period of revolutionary purges, Western donors cut off long-term development assistance in 1977, limiting the aid package to emergency relief. The discontinuation of aid was one of the factors contributing to the famine of 1984.[13]

In the case of Sri Lanka, such linkage has become commonplace. Since 1983 the country has been the theater of a bitter ethnic war that is compromising the economic recovery that began in 1977 after a long period of stagnation and brought a decade of development based on protectionism and import substitution. The Sri Lankan state and Tamil militant groups are engaged in violent acts that discourage foreign investment and try the patience of human rights organizations. But the government's renewed commitment to giving priority to private initiative in a market economy has produced a real growth of 6 percent in the 1990s. This growth has been fueled by a massive public investment program, largely financed by foreign assistance. Multilateral aid to Sri Lanka is of two types: outright grants and loans on concessionary terms. Both grant aid and concessionary loans come from Western Europe, the United States, Japan and international organizations. Most foreign aid is pledged at the meetings of the Aid Sri Lanka Consortium, which is organized by the World Bank on behalf of the major donor countries. The Sri Lanka government sends the World Bank an annual request outlining its needs. The member donors then meet to consider these requests and coordinate their aid policies.

Sri Lanka's recent past has been marked by frequent occurrences of torture and deaths in custody, extrajudicial killings, and reprisal massacres. Arbitrary arrests and detentions for long periods are also common. Sri Lanka has been under a state of emergency since 1983 except for a period of five months. In 1994, the new left-of-center government of Chandrika Kumaratunge lifted the emergency in the South. In the north and the east, the security forces are still invested with extraordinary powers under the Emergency Regulations and the Prevention of Terrorism Act (P.T.A.).[14] Partly as a response to the human rights situation and partly because of nonutilization of funds – a substantial portion of the aid provisions (funds earmarked for the rehabilitation of the north and northeast provinces for 1989–90) were not spent because of the military situation – many donors decided not to increase their budgets for 1990–91. Donor pressure since April 1990, after the death of Richard de Soyza, a prominent journalist, has resulted in an improvement in the human rights situation. The fact that by placing conditions on aid, aid-giving governments put pressure on Sri Lanka to improve its human rights record is not seen as a loss-of-sovereignty problem by many human rights activists.[15] Indeed they argue that when nations subscribe to the International Covenant on Civil and Political Rights, and the International Covenant on Economic, Social and Cultural Rights they agree in effect to cede a part of their sovereignty. Governments have agreed to answer to the U.N. Commission on Human Rights and to the Human Rights Committee. The first institution is composed of about fifty members appointed by governments selected by the United Nations Economic and Social Council. The second, set up under the Covenant on Civil and Political Rights, is a group of persons elected by the parties to the covenant and serving as individuals.

In the North European countries where interest in human rights has been strongest and its translation into political acts most immediate, the main concern has been to avoid accusations of sovereign interference. The states' formal position has been that aid should relate to the needs of people and not to the conduct of their governments. But in reality Norway has been taking human rights considerations into account since 1986 and Denmark since 1987. Donor countries, and especially the Nordic states, rely on the reports and statements of both international organs and nonstate-level organizations before forming their policy on aid. All governments have to submit regular five-year reports to the United Nations. Sri Lanka's turn was in 1991, and the representative of the government had a difficult time at the hearings. The Commission on Human Rights may receive representations and (when it deems necessary) send working groups and rapporteurs to investigate the situation in a country. In 1991, a Working Group on Disappearances visited Sri Lanka. The Sri Lanka government agreed to accept and implement most of the group's recommendations and encouraged further visits in order that an external evaluation could be effected. Among other measures, the government appointed a Presidential Commission on Disappearances to investigate complaints and set up a Human Rights Task Force.[16] Other organizations concerned with the advancement and promotion of human rights such as Asia Watch and the International Commission of Jurists exert similar pressure on the government. The concern that donor countries will cut or reduce aid puts the government in a situation where it is answerable to them as well. In the period before the aid meeting, the government acts with a certain amount of circumspection.

In 1985, Margaret Thatcher became the first European leader to attempt, if unsuccessfully, to build human rights conditions into the provisions for European Community aid to Africa, the Caribbean, and Pacific countries under the Lomé Conventions. Although that attempt was initially rejected by A.C.P. leaders as an unwarranted infringement on their domestic sovereignty, by the time of the Lomé IV Convention of 1990 an explicit reference to human rights in the context of E.C. aid could no longer be avoided.[17] More recently, the European Union has, because of its high level on internal cohesion, been fairly successful at linking human rights and development. A recent example is the freezing of Lomé IV funds to Sudan by the European Commission based on a recommendation resulting from a European Parliamentary resolution. The reason given was the existence of widespread human rights abuses.

### U.N. Human Rights and Development: Parallel Processes

There is a clear division of tasks and responsibilities between the agencies in the U.N. system that deal specifically with human rights (the Human Rights Commission, the General Assembly, and the Secretariat) and those that come under the broad heading of the promotion of social and economic rights. Although multilateral institutions of the United Nations such as the World Health Organization (WHO) and the United Nations Development Program (UNDP) have adopted development policies based on human needs, they are not articulated using rights language.[18] The first Human Development Report did show some innovation by trading the newly minted concept of "economic development" for the concept of "human development."

In the field, it is clear that human rights considerations are not taken into account in the context of U.N. development assistance. Aid is channeled in an indiscriminate way to countries governed by regimes that violate human rights. The question today is whether the United Nations has a mandate to make its aid conditional on the human rights situation in the recipient country. Article 2(7) of the Charter of the United Nations is quite explicit:

> Nothing contained in the present Charter shall authorize the United Nations to intervene in matters which are essentially within the domestic jurisdiction of any state or shall require the Members to submit such matters to settlement under the present Charter; but this principle shall not prejudice the application of enforcement measures under Chapter VII.[19]

Although Article 2(1) of the charter reflects very clearly the duty of states and the organization to refrain from intervention in each other's internal affairs – "the Organization is based on the principle of the sovereign equality of all its members" – the collective voice of sovereign states in the context of deliberations of the legislative body of the General Assembly has often stigmatized certain individual states. Indeed the prohibition in Article 2(7) is qualified by its reference to "enforcement measures under Chapter VII" (i.e., the chapter dealing with the powers of the Security Council to maintain or restore international peace and security).[20] Arguably, the application of sanctions in the form of an arms embargo against apartheid regimes (for which the council took an inclusive view of "threats to peace" in order to act under Chapter VII) is another form of collective enforcement of human rights obligations. Article 41 of the charter grants the Security Council the power to impose trade embargoes for the maintenance of international peace and security. Trade sanctions have until now been applied sparingly and only in very extreme cases of human rights abuses, such as Iraq's treatment of its Kurdish population. What is necessary is to build on precedents and go beyond them by formulating a mechanism by which the U.N. development agencies together with the U.N. human rights agencies follow an integrated and principled approach that links development aid to human rights and is applied to all countries receiving U.N. assistance.[21]

## Good Governance and Aid Conditionality

### Positive Linkages

When aid is used as an instrument to improve the observance of human rights in a recipient country, one speaks of positive linkages. This entails intervening directly to rectify situations that are judged detrimental to a human rights regime. The current concept of good

governance would not have been possible without the prior acceptance of positive linkages by the world community.

It is crucial, at the outset, to distinguish between governments and
the nongovernmental organizations (NGOs) as recipients of aid. The
reason why many countries engage in the promotion of human rights
within the government sector is that they consider this a middle road
between the two extreme situations of withholding aid and direct
support for an often ideologically hostile human rights sector. The
United States, for instance, tends to channel assistance directly through
the government. But increasingly, the trend is for more aid to be
channelled through NGOs.

The number of indigenous NGOs involved in human rights work
has increased over the last decade as the tendency for donors to
channel their development funding in this way becomes more pronounced.[22] The last twenty years has seen a rapid growth of indigenous
NGOs in Sri Lanka.[23] Most NGOs combine elements of service
delivery with elements of community mobilization. Most bilateral and
multilateral aid programs make explicit allocations of resources for
NGOs. This is partly a response to the equity concerns of the
donors' domestic constituents regarding recipient government
utilization of foreign funds. The new emphasis on the nongovernmental sector reflects the intellectual framework of wider changes in
macroeconomic policy, privatization and the reduced role of states in
all aspects of the economy and in the provision of services. NGOs
are seen as a dynamic privatized alternative to bloated state bureaucracies.

The change in aid policy by the Danish government reflects this
new emphasis. Denmark cut off aid to Sri Lanka at the end of 1989
when the Colombo government, in its attempt to put down the insurrection of the People's Liberation Front (JVP), encouraged massive
human rights abuses. When aid was resumed in 1993, Denmark
proposed to upgrade Sri Lanka to "Country Program" status while
assisting it in improving human rights and democratic freedoms. This
meant that aid to developmental projects would be resumed once the
first aim was achieved. Individuals and groups closer to the grassroots
would be supported in efforts to promote ethnic harmony or to promote press freedom. The Sri Lanka government was indignant at these
proposals, which were likened to a "Trojan horse" being introduced
by strategies in Sri Lanka to monitor and meddle in its internal human
rights affairs.[24]

The rise of the nongovernmental sector, which is often equated
with prodemocracy movements, together with the collapse of official
Communist regimes and the resurgence of neoliberalism, explain the

new concern with "governance" and democracy[25] on the part of the World Bank and some donor countries.

*Good Governance and the World Bank: The Primacy of Economic Issues*

The World Bank has, on the whole, shown very little concern for human rights issues. Until recently, the same structural impediments to human rights/development linkage that existed in the U.N. system also existed within the World Bank system. The major difference lies in the decision-making authority of the bank, where voting power is weighted according to the size of the donor's contribution. At present, the World Bank has 148 member countries. As with the International Monetary Fund (IMF), some members have more say than others. The "big five" control 42 percent of the votes and the industrial countries together 60 percent of the votes of the Board of Executive Directors.[26] This concentrates power in the Western states and allows for political/ideological motivations to influence fund allocation. For example, Vietnam was not eligible for World Bank funds because of a U.S. veto. The freeze on bank funds to China following the killings of June 1989 is also evidence of an awareness of the development/human rights linkage.

The majority of World Bank funds (roughly 70 percent) are disbursed as loans, the balance takes the form of concessionary loans through the IDA, as well as some technical assistance grants. In policy terms, this also means that funds are conditioned on the recipient's adoption of certain economic policies.

Recent works critical of the World Bank highlight three major shifts in its development policy. The 1950s and 1960s were characterized by large-scale infrastructure developments that required massive investments in capital projects. The bank primarily promoted planning and public sector initiatives providing for dams, schools, roads, and other infrastructure projects in the developing world. The underlying theory was that the LDC economies required a jump start after which they could "take off" following the growth pattern of European states during the Industrial Revolution. The benefits of this accelerated growth could then trickle down to the poor. The realization that these predictions were not materializing led to a change in policy and a concentration on "basic needs" in the 1970s. This included poverty alleviation, education, health and nutrition. Sprawling, inefficient bureaucracies and a changing global economic climate led to a balance-of-payments crisis in the early 1980s and another change in development policy. The World Bank became a great proponent of competition, privatization, and markets.[27]

The World Bank and its main contributor, the United States, began to use the concept of "good governance" in the period from 1985 to 1989, when referring to forms of political management that included some aspects of political representation. It started as a critique of the African states suggesting deconstructive institutional reforms. Adrian Leftwich has pointed out that the first contemporary public appearance of the notion of good governance came in a World Bank report on Africa in 1989, which argued that, "Underlying the litany of Africa's development problems is a crisis of governance."[28] The bank further defines governance as the exercise of political power to manage a nation's affairs." Good governance included some or all of the following features: an efficient public service; an independent judicial system and legal framework to enforce contracts; the accountable administration of public funds; an independent public auditor, responsible to a representative legislature; respect for the law and human rights at all levels of government; a pluralistic institutional structure and a free press.[29] The World Bank, however, never endorsed the notion of political conditionality, as this would constitute a derogation of its purely technicist grounding. In 1992, a booklet was published in which governance was quite clearly redefined in terms of development policy, as separate from politics. The problem of governance is said to involve four distinct issues: poor public service management, lack of accountability, absence of a legal framework for development, and problems of information availability or transparency. The underlying assumption was that it is possible to have a technical "solution" to these problems of governance that is independent of the form of political representation.[30]

The World Bank's lack of concern for the sanctity of representation has been highlighted in an analysis that correlates World Bank loans and democracy for the Philippines and Bangladesh. After these two countries lifted martial law, their shares in the total loans given by the World Bank declined.[31] Clearly, martial-law regimes were felt to be more stable and susceptible to improving economic development.

The ideology of good governance echoes and elaborates aspects of the modernization theory of the 1960s that held that Western economic and political liberalism represented "the good society itself in operation."[32] At the root of both modernization theories and good governance is the Weberian formulation that the world should move toward adopting the features of representative government, bureaucracy, a capitalist economy, the Protestant ethic and a scientific methodology. The outcome is a disenchanted or secular modern culture. Interestingly, the modern project, which is infused with Weberian undertones, has been largely internalized by policymakers and thinkers in LDC's and, it permeates even works critical of the post-colonial state in developing countries.

Thus, if the purpose of good governance is the development of modern institutions, such as banking systems modeled on the Bundesbank, it appears to be very similar to the ideology of modernization. One of the drawbacks of both these approaches is that they encourage the notion that only modernity has institutions and that only modernity is rational. Against these presuppositions Sudipta Kaviraj perceptively points out that modernity does not build institutions in an empty space. Rather it reworks the logic of existing structures.[33] The main difference between good governance and modernization, however, is that while modernization theorists advanced democracy as the outcome of development, growing out of new roads, bridges, rail networks, and television, the new orthodoxy postulates that democracy in its limited form of good governance is a necessary condition of development. Democracy/good governance is not an aim but the means to attaining a certain stage of development.

The World Bank is thus using the age-old script of the Industrial Revolution in its attempt to forge a New World Order where there will be governance without government. In this system, good governance means in effect less government. Governments would still operate and still be sovereign in a number of ways, but some of their authority would be relocated towards subnational collectivities. Comparing governance and government, Rosenau points to the main differences: "Both refer to purposive behavior, to goal-oriented activities, to systems of rule; but government suggests activities that are backed by formal authority, by police powers to secure the implementation of duly constituted policies, whereas governance refers to activities backed by shared goals that may or may not derive from legal and formally prescribed responsibilities and that do not necessarily rely on police powers to overcome defiance and attain compliance." He sums up governance as "order plus intentionality."[34]

### Bilateral Aid and Good Governance

An agenda of political conditionality has always been present to one degree or another in superpower dealings with LDCs. In the case of the United States, its content had always involved reference to multiparty democracy and human rights. After the breakdown of communism in Eastern Europe, political conditionality was adopted by the E.C. Council of Ministers in 1989 and elaborated by the French, British, and German governments the following year. The new agenda contained "governance issues" as enunciated by the

World Bank, with calls for reforms in the sphere of political representation as promoted by the United States. Thus these countries did not hesitate to make an explicit linkage between economic and political reforms. Leftwich has quite pointedly demonstrated that the idea of good governance is not simply the new technical answer to the difficult problems of development but an intimate part of the emerging politics of the New World Order.[35]

In the New World Order, the United States goals for South Asia are quite clearly dominated by a concern for good governance. They are: "to continue to support and promote security in the region through decreasing tensions between the states: second, to discourage a race toward acquisition of weapons of mass destruction; third, to promote and strengthen democratic institutions through economic development, encouraging privatization and assisting with the buildup of democratic structures; and, finally, to seek support for a successful winding up of the issues raised by the Gulf War."[36]

Sri Lanka can be looked on as a case study of the U.S. approach to development in South Asia. At her Senate Confirmation hearing in May 1992, Ambassador Teresita Shaffer described the aim of U.S. foreign policy in Sri Lanka as being "to take advantage of every opportunity to expand U.S. exports or investments."[37] According to the Sri Lanka desk officer at the State Department, the objectives of U.S. policy towards Sri Lanka are threefold: to encourage a political settlement with the Tamil militants, to foster human rights reforms in the country at large, and to improve economic relations and trade with Sri Lanka, especially in the area of the garment industry.[38]

Sri Lanka governmental sources indicate, however, that human rights are treated only at a general level by the U.S. administration and that the United States is satisfied with the steps taken by the Sri Lanka government to improve the nation's human rights record.

The USAID program objectives for Sri Lanka derive from a set of strategic goals that flow from a vision of Sri Lanka as a democratic, environmentally sound, newly industrializing country. It is felt that U.S. assistance can be especially helpful to the Sri Lanka government in managing the transition to a competitive market economy. Both Sri Lanka and the USAID subscribe to the vision of Sri Lanka as a democratic, greener NIC. The focus is on agricultural development-led industrialization and private initiative. USAID proposes to broker new private-public partnerships in key development sectors. In this strategic vision, the three following subgoals are defined: an effective market economy; protection of the environment and productive resource base; and an active, pluralistic society. In contrast with its approach in previous decades, USAID has in the 1990s attempted to focus its projects on clear strategic objectives. This was made possible by the conjunction of the Sri Lanka government's economic policy and social objectives with those of the U.S. government. Thus the United States continues to promote both political conditionality and good governance as defined by the World Bank.[39]

The European Community has clearly articulated similar concerns in its Resolution on Human Rights in the World and Community Human Rights Policy of 12 March 1993. The Community Policy on "Positive measures and conditionality" asserts that "the Community can be a very positive force in promoting democracy and human rights, where it has clear international obligations."[40] Unlike the U.S. approach, though, there is no linkage made between market friendly policies and human rights. Economic issues do not enter directly into the frame of reference. In the U.S. case, there is an underlying assumption that without a free market, there is no respect for human rights, no democracy, and thus no aid.

## Critique of Good Governance

There are two necessary and possible dimensions in a critique of good governance. One is qualitative. The question is whether the good governance policy preached by the World Bank is "good" in all cases. Is it the only way, and if not, are there better roads to development? Let us take a look then at the kernel of the notion of "good governance," which is the belief that "good governance" as defined by the World Bank is an essential condition for development in all societies.

### Development and Good Governance

One of the central features of "good governance" through structural adjustment programs is the gradual withering away of the state as an economic actor at the macro level. The underlying assumption is that development – taken here in its least controversial understanding, as the expression of a nation's growing economic well-being, evidenced by increasing quantity of, distribution of, and people's satisfaction with the national wealth – is caused by good governance. Is the equation that clear?

Interestingly, the structural adjustments prescribed by the World Bank for LDCs face at present strong opposition from the Japanese. This is an important development because Japan is the second largest contributor to the bank after the United States. The Japanese had begun complaining about the bank's aid policies in the early 1990s. They pointed out that Japan, Korea, and Taiwan had developed according to a far different model. The governments of the East Asian "dragons" worked closely with business to develop strategies for growth. Nationalized banks gave low-interest loans and grants to selected industries. Governments restricted foreign investment to maintain control over the direction of economic development. Subsidies were granted to business in exchange for specific performance requirements. Planners placed a high priority on becoming competitive through higher productivity rather than through lower wages. It was argued that those countries that have followed the American model have floundered since the 1960s, while Japan, South Korea, Taiwan, Malaysia, Hong Kong, and Thailand grew three times as fast as Latin American and South Asian countries and five times faster than sub-Saharan Africa.

The Japanese challenge touches a vital point – namely; the role of the government in the aid recipient countries. It has prompted many policymakers to rethink the role of the state in economic activity and particularly in central planning. Alternative models inspired by the Japanese experience, or the Scandinavian welfare state, fundamentally differ from "good" governance as defined by the World Bank, yet they may be better suited to some specific countries or situations. The argument here is not that democracy and development are incompatible but that the state can play an important role without the regime being as authoritarian as neoliberals suggest.

Sometimes the presupposition that democracy/good governance is a necessary condition for development appears in the very choice of countries studied and compared. Atul Kohli, taking the records of five diverse democracies including India, Malaysia (which hardly qualifies as a democracy), Sri Lanka, Venezuela, and Costa Rica and comparing them with countries that followed authoritarian routes to development, has argued that democracies in the developing world can boast impressive economic records in terms of income distribution, debt management, and even growth rate.[41] Might not his conclusions linking democracy and development have been quite different had he chosen as case studies countries such as Japan, South Korea, Taiwan, Hong Kong and Thailand, which do not conform to his criteria of democracy?

The link between democracy and development is complex and cannot be encapsulated in a notion such as good governance. Not surprisingly the concept of "good governance" has been subjected to scrutiny by human rights activists in Sri Lanka who have expressed doubt about the concern for "erecting the kind of juridical structure necessary for the spread of market relations."[42] For a developing country such as Sri Lanka, there is nevertheless no doubt that the main objective of aid and development policies in the 1990s should be to assist integration into the global mainstream. At the same time, aid and development policies will have to continue to serve their traditional objective of supporting long-term development programs for building infrastructures and financing projects of substantial social benefit, such as investment in rural development, health, nutrition, education, and the alleviation of poverty.[43] Just as there is no clear causal relationship between democracy/good governance and development, the linkage between economic growth and social advancement is not self-evident.

## Good Governance as Totalizing Discourse

The second dimension of this critique of good governance is of a more fundamental nature. We must ask ourselves why, when all grand narratives or the totalizing or foundational theorizing of modernity have given rise to so many critical responses, a concept such as "good governance," so anchored in Western history and tradition could ever have been proposed, or flourish. In an era characterized by the loss of paradigmatic guidelines, the concept of "good governance" has not remained unchallenged. Social scientists are increasingly stressing the need to get away from oversimplified models. Their works indicate that the main problem of political development theories has been their tendency to conceive of political development in terms of two general dichotomies: modern vs. traditional societies, and democratic vs nondemocratic political systems. Thinking in terms of dichotomies or binary sets of categories prevents us from realizing that many states encompass within themselves many apparently contradictory characters and structures. For example, development and underdevelopment, democracy and authoritarianism, civilian and military rule at the same time.

The development myth is a powerful one. In its name modernizing elites have shed all sensitivity to indigenous systems of thought, totally cast away during the great "development decades" of the U.N. system and the transfer of Western science and technology. This particular aspect has been subjected to serious examination by scholars in the developing countries who have investigated the power of the development myth and the creation of a Republic of Science where capitalism had lost its poetic power to a Baconian-scientific worldview.[44] The concept of "good governance" falls within the tradition of dichotomizing models, which should be once and for all put aside, while the widely accepted concept of "democracy" must be submitted to the same scrutiny.

At the level of discourse, there is indeed a tendency to confuse deep democracy, embracing all three components of the motto of the French Revolution and based on a complex, multidimensional array of human rights (political, civil, economic, social and cultural), with good governance, which is nothing more than political liberalization – that is, a process of political change controlled from the top while the social status quo remains unchanged. Democracy confined to good governance entails a change in the shell, not in the fruit. No change in social relations follows. Formal democracy, where democracy is confined to the level of formal electoral participation, is not sufficient. Instead, a return to the notion of human rights that prioritizes basic social rights, or what is commonly known as second-generation rights of the individual (education, health, and well being) may be more useful in any attempt to build deep or progressive democracy that entails profound social reform rather than formal liberties.

One encouraging trend is that development economists at the United Nations have ceased to use a narrow concept of development as growth and have begun to concern themselves with the qualitative improvement of life. This trend is reflected in the concept of "human development indicators" such as freedom of expression, association and movement, the preservation of human rights, and safeguards against intrusion into individual liberty, as preconditions for development.[45] They accept that "development must be woven around the people, not people around development."[46] A more difficult task will be to convince the financial institutions that sound democratic institutions are not enough and that the benefits must seep down to the people. The incidence of IMF riots in some countries has shown that democracies cannot be created from outside and that a government which is too evidently dependent on external support is liable to lose legitimacy at home.

## Conclusion

To paraphrase Sugata Bose, "somewhere between Sri Lanka and world capitalism lies an interregional arena of social politics and political economy"[47] molded largely by the politics of aid, concepts of human rights, and ideas of good governance. In this arena, the world financial institutions are hegemonic and have stripped away economic sovereignty. The most important decisions, those concerning the economy, are beyond the control of national power holders. The solution is surely not to delink, but rather if one borrows the Hegelian metaphor, to form a circle of circles delineating areas of sovereignty. The outer circle would be formed by circles touching each other while remaining independent. These would be U.N. institutions, the World Bank, the IMF, and the EU and similar organizations. Inside this circle of circles would be all the sovereign states in perpetual movement and interacting between themselves.[48] The role of the United Nations as the conscience of the world has declined while the economic institutions have acquired supranational powers. One of the main reasons why the United Nations, the IMF, and the World Bank have not succeeded in reducing conflicts, bringing about peace, and generating equitable world development is that these international organizations were not created with a democratic structure. Another important reason is that the United Nations, the IMF, and the World Bank do not operate as if they form part of the same system. The World Bank, for instance, does not involve the U.N. in the elaboration and subsequent implementation of economic stabilization and structural adjustment programs.

There is a possibility that the United Nations may play a new role in the formulation of a harmonious, cogent, and integrated approach to human rights and development, that of the watchguard of the powerful institutions that lack sensitivity to the human dimension of development.[49] If a reform of the Security Council takes place and if real efforts are made to eliminate wastage, the U.N. with its egalitarian premises is the best arena where notions of "good governance" and "political conditionality" can be discussed and where the smaller and weaker states could have a voice against the hegemonic tendencies that prevail in the aid regime. One can think of a world government in the spirit of Keynes' national economic stabilization formulation, which takes responsibility for managing the world development through a participative and co-operative method of taking decisions and resolving conflicts.[50]

In this type of world order, there would be no place for single-track and technicist approaches such as good governance. Instead, lending institutions as well as aid agencies and development programs would be "mindful" of the social, cultural and political consequences of their intervention. For such a scenario to take place, the relationship between national governments and international institutions must cease to be a power relationship. Such a change can come from many quarters, but there is reason to believe or at least to hope that as more people become aware that all states are interdependent in crucial areas such as the environment, arms control, or communication, more civil society initiatives will emerge to push for human rights regimes in their own countries and for a more equitable rate of exchange in international aid and development.

## Notes

1. For a lucid account of the notion of "world responsibility" as a rationale of American foreign policy, see Edward Said, *Culture and Imperialism* (New York: Alfred. A. Knopf, 1993), 285–291.
2. Jayati Gosh, "The Impact of Integration: India and the World Economy in the 1980s," in Sugata Bose (ed.) *South Asia and World Capitalism,* (New Delhi: Oxford University Press, 1990), 338–339.
3. The rationale and role of aid has been subject to scrutiny. Critics of aid have emphasized the abuses and damaging effects on the recipient society. Others have argued in favor of aid as a catalyst for development. See for instance Robert Cassen and Associates, *Does Aid Work?* (Oxford: Clarendon Press, 1986).
4. According to *the Human Development Report 1994* (New Delhi: Oxford University Press, 1994), pp. 72–73: "Aid is not targeted at the poor. Donors send less than one-third of development assistance to the ten most populous countries, which are home to two-thirds of the world's poor. As a result of these distortions, the richest 40% of the developing world receives as much aid per capita as the poorest 40%."
5. Katharine Tomasevski, *Development Aid and Human Rights. A Study for the Danish Center of Human Rights* (New York: St. Martin's Press, 1989).
6. Adrian Leftwich, "Governance, Democracy and Development in the Third World," *Third World Quarterly*, Vol.14, No.3, 1993,: 605.
7. Stansfield Turner, "Intelligence for a New World Order," *Foreign Affairs*, (Fall, 1991), :151.
8. J.C. Clad and Roger D. Stone, "New Mission for Foreign Aid," *Foreign Affairs*, 1992–3, 72, 1: 196.
9. Interview with George Lister, Senior Policy Advisor, Human Rights and Humanitarian Affairs Bureau, 4 March 1993.
10. Diane F. Orenlichter, "The United States Commitment to International Human Rights" in Richard Pierre Claude and Burns

H. Weston (eds), *Human Rights in the World Community, Issues and Action*, (Philadelphia: University of Pennsylvania Press, 2d ed. 1992), 340–352.

11. *Human Development Report 1994*, 76.
12. David P. Forsythe, *Human Rights and Peace. International and National Dimensions* (Lincoln and London: University of Nebraska Press, 1993), 33–54.
13. Gillian Kettaneh, "Human Rights and the Provision of Development Assistance," Unpublished paper presented at the conference, South Asia – An Agenda for the Nineties Oct. 1990, Ahungalle, Sri Lanka.
14. See for instance, *Report of the Working Group on Enforced or Involuntary Disappearances* (7–18 Oct. 1991), Commission on Human Rights, 48th session, 8 Jan. 1992.
15. *Report of the Canadian Human Rights Mission to Sri Lanka*, January 1992, 22.
16. Statement of Mr. Bradman Weerakoon of Sri Lanka Delegation, Commission on Human Rights, 48th Session, Geneva; Statement by Ambassador Neville Jayaweera, Delegation of Sri Lanka, 12 Feb. 1992.
17. Christopher Clapham, "Democratization in Africa: Obstacles and Prospects," *Third World Quarterly*, 14, 3, 1993, :432.
18. Gillian Kettaneh, "Human Rights and the Provision of Development Assistance," op. cit.
19. *Charter of the United Nations and Statute of the International Court of Justice* (United Nations, New York, 1993), :5.
20. Lori Fishler Damrosh, "The Civilian Impact of Economic Sanctions" in Lori Fishler Damrosh (ed.), *Enforcing Restraint. Collective Intervention in Internal Conflict,* (New York:Council on Foreign Relations Press, 1993) 275–291–294.
21. Some donor countries follow the example set by the U.N. in delinking development aid and human rights. Japan, which is Sri Lanka's principal donor has consistently refused to link aid with human rights. In other cases it is less a question of unwillingness than of inability. South Asian regional organizations (A.D.B., A.S.E.A.N., S.A.A.R.C.) have not elaborated policies to deal with the human rights/development linkage.
22. *Our Voice. Bangkok N.G.O. Declaration on Human Rights* (Bangkok, Asian Cultural Forum, 1993)
23. This section draws from Sunil Bastian, "N.G.O.s in Development," *The Thatched Patio*, 18 (April 1988) :12–18.
24. *Counterpoint* (April–May 1994) : 26–28.
25. Adrian Leftwich, op. cit.,: 606.

26. R. Herbold Green, Kim Hong Pyo, D. Tong Ka Wing, "The Language of Money", *Asian Exchange*,VII,3/4:1990,:14.

27. Peter Gibbon,"The World Bank and the New Politics of Aid," Pt.2, *Pravada,* 2, 1, Jan. 1993 :28–35.

28. Leftwich, op. cit., 610–611. For more details see *World Bank, Sub-Saharan Africa: From Crisis to Sustainable Growth* (Washington D.C.: World Bank, 1989).

29. Ibid, 60–61–192.

30. World Bank, *Governance and Development* (Washington D.C.: World Bank, 1992) :1.

31. *Human Development Report 1994,* 76, Table 4.9. World Bank Loans and Democracy.

32. S.M. Lipset, *Political Man* (Paperback edn, London, Mercury, 1963): 403. Among the political scientists and sociologists who in the 1950s and 1960s put forward modernization theories one can single out the following: Karl Deutsch, *Nationalism and Social Communication. An Inquiry into the Foundations of Nationality,* (Cambridge, Mass: Harvard University Press, 1953); David E. Apter, *The Politics of Modernization* (Chicago: Chicago University Press, 1965); Daniel Bell, *The End of Ideology* (Glencoe, Illinois: Free Press, 1960); Talcott Parsons, *Societies: Evolutionary and Comparative Perspectives* (Englewood Cliffs, N.J. Prentice Hall, 1966).

33. Sudipta Kaviraj, "On State, Society and Discourse in India" in James Manor (ed.), *Rethinking Third World Politics* (New York: Longman, 1991), 72–99.

34. James N. Roseneu, "Governance, order and Change in World Politics," in James N. Rosenau and Ernst-Otto Czempiel (eds), *Governance without Government: Order and Change in World Politics,* (Cambridge University Press, 1992), 3–4.

35. Adrian Leftwich, op.cit.,:613.

36. Statement of Teresita Shaffer, Deputy Assistant Secretary of State, Bureau of Near Eastern and South Asian Affairs, 7 March 1991, Hearings before the Sub-Committee on Asian and Pacific Affairs. See also Selig H. Harrison, "South Asia and the United States: A Chance for a Fresh Start," *Current History* (March 1992): 103.

37. *Human Rights Watch World Report 1993* (Washington, 1993): 187–188.

38. Conversation with Alison Krupnick, Desk Officer, Sri Lanka Bureau, State Department, 15 March 1993.

39. Annual Budget Submission, FY–1994, Sri Lanka, U.S.A.I.D., June 1992; U.S.A.I.D./Sri Lanka. Strategic Framework FY 1992–96, April 1991; U.S.A.I.D./Sri Lanka. Development in Sri Lanka.

A review. April 1991; Sri Lanka. Country Development Strategy Statement FY–1983, Jan. 1981.

40. *Human Rights Law Journal,* 14(7–8) 1993: 286.
41. Atul Kohli, "Democracy and Development" in J.P. Lewis and V. Kallab (eds), *Development Strategies Reconsidered* (New Brunswick: Transaction Books, 1986) :153–182.
42. Charles Abeysekere, "The Limits of Space: Human Rights and Foreign Aid" *Index on Censorship*, 21, 7 (July–August 1992) : 28.
43. Arjun Sen Gupta, "Aid and Development Policy in the 1990s" *Economic and Political Weekly,* 28, 11 (13 March, 1993): 453.
44. Ashis Nandy (ed.), *Science, Hegemony and Violence. A Requiem for Modernity* (New Delhi: Oxford University Press, 1990).
45. U.N.D.P. Human Development Report 1993: Human Development Indicators.
46. Ibid.: 1 (note 37).
47. Sugata Bose, "The World Economy and Regional Economies in South Asia: Some Comments on Linkages," in ed. Sugata Bose, 357.
48. Samir Amin, *Delinking: Towards a Polycentric World* (London: Zed, 1990).
49. A special institutional link between the U.N. and the financial institutions was established in 1961 with the formation of a "Liaison Committee" composed of the Secretary General of the United Nations, the President of the World Bank and the International Development Association and the heads of the predecessors of the U.N.D.P. They were to meet periodically and no less than four times a year to coordinate development activities. The Committee never operated formally due to opposition from the World Bank.
50. T. Krishna Kumar, "Fund-Bank Policies of Stabilization and Structural Adjustment. A global and historical perspective" *Economic and Political Weekly*, 28, 17 (24 April, 1993) : 822.

# Index

# Index

# Index

Muhammad, 118–122, 124, 126–127, 129,
133, 134, 142, 147
*mujtahidin*, 129
Mukti Bahini, 140
Murad, Khurram Jah, 140
Muslim, *see* Islam
Muslim League, 136, 137
Myanmar, 204
see also Burma

Nagorno-Karabakh, 74
Namibia, 17, 185, 203, 204, 208, 277, 282, 285, 287–288, 290–293
Constituent Assembly, 291, 292
Constitution, 292–293
National Assembly, 292
National Council, 292
see also South West Africa
Nash, Manning, 156–157
National Federation Party (Fiji), 166
National Front for the Liberation of Angola, *see* FNLA
National Front for the Liberation of Mozambique, *see* FRELIMO
National Resistance Council (Iran), 146
National Socialism, 47, 103, 160
National Union for the Total Independence of Angola, *see* UNITA
NATO, *see* North Atlantic Treaty Organization
Nazi, *see* National Socialism
Ndebele, 280
Netherlands, 39, 239, 279
Neuberger, B., 44
New Caledonia, 160
New Hebrides, 277
New Zealand, 160, 280
NGOs (nongovernmental organizations), 315
NICs (Newly Industrialized Countries), 319
Nicaragua, 186, 198, 210, 214, 282, 285–286, 290, 308
*Nicaragua v. United States*, 210, 214
Nigeria, 55, 154, 194, 198, 244
Nice, 275
Niue, 277
Nkomo, Joshua, 280
nongovernmental organizations, *see* NGOs
North Africa, 133, 141
North America, 160
North Atlantic Treaty Organization, 248

North Korea, 276, 277
see also Korea
North Solomons, *see* Bougainville
North Vietnam, 183, 199
Northern Ireland, 25, 51, 154, 194
Norway, 310
Nujoma, Sam, 285, 292
Nuremberg Trials, 1

OAS, *see* Organization of American States
OAU, *see* Organization of African Unity
Ofodile, Anthony, ix
Ogadan, 211
OIC, *see* Organization of the Islamic Conference
Olson, Mancur, ii
Oppenheim, Lassa, 180
Ona, Francis, 161–162
ONUC (Organization des Nations Unies au Congo), 275, 278, 281
ONUCA (United Nations Observer Group in Central Africa), 285, 286
ONUMOZ (United Nations Operation in Mozambique), 284, 287–288
ONUSAL (United Nations Observer Mission in El Salvador), 283, 286
ONUVEH (United Nations Observer Group for the Verification of the Election in Haiti), 286
ONUVEN (United Nations Observer Group for the Verification of the Election in Nicaragua), 285–286
Operation Restore Democracy, 287
Organization des Nations Unies au Congo, *see* ONUC
Organization of African Unity (OAU), 187, 203, 204, 205, 208
Committee for the Coordination of the Liberation of Africa, 205
Organization of American States (OAS), 215, 244
General Assembly, 215–216
Organization of the Islamic Conference (OIC), 117, 118, 136, 138, 144
Council of Foreign Ministers, 138, 144
Orient, 96
see also Asia
Ortega Saavedra, Daniel, 286
Ottoman Empire, 100, 134, 135, 141, 142, 143
see also Turkey

Pacific Islanders, 165
Pahlavi, Mohammad Reza, 145

# Index